TRANSFORMING COMMUNICATION ABOUT CULTURE

INTERNATIONAL AND INTERCULTURAL COMMUNICATION ANNUAL

Volume XXIV 2001

Editor
Mary Jane Collier
University of Denver

Editorial Assistant
Katia Campbell
University of Denver

INTERNATIONAL AND INTERCULTURAL COMMUNICATION ANNUAL
VOLUME XXIV
2001

TRANSFORMING COMMUNICATION ABOUT CULTURE

Critical New Directions

editor
Mary Jane Collier

Published in Cooperation with
National Communication Association
International and Intercultural Division

Sage Publications
International Educational and Professional Publisher
Thousand Oaks ▪ London ▪ New Delhi

For information:

Sage Publications, Inc.
2455 Teller Road
Thousand Oaks, California 91320
E-mail: order@sagepub.com

Sage Publications Ltd.
6 Bonhill Street
London EC2A 4PU
United Kingdom

Sage Publications India Pvt. Ltd.
M-32 Market
Greater Kailash I
New Delhi 110 048 India

Printed in the United States of America

Library of Congress Cataloging-in-Publication Data

Series: International and intercultural communication annual, Vol. 24.

Published: [Washington, DC] National Communication Association
ISSN: 0270-6075

Title: Transforming communication about culture / edited by Mary Jane Collier.
ISBN: 0-7619-2487-6 (cloth)
ISBN: 0-7619-2488-4 (paper)

01 02 03 04 05 06 10 9 8 7 6 5 4 3 2 1

Acquiring Editor: Margaret H. Seawell
Editorial Assistant: Alicia Carter
Copy Editor: D. J. Peck
Production Editor: Claudia A. Hoffman
Typesetter/Designer: Janelle LeMaster
Indexer: Molly Hall
Cover Designer: Michelle Lee

Contents

Acknowledgments

First, I thank my editorial assistant, Katia Campbell, doctoral student in the School of Communication at the University of Denver. Katia made certain that the review process occurred in a timely manner, kept authors informed, and provided insightful commentary regarding the introductory and concluding dialogue chapters. In addition, Teresa McPhee, master's student in international and intercultural communication, deserves my thanks for her eye to detail and thoughtful feedback during final copy-editing. I also am grateful to the dean of Arts, Humanities, and Social Sciences, as well as to the provost at the University of Denver, for continuing to provide me with funding for an editorial assistant. I appreciate the voice of Margaret Seawell, executive editor at Sage Publications, who continues to advocate for the annual as a site of outstanding scholarship in international and intercultural communication.

The reviewers for Volume 24 earned my respect and admiration; they ensured that each chapter received rigorous and thorough commentary. They not only contributed their expertise to strengthen the work of more senior scholars but also took the time necessary to give supportive feedback to beginning scholars. My sincere appreciation goes to Guo Ming Chen, Victoria Chen, Fernando Delgado, Jolanta Drzyewiecka, Mitch Hammer, Marouf Hasian, Michael Hecht, Radha S. Hegde, Tamar Katriel, Young Kim, Wenshu Lee, Casey Lum, Judith Martin, Thomas Nakayama, Kent Ono, Diana Rios, Raka Shome, Dolores Tanno, Diane Waldman, Richard Wiseman, and Gust Yep.

Finally, I thank Radha Hegde, Wenshu Lee, Thomas Nakayama, and Gust Yep for collaborating on the "Dialogue on the Edges" chapter (Chapter 9). Each of the four is an example of intellectual breadth and depth that is charting our course and transforming our views of culture and communication. Each voices an unceasing commitment to overcoming injustice with an authenticity and humility that is extremely powerful. Each was willing to fully engage in the risky terrain of a critically engaged, reflexive, unfolding conversation. I respect, admire, and thank them for what they are contributing individually and collectively to the field of communication and culture.

Transforming Communication About Culture

An Introduction

Volume 24 of the International and Intercultural Communication Annual addresses the theme of transformation. This idea connotes the ways in which people's lives and experiences across the globe are being transformed by technological changes, media institutions, political ideologies, and social forces. In the midst of such enabling and constraining forces, individuals and groups also are redefining communities, redrawing the boundaries of identity groups, and co-creating new ways of relating with each other. Rather than being a sequence of time or identifiable phase with a beginning or end, transformation is a continuous process of changing and evolving, with all of the paradoxical blockages, backward slides, blind advances, and false starts that accompany a sense of potential and renewal.

The kind of global and local transformation that characterizes the worlds in which we live contains issues that are modern and postmodern as well as a healthy skepticism and critique about our knowledge-building processes and resulting claims. As scholars/teachers/practitioners, we are being called on to rethink our assumptions about what drives our scholarly work, what constitutes scholarship, and who benefits from it. We have entered into a space in which we are beginning to address these and other such issues, and as a result, ideas about who we are and what we do are changing in fundamental ways. A critical turn is thus becoming evident in scholarship about (inter)cultural/national communication, and the chapters in this volume are exemplars of situated examinations of hierarchy and privilege, agency, and voice. In particular, the various authors question the politics of our scholarship and the nature of knowledge-building endeavors and ask that we pay more attention to the consequences and implications of our work.

BROADENING THE SCOPE OF (INTER)CULTURAL/NATIONAL COMMUNICATION

The chapters in this volume demonstrate the value in broadening what traditionally has been known as "international" scholarship and was defined as messages that have particular form (usually mediated or institutional policy) and cross particular geographic places (national borders). The first eight chapters, for example, include a critique of *kokusaika* as a privileging of white, Western, and Japanese ethnic positions; liminal identifications of relocated Arab-American diaspora group identifications that are socially constructed through communicative performances of humor; the rhetorically based identifications crafted by Taiwanese political leaders and poets; the hybridity of positions evident in group discourse of Indian young adults in discussions of international television; and portrayals of femininity and diverse audience responses to the film *Fire*.

In addition, the research projects compiled in this volume examine diverse texts and discourses and employ a variety of analytical frameworks. For example, authors focus on the press, films, television, Internet sites, poetry, literature, interviews with groups and individuals, observed community meetings, and recalled personal conversations. As would be expected, the authors choose a variety of analytical orientations to orient their gaze toward the texts of interest. For example, authors in the first eight chapters use combinations of rhetorical analysis of political speeches and newspaper texts, diverse critical approaches (for the most part using critical humanist rather than critical structuralist approaches[1]) to discourses and images, a particular type of engaged critical ethnography, and interpretive orientations to mediated texts and public speeches.

PROBLEMATIZING NATION AND CULTURE

The scholars agree that talking about culture and nation as solitary constructs rather than as multiple forces and enactments no longer is useful. Nor is it theoretically valid to assume that culture can be easily synthesized into that which is produced or constituted in a particular geographical place or by a group of people who have similar ancestry or traditions. For example, to assume that ethnic categories such as Arab-American and Latino may be equated with political and identity locations, or with normative patterns in generic use by group members, neglects the vast differences in voices and experiences of the group members and the broader historical and social structures that contribute to and constrain Arab-American and Latino identifications.

The work in this volume demonstrates the recognition that scholars, teachers, and practitioners construct and produce what nation and culture are known to be in historically situated sites and moments of time.

> Nation-ness, as well as nationalism, are cultural artifacts of a particular kind. To understand them properly, we need to consider carefully how they have come into historical being, in what ways their meanings have changed over time, and why, today, they command such profound emotional legitimacy.
>
> . . . Once created, they became "modular"—capable of being transplanted, with varying degrees of self-consciousness, to a great variety of social terrains, to merge and be merged with a correspondingly wide variety of political and ideological constellations. (Anderson, 1991, p. 4) . . . Nation is an "imagined political community." (p. 6)

The scholars in this volume, through situated studies and in the concluding "cyber-dialogue," argue that the world and the ways in which we relate to each other and the media have changed over the past few decades, and scholars of (inter)cultural/national communication need to incorporate those changes into what we study. The ways in which scholars think about and engage culture also are being transformed to bring embodied ideas of the "doing" of culture into the study of culture. Culture is being recognized as imagined, constituted in communication, and constrained by social structures and ideologies over a trajectory of time by people and institutions. Such reformulations of culture require us to rethink, reframe, and add to our previous orientations to culture.

More specifically, authors in this volume approach culture as liminal space and contested identifications. For example, Hay and Kline (Chapter 8) describe culture as that which is constructed by Arab-American diaspora group members through humor and narrative. Chang (Chapter 2) describes the imagined community evident in varied rhetorical forms establishing what it means to be Taiwanese. Schiffman and Subervi-Vélez (Chapter 7) point to how overarching stereotypes of Latinos and their politics are contested by various voices in print media. And Supriya (Chapter 5) uncovers the tensions between codes of "honorable" and "shameful" conduct and the contradictory voices of abused Indian women and the broader Indian communities in the United States.

IDENTIFICATIONS AND LOCATIONS

The authors in this volume have taken up the challenge to move beyond a focus on isolated cultural groupings based on place or peoples to begin to scrutinize intersections of nationality, race, ethnicity, gender, and classes. They point out that the level of knowledge may be too abstract and essentializing and may mask issues of hierarchy and privilege when focusing on overly broad groupings such as nationality without considering intersecting locations of ethnicity and gender/sexualities. West and Fenstermaker (1995) note, "Conceiving of race and gender as ongoing accomplishments means we must locate their emergence in social situations rather than within the individual or some vaguely defined set of role expectations" (p. 25). They add, "An understanding of the accomplishment of race, gender, or class constituted in the context of the differential 'doings' of the others" (p. 32) is essential to pinpoint how intersecting categorizations become a means of exerting domination.

In this volume, Malhotra and Crabtree (Chapter 3) and Supriya (Chapter 5) examine (inter)national and gendered identities among Indians in India and in the Asian Indian community in the United States, respectively. Hay and Kline (Chapter 8) address national, ethnic, class, and gender identities among Arab-Americans as they are accomplished in situated discursive events. Fujimoto (Chapter 1) aptly illustrates how nationality and ethnicity may be conflated and the importance of viewing not only how that is accomplished but also who is served by such positionings. Moorti (Chapter 6) studies enactments of hybridity in her examination of the contested responses of the Indian community to the film *Fire.*

Identifications are approached by the authors in this volume as structural impositions evident in institutional voices, media influences, and community hierarchies in combination with situated constructions of individual voices. Each chapter illustrates the importance of acknowledging a range of contexts of study—historical trajectories, institutional and structural forces, social and material conditions, and immediate situations —related to identifications. Identity locations are presented as combinations of involuntary reactions as well as proactive redefinitions demonstrating individual agency and counterhegemony.

There are several analyses that point us to tensions between individual identification and group identifications and issues of agency. The responses of Supriya's (Chapter 5) informant/research collaborator residing at a women's shelter illustrate her personal and public struggle to survive and escape the abuse of her husband in the midst of being ostracized as shameful by the patriarchal voices in the Indian community. Ambivalence and appropriation of identity groupings are evident in the work of Hay and Kline (Chapter 8) and their examination of how humor is used to reinforce a particular Arab-American community's liminal and traveling identities.

Moorti (Chapter 6) and Supriya (Chapter 5), among others in this volume, demonstrate that Indian group and personal identifications are complex and dynamic and that language practices occur within a matrix of power relations. Schiffman and Subervi-Vélez (Chapter 7) illustrate the dangers of attempting to generalize about ethnic group membership based on "experts" or "objective" media spokespersons or to generalize about people or political views held by those identifying as Latino in the United States. All of the chapters exemplify views that reflect movement beyond the traditional idea that intercultural communication is that which occurs between two people who come from different places, between people who have different ancestries, or between group members who have different worldviews. Communication involves, more often than not, the engagement of multiple cultural identifications and occurs in a space of intersecting historical and social forces.

CRITICAL PERSPECTIVES

The authors in this volume generally orient their studies through the use of a critical theoretical perspective or conclude interpretive and rhetorical analyses with a call for critical research. Viewed collectively, the authors make some similar claims and arguments. For example, one claim made directly by the contributors to the cyber-dialogue (Chapter 9) is that we miss a large part of the picture when we ignore issues of social justice and ethics and when we discount or overlook the broader historical and political context in which communicative phenomena are placed. Fujimoto (Chapter 1), in her chapter on Japanese-ness, whiteness, and the other, illustrates that group alignment is inherently hierarchical, occurs along multiple trajectories and for multiple groups in local and global placements simultaneously, and functions to marginalize groups such as the *burakumin*. It clearly is not appropriate, therefore, to predict from or assume similarity among people on the basis of their Japanese residency or ancestry.

We are better served as scholars and/or practitioners by asking who has the privilege of defining the criteria for group or community membership location, what is the means through which hierarchy and status are established, and who benefits from particular locations. The contributors to the cyber-dialogue in the concluding chapter note as problematic that our camera lenses that capture communicative phenomena often are pointed at those subjects who can be objectified, are most accessible, have the least to lose by participating, and are willing to pose for close-ups. The scholars in this volume provide examples of ways of broadening our gaze and increasing the relevance of our work to the lived experiences of more of us.

What is common across the chapters, including the cyber-dialogue at the end of the volume, is attention to description and critique of nationalized discourse and communicative texts that promote nationalism as dominant group ideology. Several authors address how the discourse of dominant groups—whether national, ethnic, religious, or patriarchal—functions to suppress other groups. Malhotra and Crabtree (Chapter 3) and Moorti (Chapter 6) address the use of such discourse in accomplishing the establishment of constraints on the actions of Indian women. Supriya (Chapter 5) points to cultural codes and core symbols used by community voices to attempt to control Indian women by constructing them as having "no shame."

Chang (Chapter 2) describes the ways in which political leaders, working alongside other writers and artists, construct the character of Taiwanese national identity. Fujimoto (Chapter 1) points the readers to multiple sites—including educational textbooks, Internet forums, media reports by political analysts, and scholarly forums—in which institutional voices establish hierarchical relationships and distancing of others. Schiffman and Subervi-Vélez (Chapter 7) describe the ways in which Latinos and their political standpoints are constructed and their roles and resources are positioned by the English-language print media.

The discussions of Schiffman and Subervi-Vélez (Chapter 7), Chang (Chapter 2), Roy (Chapter 4), and Moorti (Chapter 6) clearly illustrate and reinforce the need to uncover essentializing, homogenizing, and negative representations of others. The contributors to the cyber-dialogue (Chapter 9) argue convincingly that who we are as cultural beings is first and foremost political because some of us have more agency and resources to define ourselves than do others, and they issue a call for scholars/teachers/practitioners to acknowledge that what we do and how we do it have unequal consequences and impacts.

INCORPORATION OF CONTEXTS OF HISTORY AND STRUCTURAL FORCES

All of the authors in this volume include discussions of history in their examinations of culture and communication. The scholars in the cyber-dialogue (Chapter 9) point out that it is important to reflexively examine and carefully interrogate the history and development of (inter)cultural/national communication into a subdiscipline to recognize the context from which many of us speak. More than 50 years ago, Edward T. Hall began to work with the Foreign Service Institute in the United States.[2] Largely as a result of Hall's work, ideas about culture were linked to communication, a partnership of business and corporate interests within and outside of the United States was born, and a new academic specialization of intercultural communication emerged. The roots of this area of the discipline thus came about through collaborations between anthropologists and international corporate interests (including the Peace Corps) that needed personnel who were prepared to relocate to countries outside of the United States. It is important to remember that economic and political circumstances such as these produced an emphasis on views of culture as styles of communicating shared by groups of people in particular places and contributed to the value placed on social psychological prediction of successful adaptation behaviors and competent skills.

Scholars in this volume advocate for strengthening the role of context (historical, institutional, social, normative, and situated) to enable us to better understand communicative phenomena related to culture. Not only are gender, race, and class ongoing accomplishments, but "we cannot determine their relevance to social action apart from the context in which they are accomplished" (West & Fenstermaker, 1995, p. 30). The authors in this volume replace etic generalizability with situated contextual accounts that also include reflexive examination of author positionality and location. Roy's analysis of the ways in which international forces and satellite television are "demonized" in the Indian press (Chapter 4) moves beyond content analysis of press coverage by showcasing the need for including attention to historical, economic, and political contexts so as to understand the ways in which metaphors can be hegemonically used by institutional media. Malhotra and Crabtree's discussion (Chapter 3) features the ways in which Indian audiences, given their varied sociopolitical locations, construct localized interpretations of some satellite television programming in counterhegemonic ways.

The role of ideologies and institutional policies and practices addressed in this volume comprises legislative outcomes, legal rulings, economic forces, constructed histories passed down through educational texts and lectures, government, mediated and institutional policies, and social norms related to who is an acceptable member of the group. The authors of the cyber-dialogue (Chapter 9) at one point remind the readers about the importance of multivocality and multiple contexts. They note that defining oneself as "American" means something different to the African American Democrat who was denied access to the ballot box in Florida in the 2000 U.S. presidential election from what it means to the white, European American Republican who voted for George W. Bush and celebrated the U.S. Supreme Court decision of the outcome of the election.

DIALECTIC TENSIONS AND DUALISTIC CONTRADICTIONS

Martin and Nakayama (1999) argue that dialectic approaches provide one window through which scholars may theorize and better engage the contradictory forces that characterize culture and communication. Whereas Baxter and Braithwaite (in press) describe social dialectics as unified opposites in dynamic interplay and as relationally and dialogically constructed in discourse, several authors in this volume address competing social and structural dualities and dialectic forces that emerge in a variety of communicative forms and texts. The authors' approaches are consistent with Baxter and Braithwaite's claim that relating and social interaction are processes of contradiction.

More specifically, Roy (Chapter 4) uncovers mediated claims about the homogenizing forces of globalization, on the one hand, and the heterogeneity of localization, on the other, that emerge in the print media coverage of satellite television in India. He notes that both are required oppositions in the production of Indian nationalism today. Fujimoto (Chapter 1) addresses insider-outsider distinctions among Japanese identifications. Supriya's (Chapter 5) analysis delineates how honor and shame implicate one another in positioning and group alignments. Malhotra and Crabtree (Chapter 3) contrast dualistic forces such as spiritual and material, home and outer world, and traditional (uncolonized) and politically charged (contemporary) in their interview discourse from media executives and audiences of privatized satellite television. Rather than reifying overly dualistic assumptions and interpretations, they illustrate how the young adult television audience in India ruptures the binaries of local and global.

Moorti (Chapter 6) provides evidence of the alternative positions and multiplicity of voices across religious, political, and gendered positions among those who supported the release and viewing of the film *Fire,* those who argued for taking it out of theaters, and those who argued for alterations in the film such as changing the names of characters. In addition, Schiffman and Subervi-Vélez (Chapter 7) provide media quotes from various Latino spokespersons developing arguments for the heterogeneity of Latinos in the United States and offer evidence of contradictory portrayals of Latinos as either a strong economic force or economically poor. Chang (Chapter 2) analyzes the contradictory metaphors of being an "orphan of Asia" and becoming "Moses" as evidence of very different Taiwanese identity locations and illustrations of different levels of agency.

DIALOGUE ON THE EDGES

The concluding chapter features a different form of scholarly engagement, an unfinished conversation that took shape and form as a cyber-dialogue among five scholars about the study of, instruction about, and praxis in a world of cultures. In the cyber-dialogue, five scholars whose work and itineraries have taken a critical turn, and whose involuntary identifications and embodied experiences differ, engage the issues that characterize the ferment and transformation occurring in many academic disciplines today and are specifically evident in scholarship about culture and communication. In the chapter, the authors interrogate existing conceptualizations of culture and propose alternative situated orientations to culture that are politically situated, historically contexted, and socially contested.

The final chapter is a call to continuously interrogate our assumptions through a particular kind of dialogue about difference—a dialogue with those speaking from different identity locations and having different itineraries. It is a demonstration of moving beyond categorical judgments of others and ourselves through a sustained discussion over many months and the value of requesting and providing clarifications and explanations. The contributors describe personal narratives of how power and privileged locations become enacted as the means through which dominating occurs, how the establishing of political hierarchies left them feeling marginalized as individuals and group members, and how they exerted individual agency to reject and reform cultural locations and itineraries. Our discussion in the cyber-dialogue is a celebration of the importance of personal narrative and auto-ethnographic reflecting coupled with deliberate and invitational dialogue with each other.

What emerges from the cyber-dialogue is not only an argument for recognizing the politics of our intersecting cultural identifications but also the necessity of a commitment to social justice and ethics similar to that described by Frey, Pearce, Pollock, Artz, and Murphy (1998): "A concern with social justice from a communicative perspective thus identifies and foregrounds the grammars that oppress or underwrite relationships of domination and then reconstructs those grammars" (p. 112). Our chapter also is an illustration of what can be accomplished in a collaborative and stimulating relationship based on the ongoing participation of five histories, intellectual positionings, hearts, and voices.

Four broad sets of questions emerged and helped to structure our cyber-dialogue. First, what is the nature of international/cultural communication scholarship? What are key issues that scholars/teachers/practitioners need to engage in their work? Second, what is (are) the problem(s) that need(s) to be addressed in this dialogue? How is the field of scholarship around internationalization, culture, and communication shifting? How can we characterize this current ferment in the field? Third, how does this shift and ferment affect us as scholars, and how does it affect people in our field? Why should we care about this ferment? Fourth, what can we do to address these concerns? What should be the agenda for scholars of international/cultural communication?

What the readers will find is that we did not systematically answer each question in sequential order, although each scholar did respond to all of the questions. Our cyber-dialogue reflects a process that was much more messy and complex than orderly. The collaborators concur that our unfinished cyber-dialogue illustrates the nature of rich intellectual conversation that is lived and engages each of us on a deep level; there always is more to say and more to ask of each other. Most certainly, there always is more to learn. The current volume of the International and Intercultural Communication Annual exemplifies such an opportunity.

NOTES

1. See Martin and Nakayama (1999) for a discussion of the distinction between these two approaches.
2. See Leeds-Hurwitz (1990) for a historical overview.

REFERENCES

Anderson, B. (1991). *Imagined communities: Reflection on the origin and spread of nationalism.* London: Verso.

Baxter, L., & Braithwaite, D. (in press) Social dialectics: The contradictions of relating. In B. Whaley & W. Samter (Eds.), *Contemporary communication theories and exemplars.* Mahwah, NJ: Lawrence Erlbaum.

Frey, L., Pearce, W. B., Pollock, M., Artz, L., & Murphy, B. (1998). Looking for justice in all the wrong places: On a communication approach to social justice. *Communication Studies, 47,* 110-127.

Leeds-Hurwitz, W. (1990). Notes on the history of intercultural communication: The Foreign Service Institute and the mandate for intercultural training. *Quarterly Journal of Speech, 76,* 262-281.

Martin, J., & Nakayama, T. (1999). Thinking dialectically about culture and communication. *Communication Theory, 9,* 1-25.

West, C., & Fenstermaker, S. (1995). Doing difference. *Gender & Society, 9,* 8-37.

1

Japanese-ness, Whiteness, and the "Other" in Japan's Internationalization

ETSUKO FUJIMOTO • *Southern Oregon University*

During my early years at a graduate school, I was involved in many projects led by the English Language Institute (ELI) on campus. Knowing that I was from Japan, the ELI coordinators and teachers wanted me to help Japanese students who spend several months as exchange students and visitors. Every summer, the ELI welcomes various student groups mainly from Asian and European countries to provide the groups with opportunities to experience "American life." The student groups spend a busy 4 to 6 weeks studying English, visiting various organizations of interest, taking trips to scenic places, and shopping. They stay in the residence halls on campus during weekdays and spend weekends with host families that are arranged by the ELI. The group that I helped during the summer of 1994 consisted of 20 young Japanese women who, at the time, were students in a women's junior college in Tokyo. Although these students generally enjoyed their experiences, one student was not happy with her host family. She complained to the program coordinator that she did not want a Chinese family as her host family given that all of the other students had "American" families.

The following winter, I again worked with a group of Japanese female exchange students. Because it was the first visit to the United States for many of them, the program coordinator thought that it would be a good idea for me to work with them as a counselor so that they could express any concerns and problems freely to me. I set up a weekly meeting with them and also visited with them on an individual basis. They stayed with U.S. American roommates in the college residence halls to furnish them with ample opportunities to practice English and form friendships. After a couple of weeks into the program, two of the Japanese students came to talk to me about their dissatisfaction with their roommates. Both students told me that they did not care much for their roommates because the roommates' personalities did not quite match theirs. I called the resident assistants of the dormitories and met with the roommates just to have casual talks. Both roommates seemed very friendly and excited about their Japanese roommates. One was an African American, and the other was a Vietnamese American. I found out later that the rest of the exchange student group had white U.S. American roommates and that the two dissatisfied students had told their Japanese friends that they envied the rest of the group for having "cute *hakujin* [white]" roommates.

I do not wish to make a sweeping generalization about racial and ethnic prejudices held by Japanese about U.S. Americans based on these two personal accounts. Those accounts, however, present a glimpse of some consistent and pervasive representations of U.S. Americans in Japan and how white the image of U.S. Americans is to Japanese. I am no exception. I remember fantasizing about meeting many U.S. Americans and making friends with them when I left Japan 9 years ago to study in the United States. What I pictured were the smiling friendly faces of young, blond, blue-eyed women and men, which fit the image of U.S. Americans that I saw time and again in Hollywood films, in popular fashion magazines, and in the textbooks that my schools used to teach English and about the United States. This image, of course, has changed over time as I came to meet and learn from U.S. Americans of different races, ethnicities, ages, sexualities, and so on. But when my international friends tell me that they have met new U.S. American friends, boyfriends, and girlfriends, or when they tell me that they are getting married to U.S. Americans, I still picture white U.S. Americans in my mind unless they tell me otherwise.

This equation between the racial category (white) and the nationality (U.S. American) often is subtly but persistently taught to Japanese through personal, institutional, and mediated contacts with non-Japanese people and cultures. Selective racialized representations of U.S. Americans and other Westerners often have helped to shape certain ways in which Japanese come to perceive and relate to non-Japanese people within and outside of Japan. One of the central points that I demonstrate in this chapter, therefore, is that a discourse of whitenization has been pervasive in the ways in which Japan's internationalization has occurred. I use the term *whitenization* to mean the process of identifying with white Westerners and privileging white bodies. In addition, I wish to demonstrate that the conflation of Japanese ethnicity with Japanese nationality also has played a significant role in navigating Japan's internationalization and in allowing the nation a tendency to neglect groups and individuals that have long been part of the nation.

THEORETICAL FRAMEWORK

To the extent that I wish to talk about whitenization, Japanese-ness, and the "other," some central concepts need to be clarified. In response to a critique regarding the lack of discourses on whiteness (hooks, 1990), non-white and white scholars began to put whiteness under critical scrutiny during the 1990s. Some common themes that emerged from those works include whiteness as a socially and historically constructed location that is dominant, normative, privileged, and invisible (Chambers, 1997; Collier, 1998; Frankenberg, 1993; Harris, 1995; Martin, Krizek, Nakayama, & Bradford, 1996; McIntosh, 1998; Moon, 1998). Whiteness is dominant and normative in that the values, practices, and behaviors of white U.S. ethnics are used as the expected standard across various institutions. The privileges of whiteness tend to be invisible to white persons precisely because they are the norm. This view of whiteness as an invisible standard is upheld when U.S. American ideas, products, and people enter Japan. However, white individuals are both unmarked and marked in Japan's internationalization. Similarly, Japanese-ness is simultaneously unmarked and marked, but differently, from whiteness.

In addition to whiteness, the concept of center/margin (or insider/outsider) is helpful in understanding the ways in which Japanese-ness meets non-Japanese-ness. Japanese-ness has been discussed most often in terms of authentic uniqueness that the identity embodies. This modernist view of identity, however, includes little about how Japanese-ness has in fact been constructed and expressed by distancing from the other. Identity is first and foremost a contested concept (Hall, 1996; Lavie & Swedenburg, 1996; Wong, 1998; Woodward, 1997). Hall (1996), for example, illustrates this idea of "identity and difference":

> Identities are constructed through, not outside, differences. This entails the radically disturbed recognition that it is only through the relation to the Other, the relation to what is not, to precisely what it lacks, to what has been called its *constitutive outside* that the "positive" meaning of any term—and thus "identity" —can be constructed. . . . Throughout their careers, identities function as points of identification and attachment only *because* of their capacity to exclude, to leave out, to render "outside," abjected. Every identity has at its "margin" an excess, something more. (pp. 4-5)

As I discuss later, Japanese-ness needs non-Japanese-ness to define itself. Then, this framework of identity and difference helps scholars to explore the relationship between the supposedly binary concepts of self and other.

This framework, however, is yet insufficient to understand Japan's internationalization, for it seems to assume singularity of Japanese-ness and non-Japanese-ness. Trinh (1990) argues that differences exist not only in the self-other relationship but also within the self or within the other. Although Trinh is referring to the paradoxical construction of postcolonial women's identity, her point is instructive in understanding the relationships between and within identity locations in Japan's internationalization. I argue that Japanese-ness and non-Japanese-ness cannot be considered as single homogeneous spaces and that differential relationships exist within and across the insider-outsider boundaries.

My analysis necessarily reflects my personal and professional experiences in Japan and in the United States. My orientation is from the view of someone who stepped out from the cultural and geopolitical boundaries of naturalized Japan and Japanese, someone who is not quite an insider or an outsider (Trinh, 1990). It also is a view of someone who struggles to de-essentialize her cultural identity. In what follows, I briefly introduce common definitions of internationalization to provide context and then illustrate some ways in which a discourse of whitenization occurred in Japan's internationalization. Then, I discuss how the dominant discourse of Japanese-ness has contributed to the continuation of domestic intercultural struggles.

GENERAL MEANINGS OF *KOKUSAIKA* IN JAPAN

Kokusaika (internationalization) is a term that has not ceased to capture Japanese people's interest and fascination since the term joined Japan's everyday vocabulary several decades ago. Befu (1983) examines ways in which the term *kokusaika* is used in Japanese newspapers and popular magazines. Mouer and Sugimoto (1986), who led discussions on internationalization in several major Japanese cities during 1980 and 1981, analyze the meanings that participants attached to the term.

Some common meanings of kokusaika that emerged from the studies include the following: learning about foreign cultures (languages, customs, and people), learning foreign languages, traveling overseas, foreigners traveling in Japan, promoting world peace, and teaching Japanese language and culture to foreigners. In addition to definitions that focus on the individual, Befu (1983) describes national-level changes such as foreign investment in Japan, Japanese investment abroad, liberation of trade policy, lenient immigration laws, and contribution to the world order. More recent writers on Japanese society (Kumagai, 1996; Stronach, 1995) suggest that these views persist.

Some conclusions may be drawn from those definitions. First, kokusaika points to social conditions and activities occurring both in Japanese society and overseas, and influences are mutual between Japan and other countries. Second, the list of the definitions shows that kokusaika seems to have positive connotations to Japanese people; it refers to desirable changes. A closer examination of Japan's internationalization, however, reveals problematic aspects in these assumptions, for the Western influence was powerful in the history of Japan's internationalization, and there are many elements in the process, including whitenization, that are hidden behind the positive image of kokusaika.

WHITENIZATION: A DOMINANT DISCOURSE IN JAPAN'S KOKUSAIKA

Befu (1983) observes that Japan's internationalization glosses over concepts such as Westernization, modernization, and liberalization and presents them as almost synonymous.[1] This interchangeability is rooted in the way in which kokusaika began. Japan's internationalization generally is traced back to the mid-19th century, when the new Meiji government defeated the Tokugawa Edo Shogunate that kept Japan isolated from the rest of the world for 220 years (Befu, 1983; Koshiro, 1999; Stronach, 1995). The Meiji government began to modernize the nation by importing new ideas, technology, and fashions from the West. In her critical historical analysis of transnational racism between the United States and Japan, Koshiro (1999) refers to the Meiji emperor's 1888 engraving that portrayed the emperor as looking somewhat Caucasian. The emperor in the engraving wore Western clothes, was surrounded by Western decorations, and (most important) had visible Caucasian physical features such as thicker eyebrows, double eyelids, and rounder and bigger pupils. This white Westerner's image became "the official royal image of modern Japan, deeply embedded in people's minds as a proud symbol of Japan's successful enlightenment" (p. 228).

Westernization not only means adoptions of Western technology, architecture, and fashions but also means Western ideas about race and ideology. Koshiro (1999) uses the term *mutual racism* to characterize U.S.-Japanese relations. The United States accepted the Japanese as an "assimilable race" that was more apt to learn Western civilization than were other Asians, and Japan internalized this belief and transformed itself into a colonial power over other Asian nations. Hence, Westernization (or, more accurately, whitenization) was a defining characteristic of Japan's internationalization from the 19th century onward.

After World War II, Japan began to use the term *kokusaika* (Befu, 1983). During the 1950s and 1960s, when Japan was still recovering from its defeat in World War II, kokusaika generally referred to transferring Western technology into Japan and opening Japan up to Western ideas (Befu, 1983; Sugimoto & Mouer, 1989). The postwar restoration of Japan occurred under the subsequent 7-year occupation by Allied forces, particularly under the control of the U.S. government. Under the occupation, Japan underwent substantial institutional reforms including political reforms such as equal rights for women, K-12 education systems and curricula, and capitalism. Many of these reforms contributed to the involuntary Westernization of Japan. Noticeable changes occurred in the education reforms. For example, English was added as an important subject in the junior high school[2] curriculum, and the subjects and books that included descriptions of positive influences of imperial Japan were eliminated.[3] In short, the early internationalization of Japan was a discourse of learning from the West.

The discourse established not only the obvious power difference between the United States (conqueror) and Japan (conquered) but also a racial hierarchy. Koshiro (1999) observes,

> In the early stage of the Occupation (1945-1948), race functioned as a punitive tool used to instill among the Japanese people a proper sense of relations between the white conqueror and the colored vanquished. In the second stage (1949-1952), along the line of the so-called Reverse Course, race expedited the radical change in their relations by upgrading the Japanese status to that of honorary whites and an ally of strategic value. Mutual racism displayed extraordinary maneuvering power in restoring proper U.S.-Japanese relations. (p. 16)

I argue that the racial hierarchy, palpable during the war and postwar periods, also continues to play a significant role in framing Japanese perceptions of and relations to white Westerners and nonwhite migrants.

Beyond Japan's Geopolitical Borders

As Japan began to show its rapid growth in economic and technological sectors during the 1970s, the meaning of kokusaika mirrored the change. In addition to Westernization, the term also began to take on the meaning of "exporting" Japanese ideas, products, and people to the rest of the world (Sugimoto & Mouer, 1989). This was reflected in the increasing number of people traveling overseas, studying abroad, and working on business assignments. Japanese investment and business ventures abroad increased, and Japan began to play a role in the world order by making monetary contributions to international organizations (e.g., the United Nations) and by participating in international programs (e.g., the Japanese Overseas Youth Corps).

This overseas visibility has produced conflicting responses from other nations. Some critics view the ways in which Japan asserts its international presence as a discourse of revived nationalism or what Stronach (1995) refers to as "Japanizing the world" (p. 54). Sugimoto and Mouer (1989) further summarize this view:

> While the word "internationalization" suggests that there is a move toward more cosmopolitan values, it is also used to indicate a kind of neo-nationalistic push beyond the shores of Japan. This facet of internationalization is symbolized by the establishment of an increasing number of full-time Japanese schools for Japanese children overseas to maintain their "Japaneseness," by the appearance of Japanese medical teams abroad exclusively for Japanese businessmen and their families, and by the mushrooming of Japanese tourist facilities designed specifically for Japan's international travelers. The trend is reminiscent of the American enclaves abroad which accompanied America's move into the international arena three or four decades ago. It is as though the "Hilton Hotel syndrome" is giving way to the "*karaoke bar syndrome.*" (p. 19)

Internationalization and nationalism, therefore, are not necessarily oppositional concepts but rather two sides of a coin. Japan's increasing visibility overseas can be interpreted as cultural and economic invasions from the point of view of the receiving nations; such sentiments were articulated in the trade frictions and "Japan-bashing" of the 1980s. If Koshiro's (1999) observation about U.S.-Japan power and racial relations and whitenization is correct, then Japanese-ness always was defined in relation to the United States. Japan needed the United States to understand what it was lacking so that Japan could strive to attain the missing qualities. Japan's overseas visibility might have suggested to the United States and the West in general that Japan was upsetting the power relations established earlier between the West and Japan. Westernization may have meant internationalization to Japan, but Japanization did not—and *can*not—suggest the same to the West. This, I believe, also was a view internalized by many Japanese because Japan never has ceased to be an active consumer of Western cultures. As much as Japan increased its presence overseas, the ways in which Japan opened its doors to international influence was very much characterized by a discourse of whitenization. One way in which this continues to be accomplished is through mediated communication.

Echoing U.S. Racial Representations

International circulation of Western (especially U.S.) pop culture serves as a powerful means for the distribution of the Western discourse on race to other countries. For example, as an eager consumer of the U.S. culture, Japan has blindly accepted many of the media representations of African Americans. Russell's (1996) extensive historical analysis of the representation of blacks in Japanese popular culture shows how closely Japan mirrors the black stereotypes found in the U.S. media texts. For example, Russell refers to grossly deformed black physical stereotypes (e.g., thick bulbous lips, banjo eyes, flaring nostrils) in cartoons and mannequins. He concludes that the overpowering U.S. American popular culture "resulted in Japan's uncritical acceptance and indigenization of the racial hierarchies they [American popular culture] project. One sees in these representations of black otherness a repetition of the discursive strategies . . . employed by the West in its construction of the Orient" (p. 20).

The images of blacks are not necessarily all negative; the popularity of hip-hop styles and of black U.S. American musicians and athletes has spawned many examples of positive images of blacks among Japanese youths (Cornyetz, 1994). Having black boyfriends and adopting black physical characteristics (e.g., hairstyles, dark skins) have become popular among the young generation as a "black boom." Many recent magazines for youths such as *Ollie, Boys Rush,* and *Boon* reflect the popularity of "black-associated" fashion and music. Cornyetz (1994) cautions, however, that blacks and blackness are made "fads" precisely because of the phallic power that blackness is supposed to embody. Support to her claim is easily found in fashion magazines. *Boon,* for example, includes an ad for a brand of sportswear called Discus. The ad shows two young black men accompanied by the following phrases: "America's properly built muscle. Joggers in Central Park. Street kids on 5th Street. Discus is always their number one choice."[4] Browsing through other ads in the same magazine, an association of blackness with music and sports is apparent. Blackness in this light is yet another expression of otherness, however popular it is.

In contrast to the selective, stereotypically negative representations of black U.S. Americans, there are numerous positive representations of white U.S. Americans in various sites of Japanese media. For example, the use of white U.S. American actors in television commercials is very common (e.g., Leonardo DiCaprio advertises a Visa credit card, Jodie Foster appears in a shampoo commercial). Television commercials for cars show white men and women in professional attire driving the cars while verbally emphasizing the elegant and smart performance of the cars. Women's fashion magazines eagerly use white models; there are at least 35 women's fashion magazines in Japan, many of which regularly use blond, white-looking persons on the covers. The ads of English-language schools placed at train stations predominantly use white individuals' pictures along with phrases that urge Japanese people to become *kokusaijin* (internationalist) by acquiring conversational English skills. White individuals, from celebrities to ordinary persons, take part in a variety of Japanese popular culture scenes, whereas the appearance of black Americans, except for celebrities (e.g., Tiger Woods appears in a coffee commercial, Scottie Pippen appears in a car commercial), is likely to be limited to music and sports advertisements. Representations of other U.S. racial minorities are extremely rare.

The skewed representations of whites and blacks in Japan not only suggest a heavy influence of U.S. discourse about racial and ethnic minorities but also illustrate how whiteness is unmarked just as it is in the United States. Russell articulated this point when he spoke at a gathering in celebration of African Descendants Friendship Day (October 14) in Tokyo in 1995. Russell (1995) states,

> Millions of Japanese—young and old—flock to see the latest films of Steven Spielberg, Kevin Costner, Tom Hanks, Tom Cruise, Julia Roberts, and Sharon Stone. Japanese youth [listen to] white bands such as Bon Jovi, KISS, and the Rolling Stones, but no one in Japan calls this a hakujin bumu [white boom]. . . . White Euro-American culture has become such a part of Japanese culture that few question it or perceive it in color-coded [terms].

Both whiteness and blackness may represent the other or "outsider" from the point of view of Japanese consumers of U.S. popular culture. As Trinh (1990) points out, however, the outsider is not one single space. The multivocal and ubiquitous representations of white persons contribute to more realistic and more normative (Collier, 1998) construction of whiteness, whereas the limited and skewed representations of black persons help to name and objectify blackness. In this way, blackness is kept at a far margin that Japanese may "visit."

Although media texts certainly are not the only sources of intercultural knowledge, they can help to shape views of what other cultural groups are like and whether or not contact is desirable. The skewed representations can profoundly affect the kinds of communicative relationships that Japanese have with people from other cultures. I briefly discuss some of these influences in the next section.

"Westerner," "U.S. American," and Gaijin, as Equated With "White"

The term *gaijin* has been cited as primary evidence of the Japanese insider-outsider mentality and unwillingness to allow non-Japanese persons into the insider's circle (Befu, 1983; Kumagai, 1996; Woronoff, 1997). Aldwinckle (1996), a U.S. American writer who is married to a Japanese woman and has become a permanent resident of Japan, confirms this view of the term. Because anyone who is not Japanese is a gaijin, Aldwinckle believes that that the term represents a binary view of the world.

Aldwinckle (1996) describes a number of situations in which the concept of gaijin negatively defines many non-Japanese people in ways that they do not like. For example, he remembers that his U.S. American friend was introduced by a Japanese person as gaijin, not even as an American, at an international symposium. He also recalls, from a trip to Venice, a young female traveler who told her friend to wait until some gaijin entered the picture frame so that the pictures would look more exotic. Aldwinckle argues that seeing non-Japanese persons as gaijin is racist because even if gaijin persons choose to naturalize and become Japanese citizens, they still will be treated as gaijin and not as Japanese. Thus, "once a gaijin, always a gaijin."

Aldwinckle's (1996) argument is well warranted; the use of the term *gaijin* perhaps exemplifies the binary mentality that is insensitive to individuality of international migrants and Japan's unwillingness to expand the inner circle of who may be Japanese. The pervasive use of the term continuously reproduces monolithic representations of foreigners who have heterogeneous experiences and voices (Hegde, 1998). Under this binarism, any foreigner, even a white person, is marked and gazed at as the other.

As much as the term *gaijin* "others" non-Japanese persons, it is too simplistic to conclude that it is the only way in which Japanese-ness/non-Japanese-ness is defined. The term implies white Westerners more often than it does nonwhite foreigners, and it connotes positive attitudes such as curiosity, awe, and admiration more often than it does negative attitudes (Koshiro, 1999; Russell, 1996). March's (1992) study reveals the same signifier-signified relationship. He surveyed a total of 270 Japanese in Tokyo in 1983 and 1987 to understand the extent and nature of Japanese people's "gaijin complex." In the studies, 60% to 70% of the participants reported that they were apprehensive about interacting with gaijin. In examining the reasons for their apprehension, March found that the respondents were referring to Caucasian people when they thought about the reasons; they were intimidated by gaijins' blond hair, attractive looks, and tall and well-proportioned bodies and because they felt inferior due to their own poor English and communication skills.

In the process of Japan's kokusaika, "white" was assumed to represent not only "U.S. American" but also "Westerners" and "gaijin" (Koshiro, 1999; Russell, 1996). Mouer and Sugimoto (1986) point out that Japan's heavy reliance on the West and the United States as the major reference groups severely undermines Japan's effort to be internationalized. The reliance has included uncritical adoption of the dominant U.S. racial non/representations as discussed in the previous section. In other words, these four concepts—white, U.S. American, Westerner, and gaijin—often have been imagined to be synonymous. This assumed link among different identity locations manifests in a number of ways in Japan's non/acceptance of international residents and tourists in Japan.

More recent evidence of presumptions about and favoritism toward white persons in Japan's internationalization comes from an ethnography of the Japan Exchange and Teaching (JET) Program (McConnell, 2000). The Japanese government began the JET Program in 1987 to promote international exchange and foreign-language learning in local governments and schools throughout Japan (Council of Local Authorities for International Relations, 2000). About 90% of the participants work as assistant language teachers (ALTs) who "team-teach" foreign-language classes with Japanese teachers, and the rest work for local governments as coordinators of international relations (CIRs). McConnell (2000) conducted a long-term field study of the JET Program to examine how contemporary Japanese society is dealing with the struggle for cultural and educational change through a program that is "the centerpiece of a top-down effort to create 'mass internationalization' " (p. x).

McConnell's (2000) study reveals racial favoritism and presumptions in a number of ways. For example, he found that program coordinators rarely placed nonwhite ALTs and CIRs in rural schools and local governments because people were expecting white faces. Schools also preferred ALTs who spoke North American English to those who spoke other variations of English. One African American participant, for example, shared her experience that she was repeatedly asked whether she could speak standard English. Caucasian participants from various countries also commented that they usually were assumed to be from the United States. McConnell notes that those problems with racial, language, and regional favoritisms improved as years passed, and in 1997 about 35% of CIRs were from non-English-speaking countries such as China, South Korea, and Russia. He cautions, however, that the changes should not be taken with too much optimism given that "Japan has largely defined itself in relation to the United States as the embodiment of 'Western' culture and perceive 'American English' as the most desired form of English for the foreseeable future" (p. 236).

International migrants in Japan may experience difficulty in living in Japanese society. As the preceding examples show, the racial hierarchy can situate the experience of nonwhite persons as qualitatively different from that of white Westerners in Japan. Such differential approaches to international migrants are most blatant when race and class intersect. For example, Japanese affluence has resulted in a labor shortage in labor-intensive factories and construction sites. Asian migrants—including Pakistanis, Thais, Chinese, Malays, Bangladeshis, and Iranians—have filled positions. Despite their growing importance and necessity to Japan's industries, their physical presence often is considered undesirable and disruptive to the social order. A number of cases have been reported of verbal and physical abuse experienced by Asian migrants at work (Higuchi, 1998; Utsumi & Matsui, 1989).

According to Tony Laszlo, director of ISSHO Kikaku (a nonprofit organization that facilitates multiculturalism in Japan), in some local cities with growing numbers of nonwhite and non-Western immigrants, local businesses have posted signs explicitly refusing service to foreigners (Laszlo, 2000). Immigrants have begun to take actions to resist such overt discrimination. For example, *Mainichi Interactive,* an online Japanese newspaper, reported a recent court case of racism in which Ana Bortz, a Brazilian reporter for a Tokyo-based television station, sued a jewelry store for forcing her out of the store because she was a foreigner ("Foreigner Wins," 1999). Because the abuse and discrimination are, for the most part, against nonwhite migrants, it is imperative that the role of hegemony in privileging or marginalizing certain differences be acknowledged (Hegde, 1998). The favoritism toward white Westerners often has worked as hegemony that allowed Japan's discriminatory approaches toward migrants to emerge along racial lines. Reducing the relationships between Japanese and migrants to the binary positions of insider-outsider or to Japanese-gaijin does not completely account for this difference. Interrogating whiteness in Japan's movement toward internationalization helps to uncover the disparate locations that Japan's international migrants occupy. Similarly, it is important to examine the construction and the functions of Japanese-ness in Japan's internationalization because the insider is not singular but rather includes multiple social formations.

INTERNATIONALIZATION AND JAPANESE-NESS

"Japanese" as Equated With "Japanese Ethnicity" and "Japanese Nationality"

Japan's internationalization has been skewed not only because of its heavy reliance on the discourse of whitenization but also because of the "inherent" link between Japanese ethnicity and Japanese nationality. The concept of *minzoku* is relevant here. In a strict literal sense, minzoku refers to ethnicity, but as Yoshino (1998) points out, the word can mean ethnic community, race, nation, or a combination of all of these; thus, "racial, ethnic, and national categories rather vaguely overlap in the Japanese perception of themselves" (p. 24). It is important to note, therefore, that the term *Japanese* that has appeared in this chapter thus far reflects that conflation found in the literature. The naturalized overlaps among the terms must be scrutinized because equating race, ethnicity, and nationality also has undermined Japan's internationalization.

Nihonjinron, or theories of Japanese-ness, are in large part responsible for naturalizing the conflation of Japanese ethnicity and Japanese nationality. According to Dale (1986), from 1946 to 1979, approximately 700 titles were written by Japanese and non-Japanese on Nihonjinron, many of which were published during the latter part of the 1970s. Whereas

Nihonjinron is discussed in a variety of ways for different purposes, the recurrent themes are group orientedness, social harmony, and homogeneity. Advocates of Nihonjinron underscore these traits as the major contributors to the miraculously rapid postwar recovery and industrialization (Mouer & Sugimoto, 1986). Vogel's (1979) best-seller, *Japan as Number One,* represents a typical Nihonjinron discourse; he delineates how a group-oriented mentality and behaviors helped Japan's postwar success in its economy, education, and control of crime. Vogel also suggests how U.S. Americans can adopt these Japanese cognitive and behavioral patterns.

Perhaps it is in the business and management realm that Nihonjinron became most popular. Numerous books have provided U.S. Americans with manuals on how to work with the Japanese by comparing and contrasting their management styles. For example, in his popular book, *Theory Z,* Ouchi (1981) identifies Japanese communication-related features such as implicit control mechanisms, collective decision making, collective responsibility, and holistic concerns. In accordance with Hofstede's (1980) description of cultural characteristics of Japan, many other management-related books (e.g., Byham, 1993; Howard, Shudo, & Umeshima, 1983; Imai, 1986; Okabe, 1983) during the 1980s and early 1990s consistently assert the Japanese group values and underlying cultural homogeneity.

Although Nihonjinron was later severely criticized for its weak theoretical framework,[5] the persistence of these assumptions is revealed in the language of political leaders as well. The infamous remark that former Prime Minister Yasuhiro Nakasone made in a National Study Council meeting of his ruling Liberal Democratic Party in September 1986 is illustrative of the assumptions. The prime minister commented that the average intelligence level in the United States is lower than that in Japan because of the presence of blacks, Mexicans, and Puerto Ricans (Koshiro, 1999; McConnell, 2000; Russell, 1996). When appalled critics demanded the source of the statement, he was not able to provide any but apologized for his racial insensitivity and emphasized that his earlier comment was not based on prejudice but rather meant to point out the difficulty of educational reforms in the United States due to racial diversity. This incident is particularly noteworthy because, in comparison to earlier Japanese leaders, Nakasone's strength rested in having an internationalist orientation and his ability to discuss intercultural issues with other world leaders.

This incident is not an isolated event from the past.[6] According to the *Buraku Liberation News,* Tokyo Governor Shintaro Ishihara's use of the word *sangokujin* at a Self-Defense Force garrison stirred up controversy in the country ("Tokyo Governor's," 2000). He stated that "atrocious crimes have been committed again and again by 'sangokujin' (people from Taiwan, Korea, or their descendants) and other foreigners. We can expect them to riot in the event of a disastrous earthquake." *Sangokujin* is a label used before World War II to refer to Taiwanese and Koreans who were living in Japan. Currently, use of the label is linked with prejudiced attitudes. Ishihara later held a press conference in response to heated protests by human rights groups. *Mainichi Interactive* reported that Ishihara explained that he was from an old generation when the term had been used as slang and that he was referring to illegal aliens and not to the Koreans and Taiwanese who live in Japan legally ("Ishihara Chiji," 2000).

Whatever their intentions, the political leaders' remarks signify prejudicial attitudes toward ethnic minorities and perhaps ignoring the historical existence of cultural groups other than ethnic Japanese. There is little argument that Japan's majority population is ethnic Japanese, but it also is a culturally heterogeneous group of multiple social and cultural identities and histories. The persistent myth of Japan's cultural homogeneity and thus the assumed equation between Japanese ethnicity and Japanese nationality have allowed Japanese society to trivialize domestic intercultural issues that involve "internal others." Korean residents are but one example of a group whose members have a long history in Japanese society but who have been marginalized.

Korean Residents and the Problem of Blurred Nationality and Ethnicity

One of the intercultural issues is the social stratification that Korean residents experience in Japan. There currently are about 640,000 North and South Korean residents in Japan, constituting the largest ethnic minority in Japan (Ministry of Justice, 2000).[7] After Japan's annexation of Korea in 1910, many Koreans were forcibly brought to Japan to work as cheap laborers for coal mines, railroads, and other construction projects. Many other Koreans also migrated to Japan, leaving behind a country where Japan imposed colonial policies to make their lives severely difficult and controlled agricultural production (Fukuoka, 1996; Weiner, 1994).

The majority of the North and South Korean nationals today are second to fifth generation. The majority of the Japan-born Koreans never have been to their homeland of South or North Korea. Many do not speak

Korean. They have lived all of their lives in Japan and will continue to live in Japan. Unlike U.S. American-born ethnic minorities, however, the majority of Japan-born Koreans are Korean nationals because Japanese citizenship is granted to children according to their family "bloodlines." Thus, although Korean residents are an integral part of Japanese society, their legal status claims otherwise.

Maintaining Korean nationality and asserting Korean heritage often come with costs. Although they may take different approaches to their Korean-ness and have varying relationships with members of Japanese society, Korean residents share similar experiences of discrimination in employment, suffrage, housing, and social lives. The constitution of Japan and Japanese laws do not limit positions of national civil service to Japanese citizens. Nevertheless, in practice, the government claims that it is only natural that employment opportunities in the national civil services are open only to Japanese citizens (Den, 1996; Ebashi, 1998). Thus, the Koreans who were born and raised in Japan are excluded because of their Korean nationality.

Many corporations that have no obligation to follow the law often are reluctant to hire Korean nationals (Den, 1996; Kyo, 1996). According to *Mainichi Interactive,* in a recent survey conducted by the Board of Education in the Osaka prefecture, about 30% of some 2,000 foreign-national college graduates reported that they experienced employment discrimination ("Shushoku Sabetu," 2000). The vast majority (98%) of the respondents were Korean residents. Their responses showed shockingly blatant discrimination such as "the company said that they wanted someone from a good family because they deal with money," "the company said that foreigners couldn't join a labor union," and "they asked me if I would naturalize. When I said 'no,' the interview was terminated and I was turned down."[8]

Despite the continuing discrimination, many Korean residents maintain Korean nationality for reasons such as the salience of their Korean heritage and the complexity of the naturalization process. Not only does naturalization take a long time, but the applicants often are asked to minimize their ties to their homeland, reducing their communication with Korean relatives and transferring the assets they have in Korea to Japan (Den, 1996). When browsing through a Web site called the *Han World* that aims to promote understanding between Korean residents and ethnic Japanese, it becomes instantly clear that the conflation of Japanese ethnicity and Japanese nationality is a defining reason why many Korean residents are hesitant to give up their Korean nationality. A comment made by a third-generation Korean resident illustrates this point:[9]

> In the United States, nationality means citizenship, and ethnicity can be anything. In Japan, nationality means ethnicity, so Japanese nationality means Japanese ethnicity. So Korean residents are expected to become Japanese once they are naturalized. . . . This may be fine for those Korean residents who want to become Japanese, but there are many others who don't want to lose their Korean heritage. ("Kokuseki ha Minzoku," 1998)[9]

Ono (1998) argues for problematizing "nation" and "national identity" because the homogeneity presumed for each does not reflect the experience, existence, and identity of those who are not part of the dominant group. For most of us who are ethnic Japanese growing up in Japan, equating Japanese nationality with Japanese ethnicity is a practice that is too normalized to notice. The omissions, however, are obvious to Korean residents whose socialization is characterized not by references to a national identity in which they are included but rather by daily reminders of being at the margin of Japanese-ness.

Although Korean residents and international migrants both are categorized as foreigners by nationality, they are situated differently in the dominant discourse on Japanese-ness. Korean residents are considered by the dominant group of ethnic Japanese to be "assimilable" by virtue of naturalization. This contrasts with the location given to gaijin persons who are physically and culturally marked as outsiders and do not have the option of naturalization. The discrimination and identity issues that are salient to Korean residents, however, continue to exist because of the difficulties of naturalization and the taken-for-granted equation between Japanese nationality and Japanese ethnicity.

Burakumin: Japanese Ethnic, yet the Other

Being a Japanese ethnic and a Japanese national, however, does not guarantee one's privileged place in the dominant group. Another group of people that embodies the "internal other" hidden from the dominant discourse on Japanese-ness is *burakumin.*[10] Burakumin are ethnic Japanese but are said to be descendants of outcast populations in the feudal system who made their living by burying the dead, killing and butchering animals, tanning hides of animals, and other works that are regarded as filthy and despicable under the tenets of Buddhism and Shinto. A newspaper article in *Hokkaido Shinbun* reported on October 22, 1986, that Prime Minister Nakasone stated to the Lower House, "In Japanese society, I believe there is no single minority group who suffers from so-called discrimination as long as they have Japanese nationality" (quoted in Enomori, 1987, p. 226). This statement ignored entirely the continuing discrimination that at least 3 million Japanese citizens face today (Neary, 1997) due to a caste system that existed centuries ago. Buraku communities began to desegregate during the 1960s, and their living conditions, education, and employment situations have slowly improved (Takagi, 1998). But discrimination against burakumin continues.

Similar to Korean residents, burakumin represent an internal other, but their otherness is defined based on class-based stratification rather than on ethnic and nationality differences. Class in this context does not refer to the level of education, occupation, or socioeconomic status as it is commonly understood. Rather, class is based on the assumed "genetic" inferiority and impurity of burakumin, and this assumption is apparent in the ways in which discrimination continues against them. For example, according to the Buraku Liberation and Human Rights Research Institute (BLHRRI), about 1,400 companies registered membership with an investigative agency, and at least 430 of the companies requested the agency to secretly investigate the backgrounds of job applicants to determine whether the applicants were burakumin, Korean residents, members of Sokagakkai (a religious sect), or trade union activists (Tomonaga, 2000).

This incident, revealed in June 1998, demonstrates that little improvement in employment has been achieved since 1975, when more than 200 companies purchased illegal lists of names of burakumin so as to avoid employing them (Schoolland, 1990). Non-burakumin families hire private investigators to interrogate the family histories of potential spouses of their children for buraku backgrounds. Although it is misleading to assume that these discriminatory practices reflect the whole of Japanese society, the very existence of the practices is significant. Despite the obvious violation of human rights, only 5 of the 47 prefectures restrict discriminatory investigations into family backgrounds, and there is no federal law prohibiting such practices (Tomonaga, 2000).

In Japan, class often is considered to be a category of social differentiation that can be changed; for example, a person may move out of a lower class to a middle class if he or she works hard enough or acquires a higher education and a respected career. However, burakumin becoming a reference to class resembles the way in which race was attributed to biological traits. The otherness embodied in burakumin has come to be considered as innate impurity (Schoolland, 1990). But the difficulty of non-burakumin in distinguishing burakumin apart from the rest of ethnic Japanese points precisely to the "social construction" of burakumin as a class and an internal other. Furthermore, the dominant discourse on Japanese-ness refuses to acknowledge burakumin and has constructed Japanese-ness by silencing the other and excluding "undesirable" differences.

INTERNATIONALIZATION: (UN)LEARNING THE NATURALIZED ASSUMPTIONS

Shun Den, a South Korean national critic who has lived in Japan since the 1950s, argues that Japanese politicians tend to think that establishing a close relationship with South Korea would solve the problems that Korean residents face in Japanese society (Den, 1996). This is placing responsibility in the wrong place. The situation of Korean residents in Japan must be improved first if the relationship between the two nations is to improve. I believe that this argument is important beyond the immediate context. In many ways, Japan's orientation to internationalization defines Japan as a single homogeneous entity and focuses on relationships with other countries, particularly the United States. With this orientation, intercultural challenges and tensions within its geopolitical border have not received the attention they deserve.

Japan's internationalization brought many changes to the country. Some changes are perceived to be positive, as reflected in the general meanings of kokusaika, but changes also have meant conflicts, struggles, and problems. It is the ways in which a country defines and handles such changes, I believe, that determines whether the country is becoming a part of the international community. An important part of facing the challenge is to examine the ways in which Japan's kokusaika has occurred because it has not been based on an open or color-blind acceptance of any foreign ideas, products, or people. Rather, kokusaika has been constructed through a discourse of whitenization and the myth of Japan's homogeneity. In addition, Japanese-ness has been created and performed variously in relation to socially and historically differentiated identity locations that embody non-Japanese-ness.

Resonating with Ono's (1998) critique about "nation," it is imperative for ethnic Japanese in particular (and all readers in general) who wish to understand Japan's internationalization to examine taken-for-granted assumptions about frequently used terms such as "Japanese culture," "Japanese society," and "Japanese people." These terms should not be taken as a priori inclusive categories; rather, they must be examined reflexively because, for those who are reminded of their otherness in their daily lives, those words are not natural, nor do they imply harmony and one-ness as the myth of Japanese-ness insists. For the same reason, it is important to interrogate the ways in which discourses of whiteness often have subsumed concepts such as Westerner, American, and gaijin.

Examining these naturalized assumptions is a difficult task for those of us who have privileged status and no immediate need to look beyond the assumptions. It is especially difficult if we have few opportunities to physically step out of the boundaries of Japan and Japanese. This is precisely the reason why it is critical that media and educational texts should strive to present multivocal and multifaceted existences within and across national cultural boundaries. After 9 years of living outside of Japan, I still struggle with deconstructing naturalized assumptions that I learned as I grew up in Japan. My dearest 7-year-old niece has been learning English at a Christian school, and she tells me that she wants to become an internationalist person. I wish for her socialization to be filled with opportunities that help her to cultivate an internationalist vision that is different from what I was given.

NOTES

1. The work of anthropologist Harumi Befu is widely recognized among scholars who specialize in Japan and Japanese society. His perspective on Japan contrasts with the popular view of the nation as collectivistic.

2. Dividing education levels into elementary, junior/middle, and high school also was adopted during the postwar reforms.

3. My mother-in-law, who had begun seventh grade at the time of Japan's defeat, vividly remembers the substantive changes that she experienced. For example, she recalled that right after the defeat, she and other students were told to browse through textbooks and cross out all words and sections that spoke ill of the West.

4. This is my translation.

5. Nihonjinron has been criticized for theoretical weaknesses (e.g., exaggerations, oversimplifications, unsupported claims) and for perpetuating the myth of Japan's homogeneity. Critics, many of whom are members of non-Japanese ethnic groups, deconstruct Nihonjinron by stressing the existence of racial, ethnic, and class minorities in Japan and also present evidence against social harmony (e.g., labor conflict, social stratification, crime). See, for example, Dale (1986), Henshall (1999), Smith (1995), Sugimoto and Mouer (1989), and Woronoff (1996).

6. According to McConnell (2000), Michio Watanabe, a politician, commented during a political action meeting in 1988 that blacks are indifferent to bankruptcy. In 1990, another

Japanese political leader, Kajiyama Seiroku, lamented the increasing number of foreign prostitutes in Japan and compared the situation to blacks moving into white neighborhoods in the United States.

7. The North and South Korean nationals in Japan include not only children with Korean national parents but also children who are offspring of interethnic marriages between Korean nationals and Japanese nationals. In addition to some 700,000 North and South Korean nationals who reside in Japan, there are other Koreans who are naturalized. There also are many offspring of interethnic marriages who adopt Japanese nationality.

8. This is my translation. The message was posted in Japanese.

9. This is my translation. The message was posted in Japanese.

10. *Buraku* and *-min* literally mean village and people, respectively. However, the term *burakumin* usually is understood to mean people who are descendants of the outcasts from feudal systems in the past. Historically, they lived in largely segregated buraku or separate communities.

REFERENCES

Aldwinckle, D. (1996, October, 23). *What's all the fuss about?* [Online]. Available: www.voicenet.co.jp/~davald

Befu, H. (1983). Internationalization of Japan and Nihon Bunkaron. In H. Mannari & H. Befu (Eds.), *In the challenge of Japan's internationalization* (pp. 232-266). Tokyo: Kodansha International.

Byham, W. C. (1993). *Shogun management: How North Americans can thrive in Japanese companies.* New York: HarperCollins.

Chambers, R. (1997). The unexamined. In M. Hill (Ed.), *Whiteness: A critical reader* (pp. 187-203). New York: New York University Press.

Collier, M. J. (1998). Researching cultural identity: Reconciling interpretive and post-colonial perspectives. In D. V. Tanno & A. Gonzalez (Eds.), *Communication and identity across cultures* (pp. 122-147). Thousand Oaks, CA: Sage.

Cornyetz, N. (1994). Fetishized blackness: Hip hop and racial desire in contemporary Japan. *Social Text, 41,* 113-140.

Council of Local Authorities for International Relations. (2000). *JET programme* [Online]. Available: www.clair.nippon-net.ne.jp/html_e/jet/general.htm

Dale, P. (1986). *The myth of Japanese uniqueness.* Sydney, Australia: Croom Helm.

Den, S. (1996). *Nikkan no hazama ni ikite.* Tokyo: Jiyuu sha.

Ebashi, T. (1998). Zainichi Gaikokujin. In *Gendaiyogo no Kisochishiki 1998* (pp. 768-772). Tokyo: Jiyuu Kokumin Sha.

Enomori, S. (1987). *Ainuno rekishi: Hokkaido no hitobito, 2.* Tokyo: Sanseido.

Foreigner wins racism case. (1999, October 13). *Mainichi Interactive* [Online]. Available: baseball.mainichi.co.jp/english/news/archive/199910/13/news01.html

Frankenberg, R. (1993). *White women, race matters: The social construction of whiteness.* Minneapolis: University of Minnesota Press.

Fukuoka, Y. (1996). Koreans in Japan: Past and present. *Saitama University Review, 31*(1). [Online]. Available: www.han.org

Hall, S. (1996). Who needs identity? In S. Hall & P. du Gay (Eds.), *Questions of cultural identity* (pp. 1-17). London: Sage.

Harris, C. I. (1995). Whiteness as property. In C. West, K. Crenshaw, N. Gotanda, G. Peller, & K. Thomas (Eds.), *Critical race theory: The key writings that formed the movement* (pp. 276-291). New York: New Press.

Hegde, R. S. (1998). Swinging the trapeze: The negotiation of identity among Asian Indian immigrant women in the United States. In D. V. Tanno & A. Gonzalez (Eds.), *Communication and identity across cultures* (pp. 34-55). Thousand Oaks, CA: Sage.

Henshall, K. G. (1999). *Dimensions of Japanese society: Gender, margins, and mainstream.* London: Macmillan.

Higuchi, K. (1998). Zainichi Gaikokujin. In *Gendaiyogo no Kisochishiki 1998* (pp. 786-872). Tokyo: Jiyuu Kokumin Sha.

Hofstede, G. (1980). *Culture's consequences: International differences in work-related values.* Beverly Hills, CA: Sage.

hooks, b. (1990). *Yearning: Race, gender, and cultural politics.* Boston: South End.

Howard, A., Shudo, K., & Umeshima, M. (1983). Motivation and values among Japanese and American managers. *Personnel Psychology, 36,* 883-898.

Imai, M. (1986). *Kaizen: The key to Japan's competitive success.* New York: Random House.

Ishihara Chiji: "Sankokujin ga kyoaku hanzai." (2000, April 10). *Mainichi Interactive* [Online]. Available: www12.mainichi.co.jp/news/search-news/817132

Kokuseki ha minzoku. (1998, May 2). *Han World* [Online]. Available: www.han.org/hanboard3

Koshiro, Y. (1999). *Trans-Pacific racism and the U.S. occupation of Japan.* New York: Columbia University Press.

Kumagai, F. (1996). *Unmasking Japan today: The impact of traditional values on modern Japanese society.* Westport, CT: Praeger.

Kyo, N. (1996). *Goku futsuuno zainichi kankokujin.* Tokyo: Asahi Shinbun Sha.

Laszlo, T. (2000, September). *Businesses excluding non-Japanese customers Issho project* [Online]. Available: www.issho.org

Lavie, S., & Swedenburg, T. (1996). Introduction: Displacement, diaspora, and geographies of identity. In S. Lavie & T. Swedenburg (Eds.), *Displacement, diaspora, and geographies of identity* (pp. 1-26). Durham, NC: Duke University Press.

March, M. R. (1992). *Working for a Japanese company: Insights into a multicultural workplace.* Tokyo: Kodansha International.

Martin, J. N., Krizek, R. L., Nakayama, T. K., & Bradford, L. (1996). Exploring whiteness: A study of self labels for white Americans. *Communication Quarterly, 44*(2), 125-144.

McConnell, D. (2000). *Importing diversity: Inside Japan's JET Program.* Berkeley: University of California Press.

McIntosh, P. (1998). White privilege: Unpacking the invisible knapsack. In P. S. Rothenberg (Ed.), *Race, class, and gender in the United States* (4th ed., pp. 165-169). New York: St. Martin's.

Ministry of Justice. (2000). [Number of non-Japanese residents in Japan by country, as of 1999]. *Statistics on Foreign Residents* [Online]. Available: www.jinjapan.org/stat/stats/21mig22.html

Moon, D. (1998). White enculturation and bourgeois identity: The discursive production of "good (white) girls." In T. K. Nakayama & J. N. Martin (Eds.), *Whiteness: The communication of social identity* (pp. 177-197). Thousand Oaks, CA: Sage.

Mouer, R., & Sugimoto, Y. (1986). *Images of Japanese society: A structure of social reality.* London: Kegan Paul.

Neary, I. (1997). *Political protest and social control in pre-war Japan: The origin of buraku liberation.* Manchester, UK: Manchester University Press.

Okabe, R. (1983). Cultural assumptions of East and West: Japan and the United States. In W. B. Gudykunst (Ed.), *Intercultural communication theory* (pp. 21-44). Beverly Hills, CA: Sage.

Ono, K. A. (1998). Problematizing "nation" in intercultural communication research. In D. V. Tanno & A. Gonzalez (Eds.), *Communication and identity across cultures* (pp. 193-202). Thousand Oaks, CA: Sage.

Ouchi, W. G. (1981). *Theory Z: How American business can meet the Japanese challenge.* Reading, MA: Addison-Wesley.

Russell, J. G. (1995, October 14). *Playing with race: Racial myths and the exploitation of blackness in Japan and the United States* [Online]. Available: www.jafa.org/membersonly/education2/johnrussel

Russell, J. G. (1996). Race and reflexivity: The black other in contemporary Japanese mass culture. In J. W. Treat (Ed.), *Contemporary Japan and popular culture.* Surrey, UK: Curzon.

Schoolland, K. (1990). *Shogun's ghost: The dark side of Japanese education.* New York: Bergin & Garvey.

Shushoku Sabetu. (2000, August 26). *Mainichi Interactive* [Online]. Available: www12.mainichi.co.jp/news

Smith, H. (1995). *The myth of Japanese homogeneity: Social ecological diversity in education and socialization.* New York: Nova Science.

Stronach, B. (1995). *Beyond the rising sun: Nationalism in contemporary Japan.* Westport, CT: Praeger.

Sugimoto, Y., & Mouer, R. E. (1989). Cross-currents in the study of Japanese society. In Y. Sugimoto & R. E. Mouer (Eds.), *Constructs for understanding Japan* (pp. 1-35), London: Kegan Paul.

Takagi, M. (1998). Gakusei and Taishu Undou. In *Gendaiyogo no Kisochishiki 1998* (pp. 773- 782). Tokyo: Jiyuu Kokumin Sha.

Tokyo governor's discriminatory remarks regarding foreign residents arouse criticism. (2000, March). *Buraku Liberation News* [Online]. Available: blhrri.org/blhrri_e/news/new113/new11301. html

Tomonaga, K. (2000, May). BLHRRI sent information to the UN Committee on economic, social, and cultural rights prior to examination of Japanese government's report. *Buraku Liberation News* [Online]. Available: blhrri.org/blhrri_e/news/new113/new11301.html

Trinh, M. (1990). Not you/like you: Post-colonial women and the interlocking questions of identity and difference. In G. Anzaldúa (Ed.), *Making face, making soul* (pp. 371-375). San Francisco: Aunt Lute.

Utsumi, A., & Matsui, Y. (1989). *Ajia kara kita dekasegi roudousya tachi.* Tokyo: Akashi.

Vogel, E. (1979). *Japan as number one: Lessons for America.* Cambridge, MA: Harvard University Press.

Weiner, M. (1994). *Race and migration in Imperial Japan.* London: Routledge.

Wong, K. (1998). Migration across generations: Whose identity is authentic? In J. N. Martin, T. K. Nakayama, & L. A. Flores (Eds.), *Readings in cultural contexts* (pp. 127-134). Mountain View, CA: Mayfield.

Woodward, K. (1997). Concepts of identity and difference. In K. Woodward (Ed.), *Identity and difference* (pp. 7-62). London: Sage.

Woronoff, J. (1996). *Japan—as anything but—number one* (2nd ed.). London: Macmillan.

Woronoff, J. (1997). *The Japanese social crisis.* New York: St. Martin's.

Yoshino, K. (1998). Culturalism, racialism, and internationalism in the discourse of Japanese identity. In D. C. Gladney (Ed.), *Making majorities: Constituting the nation in Japan, Korea, China, Malaysia, Fiji, Turkey, and the United States* (pp. 13-30). Stanford, CA: Stanford University Press.

2

From "Orphan of Asia" to "Moses Coming Out of Egypt"

A Metaphorical Analysis of the Transformation of Taiwan's Political Identity

HUI-CHING CHANG • *University of Illinois at Chicago*

Since his election as the new president of Taiwan, Republic of China (ROC), Chen Shui-bien has been calling for the People's Republic of China (PRC) to peacefully negotiate its relations with Taiwan. Chen's somewhat conciliatory gestures toward China stand in contrast to the pro-independence position he took prior to being elected. This "softer" position seems to reflect Chen's attempt to, on the one hand, consolidate diverse voices in Taiwan and, on the other, to avoid further straining the relationship between Taiwan and China.

Why is it necessary for Chen to establish an equilibrium between the ROC and the PRC? The title of Copper's (1996) book, *Taiwan: Nation-State or Province?*, highlights the ambiguity and uncertainty of Taiwan's situation. An island with more than 20 million people, and a lengthy history as an independent political entity that practices democracy, Taiwan has nevertheless been claimed by the PRC as a part—or, more specifically, a province—of its territory. The PRC has consistently isolated Taiwan in the international political arena and has repudiated attempts of foreign governments to support Taiwan,[1] claiming that it will not hesitate to use armed force if Taiwan ever tries to become independent.

The political tension between Taiwan and China came to a head in a recent interview with ex-President Lee Teng-hui by a German radio station

---

AUTHOR'S NOTE: The author thanks the editor and reviewers for their helpful comments. David Frank was particularly helpful in providing insightful comments and encouragement throughout the development of this research project.

on July 9, 1999. In this interview, Lee said that the relations between Taiwan and China should be considered "state to state," thereby abandoning the "one China" policy that Taiwan officially has endorsed in the past (Mong, 1999a). Lee's comments infuriated the PRC officials, who criticized Lee's position as reckless and as amounting to an assertion of Taiwan's independence. According to the PRC, in light of Lee's purported attempt to "split the motherland," Chinese officials delivered their most severe military threats to Taiwan since 1996 (Faison, 1999a, 1999d). Taiwan was forced to tone down some of its "contentious" language—such as "two states," "two Chinas," "one China, two states," and "one nation, two countries"—to avoid further straining the relationship with China (Parker, 1999).

Nevertheless, despite political pressure from the PRC and the past official endorsement of the "one China" policy by the Taiwanese government, Taiwan has managed to create a distinctive identity by establishing relationships with foreign governments through practical diplomacy and commercial contacts. One way of exploring the cultivation of Taiwan's identity is to examine the discursive forces and symbolic acts, such as metaphors (Foss, 1989; Ortner, 1973), that integrate and solidify the feelings and emotive reactions of Taiwanese toward the problems of the Taiwan-China relationship.

In the case of Taiwan, development and transition of two key metaphors (Ortner, 1973)—"orphan of Asia" and "Moses coming out of Egypt"—provide a useful vantage point from which to examine Taiwanese political discourse. For the people in Taiwan, "orphan" has long served as a key metaphor to contemplate the meaning of being Chinese, highlighting Taiwan's struggle to carve out a sense of identity. As the sociopolitical context has gradually changed and no longer supports the orphan metaphor as a symbolic template for Taiwanese[2]—that is, as the orphan metaphor has become dormant (Perelman & Olbrechts-Tyteca, 1969)—it has yielded to the "Moses" metaphor, which eventually has led to the articulation of the two-state theory by Lee. When metaphors change, so do our perceptions and constructions of political reality (Miller, 1979). From the sense of "no identity" (as implied in the orphan metaphor), to the sense of "identity in sight but yet to be achieved" (as implied in the Moses metaphor), these two metaphors provide alternative frameworks for people in Taiwan to express and define themselves while enduring political uncertainty and pressure. By delineating the historical and cultural contexts within which these metaphors have been developed, modified, and transformed, this study shows how these symbolic vehicles provide

Taiwanese with the means to walk a fine line between being essentially "Taiwanese" and being "Chinese."

METAPHOR AND POLITICAL DISCOURSE

Metaphors have been explored in various fields of inquiry including philosophy, anthropology, social psychology, and sociolinguistics as well as symbolism and literary criticism. Metaphor, in its broadest sense, can be explained as a situation in which one thing is seen or experienced in terms of another (Brown, 1976; Lakoff & Johnson, 1980; Schön, 1979) or as a "condensed analogy" (Perelman & Olbrechts-Tyteca, 1969, p. 399). To put it simply, "Metaphor is a device for seeing something *in terms of* something else. It brings out the thisness of a that or the thatness of a this" (Burke, 1969, p. 503). This connection may depend on structural analogy or the analogy of an emotional dimension (Thaiss, 1978). By building connections between two unrelated events, metaphor helps to simplify complex and bewildering sets of observations through organizing perceptions (Edelman, 1971) while at the same time possessing ambiguity that allows for multiple interpretations to suit the needs of specific situations or changing interests (Graves, 1983; Johnson, 1978).

Although metaphor may be created purposefully as ornament to embellish a text, more important, as Lakoff and Johnson (1980) put it, metaphor "is pervasive in everyday life, not just in language but in thought and action" (p. 3). Because we can access "reality" only through language, and language is what enables us to connect symbol with experience, whatever is used to describe reality is necessarily metaphorical (Edelman, 1971; Foss, 1989; Lakoff & Johnson, 1980). Hence, thoughts are by nature metaphorical, and metaphor is "the basic process by which humans understand their world" (Foss, Foss, & Trapp, 1985, p. 156; see also Edelman, 1971; Lakoff & Johnson, 1980).

In Western rhetorical tradition, Aristotle initiated the extended treatment of metaphors. However, from Aristotle until the 19th century, metaphors were seen by many theorists as merely ornaments of language that deviated from its normal use. Moreover, given their supposed decorative function, various rules were formulated to ensure appropriate use of metaphors as linguistic embellishment. This narrow view was later transformed into an extended view—particularly through the contributions of Richards (1936, 1950, 1952)—that treats metaphors as intrinsic to thought and reality:

> Whatever vocabulary we use to describe reality is a metaphor because it enables us to see reality *as* something. Phenomena in the world become objects of reality or knowledge only because of the symbols/metaphors that make them accessible to us. (Foss, 1989, p. 188)

Richards (1950) notes that metaphor provides "a concrete instance of a relation which would otherwise have to be stated in abstract terms" (p. 239); hence, metaphor is "a shift, a carrying over of a word from its normal use to a new use" (Richards, 1952, p. 221). One word or phrase serves to bring two thoughts together, and meaning is derived from such interaction (Foss et al., 1985).

Metaphor is not simply a feature of language but rather a mode of communication whose enactment depends on the interaction between reader and context, invoking systems of thought and meaning (Black, 1962; Koestler, 1964). As Thaiss (1978) puts it, "The hearer is asked to make imaginative completion from within his own experiences of what the metaphor figuratively suggests. The hearer must become involved, he must intellectually do something, to join in, in order to comprehend the message" (p. 7). Use of the metaphor invites audiences to see things in new ways, highlight specific viewpoints, structure audiences' perceptions, and construct social realities (Burke, 1969; Ivie, 1987; Lakoff & Johnson, 1980). For this reason, Burke (1969) said, "For metaphor we could substitute *perspective*" (p. 503). According to Richards (1950), such fusion affects "attitude and impulse which spring from their collocation and from the combinations which the mind then establishes between them" (p. 240). Thus, metaphors are particularly useful in areas of unnamed experience (Thaiss, 1978).

Although this fusion invites those who perceive the metaphoric analogy to participate in cocreating new ways of thinking and understanding, at the same time, it constrains the way in which one comes to think about the things described (Schön, 1979). The operation of metaphor depends not only on similarities and resemblance but also on disparity and dissimilarity (Foss et al., 1985). Because the two realms never are identical, as Burke (1969) notes, varying degrees of incongruity can be expected. To deal with such incongruity, aspects that are inconsistent with the metaphor often are ignored (Lakoff & Johnson, 1980); hence, whereas the desired aspects are highlighted, limitations are concealed (Edelman, 1971).

By constructing reality in specific ways, metaphors also inform attitude and direct actions. As rhetorical devices, metaphors help us to "focus our attention on certain features, exhibit an evaluation or attitude toward those features, and thus encourage us to experience the concept in a particular way" (Foss, 1989, p. 5). Specifically, metaphors help us to summarize and elaborate information (Ortner, 1973) and also function as an inventional tool (Graves, 1983).

Hence, metaphors can be treated as pivotal points of entry for insight into political discourse. Metaphors take on new meanings and new interpretations as situations warrant, and they create an alternative arena within which new political discourse can take root and grow. As Edelman (1971) contends, metaphorical modes of examining the political scene "are central to the shaping of political values, attitudes, . . . perceptions, and sometimes personality formation" because they "help promote conformity to organization, movements, and leadership, though they are also central to arousal and rebellion" (p. 65; see also Miller, 1979). Particularly in times of social change, metaphors help to create beliefs and provide guidance on values as well as proper actions (Thaiss, 1978). Of course, beyond creating and sustaining political realities, metaphors derive their substance from their unique sociopolitical contexts. To use Miller's (1979) words, "Metaphors can take us beyond the observable and also make manifest the intelligible structure of the unobservable" (p. 169).

Analysis of key metaphors allows us to understand the dominant themes of a given culture (Johnson, 1978; Miller, 1979; Ortner, 1973). Key or root metaphors, according to Ortner (1973), are "symbols with conceptual elaboration power" because "many aspects of experience can be likened to, and illuminated by the comparison with, the symbol itself" (p. 1340). They help to formulate unity of cultural orientation by sorting out experiences and building interrelationships among them and by suggesting effective orderly action. The metaphor is considered "key" to the cultural system "insofar as it extensively and systematically formulates relationships . . . between a wide range of diverse cultural elements" (p. 1343).

In the past, various scholars have used metaphorical criticism to examine metaphors developed in various arenas of political discourse (Johnson, 1978; Thaiss, 1978), particularly those created and sustained by specific speakers (see, e.g., Daughton, 1993; Graves, 1983; Ivie, 1987; Jamieson, 1980; Lee & Campbell, 1994). The purpose of this study, then, is to use metaphorical criticism (Foss, 1989) to examine Taiwan's political discourse about its changing identity, as expressed in two key metaphors. One metaphor, "orphan of Asia" (introduced toward the end of Taiwan's occupation by Japan from 1895-1945), has gradually been supplanted by another metaphor, "Moses coming out of Egypt" (introduced by Lee in a 1994 interview with a Japanese reporter).

According to Ortner (1973), a metaphor may be considered as a key symbol of a given culture if it fulfills any or some of the conditions that (a) people consider it culturally important; (b) people react to it either positively or negatively; (c) the symbol manifests itself in many different contexts and domains, whether behavioral or symbolic; (d) the symbol receives great elaboration; and (e) there are cultural rules restricting the symbol's proper use. People in Taiwan are well aware of discourses concerning these two metaphors. In addition, both popular media and scholarly research feature discussions of the metaphors, regardless of whether the discussants embrace or challenge the metaphors' implications. Hence, from both qualitative and quantitative perspectives, the orphan and Moses metaphors may be considered as key or root metaphors for Taiwan's political discourse (see also Graves, 1983).

It should be noted, however, that the analysis conducted in this study focuses not only on the creators and audiences for metaphors but also on the historical contexts and situations that call for development, discussion, and debates about them (Foss, 1989). These metaphors thrive in Taiwan's historical context—from its colonial past to its more recent status as an economically successful, democratic, modern political entity—and provide distinctive frames of reference that outline Taiwan's changing sense of identity. Specifically, this study analyzes various forms of cultural texts—including media presentations through newspapers and the Internet, popular and scholarly books, and popular culture as well as speeches delivered by various government officials—to show how the metaphors have been constructed and sustained, their pervasiveness, and their potential influence. Before a detailed metaphorical analysis is presented, however, a short history of Taiwan is in order.

TAIWAN, ISLAND OF FORMOSA

Taiwan's Story: A Brief History

Taiwan is an island located in the South China Sea, about 100 miles east of the Asian continent, and about the size of Delaware (Hsu, 1990). During the 16th and 17th centuries, Taiwan was controlled by several Western European governments (Portugal, Spain, and Holland). It was ruled by the Cheng family for more than 20 years and then by the Ch'ing dynasty for more than 200 years (Copper, 1996). Taiwan was ceded to Japan by the

Ch'ing dynasty after the war of 1894-1895 and was ruled by the Japanese until 1945. Following the defeat of Japan in World War II, in accordance with the terms of the Cairo Declaration of 1943 and the Potsdam Proclamation of 1945, Taiwan was restored to the Chinese Nationalists (Hsu, 1990).

Four years later, after the Communist Party seized power on the mainland in 1949, the leader of the Nationalists, Chiang Kai-shek, moved to Taiwan, formed a Chinese government, and declared the occupation of mainland China by the Communist Party illegal. Chiang also brought more than 1.5 million Chinese with him to Taiwan; these "late immigrants" usually were referred to as "outside province people" (*waishengren*) by the early Chinese immigrants, who sometimes call themselves "native Taiwanese" (Copper, 1996) or "own province people" (*benshengren*).[3]

Politically, Chiang's Nationalist government positioned itself against what it termed the "illegal" PRC, stating its aim of one day "recovering" the "divine land"—that is, the mainland—and punishing anyone found advocating Taiwan's independence. Martial law also was established, and the ROC's constitution was temporarily suspended—moves that significantly restricted political rights and ensured the stability of the Nationalist government in Taiwan. It was not until 1987, after Chiang's son (Chiang Ching-kuo) succeeded him as president in 1978, that martial law was lifted and Taiwan gradually opened its doors to democracy.

Chiang Ching-kuo made a number of political changes, gradually allowing Taiwanese to participate in governmental affairs and bridging the gap between early and later immigrants. After having lived under the rulership of Japan for the first half of the 20th century and having operated under the influence of Nationalist socioeconomic policies, Taiwan has managed to become one of the most powerful economic entities in the world. Taiwan's degree of democratization is particularly impressive, leading some observers to claim that Taiwan is the first free Chinese political entity ever to exist (Garver, 1997). In 1996, Lee became the first "native" Taiwanese to be elected ROC president. Lee abolished the "temporary provisions of the constitution" (the law under which civil rights had been suspended), granting political and civil rights to all of Taiwan's citizens. He also officially ended the war with China and further promoted contact between Taiwan and China[4] (Copper, 1996). In 2000, Chen Shui-bian, also a native Taiwanese, became the first president of Taiwan not to be affiliated with the Kuomintang (KMT, the ruling Nationalist party in Taiwan).

Two Sides of the Taiwan Straits

The question of who should represent the "legitimate China"—or, indeed, whether there should even be such a discussion—has long been an unresolved issue for scholars of international politics and law (Chen & Reisman, 1972). Since the establishment of Chiang's regime, and for nearly 30 years thereafter, the ROC was widely considered to be the only legitimate Chinese government (Hsu, 1990). The situation was reversed when China replaced Taiwan in the United Nations' General Assembly and the Security Council in 1971 and when the United States cut its formal ties with Taiwan, extending diplomatic recognition to the PRC as the "only China" in 1978.

In response to its diplomatic exclusion, and to assert that it would not surrender to China, Taiwan banned its citizens from direct trade and investment under the "three no's" policy articulated in 1981—no contacts, no negotiation, and no compromise with the PRC (Chao & Myers, 1998; Copper, 1996; Huan, 1994). Taiwan's international political status has continued to decline; now, fewer than 30 countries, most of them small, still maintain diplomatic ties with Taiwan. With widespread recognition of the PRC as the only legitimate China, Taiwan has been constantly threatened with direct military invasion by the PRC (Harding, 1994). China claims that the question of Taiwan's status is a "domestic problem" and that it would not tolerate any suggestion of "two Chinas" or "one China, one Taiwan" (Wei, 1994) as the result of either support by the international community or Taiwan's attempts to create an independent country.

Since the mid-1980s, however, China and Taiwan have begun to narrow their differences. While gradually cultivating contacts with China, Taiwan also has softened its claim as the "only legitimate Chinese country" and has tried increasingly to pursue a course as a separate political entity (Copper, 1996; Morgan, 1993; Robinson & Lin, 1994). In 1987, when martial law in Taiwan was abolished, Chiang Ching-kuo also opened the door for Taiwanese to visit relatives on the mainland. In 1988, the Mainland Affairs Council was established to handle informal relations between Taiwan and China. In 1990, Lee established the National Unification Council to endorse national unification and actualize a policy of "one China," even though that policy was stated in Taiwan's terms rather than in those of the PRC (Chao & Myers, 1998). The council also proposed guidelines, setting three stages for eventual unification.[5] In 1990, both

Taiwan and China established "unofficial" organizations to assist in matters relating to communication between the two political entities.

Semi-official dialogue gradually developed, culminating in the unprecedented "Koo-Wang talks" in 1993 (Koo and Wang are heads of unofficial organizations in Taiwan and China). Restrictions on business activities were loosened, and even governmental employees were allowed to visit the PRC (Huan, 1994). Mainland Chinese also were allowed to visit Taiwan provided that they fulfilled certain requirements. Because these reforms were instituted, exchanges between China and Taiwan have increased at a rapid rate in areas such as cultural learning, educational affairs, arts, commerce, and technology (Chao & Myers, 1998; Clough, 1993). But the "three communication policy"—direct communication through post, through commerce, and through transportation between Taiwan and China—is officially opposed by Taiwan until China changes its hostile position toward Taiwan's status (Copper, 1996). From 1990 to mid-1995, relations between the two countries steadily improved; according to Chao and Myers (1998), "This détente never involved official contacts, but an atmosphere of goodwill and optimism ensued" (p. 292).

In 1995, however, Taiwan and China halted continuing discussions about a common political future and did not resume their dialogue until 1998 (Clough, 1999). A series of events—beginning with a white paper published by the Mainland Affairs Council in 1993, followed by messages published in *Asia Weekly*'s interview with Lee in 1994, and capped by Lee's controversial visit to the United States in 1995—apparently led China's leaders to doubt Taiwan's sincerity about the idea of a unified China.[6]

The relations between Taiwan and China reached a new critical point when, on July 9, 1999, Lee stated that relations should be treated as "state to state." In an interview with a German radio station, Lee emphasized that the ROC government has sovereignty over Taiwan.[7] Lee's redefinition of the relations between Taiwan and China as state to state is, according to Sly (1999b), "the closest Taiwan has come to a formal declaration of independence from China" (p. 8).[8] Although Lee himself did not explicitly mention that the "one China" policy was to be abolished, in a follow-up news meeting held to clarify the points Lee raised, a high official stated, "[Our] government will no longer use terms such as 'one China' and 'two equal political entities' to interpret the relation between the two sides" (Chen, 1999; see also Sly, 1999a). Nevertheless, the eventual goal of reunification was said to remain intact (Mong, 1999b). Lee's two-state view, according to a poll, was supported by 73.3% of Taiwan's people

(Lim, 1999). Not surprisingly, Lee's implication that China and Taiwan no longer are the same country of "China" led China to see Lee as favoring Taiwan's independence. China issued severe threats against Taiwan including the release of information about its ability to manufacture nuclear weapons (Faison, 1999b, 1999c). As a result, Taiwan softened its rhetoric, toning down its claim of state-to-state relations (Parker, 1999).

Similarly, China attempted to influence the March 2000 election by constantly warning Taiwan voters not to elect the Democratic Progressive Party (DPP) candidate, Chen Shui-bian, apparently in the belief that Chen appeared to be the most likely candidate to lead the Taiwanese on the road to independence, despite the fact that following Chen's election as president of the ROC, he adopted a more conciliatory position toward China. At this point, how future relations develop between Taiwan and China remains to be seen. Setting aside the issue of whether Taiwan has officially claimed independence, it is quite clear that there is a strong urge by some Taiwanese to separate themselves from China. Such an urge has not materialized overnight; rather, it has been developed over a long period of time, as can be observed in the discourse revealing the transformation of two key metaphors.

FALLACY OF CONNECTION: ANALYSIS OF TWO KEY METAPHORS

Taiwan's national identity can be understood by analyzing the Taiwanese sense of "Chinese-ness." Although the Nationalist government has for some time stressed the role of Taiwan as the true bearer of "Chinese cultural heritage" (Gates, 1987), more recently this construction of identity has been transformed as many Taiwanese increasingly feel the need to distinguish themselves from Chinese on the mainland. As Garver (1997) puts the question, "Were they Chinese or Taiwanese? If they were Chinese, what exactly did this mean?" (p. 16; see also Tu, 1994b). Answers to these questions are complicated with issues relating to race, ethnicity, cultural heritage, historical contact, locality, and even blood connections between the two peoples.

People in Taiwan use various symbolic means to walk a fine line between being essentially "Taiwanese" and being "Chinese." Close examination of two key metaphors articulated in Taiwanese political discourse —"orphan of Asia" and "Moses coming out of Egypt"—reveals attempts to redefine what it means to be Chinese in terms of a unique Taiwanese identity as they try to move from a feeling of being abandoned and unable to partake of the grandeur of being part of the "central nation"[9] to a search for an identity separate from the PRC.

"Orphan of Asia"

The Orphan of Asia is the evocative title of a novel by Wu (1995) portraying the struggle of Taiwanese intellectuals under Japanese occupation.[10] Originally written in Japanese in 1945 toward the end of Japanese colonization, *The Orphan of Asia* was published only after Taiwan was released from Japanese control (Dai, 1994). The book, later revised and translated into Chinese (Wu, 1995),[11] describes the lifelong search for identity by one Taiwanese intellectual working under a Japanese government that Copper (1996) describes as "beneficial and progressive, on the one hand, yet discriminatory and predatory, on the other" (p. 30). Much like an orphan, the main character, Hu Tai-ming, struggles with the ambiguous and contradictory relations among Taiwan, Japan, and China, exacerbated by Japan's invasion of China and the placing of Taiwan under Japanese control. Rather than finding his identity and dignity, Hu eventually succumbs to insanity, providing an emotional indictment of the absurdity and cruelty of political power and history.

Because it so powerfully outlines the suffering, uncertainty, and struggle of Taiwanese who tried to make sense of their existence before, during, and after Japanese rule, Wu's (1995) writing is highly regarded by many Taiwanese (Lin, 1989). Specifically, Wu's creation of the orphan metaphor is one factor that has made the novel an important part of the political and cultural discourse of Taiwan's people (Lin, 1989).[12] The pervasiveness of the image of the orphan can be discerned in various channels of discourse. For example, Chen (1984), a writer who supports Taiwan's unification with China, published a book in 1984 titled *Orphan's History: The History of an Orphan.* The orphan, to paraphrase Edelman (1971), becomes a form of social cuing whose potency sometimes easily dominates testable reality (p. 67).

The metaphor serves as "a semi-surreptitious method by which a greater variety of elements can be wrought into the fabric of the experience" (Richards, 1950, p. 240), and the orphan metaphor evokes a feeling of deep sorrow (*beiqing yishi*) that Taiwanese may have experienced but that otherwise would remain unnoticed. (This characteristic of some metaphors also is explored in Black, 1962.) Through the orphan metaphor, Taiwan's fate is conceptualized as a human life in the course of which all kinds of emotions, for better or for worse, are experienced. The orphan image is particularly powerful because of the close blood connections of Chinese kinship that have led Taiwanese to view the fate of orphans as among the most miserable and pitiful examples of human suffering. Orphans grow up in orphanages or are left to survive on their own, with abuse and mistreatment being the norm rather than the exception. Various folk stories and television programs in Taiwan provide ample evidence of the sufferings of orphans. Without the love and concern of one's parents, it is unlikely that orphans ever receive any kind of love and compassion.

The "orphan of Asia" metaphor, without explicating the similarity of Taiwan's fate to that of an orphan, brings forth its past struggle and suffering. Although many see such a sorrowful feeling as having been occasioned primarily by Japanese rulership (Dai, 1994; Long, 1996), Xiang (1996) notes that any understanding of the sorrow Taiwanese feel about themselves must go back through Taiwan's history of being oppressed by foreign colonialism—back to the 17th and 18th centuries or even earlier. During this period, Chinese immigrants journeyed to Taiwan to avoid harsh lives in China, as a result becoming regarded by Chinese rulers as "wanderers." According to Xiang, "The sorrowful feeling cultivated in their migration to Taiwan came not from their being oppressed, but from their being abandoned" (p. 42).

Harding's (1994) observation that "Taiwan is an instance of both of the processes—foreign colonialism and civil war—that created a divided China" (p. 236) well delineates the complex sociopolitical environment within which Taiwan's sense of being an orphan has developed. As Lin (1989) puts it, "We are like an orphan without parents to cherish us, and we are chased around by people" (p. 112). Particularly for those who support an independent Taiwanese identity, throughout its history, Taiwan never has decided its own destiny and its people have been unsuccessful in their repeated attempts to struggle against colonialism (Zhang, 1992).[13] As an orphan, Taiwan has been "abandoned," later having its destiny decided by different nations including the Nationalist government that Lee has described as an "alien regime" (Garver, 1997).[14] The notes on the back cover of Zhang's (1992) book on Taiwan's history illustrate this line of thinking: "All those changes were entirely due to wars among powerful nations and had nothing to do with the quality of Taiwanese governmental administration or the people's will. However, each time, the Taiwanese paid a steep price in either their lives or their possessions."

Taiwan's feeling of being an orphan became particularly acute in light of the Japanese takeover that completely severed its ties with the mainland—that is, the "motherland" (*zhuguo*)—for half a century (1895-1945):

> Whether it is positive or negative, people in Taiwan could not have the same common basis and experience to walk with people in the Mainland toward a modern nation. Also cut off is whatever could have happened "on the road," whether it is the experience of love, hate, fortune, suffering, happiness, or sorrow. The opportunity of having a common experience between people in Taiwan and in the Mainland was taken away by Japanese imperialism. (Dai, 1994, p. 17)

Having failed to combat Japanese rulership, some Taiwanese advocated going "back to the motherland," even though the motherland had surrendered to Japan and had "abandoned" Taiwan. Unfortunately, the "divine land" (*shenzhou,* one of several elevated names for the "central nation" [Tu, 1994b]), at that time governed by Nationalists, had fallen prey to Western and Japanese imperialism. Because Nationalist rulers were in conflict with external powers and caught up in an internal political struggle with the Communists and other military forces, the motherland could do little to help its "abandoned child." As part of an "orphan nation" that dictated ambiguous roles, some Taiwanese chose to fight against Japan simply by following Nationalist leadership, some curried favor with Japanese in Taiwan, and some were forced by Japanese to join the military to fight against the Nationalists. These contradictory roles produced in Taiwanese a sense of being directionless, thereby aggravating the "Taiwan complex," particularly among the middle class and intellectuals (Dai, 1994).

Because for most of their history the people of Taiwan have been predominantly *Han* people from the southern provinces of China, it is understandable that the orphan would want to free itself of control by Japan and to return to the kindness of the motherland. Chen (1998) contends that if Wu's (1995) book symbolizes the beginning of "Taiwanese consciousness" (*taiwan yishi*), then such consciousness is defined by and integrated with—rather than separate from—the "Chinese consciousness" (*zhongguo yishi*). Although such sentiments for the motherland lack practical foundation, they nevertheless are blood connected, almost instinctual, and even irrational (p. 111). In other words, the motherland symbolizes Han people, and Taiwan consciousness is "Han people consciousness" with its bases in Chinese culture. Wu (1988), commenting on his own work, elaborates as follows:

> Although the affection for the motherland cannot be seen with one's eyes and exists only as a notion, it is very subtle and always attracts my heart. It is just like an orphan, separated from his or her parents, would admire the unknown parents. It does not matter what kinds of parents they are. The child just admires his/her parents, thinking that as long as s/he can be together with the parents, life would be good. It is almost an instinctual feeling that one loves the motherland and admires the motherland. (p. 40)

The orphan image and its derivative motherland image collaborate in expressing the racial and ethnic connection between being Taiwanese and being Chinese; together, to use Jamieson's (1980) words, they weave "a pattern that is at least coherent and at best compelling" (p. 51). The Chinese sense of racial identity and ancestry makes them "feel that they have a bond with all people of Chinese blood" (Pye, 1985, p. 185). The designation as people of the central nation (*zhongguoren*),[15] Wu (1994) notes, "carries the connotation of modern patriotism or nationalism . . . , a connectedness with the fate of China as a nation. Associated with this is a sense of fulfillment, of being the bearers of a cultural heritage handed down from their ancestors, of being essentially separate from non-Chinese" (p. 149).

This "mother complex" exemplified by the orphan metaphor well illustrates Chen's (1998) contention that it was not until World War II that Taiwan intended to separate itself from China and claim independence. Rather than treating the Chinese mainland as an enemy and as a target to fight against, the orphan wanted to return to the bosom of its parents. When Taiwan finally was restored to the Nationalist government in 1945, Taiwanese activated a mother complex, eagerly welcoming the arrival of the central government from China (Dai, 1994).

Unfortunately, the orphan's eagerness to return to the embrace of the motherland soon was met with consternation and dismay when occupation by Chiang's military troops—aided by widespread incompetence, greed, bribery, and illegal behavior by various government officials and exacerbated by cultural differences between early and later immigrants—led to fierce conflict. In addition, most governmental positions were filled by late immigrants. These conflicts reached critical proportions when on February 28, 1947, the Nationalist government used armed force against native Taiwanese and thus began the "white terror" regime (Kerr, 1965). Particularly for many early immigrants, Chiang's government was just as foreign as, and even harsher than, the Japanese colonialist government (Hong, 1997; Kerr, 1965; Zhang, 1992). This unfortunate encounter between the early and late immigrants was crystallized by what happened on February 28, known to many Taiwanese as the "2-2-8 event." It led to the death of the image of a motherland that had come from the notion of the mainland as the divine land. From the time of Chiang's government, some Taiwanese started to be more interested in Taiwan's independence as well as in separating themselves from the Chinese. But none of these attempts was successful (Zhang, 1992).

Others, however, continued to endorse a Chinese-centered construction of identity, as facilitated by Taiwan's educational practices. It was not until after the abolition of martial law that education in Taiwan began to focus on indigenous Taiwanese culture. Until that time, although the history and geography of China were required courses from elementary school through high school, the Nationalist government forbade the teaching of Taiwanese history and geography. Moreover, because the government's program of historical education always had focused on China, many Taiwanese found it difficult to form a conception of a "home" in any place other than the mainland. Lin (1989), for example, writes that the textbooks used in Taiwan's elementary schools misled Taiwanese children into thinking that the central nation cherishes Taiwanese "as hearts and treasure" (*xingan baobei*) (p. 178), a phrase generally reserved for describing the love that parents have for their children.[16]

To the orphan, the idea of the Chinese motherland always has been imagined and idealized; the orphan can return to the warmth of the motherland only if the Nationalist government were to lead Taiwanese to "recover" the mainland. Although the central nation never has been stabilized and, given its diverse ethnic groups, multiple languages and religious practices, and even fluctuating boundaries, always has been in a state of chaos, the act of orienting toward the "center" and respecting common traditions helps Chinese to build their collective identity. The identity that is being constructed is based on cultural and historical fulfillment rather than on the more modern view that national identity is a matter of citizenship (Dai, 1994; Wu, 1994).

The uncertainty of the status of the orphan remained as the concern over whether Taiwan had its own unique culture became more and more acute and the orphan status became more and more ambiguous. In 1983, uncertainty was further intensified when a famous singer, Ho De-jian, went back to China to search for his motherland. Ho had composed and sung a popular song titled *The Descendants of the Dragon* (*Long de Chuanren,* an expression of a Chinese-centered view, given that "dragon" is the symbol for Chinese or Han people), and his journey to China sparked fierce debates concerning the intersection between the "Taiwan complex" and the "China complex." These debates and references to complexes were evident in various publications and political demonstrations, climaxing in 1987 when a group of people stood up to challenge the authority of the KMT, referred to as the "Formosa Event" (Chen, 1998).[17]

The orphan metaphor, therefore, consolidates the sense of sorrow cultivated throughout Taiwan's long history, accentuated during Japanese rulership, and then expanded by the imposition of the Nationalist government. According to Xiang (1996), the Taiwanese feeling of sorrow includes the following features: (a) the feeling of being discarded by the motherland, (b) the feeling of being oppressed by various alien regimes, (c) the feeling of "no motherland," (d) the feeling of frustration at futile attempts to change the situation, and (e) the feeling of being distorted (because Taiwanese know little about Taiwan). Even after 400 years, Taiwan has not established its own self-reliant, healthy culture; it remains dominated and unable to provide a worldview that encompasses people of different ethnic groups in Taiwan (Xiang, 1996).

The orphan mentality continues to exert its influence in the modern era. For example, during the early 1980s, one well-known Taiwanese singer, Dayou Luo, wrote and performed a widely influential song titled *Orphan of Asia:*

The orphan of Asia cries in the wind,
Her yellow face has red dust,
Her black eyeballs have white terror,
The West wind in the East, sings sad songs.

The orphan of Asia cries in the wind,
No one wants to play an equal game with you,
Everyone wants your cherished toy.
Dear children, why are you crying?

How many people are searching for the unsolvable question?
How many people have no alternative but to sigh in the flow of time?
How many people wipe their tears in silence?
Dear mother, what kind of reason is this?

The orphan of Asia cries in the wind,
Her yellow face has red dust,
Her black eyeballs have white terror,
The West wind in the East, sings sad songs.

Does the singer regret Taiwan's history? Is he complaining about the irresponsibility or powerlessness of the imagined motherland? If Taiwan has returned to the motherland—a Chinese government—then why does the singer still complain about being an orphan? Is the mother an imagined and idealistic, but never extant, sense of a Chinese world or a government established by Taiwanese themselves? Perhaps we never will find definitive answers to these questions given that "ambiguity is a necessary by-product of the metaphor's suggestiveness" (Black, 1990, p. 62). Although some criticize the "orphan of Asia" metaphor and its implications (see, e.g., Dai, 1994; Long, 1996), the fact that it continues to invite debate and elaboration testifies to its powerful impact in shaping political discourse about Taiwan's sense of identity.

Since the creation of the orphan metaphor, Taiwan's sorrowful "orphan consciousness" has become part of its political discourse to be adapted, modified, interpreted, and evaluated by future generations (a process described by Black, 1990). This metaphor provides the root from which "grow many shoots which, taken as a whole, constitute an entire system or way of looking at things" (Ortony, 1979, p. 4). It contains many different layers of meaning as well as varying levels of reference (Johnson, 1978). Such a system of thought, which structures Taiwan's political discourse and sense of identity, can be observed in how the root metaphor encompasses other metaphors or, to use Jamieson's (1980) notion of "metaphorical cluster," how such a cluster co-creates a system of meanings and corroborates inclusive rhetorical cues.

Dai (1994), for example, describes Taiwanese feelings of helplessness, complaining, and self-pity as well as their cultivation of a negative self-identity that reflects the mentality associated with being an "adopted daughter" (p. 18). Being born female in a traditionally patriarchal society often means one's "adoption" is considered a burden, and an "adopted daughter" stands an even greater chance of being abused and exploited. Much like the orphan who enjoys no love from his or her natural parents, the adopted daughter metaphor supplements the implied meaning of the orphan metaphor by further highlighting the "child's" sorrow and helplessness (Perelman & Olbrechts-Tyteca, 1969).

"Orphan of Asia" has become shorthand for some Taiwanese to summarize their feelings of being abandoned and helpless, of suffering, of humiliation, and of the futility of their attempts to reassert their Chineseness (Dai, 1994; Tu, 1994a). It is not surprising to find that an interview with ex-President Lee, conducted by late Japanese reporter Ryotaro Shiba in 1994 for a book on Taiwan, was titled "The Sorrow of Being a Taiwanese." Interestingly, the interview, as published in Japan, originally was titled "The Sorrow of the Situation." When the interview was translated into Chinese by the *Independent Evening News,* the title was changed to "The Sorrow of Being a Taiwanese" (*shengwei taiwanren de beiai*) (Lee, 1999).

Of course, not everyone in Taiwan shares this feeling of sorrow.[18] Although the contemporary Taiwan complex reflects the overlaying of the old Taiwan complex (produced throughout its history) with the experience of new political realities, the historical underpinning has established the roots for Taiwanese experience in the present time (Dai, 1994). Although the "Orphan of Asia" metaphor and its derivatives have gained prominence in Taiwanese political discourse, with the continual economic and political progress of Taiwan and the further distancing between people on the two sides of the Taiwan Straits, it has become obvious that the orphan metaphor no longer is sufficient to provide the frame of reference that some Taiwanese need to express their urge for an identity separate from China. As Miller (1979) puts it, "A dominant metaphor thus tends to become self-perpetuating, although competing metaphorical definitions of political reality can arise to supplant it and create a new orthodoxy" (p. 161). Gradually, there has emerged another provocative root metaphor used to describe the relationship between Taiwan and China—the metaphor of "Moses coming out of Egypt."

"Moses Coming Out of Egypt"

As noted previously, the Moses metaphor was introduced by Lee in 1994 in an interview with Shiba. Before being interviewed, Lee asked his wife what would be a good topic to talk about. She replied that he could talk about "the sorrow of being a Taiwanese." Lee recalled, "And then, we started talking about the Old Testament story of 'coming out of Egypt' " (Lee, 1995, p. 471). That the title of this interview remained "The Sorrow of Being a Taiwanese" testifies that the orphan metaphor, to this point, had not totally disappeared from the scene; rather, it had merely waned in its application to the changing, ever self-asserting, Taiwanese political realities.

Moses, a figure in the Old Testament, was a Hebrew prophet who led the Israelites out of their enslavement in Egypt. Lee, like Moses, saw himself as called on by God to perform a sacred duty, that is, to bring Taiwanese to a new place where they would be free. In his interview, Lee mentioned this story twice to describe his mission toward the Taiwanese people (Garver, 1997; Lei, 1995). "Yes, [we] have already started," Lee asserted in the interview. "From now on Moses and all his people have a lot to fight for. To put it simply, [we] have already started" (Lei, 1995, p. 91). Thus, the image of Moses did not simply inspire hope; it provided a goal whose pursuit will lead Taiwanese toward the "promised land." Lee implied that people in Taiwan should leave the land of enslavement to become their own masters and thus cease to be orphans. By using the Moses metaphor, Lee signaled his reconceptualization of the motherland for the orphan away from the grand and idealized central nation and toward the implication that the model for Taiwanese self-rule should be sought in current Taiwanese sociopolitical reality.

In this interview, Lee also mentioned that even the KMT is an "alien regime," effectively including the KMT as one of the oppressors who have "enslaved" Taiwan. This characterization created the context needed for Lee to present himself as a religious and political leader. Given the invasion of an alien regime that still maintained its control over Taiwan, it is only logical to endow the leader with a heavy responsibility for helping his people. Although Lee's view of the KMT, given his role as leader of that party, might seem ironic, it does not contradict his assuming the role of Moses given that Lee was the first "Taiwanese president" ever to have been elected in the ROC's history. In fact, this context allowed Lee more —not less—credibility as a leader who is working to save his people from an alien regime.[19]

The alien regime comment also is noteworthy because of its consonance with Shi Ming's account of Taiwan's history. Those who support the independence movement endorse Ming's book, *Four Hundred Years of History of the Taiwanese* (Shi, 1980), because its Taiwanese-centered viewpoints are seen in contrast to what some believe is the more "official" (i.e., KMT-endorsed) version of Taiwan's history written by Lien Hen (Chen, 1998). In a later portion of the interview, there is a final piece of evidence showing how Lee completed the Moses metaphorical cluster: "Yes, when [I] think about the 2-2-8 event [i.e., the massacre and imposition of martial law that brought the KMT to power in Taiwan] that sacrificed many Taiwanese people, 'coming out of Egypt' has become the conclusion" (Lei, 1995, p. 91). What prompted Lee's use of the Moses metaphor was not the action of the PRC but rather the 2-2-8 event, which served as a prelude to the white terror enforced by the alien regime of the KMT and which marked the beginning of the conflict between Chiang's KMT government and the early immigrants.

Thus, the image of the KMT as an alien regime, and the endorsement of a Taiwanese-centered reading of history, implicitly reinforced and provided concrete support for the construction of the Moses metaphor, advocating the separation of Taiwan consciousness and China consciousness. Among the bewildering number of possibilities for interpreting Taiwan's identity, use of the Moses image clearly pointed to the need for Taiwanese to differentiate and disconnect themselves from the idealized "Chinese world," whatever that world might be.

Lee's use of the Moses metaphor was particularly meaningful in that the Book of Exodus, as a description of revolutionary politics deeply rooted in the Western cultural consciousness, legitimizes and constructs the perception of revolution as moving forward from oppression, to liberation, to social contract, to political struggle, and (eventually) to a new society (Walzer, 1985). Through endless tellings, retellings, and reinvention by people in different places and times, the story in the Exodus helps to sustain the spirit of, and even inspires resistance among, people who experience oppression. So powerful is the "this worldly" biblical story that "revolution has often been imagined as an enactment of the Exodus and the Exodus has often been imagined as a program for revolution" (p. ix). Indeed, "The concept of a holy war has been invoked throughout the centuries by English speakers on both sides of the Atlantic to justify or motivate 'real' violence as well as to inspire dedication to battles that are 'only' symbolic" (Daughton, 1993, p. 429).

Nevertheless, although Moses might be familiar to Western cultures, it never had been a cultural archetypal metaphor for people in Taiwan. One only needs to read the variety of Taiwanese newspaper articles published during the time to note how most began by explaining the biblical story before discussing Lee's interview. Civil religious tradition that combines religion (particularly that of Judeo-Christianity) with politics (Daughton, 1993; Ivie, 1987) seldom has become part of Taiwanese political discourse. Instead, the impact of Christianity on Taiwan's politics can be discerned through alternative channels. On the one hand, all three of the ROC's past presidents converted to Christianity, confirming the influence of the West on them; on the other hand, Taiwan's Presbyterian denomination, to which Lee belongs, firmly supports "Taiwanese interests" and is accused by some of being "pro-independence" (Copper, 1996, p. 63).

Because Lee did not explicitly state who Moses was, he had to rely on his audience's previous knowledge of the Exodus story. As the metaphor unfolded in the interview, presumably it was only the interviewer who needed to know the allusion to Moses. However, once Lee's interview was transcribed, printed, and publicized—a process whereby the initial rhetorical act of speaking becomes a rhetorical artifact expressed in various forms of discourse (Foss, 1989)—his audience was extended far beyond his interviewer. Indeed, his mode of expression through the interview may be seen as more effective in formulating the Moses metaphor than a formal speech would have been given that many people in Taiwan view government officials' speeches as nothing but formulaic policy statements devoid of substance.

Although metaphorical application often relies on one's knowledge of the familiar to help apprehend the unfamiliar (Edelman, 1971), in the case of Moses, the situation is somewhat reversed. Even though the Moses story becomes "a *way* of *seeing* certain political behaviors and persons in the terms, contexts, and roles normally associated with the religious realm" (Daughton, 1993, p. 428), contrary to what might be expected, unfamiliarity with the biblical story (i.e., audiences' lack of connection to scriptural and historical references) actually makes the metaphor more—not less—persuasive (Martin & Martin, 1984). As Richards (1936) puts it, "A metaphor may work admirably without our being able with any confidence to say how it works or what is the ground of the shift" (p. 117) because the mind can exercise its power to connect elements that may at first appear to be disparate.

As soon as some Taiwanese accept the linkage between Moses' role as a leader in a grave undertaking and Lee's role as Taiwan's president, to use Foss's (1989) words, "the audience accepts the argument" (p. 190). Taiwanese found it useful to appropriate the Moses metaphor in ways that suited their political needs. For this audience, the religiosity implied in the metaphor does not incite violence or zealotry, as is often the case in Western religious crusades (Ivie, 1987); rather, it incites a feeling of power. Particularly, there seems to be the belief that such a religiously inspired movement is an ordeal that comes at the behest of a supreme being and presumably is morally justified and necessary (cf. Daughton, 1993, pp. 432-433), an orientation that is quite in line with Chinese cultural beliefs. Hence, in the case of the Moses metaphor, "what seems an impossible connection, an 'impracticable identification,' can at once turn into an easy and powerful adjustment if the right hint comes from the rest of the discourse" (Foss, 1989, pp. 125-126).

The timing of the introduction of the Moses metaphor also was right given that Taiwan's political nativism had reached its apex, thus allowing the metaphor and its context (Foss, 1989) to mutually reinforce each other. According to Chen (1998), from the KMT's perspective, political nativism began when the late president, Chiang Ching-kuo, started calling himself a Taiwanese and reached its climax when Lee, the "real Taiwanese," assumed the presidency (p. 102). In tracing historical processes back to the Japanese occupation, this nativistic movement can be divided into three stages: from being against Japan (since 1895), to being against Westernization (since 1949), to being against China (since 1983) (p. 103). Chen (1998) notes that during the 1990s, Taiwanese consciousness became too ambiguous and was replaced by the sense of "Taiwanese identity." Much as Taiwanese consciousness has been part of the ramifications of the orphan metaphor, Taiwanese identity has come to be supported by the Moses metaphor.

Increased contact between the ROC and the PRC, although in a way fulfilling the dream of Taiwanese to go back to the motherland, also made it clear to some Taiwanese that this goal is illusory. Although agreeing that people of China and Taiwan both speak the same official language and have similar cultural traditions, many Taiwanese now claim to have established a unique Taiwanese culture that is noticeably different from that of the PRC.

Lee's introduction of Moses may thus be seen as a case of a metaphor living up to its rhetorical potential. Although no specific details about the story of Moses were provided, the metaphor nevertheless has gained prominence and emerged as a key symbol for many to contemplate Taiwan's identity. It became an instrument that helped to shape political support as well as opposition (Edelman, 1971). The image of Moses provided an effective channel of expression for those interested in promoting, either culturally or politically, an independent Taiwan. Not only was Lee nicknamed "Taiwan Moses" and "Lee Moses" (*li mo xi*) as the powerful leader of a new order, new possibilities, and new directions for Taiwan, but Taiwan's current president, Chen Shui-bian, who at the time of Lee's comments was a member of the opposition DPP and former mayor of Taipei, stated that if Lee is Moses, then Chen will be the "Joshua" to follow in Lee's footsteps and help to complete the sacred mission of getting out of "Egypt" (China) ("China Throws," 2000). The Moses image not only stimulated conceptual thinking but also, and more important, led to personal commitment and action (Graves, 1983).

Chen capitalized on the Moses metaphor, introduced in 1996, to effectively fashion a discourse that facilitated his political campaign for the presidency in 2000. Although Chen's party, the DPP, is officially in opposition to Lee's party, the KMT, concerning issues of Taiwan's identity, thanks to the Exodus story, Chen nevertheless is seen as the "true heir" to Lee's mission. The *Taipei Times* noted, "We cannot help notice that in attacking Chen, Beijing is of the opinion that the DPP presidential candidate is Lee's real spiritual heir—as Chen himself once said, he is playing Joshua to Lee's Moses." Hence, the message to Lee's supporters is, "If you loved Lee in 1996, you should like Chen in 2000" ("China Throws," 2000). Despite the dissimilarities between Lee and Chen, the link between the two is made possible through the Moses metaphor because "each metaphor intensifies selected perceptions and ignores others, thereby helping one to concentrate upon desired consequences of favored social policies and helping one to ignore their unwanted, unthinkable, or irrelevant premises and aftermaths" (Edelman, 1971, p. 67).

Another example of the extension of the Moses metaphor is explained by Hu (1999). In his elaboration of the "Moses coming out of Egypt" metaphor, Hu notes that after Moses passed leadership to Joshua, Joshua was able to capture Jericho, not by direct confrontation but rather by following the advice of God, who said, "You cannot cry, cannot make a sound, not even a sentence should come out of your mouth. . . . With the faith of the Israelites, they surrounded the walls of the city for seven days, and the walls tumbled" (p. 15). Hu calls for a "second-generation leader" to take to heart the lessons of this story:

> Jericho is the PRC's regime. We will never surrender ourselves to Jericho. We will not worship, not cry, and not make a sound. We insist upon Taiwan's self-determination, hold onto democracy, market economy, and civilized mechanism of citizen society. Based upon such faith, we will "surround the walls for seven days, and the walls will tumble." . . . Only if we insist on such eventual values will we complete the historic poem of "Coming Out of Egypt," entering the land of Canaan, and building a new place. (p. 15)

For Hu (1999), the Moses metaphor aptly describes Taiwan's urge to separate itself from the PRC, an idea that can be extended beyond the leadership of Lee. Just as Moses did not live long enough to reside in the promised land, people in Taiwan are urged not to resort to force but to insist on their spirit and their practice of democracy to help them achieve their final goal.

At the same time, there also has been strong dissent to these ideas from both the PRC and some Taiwanese. Given Taiwan's complex political situation, the Moses metaphor invited debate and has generated a good deal of controversy. For example, when Lee talked in the interview about contemplating passing on his regime while still alive, Long (1996) voiced her objection, arguing that Lee had no right to decide who was going to be the next leader because in a sound democratic system, according to Long, there would be no need for a Moses. For Long, the image of Moses is not compatible with democracy. This confirms a point made by Ivie (1987): "Regardless of how compelling any metaphor may be, however, its limitations eventually are encountered in its application" (p. 179). Lei (1995), although not commenting on the metaphor specifically, contends that the contents of the interview amounted to a negation of all of Lee's past talk about unification with China:[20]

> Even if one wants to use political power to erase these words, it would be very difficult, since the U.S. Congress has included this interview in its congressional report. . . . As soon as "Taiwan as an independent nation" succeeds, these words will be the "declaration of independence." (p. 75)[20]

Metaphors, once adopted, become subject to extension, erosion, criticism, and even reversal or replacement.

One reason why the Moses metaphor generated so much controversy is that it is simultaneously clear in articulating the need to become independent and the need to become ambiguous in allowing for alternative interpretations. As the metaphor is subjected to multiple interpretations, it becomes possible for it to function as a common medium of political discourse (Johnson, 1978). Although the analogy of Lee as Moses and the Taiwanese as the Israelites seems quite clear, the question of who represents the Egyptians may be interpreted in multiple ways, even though such readings may be partially conflictual (Black, 1990, p. 55). If the Taiwanese, like the Israelites, must deliver themselves from enslavement, then who is it that has enslaved them?

Although Lee hinted at the KMT's role as one among several parties that have enslaved Taiwan, some see Egypt as symbolizing the powerlessness and oppression that the Taiwanese people have endured throughout their long history. Other commentators, however, view Lee's appropriation of the Moses metaphor as an attempt to be rid of China's influence. Hu (1999) contends that future historians might agree with an interpretation that views "Lee as the Taiwan Moses 'Coming Out of Egypt' who will lead Taiwan away from the 'black hole' of Chinese politics" (p. 15). The PRC's political analysts also "believed that 'Egypt' symbolized China and that Lee's self-styled mission was to lead the people of Taiwan out of China" (Garver, 1997, p. 24). Lee's application of this metaphor might have led China to think that Lee was actually working toward Taiwan's independence even though, as leader of the KMT, Lee had consistently asserted that the ROC government would not support or tolerate any move in that direction (Clough, 1999).[21] The analogies between the PRC and the Egyptians and between the ROC and the Israelites suggest a highly negative judgment of the PRC, implying that it has exploited and abused Taiwan, much as the Egyptians did the Israelites. Through the symbolic power of the Moses metaphor, China is framed as a foe, as an enemy, or (at the very least) as an unworthy neighbor.

In a way, these interpretations do not conflict with one another. Even if the category of "Egyptians" were to be broadened to include all people, past and present, who have enslaved Taiwan, the PRC, although never ruling Taiwan, might conceivably be included in that category because of its constant military threat. Regardless of how people of different political persuasions choose to decode the meanings of this particular metaphor, metaphor in general organizes our view of reality by highlighting some details and suppressing others (Black, 1962), and the reality alluded to is parsed according to the vantage point from which one chooses to describe it (Schön, 1979). As the metaphor unfolded, not only did there seem to be little need for the PRC and the ROC to continue to be connected, but the Taiwanese, as an oppressed people, were called to fight for their freedom.

Specifically, the Moses metaphor argues against the "collective identity" that supporters of the "one China" policy so strongly advocated. As Garver (1997) points out,

> One hoary Chinese idea . . . was the proposition that all Chinese should be united under a single emperor, the Son of Heaven, ruling over all under Heaven (*Tian Xia*). . . . The division of Chinese-populated territory into several states was considered an abnormality, an abomination, to be overcome as quickly as possible. (p. 17)

Lee's use of the Moses metaphor, however, made it clear that such a division is not only not an abnormal state but also a victory for which to fight. Through the symbolic implication of the Moses metaphor, "getting out of China" became a plausible scenario, whether this getting out implies an independent Taiwan or not.

The Moses metaphor also effectively discounted the PRC's position that reunification is a "historical trend" (Garver, 1997; Wang, 1985). Returning to one's motherland, an idea that implies political power as well as moral influence (Tu, 1994a), has long been advocated as a sacred historical responsibility because it "is a matter of finishing the civil war, completing a Nationalist tryst with Chinese history, and finally triumphing over the demeaning effects of past humiliations at the hands of Western powers" (Yahuda, 1993, p. 698; see also Faison, 1999d). Although the vision of a new reinvigorated China may have aroused much emotion, the Moses metaphor suggested that some Taiwanese no longer feel like orphans searching for unknown parents and no longer are interested in being part of the central nation. If anything, this suggested that the direction of the "historical trend" ought to be changed. Even though all Chinese are descendants of the Han people, there were compelling reasons why they should go their separate ways.[22]

Although China often uses the rhetorical construction "mandate of heaven," the Moses metaphor articulates a different kind of mandate, one that points toward separation. If returning to the motherland is viewed as the responsibility of all Chinese people, then the act of ridding oneself of enslavement can be viewed as a sacred duty of the Taiwanese people. From a source of authority based in nature for mandate of heaven to the personified God for the Exodus story, the actions to be taken concerning the relations between Taiwan and China transcend matters of desire or volition on the part of their respective leaders and people, even as they answer to the call of a higher order.

The Moses metaphor also suggests the equally provocative implication that Taiwan could become a center of its own rather than taking the peripheral position that it has assumed throughout its long history. Because Taiwan already has claimed important status in the world economy, political independence could bring further equality of status between Taiwan and China. To draw implications from the Moses metaphor, once having come out of Egypt, the Israelites were free to build their own world and create their own motherland. Thus, the center and peripheral could be balanced, permitting the peripheral elements to undermine the center's political effectiveness (Tu, 1994a).

The story of Exodus aptly highlights the struggle of Taiwan in seeking its own identity. It not only frames how the problem of Taiwan's political identity should be conceived but also lays out the direction for solving the problem. Although official policy statements by both the PRC and the ROC champion reunification, use of the Moses metaphor hints at a path toward separation. The story of Moses reflects "a march toward a goal, a moral progress, a transformation" that seeks not an *improved* beginning but rather a *different* beginning (Walzer, 1985, p. 12). Such a path, however, is not easily attainable. As Walzer (1985) notes, although miracles play a part in the Exodus story, the event itself was not miraculous. Rather, the path toward deliverance was full of danger, difficulties, and struggles including events that occurred as a result of the Israelites' rebellion against Moses and their uncertainty in making the march. Nevertheless, the Hebrew refugees eventually succeeded; for example, they were able to cross the Sea of Reeds (Wilson, 1985). Much like the Israelites who had to march through the desert wilderness for 40 years to get to the promised land, the Moses metaphor implies that Taiwanese must be prepared to cope with struggles and crises en route to their achievement of a separate political identity.

If, as Black (1990) notes, "every metaphor is the tip of a submerged model" (p. 62), then this visible referent of Moses reflects a great deal about what has transpired in Taiwan's polity. Although Lee introduced the Moses metaphor in 1994, advocacy for the separation of Taiwan from China has extensive roots. Chiang Ching-kuo's democratization of Taiwan "promoted the reality of a separate and sovereign Taiwan" (p. 43). Lee's metaphor thus made concrete the feeling of some Taiwanese of being different from China and actualized this urge to become an independent political entity. Lee's recent "two states" position further confirmed that this urge is still an important part of Taiwanese political discourse.

Six years after the introduction of the metaphor, newspaper commentaries still continue to employ it in commenting on Chen's performance as president. For example, the *Taipei Times* reported, "Perhaps Chen has no choice but to play along with Lee's unfinished cross-strait plan. And that, perhaps, was the most tragic aspect to Joshua's following in Moses' footsteps: He never had a plan of his own" ("Chen Is Shooting," 2000). Thus, the Moses metaphor continues to engage Taiwanese political discourse and to develop and take on new substance as Taiwan's political situation continues to evolve in directions few can predict with certainty.

FROM "ORPHAN OF ASIA" TO "MOSES COMING OUT OF EGYPT": IDENTITY TRANSFORMATION

The two key metaphors—"orphan of Asia" and "Moses coming out of Egypt"—together with their numerous derivatives, structure perceptions for some Taiwanese to contest the claims of others (primarily China) to Taiwan. Of course, given the divergent political viewpoints of people in Taiwan, these metaphors function differently and with different purposes for different audiences. The "reality" created through these metaphors invites debate and discussion. This inconsistency provides us with insights into how ideology may be formulated and maintained (Johnson, 1978).

Although metaphors are subject to interpretation, and although the question of whether (and the extent to which) Taiwanese are interested in building a new country remains dependent on a host of political and other factors, the transition from the orphan and Moses metaphors nevertheless outlines, as well as symbolically constructs, Taiwan's growing urge for a distinctive self-identity. They not only reflect but also transform Taiwan's political culture. As metaphors come to life and die within specific sociopolitical milieus, so do metaphoric expansions, transformations, and modifications. When metaphors are out of vogue, they are still subject to transformation, erosion, or the possibility of becoming dormant for some time only to be awakened in the future (Perelman & Olbrechts-Tyteca, 1969).

The sense of helplessness, of being discarded, and of wearing the yoke of the pitiful orphan image, sustained through various forms of text, seems to have gradually given way to a new image of "Moses coming out of Egypt" toward a better (i.e., self-determined) future. This apparent transformation also is in line with Taiwan's domestic political circumstances. Although some Taiwanese have long nurtured dreams of independence, it was not until the lifting of martial law in 1987 that they were able to openly challenge the idea that China and Taiwan would one day be unified. Thus, it is not surprising that Chen (2000), in his inaugural speech, stated, "In whatever difficult environment, Taiwan will be like a selfless loving mother who never stops giving her children opportunities and who helps them realize beautiful dreams." The mother no longer is an idealized central nation as implied in the orphan metaphor; rather, it is a mother to be found in Taiwan in the present.

The transformation also redefines the notion of what it means to be Chinese. The meaning of Chinese-ness is constructed out of the longevity of various historical contexts in which Chinese have found themselves (Dai, 1994) that have led to China's turbulent modern history including Western imperialism, the end of the Ch'ing dynasty, Japanese aggression, the struggle between Nationalists and Communists, and many other political episodes. Whereas the orphan may regret the inattention from the motherland, the inattention may have led to questions about Chinese-ness. The image of Moses persuading Taiwanese to seek their own identity by separating Taiwan from the PRC's political power is a new identity linking past with present and future. Through the working of the Moses metaphor, the past humiliations that China (particularly the Ch'ing dynasty) suffered at the hands of Western and other foreign powers may be undergoing a transformation in the consciousness of some Taiwanese people.

Metaphors, with their inherent ambiguities, provide symbolic resources for Taiwan to emphasize its own unique identity without appearing to be seeking independence. This struggle is described by Tu (1994a): "In response to the threat of the independence movement, the government deems it advantageous to underscore Taiwan's Chinese-ness, but the challenge from the mainland prompts it to acknowledge how far Taiwan has already departed from the Sinic world" (p. 10). The "Moses coming out of Egypt" metaphor nicely supplements the dialectical tension between drawing the two sides closer and also setting them apart (Clough, 1999), a tension given substance by the official acknowledgment of the eventual goal of reunification and the promise not to declare independence, even while Taiwan rejects the notion of "collective identity" articulated by the PRC.

Interestingly, however, neither metaphor rejects the possibility of the coexistence of Taiwanese-ness and Chinese-ness. For the orphan, Taiwanese-ness is subordinate to, or at least integrated with, the sense of Chinese-ness; for Moses, such Chinese-ness must be made uniquely Taiwanese. This notion of "Taiwanese Chinese" maintains the feelings of Taiwan's people for being Chinese while at the same time making it clear that this notion is markedly different from that of Chinese living under the PRC's government. Whether it is due to the image of an orphan or the image of a people who strive to leave the land that enslaves them, the so-called "cultural heritage and traditions" that once bound the PRC and the ROC together seem to have become less prominent in political discourse in Taiwan. One window through which to frame the changing political and cultural identity of the Taiwanese is through the root metaphors that embody insight that cannot be expressed in any other fashion (Black, 1990).

NOTES

1. Even humanitarian contact between outside nation-states and Taiwan is viewed as problematic and has been capitalized on as political by the PRC. On September 21, 1999, Taiwan suffered one of the most serious earthquakes in its history. China claimed that all efforts by other nations to help Taiwan should be relayed through China because Taiwan is its local government. In addition, China openly thanked other nations on behalf of Taiwan, thus symbolically claiming its sovereignty over Taiwan.

2. In this chapter, the term "Taiwanese" (other than its function as an adjective) is used to refer to people residing in Taiwan rather than only to early Chinese immigrants.

3. The island of Taiwan initially was inhabited by aboriginals. These "mountain people" (as they are now called) were supplanted by Chinese from the southern Chinese provinces of Fukian and Kwangtung, primarily during the 14th and 17th centuries. By the 19th century, they had become the majority of the island's population.

4. Although some may see Taiwan's increasing contact with the PRC as an endorsement of the eventual reunification with China, it also can be argued that it represents Taiwan's effort to become an independent entity because it can maintain contact with the PRC on mutual terms.

5. According to Wei (1994), "The first stage is for mutually beneficial interchanges.... In the second stage, official channels of communication between mainland China and Taiwan would be established, following reduction of tension and hostility.... Finally, in the third stage, the mechanism for deliberation (*shieh-shang*) of national unification would be established between the two sides" (pp. 229-230, italics added).

6. At that time, China threatened Taiwan by practicing missile tests over the island between July 21 and 27, 1995; on August 15, 1995; and 2 weeks before Taiwan's presidential election in March 1996 (Chao & Myers, 1998; Clough, 1999).

7. According to Lee, the position is both legal and accurate. The ROC was established in 1912, and the constitution was revised in 1991 to define the ROC's territory as composed only of Taiwan and several small islands, not to extend to China's territory. Hence, Taiwan has long had its own sovereignty, and the PRC never has ruled Taiwan. Also, because Taiwan has been independent from China since the end of the civil war in 1949, Lee saw no need to announce independence. Although for a long time the highly sensitive issue of whether Taiwan's government has sovereignty over Taiwan had been set aside under the cover of the "one China" policy, Lee's comments brought this issue to the forefront.

8. Many commentators see Lee's comments as an attempt to use the strained relations between China and the United States—the result of NATO's accidental bombing of the Chinese embassy in Belgrade in May and the dispute concerning China's theft of nuclear weapon secrets from the United States (Faison, 1999a)—to the benefit of the ROC. Also, the timing of Lee's comments appeared to have something to do with local politics in Taiwan, oriented toward the 2000 presidential election (Faison, 1999d).

9. Here, "central nation" is used to refer to an idealized nation rather than to either the PRC or the ROC.

10. The novel has undergone several editions in both Taiwan and Japan. It originally was titled *Hu Zhi Ming* (the name of the key character) and published in Taiwan. The title was later changed to *The Orphan of Asia* and published in Japan. It was changed again to *The Distorted Island* when the work was published by another company in Japan.

11. The original Japanese and Chinese publication dates are unknown. However, according to the 1995 edition of Wu's book, the preface for the Japanese edition was written in 1956, and the preface for the Chinese edition was written in 1962.

12. "Orphan," according to *Sources of Words* (Taiwan Shang-wu Publishing, 1987), historically refers to a child whose father has died, in line with the patrilineal emphasis of ancient Chinese society (p. 597). Colloquially, however, the term refers to a child whose parents have died or have disappeared.

13. This view is different from Chen's (1998) contention that Taiwan's struggle against colonialism did not start until after the KMT took over Taiwan. Prior to that, Chen argues, Taiwan's self-identity was integrated with Chinese identity. Zhang's (1992) account also

appears to be in line with the orphan image given that the orphan would be interested in finding his or her parents.

14. Long (1996), a second-generation late immigrant to Taiwan, in an article titled "I am Taiwanese, I Am Not Sorrowful" contends that such sorrowful feelings belong only to early Chinese immigrants. She argues that late immigrants—those who came to Taiwan with Chiang's troops—did not have the experience of being under foreign rule by Japan and other nations. Long argues that, instead, her sorrowful feelings come from being separated from her roots (i.e., the mainland). Xiang (1996), however, contends that the sorrowful feeling of being abandoned is equally applicable to late immigrants, even if it is of a different kind.

15. This term was introduced by late 19th-century Chinese statesman Zhang Taiyan, who proposed zhongguoren as the authoritative definition of the Chinese people (Wu, 1994).

16. It should be noted that textbooks have undergone significant revision since the publication of Lin's book in 1989. At present, given the clear quest for a Taiwanese identity, elementary and high school textbooks adopt a Taiwan-centered approach that puts the mainland at the periphery.

17. Chen (1998) provides a detailed account of the debate during the 1980s surfacing in various journals including *Qianjin Weekly, Xiachao Tribune of Opinions, Shenggen Magazine, Taiwan Niandai,* and *Taiwan Wenyi* (pp. 142-147). More recently, Chen's article, "A Commentary on Taiwan's Nativistic Movement" (originally published in 1995 by *Zhongwai Literature* and included in his 1998 book), also has generated debate including work published in *Zhongwai Literature* and *Strait Commentary* (*haixia pinglund*).

18. Lei (1995), for example, contends that although Taiwan is small, Taiwan also is very rich and there is little that it needs to be sorrowful about. If anything, the sorrow belongs to the late immigrants because they were excluded by President Lee. Long (1996) also contends that although she is Taiwanese, she does not feel the same sorrow as is expressed by Lee: "As a second generation of late immigrants, I am sorry, I don't have your beiqing yishi. The pain I and my parents have suffered, the pain of no roots, is another historical complex that is different from your beiqing yishi" (p. 31). The real sorrow, Long contends in the letter she wrote to Lee, is that Taiwan will still chase "its own shade of the past as its target for tomorrow" (p. 30). Finally, the early immigrant Chen (1998), in analyzing the tendency of advocates of Taiwan independence to contrast China as foreign ruler and Taiwan as needing independent self-identity, dismisses such divisions as simplistic and problematic.

19. This also explains why, when the KMT candidate lost the presidential race in 2000, Lee was blamed by some KMT party members as being the one who was destroying the party.

20. Lei's (1995) negative view of the interview probably explains why, when the Japanese reporter's name was transliterated into Chinese characters according to phonetic rules, one of the characters he chose has a radical of "dog," thus belittling the Japanese reporter.

21. Despite the KMT's insistence that the public declarations of Lee are not about Taiwan's independence, some commentators believe that Lee and the DPP hold similar positions toward the relative placement of Taiwan and the PRC given that Lee is a native Taiwanese and not a late immigrant. This also explains the "spiritual connection" between Lee and Chen Shui-bian, as articulated in the metaphor.

22. There are, of course, multiple voices in Taiwan with regard to reunification with China. The New Party, for example, endorses the PRC's vision of a "greater China" and "longs for the day when China is accorded its rightful place as one of the leading nations of

the world. It desires a powerful Chinese nation-state and derives a deep satisfaction from identification with that would-be state" (Garver, 1997, pp. 19-20).

REFERENCES

Black, M. (1962). *Models and metaphors.* Ithaca, NY: Cornell University Press.

Black, M. (1990). *Perplexities.* Ithaca, NY: Cornell University Press.

Brown, R. H. (1976). Social theory as metaphor: On the logic of discovery for the sciences of conduct. *Theory and Society, 3,* 169-197.

Burke, K. (1969). *A grammar of motives.* Berkeley: University of California Press.

Chao, L., & Myers, R. H. (1998). *The first Chinese democracy: Political life in the Republic of China on Taiwan.* Baltimore: Johns Hopkins University Press.

Chen, B.-Y. (1999, July 13). Su Chi: New definition of the relation between the two straits opens up political dialogue. *Central Daily News,* p. 1. (International edition, in Chinese)

Chen, L.-C., & Reisman, W. M. (1972). Who owns Taiwan: A search for international title. *Yale Law Journal, 81,* 599-671.

Chen, S.-B. (2000, March 20). *Taiwan stands up: Advancing to an uplifting era* [English translation of inaugural speech] [Online]. Available: th.gio.gov.tw/pi2000/dow_2.htm

Chen, Y.-J. (1984). *Orphan's history: The history of an orphan* [Guer de lishi: Lishi de guer]. Taipei, Taiwan: Yuan-Liou Publishing.

Chen, Z.-Y. (1998). *Taiwan literature and nativistic movement* [Taiwan wenxue yu bentuhua yundong]. Taipei, Taiwan: Zeng-Zhong Books.

Chen is shooting himself in the foot. (2000, August 17). *Taipei Times* [Online]. Available: th.gio.gov.tw/show.cfm?news_id=4842

China throws its weight around. (2000, February 27). *Taipei Times* [Online]. Available: th.gio.gov.tw/show.cfm?news_id=2471

Clough, R. N. (1993). *Reaching across the Taiwan strait: People-to-people diplomacy.* Boulder, CO: Westview.

Clough, R. N. (1999). *Cooperation or conflict in the Taiwan strait?* Lanham, MD: Rowman & Littlefield.

Copper, J. F. (1996). *Taiwan: Nation-state or province?* Boulder, CO: Westview.

Dai, G.-H. (1994). *Taiwan complex and China complex* [Taiwanjie yu zhongguojie]. Taipei, Taiwan: Yuan-Liou Publishing.

Daughton, S. (1993). Metaphorical transcendence: Images of the Holy War in Franklin Roosevelt's first inaugural. *Quarterly Journal of Speech, 79,* 427-446.

Edelman, M. (1971). *Politics as symbolic action.* Chicago: Markham.

Faison, S. (1999a, July 15). Beijing sees U.S. hand in Taiwan shift on "one China." *New York Times,* p. A8.

Faison, S. (1999b, July 16). The China cloud: Is a bomb waved at Taiwan? *New York Times,* p. A3.

Faison, S. (1999c, July 18). Getting real in the other China. *New York Times,* p. 5 (Week in Review).

Faison, S. (1999d, July 13). Taiwan president implies his island is sovereign state. *New York Times,* pp. A1, A8.

Foss, S. K. (1989). *Rhetorical criticism.* Prospect Heights, IL: Waveland.

Foss, S. K., Foss, K. A., & Trapp, R. (1985). *Contemporary perspectives on rhetoric.* Prospect Heights, IL: Waveland.

Garver, J. W. (1997). *Face off: China, the United States, and Taiwan's democratization.* Seattle: University of Washington Press.

Gates, H. (1987). *Chinese working-class lives: Getting by in Taiwan.* Ithaca, NY: Cornell University Press.

Graves, M. P. (1983). Functions of key metaphors in early Quaker sermons, 1671-1700. *Quarterly Journal of Speech, 69,* 364-378.

Harding, H. (1994). Taiwan and greater China. In R. G. Sutter & W. R. Johnson (Eds.), *Taiwan in world affairs* (pp. 235-275). Boulder, CO: Westview.

Hong, M.-C. (1997). *"Hot hope" and "hopeless": Recovery and 2-2-8* ["Rewang" yu "juewang": Guangfu, er er ba]. Taipei, Taiwan: Yuan-Liou Publishing.

Hsu, I. C. (1990). *The rise of modern China* (4th ed.). London: Oxford University Press.

Hu, Z.-S. (1999, January 28). From Moses to Joshua: The Taiwanese historical perspective on Moses coming out of Egypt. *Freedom Time Press,* p. 15. (In Chinese)

Huan, G. (1994). Changing China-Taiwan relations. In Z. Lin & T. W. Robinson (Eds.), *The Chinese and their future* (pp. 418-441). Washington, DC: American Enterprise Institute.

Ivie, R. (1987). Metaphor and the rhetorical invention of cold war "idealists." *Communication Monographs, 54,* 167-182.

Jamieson, K. H. (1980). The metaphoric cluster in the rhetoric of Pope Paul VI and Edmund G. Brown, Jr. *Qrarterly Journal of Speech, 66,* 51-72.

Johnson, N. (1978). Palestinian refugee ideology: An enquiry into key metaphors. *Journal of Anthropological Research, 34,* 524-539.

Kerr, G. H. (1965). *Formosa betrayed.* Boston: Houghton Mifflin.

Koestler, A. (1964). *The art of creation.* New York: Macmillan.

Lakoff, G., & Johnson, M. (1980). *Metaphors we live by.* Chicago: University of Chicago Press.

Lee, S.-C., & Campbell, K. K. (1994). Korean President Roh Tae-Woo's 1988 inaugural address: Campaigning for investiture. *Quarterly Journal of Speech, 80,* 37-52.

Lee, T.-H. (1995). *Managing the big Taiwan* [Jianshe dataiwan]. Taipei, Taiwan: Yuan-Liou Publishing.

Lee, T.-H. (1999). *Taiwan's claims* [Taiwan de zhuzhang]. Taipei, Taiwan: Yuan-Liou Publishing.

Lei, M. (1995). *"Late immigrants" can no longer make it?* [Waishengren meide huen lo?]. Taipei, Taiwan: Hans Publishing.

Lim, B. K. (1999, July 18). *Wrapup: Taiwan says on normal alert amid threats* [Online]. Available: news.excite.com/news/r/990718/04/china-taiwan

Lin, S.-B. (1989). *Loudly claim that you love Taiwan* [Dasheng shuochu ai taiwan]. Taipei, Taiwan: Qian-Wei Publishing. (In Chinese)

Long, Y.-T. (1996). I am a Taiwanese, I am not sorrowful [Wo shi taiwan-ren, wo bu baiai]. In Y.-T. Long (Ed.), *Let's toast Tomasti* (pp. 29-39). Taipei, Taiwan: Times Newspaper Publisher.

Martin, D. R., & Martin, V. G. (1984). Barbara Jordan's symbolic use of language in the keynote address to the National Women's Conference. *Southern Speech Communication Journal, 49,* 319-380.

Miller, E. F. (1979). Metaphor and political knowledge. *American Political Science Review, 73,* 155-170.

Mong, R.-H. (1999a, July 10). President Lee: The relation between the two sides is special state-to-state relation. *Central Daily News,* p. 1. (International edition, in Chinese)

Mong, R.-H. (1999b, July 13). We will no longer use "two equal political entities, two China's." *Central Daily News,* p. 3. (International edition, in Chinese)

Morgan, P. M. (1993). Taiwan's security interests and needs. In G. T. Yu (Ed.), *China in transition: Economic, political, and social developments* (pp. 3-22). Lanham, MD: University Press of America.

Ortner, S. B. (1973). On key symbols. *American Anthropologist, 75,* 1338-1346.

Ortony, A. (1979). Metaphor: A multidimensional problem. In A. Ortony (Ed.), *Metaphor and thought* (pp. 1-16). Cambridge, UK: Cambridge University Press.

Parker, J. (1999, July 21). *Taiwan seeks to tone down new China policy* [Online]. Available: news.lycos.com/stories/topnews/19990721rtnews-taiwan-china.asp

Perelman, C., & Olbrechts-Tyteca, L. (1969). *The new rhetoric: A treatise on argumentation* (J. Wilkinson & P. Weaver, Trans.). Notre Dame, IN: University of Notre Dame Press.

Pye, L. W. (1985). *Asian power and politics: The cultural dimensions of authority.* Cambridge, MA: Harvard University Press.

Richards, I. A. (1936). *The philosophy of rhetoric.* New York: Oxford University Press.

Richards, I. A. (1950). *Principles of literary criticism.* New York: Harcourt, Brace.

Richards, I. A. (1952). *Practical criticism: A study of literary judgment.* London: Routledge & Kegan Paul.

Robinson, T. W., & Lin, Z. (1994). The Chinese and their future. In Z. Lin & T. W. Robinson (Eds.), *The Chinese and their future* (pp. 445-472). Washington, DC: American Enterprise Institute.

Schön, D. A. (1979). Generative metaphor: A perspective on problem-setting in social policy. In A. Ortony (Ed.), *Metaphor and thought* (pp. 254-283). Cambridge, UK: Cambridge University Press.

Shi, M. (1980). *Four hundred years of history of the Taiwanese* [Taiwanren sebainian shi]. San Jose, CA: Pengdao Cultural Company.

Sly, L. (1999a, July 13). Taiwan jettisons "one China" policy. *Chicago Tribune,* pp. 1, 8 (sec. 1).

Sly, L. (1999b, July 14). Taiwan puts troops on alert as China vents more anger. *Chicago Tribune,* p. 8 (sec. 1).

Taiwan Shang-wu Publishing. (1987). *Sources of words* [Ciyuan] (2 vols., 8th ed.). Taipei, Taiwan: Author.

Thaiss, G. (1978). The conceptualization of social change through metaphor. *Journal of Asian and African Studies, 13,* 1-13.

Tu, W.-M. (1994a). Cultural China: The periphery as the center. In W.-M. Tu (Ed.), *The living tree: The changing meaning of being Chinese today* (pp. 1-34). Stanford, CA: Stanford University Press.

Tu, W.-M. (1994b). Preface to the Stanford edition. In W.-M. Tu (Ed.), *The living tree: The changing meaning of being Chinese today* (pp. v-x). Stanford, CA: Stanford University Press.

Walzer, M. (1985). *Exodus and revolution.* New York: Basic Books.

Wang, Y.-S. (1985). The mainland-Taiwan issue and China's reunification: Road toward reconciliation. In Y.-S. Wang (Ed.), *The China question: Essays on current relations between mainland China and Taiwan* (pp. 35-49). New York: Praeger.

Wei, Y. (1994). The effects of democratization, unification, and elite conflict on Taiwan's future. In Z. Lin & T. W. Robinson (Eds.), *The Chinese and their future* (pp. 213-240). Washington, DC: American Enterprise Institute.

Wilson, L. (1985). *Exodus: The true story behind the biblical account.* New York: Harper & Row.

Wu, D. Y.-H. (1994). The construction of Chinese and non-Chinese identities. In W.-M. Tu (Ed.), *The living tree: The changing meaning of being Chinese today* (pp. 148-167). Stanford, CA: Stanford University Press.

Wu, Z.-L. (1988). *The fruit without flower: Reflections on Taiwan's seventy years* [Wuhuaguo: Taiwan qishinian de huixiang]. Taipei, Taiwan: Qian-Wei Publishing.

Wu, Z.-L. (1995). *The orphan of Asia* [Yaxiya de guer]. Taipei, Taiwan: Grass Roots Publishing.

Xiang, Y. (1996). It is the sorrow of history, and also Taiwan's powerlessness [Shi lishi de baiai, yeshi taiwan de wunai]. In Y.-T. Long (1996), *Let's toast Tomasti* (pp. 40-45). Taipei, Taiwan: Times Newspaper Publisher.

Yahuda, M. (1993). The foreign relations of greater China. *China Quarterly, 136,* 687-710.

Zhang, D.-S. (1992). *Excitement! Taiwan's history* [Jidong! Taiwan de lishi]. Taipei, Taiwan: Qian-Wei Publishing.

3

Gender, (Inter)Nation(alization), and Culture

Implications of the Privatization of Television in India

SHEENA MALHOTRA • *California State University, Northridge*
ROBBIN D. CRABTREE • *Fairfield University*

> For the first time in human history, most of the stories about people, life, and values are told not by parents, schools, churches, or others in the community who have something to tell, but by distant conglomerates that have something to sell.
>
> —G. Gerbner (1996, pp. 28-29)

A satellite television revolution began in India in 1991; within the first 5 years of the 1990s, television in India changed from a single, state-run "educational" network to including more than 40 private commercial channels broadcasting around the clock. Many of these new networks and channels were Western owned (e.g., Star TV, CNN, MTV, ESPN, NBC, Discovery). These television channels inspired the initiation of a number of private, indigenous Indian satellite television networks during the early 1990s. This chapter, based on 7 years of research, is concerned with the potential implications that privatization and internationalization of television in India has on Indian society, with particular emphasis on changing conceptualizations of gender, nation, and culture.

Not only does television reflect the society and culture of which it is a part, it also is one of the main forces in the formation of the popular culture of that society (Morgan & Signorielli, 1990). Newly available satellite television technology has helped to expand markets throughout the globe. Television programs created in one part of the world can be seen in many other nations. This wide distribution gives rise to important questions. As multinational media corporations expand across the globe, the new technology facilitates media flow from powerful nations to different cultures. The case of India is particularly useful in illuminating the implications of this latest media explosion.

The private Indian television networks, launched during the 1990s, borrow heavily from Western traditions of entertainment television. Many private Indian networks have adopted the 24-hour programming format, advertising as financing, and genres and plots that are very similar to Western programming genres (e.g., situation comedies, soap operas, action series) (Crabtree & Malhotra, 2000).

The commercialization of Indian television during the 1990s coincided with the liberalization of the Indian economy to open the doors for multinational corporations to establish operations in India. The combined impact of the new capitalistic economy and commercial television has resulted in a cultural revolution in India. One of the greatest impacts of the privatization of television in India has been on gender role constructions. Beliefs that center on gender in India are being transformed into more Westernized and/or hybrid conceptualizations (Chopra & Baria, 1996; Krishnan & Dinghe, 1990; Mankekar, 1999). But the impact of privatizing television in India is not limited to changing gender roles. The cultural values that were championed by Mohandas Gandhi are being replaced by values produced in Hollywood. Constructions of nationalism and nationhood also are changing as television becomes increasingly privatized in India.

This chapter draws on the data gathered for a long-term project (Crabtree & Malhotra, 1996, 2000, in press; Malhotra, 1993, 1999; Malhotra & Crabtree, 1994; Malhotra & Rogers, 2000). In this ongoing work, we examine the phenomenon of satellite television in India from the perspective of three essential components in any media exchange: (a) the producers of the television programming including media organizational structures and practices, (b) the television programming itself (the message), and (c) the audience (the decoders).

Accordingly, data were gathered during different phases and include (a) personal interviews with high-ranking programming executives and prominent program producers at five private television networks broadcasting in India, (b) content analysis of 10 television programs, and (c) focus group interviews conducted with audience members. The different data sets provide an opportunity to analyze the evolving situation in India in a sufficiently complex and multifaceted manner. In this chapter, we draw primarily from the interview and focus group data, focusing our discussion on the moments of production and consumption.

This study presents an opportunity to understand how the forces of globalization, made extremely potent through new technologies and advanced capitalism, may articulate certain ideologies in hegemonic formations. India is undergoing a moment of rupture, wherein a former colonial state is renegotiating its cultural identity and conceptions of gender roles in response to the neocolonial forces represented by multinational media corporations broadcasting in the country. Contradictory ideas about gender and nationhood have proliferated in the Indian media landscape since the early 1990s. We focus on issues of gender, nation, and culture as they are negotiated through the discourse of television executives and audiences to understand the conflicting images and ideas generated on Indian television. This may illustrate how cultural hegemony is manifesting during this time of globalization. A brief description of the new developments in television in India sets the stage.

THE PROLIFERATION OF PRIVATE TELEVISION CHANNELS IN INDIA

Satellite television as a direct broadcasting system burst onto the Indian scene in 1991 with the establishment of Star TV, an international television company with headquarters in Hong Kong (Tanzer, 1991). The phenomenal success of Star TV set the scene for the development of other commercial television channels in the country (Mankekar, 1999; Ninan, 1995). In 1991, the Gulf War highlighted the capability and usefulness of satellite television broadcasting in India when the Taj Hotel in Bombay used a satellite dish to catch CNN's signal. Domestic commercial television stations began proliferating. Zee TV was the first private Indian channel, starting in late 1992 (Ninan, 1995), and soon other Indian and foreign-owned networks (e.g., BiTV, ATN, SONY, NEPC, MTV, NBC Asia, ESPN, Discovery) followed suit. Before 1991, India had one government-controlled network, Doordarshan (or DD). By the late 1990s, however, there were more than 40 television channels available to Indian audiences (Melkote, Shields, & Agrawal, 1998). This spread of satellite television was facilitated by local entrepreneurs who bought small satellite dishes and charged their neighbors to share the feed (Rajagopal, 1993). These "cable television networks" multiplied rapidly, and many new commercial television organizations bought cable networks to ensure the distribution of their signals. Thus, commercial satellite television may have been initiated in India by non-Indian media corporations, but it was quickly adopted and perpetuated for profit by Indian entrepreneurs and corporations (Crabtree & Malhotra, 1996, 2000).

THEORETICAL FRAMEWORK

Our theoretical framework is informed by multiple and related critical perspectives. We primarily use a postcolonial feminist perspective to analyze the fluid conceptions of gender roles, national identity, and culture in India. Literature from the related fields of feminist media criticism and cultural studies also informs our work in significant ways, however, as we foreground gender constructions and use the concept of cultural hegemony as it is articulated within cultural studies.

Postcolonial theory articulates the impact of colonization on colonized cultures and societies (Ashcroft, Griffiths, & Tiffin, 1998). Postcolonial theory, which has some roots in cultural studies, is a particularly relevant framework for our analysis given India's colonial past and the focus of our research. India was a colony of the British Empire for more than 200 years, gaining its independence only in 1947 (Basham, 1975). There has been a fear in India since the 1990s that the television programming broadcast by way of the new satellite television technology represents a neocolonialist force in the Indian context. Postcolonial theory and criticism assists in the understanding of how new technologies may affect constructions of gender, nation, and culture in India, as postcolonial theorists recognize cultural colonialism as one of the most dangerous and long-lasting aspects of the colonial experience (Gandhi, 1998). It is telling that the privatization of television in India represented a revisiting of potential cultural colonization during the late 1990s, some 50 years after India had won its independence from the British. In what follows, we briefly summarize certain key concepts from postcolonial critic Homi Bhabha's work that guide our research.

Ambivalence. The term *ambivalence* is a psychoanalytic term that was adopted by Homi Bhabha to denote the "complex mix of attraction and repulsion that characterizes the relationship between colonizer and colonized" (Ashcroft et al., 1998, p. 12). Unlike earlier conceptualizations of submissive colonized populations, Bhabha (1994) argues that the colonized subjects both admire and resent the colonizer simultaneously. The ambivalence of the colonial subjects toward the colonizer disrupts the colonial relationship to the extent that it does not produce compliant colonial subjects (Ashcroft et al., 1998).

Appropriation. Appropriation describes how postcolonial societies take on particular aspects of the colonizer's culture in ways that help them to articulate their own social and cultural identities (Ashcroft et al., 1998). The cultural forms may include language, writing, film, theater, rationalism, logic, and so on. With the proliferation of Indian-owned-and-operated commercial television services, the degree to which their practices and programming appropriate Western models and forms is a salient concern here.

Hybridity. Hybridity is the creation of "transcultural forms" within colonial histories and relationships (Ashcroft et al., 1998). The term has been associated with Bhabha's analysis of the colonizer-colonized relations. Cultural identity and cultural systems are constructed in the "Third Space of enunciation" (Bhabha, 1994, p. 37), wherein the ambivalence and interdependence of the colonizer and colonized construct hybrid cultural identities (Ashcroft et al., 1998, p. 118). Much of this chapter documents the construction of hybrid identities in contemporary India.

These concepts are closely interrelated and are important to understanding the underlying dynamics of private television broadcasting in India since the 1990s. It is the ambivalence of the relationship between the colonizer and the colonial subjects that encourages mimicry and/or appropriation, often resulting in the formation of a media reflection of a growing hybrid identity.

Other fields also inform this chapter. One such field is cultural studies, which focuses on the study of "contemporary culture" (During, 1993, p. 1) and views the media as one of the prominent ways in which hegemonic ideologies are perpetuated and maintained within a culture (Grossberg, 1996; Grossberg, Wartella, & Whitney, 1998). Cultural hegemony is defined as the process through which "a dominant cultural order is consistently preferred, despite its articulation with structures of domination and oppression" (Grossberg, 1996, p. 161). Cultural hegemony differs from early work on cultural imperialism (e.g., Schiller, 1976) because it acknowledges a degree of agency in local media organizations and viewers. Finally, our concerns with gender roles and cultural identity in this chapter also are influenced by feminist media critics who deconstruct gender images in popular culture—particularly in the moments of production, text, and reception (van Zoonen, 1994)—to illuminate discourses of dominance (Penley, 1988; White, 1987).

Recent work by postcolonial feminist scholars advocates moving feminist communication theory to a global context "in order to make it transnationally responsive and more politically engaged with issues of difference" (Hegde, 1998, p. 271). We attempt to contribute to that goal by analyzing our data for insights into "moments" of meaning production and reception. More specifically, in this chapter we question how the new conceptualizations of Indian gender roles and cultural identity are being constructed and by whom.

RESEARCH METHODOLOGY

In this study, we take a multimethodological approach within the qualitative research paradigm (Denzin & Lincoln, 1994) to discover and analyze some of the implications of commercial television in India. The project, which began in 1992, is longitudinal and continues through various phases of data gathering and analysis. We are reporting part of this analysis here.

It is important to position ourselves in relation to the research to facilitate the readers' understanding of why the research was conducted as well as the researchers' assumptions and perspectives. The first author is an Indian native with experience in the Indian film and television industries including a position as a program executive for BiTV. Her academic research has focused on the privatization of television in India and its implications for gender, nation, and culture. Her work and contacts in the industry and her upper middle class background helped us to gain access to different sites and high-level executives. This dual academic-practitioner mode creates the critical distance necessary to conduct research as well as the insider status necessary to perceive the phenomenon at close range. Her critique of the industry is affected both by her optimism for the possibility of change that the new television programming represented and by her witnessing of the eventual lapse of television programs into reactionary nationalism and sexist gender roles fostered by the neocolonialist forces in India.

The second author is European American and has studied media and cultural imperialism as informed by neo-Marxist and Gramscian perspectives for more than a decade. Prior to this research project, her research was conducted mainly in Latin America around the themes of media, revolution, and participatory development. The "revolutionary" media landscape in India during the 1990s was attractive as a new point of departure for understanding the increasingly complex processes of globalization. Familiarity with relevant theory but lack of familiarity with Indian culture creates another insider-outsider modality from which to observe the events under investigation. Certainly, these dialectics of academic-practitioner and insider-outsider affected our readings of the data and have produced multiple instances of debate and dialogue about how to interpret and name these complex phenomena.

To collect part of the data reported here, the first author facilitated focus groups with Indian youths about their reactions to the growing presence of satellite television in India. Focus groups foster openness and range in exploring the topic on the part of participants (Lindlof, 1995; Morgan, 1988). Four focus groups were conducted with college students on two college campuses in Bangalore, India. Participants were recruited through personal friends of the first author who were students at the colleges where the focus groups were conducted. Two of the focus groups were mixed-gender groups, whereas the other two groups were women-only groups. These different gender groupings were desired to ensure a range of responses, and two groups were composed of only women to reduce the impact of gender issues in the dynamics of group interactions.

The size of the groups ranged from 6 to 12 participants between 18 and 24 years of age. Participation was voluntary. Each group began with a brief outline of the topics for discussion: the presence of satellite and commercial television, its effects on Indian culture generally and on Indian women specifically, and participants' own use and impressions of the new programming.

Focus groups were tape-recorded and transcribed using pseudonyms for the participants. Transcripts were analyzed to extract a full range of responses and to identify any patterns in those responses (Morgan, 1988; Strauss & Corbin, 1990). Both researchers read each transcript holistically first to get a sense of each interviewee's ideas and perspectives. We then analyzed and discussed the transcripts, identifying emergent themes as well as divergent views. The strategy was not to do a systematic content analysis of interview and focus group transcripts but rather to identify the widest range of responses with attention to possible patterns. This analysis is consistent with qualitative and interpretive methodology. Our goals were to foreground Indian television personnel and audience members' own interpretations of the media landscape in India and then to relate their insights and experiences to the various theoretical perspectives, bringing both into a dialogue with each other.

As a complement to audience data, we chose to conduct 23 interviews at several of the new television organizations—including BiTV, MTV India, SONY, Star TV (Star Plus and Channel V), and Zee TV—as well as with prominent television producers who had worked with these networks. The first author interviewed high-ranking network executives who oversaw programming at the network level, specific program producers, and executives who worked closely with specific programs or with the research and marketing of programs. Interviewees were selected based on their ability to observe from close range and comment on the practices and programming of the new commercial television networks operating in India as well as on their willingness to participate in the study.

Data from our in-depth case study of one television organization (Crabtree & Malhotra, 2000) is not reported in this chapter, although we might occasionally refer to issues that were illuminated by that research. Data from an analysis of new Indian television programs also have been analyzed in another study (Malhotra & Rogers, 2000). Although we are informed by the larger data set in our observations, we draw specifically on the focus groups with audience members and the interviews with network executives and producers in this chapter.

TENSIONS BETWEEN TRADITION AND MODERNIZATION

It is important to recognize and examine the social context in India at the present time to contextualize the perceptions of change and the new constructions of gender, nation, and culture about which our study offers insights. Such a discussion will aid in the comprehension of the changes wrought by the privatization of television in India, particularly regarding constructions of gender, nation, and culture.

The conflict between traditional Indian culture and modernity (often equated with Westernization) suddenly became the focus of many public discussions in India during the 1990s, particularly with regard to new communication systems and economic liberalization (Melkote et al., 1998; Thomas, 1999). India underwent rapid changes during the 1990s by opening its doors to multinational corporations and the capital they represented. The new liberal economic policies combined with transnational broadcasting generated much dialogue about the sustainability of Indian culture in the face of perceived rampant Westernization (Mankekar, 1999). But this should not be read as a unique or new development. The British colonial legacy in India historically has often manifest as an internalized "Orientalism" (Said, 1978) and as a desire for progress and modernity represented by the West that pervades all forms of Indian life (Shome, 1999). The new media images, therefore, serve to further exacerbate the complex relationship to the West that already was in existence in postcolonial India.

Indeed, the dilemma and debate over the impact of modernization on traditional Indian values can be traced back to the colonial period in India. According to Chatterjee (1993), "Modernization began in the first half of the nineteenth century because of the penetration of Western ideas" (p. 116). There was a substantial resistance to the modernizing of India during the colonial period by the Indian nationalist movement of that time, which emphasized and glorified India's rich past and defended traditional values (Chatterjee, 1993). Later, independent India negotiated modernity by claiming spiritual superiority over the West and by cultivating "the material techniques of modern Western civilization while retaining and strengthening the distinctive spiritual essence of the national culture" (p. 120). Therefore, the nationalist project formulated during the Indian independence movement, which appropriated Western modernity very selectively, set the parameters that frame the dialectical tensions and the debate that raged in India during the last decade of the 20th century.

Since the 1990s, there has been a problematic conflation of Indian national identity with Hindu identity (Mankekar, 1999; Moorti, 2000) largely orchestrated by the rhetorical and political tactics of the Bharatiya Janata Party (BJP, a Hindu nationalist political party). The BJP manifesto released for the 1998 national election had a chapter titled "Cultural Nationalism" that typifies the BJP position with the following declaration:

> Our nationalist vision is not merely bound by the geographical or political identity of *Bharat* [India], but it is referred by our timeless cultural heritage. This cultural heritage, which is central to all regions, religions, and languages, is a civilizational identity and constitutes the cultural nationalism of India, which is the core of *Hindutva* [nationalist/Hindu pride]. This we believe is the identity of our ancient nation. ("BJP Manifesto," 1998)

The construction of a monolithic and rather ethnocentric Indian national identity (as outlined by the BJP) is one of the conservative reactions to the threat of Westernization posed by the private television networks. Thus, we can see the complex demands and pressures of both modernity and tradition again taking center stage in the current public discourse in India.

CONSTRUCTIONS OF INDIAN WOMANHOOD

Indian culture is more than 5,000 years old (Singhal, 1983), with cultural values and traditions that are very different from those of Western nations (Embree, 1988). Indian women often have been cast as the "carriers" of those traditions (Bumiller, 1990; Mani, 1989). Postcolonial feminists have critiqued monolithic constructions of Indian womanhood (Mankekar, 1999; Moorti, 1998)[1] and written about gender ideologies, which help to maintain and perpetuate a culture of violence against women (Hegde, 1999) by functioning within the trope of the colonial and the patriarchal. As postcolonial critic Moorti (2000) argues, "Woman becomes the repository of difference and carries the mark of the authentic India; her body is the terrain where contested definitions of national identity are worked out" (p. 54).

Chatterjee (1993) argues that the construction of the essentialized Indian woman was partially necessitated by Indian nationalism negotiating within the contradictory forces of nationalist ideology, on the one hand, and anticolonial struggles, on the other. Such contradictions were "resolved" by separating the domain of culture into two spheres: the material (or the outside world) and the spiritual (or the inner world). Chatterjee (1993) argues that the inner-outer distinction, when applied to daily living, translates into the separation of social spaces into "home" and "world." The home is equated with true cultural identity, tradition, the inner spiritual self, and the uncolonized space. The world represents the domain of the material, politics, and the practical. Therefore, nationalist efforts to achieve parity with the West in the realm of the world or the "outer" sphere further necessitates the preservation of the unconquered, spiritual "inner" sphere of the home. "And woman is its representation" (Chatterjee, 1993, p. 120).

Prior to the 1990s, the Indian media portrayed women primarily as housewives, mothers, and daughters, defined only in relationship to men and looking to men to provide meaning in their lives (Krishnan & Dinghe, 1990; Mankekar, 1999).[2] Portrayals of women as independent, career oriented, and self-possessed were virtually nonexistent in Indian media prior to the 1990s. Currently, however, it is apparent that Indian womanhood is fast becoming the most contested site in the Indian cultural landscape. Indian media commentator Amrita Shah observes that all of the "moral controversies" of the early 1990s revolved around women (Shah, 1997, p. 187) who no longer could be contained within the old inequitable power structures. She argues,

> The forces of modernisation and powerful media such as television appeared to have given rise to a new breed of women: women who ran their own lives, women who made their own decisions. . . . It was fear of losing control that drove men to hit back with threats of abandonment, rape, violence, and more commonly exhortations of morality couched in the all-inclusive notion, "Our Indian Culture." (p. 188)

Thus, the linkages between cultural identity and constructions of Indian womanhood require Indian women to be "pure" and "self-sacrificing" so as to maintain the patriarchal and colonial status quo. However, the influx of Western mass media and the appropriation and reproduction of images by Indian media corporations provide new images that Indian women may choose to negotiate, appropriate, or reinterpret in myriad ways. Our interviews provide a portrait of the tensions produced by the hybridity and ambivalence of a postcolonial society in transition. The discussions permitted in one chapter merely create a snapshot, but they may provide some insight into the tensions that characterize Indian society today.

CHANGING CULTURAL LANDSCAPES: HYBRIDITY AND AMBIVALENCE

From the analysis of the interviews we conducted with the producers of television programming and the college focus groups, various vital issues and themes came into focus, but none as prominently as the changing cultural landscape of India. There were many instances in which focus group participants expressed concern over the potential loss of Indian culture that the Westernization of television represented. For example, one woman said, "I think that Indian culture is on the way to becoming a thing of the past . . . more of the West and less of the Indian stuff" (Sheila, Focus Group 4).[3] There also was a discomfort about the images that suddenly were appearing in their living rooms. In an all-women focus group, one participant stated, "I'd hate to watch Star TV or MTV in front of my father and grandfather. It's a real culture shock" (Roma, Focus Group 4).

In their comments, focus group members appeared to construct a monolithic Indian culture that was conflated with morality and self-sacrificing values, whereas the West was constructed as consumerist and sexually permissive.[4] A few participants in the focus group interviews, however, seemed to believe that although satellite television posed a cultural challenge, ultimately Indian culture would prevail because of its resilience. "That's one way of looking at it—we've gone materialistic. But another way of looking at it is, after seeing the other side of the world . . . , we've become stronger about what we really believe in" (Priya, Focus Group 2). Although none of the focus groups was able to resolve the issue of whether the challenge to traditional Indian culture and its cultural values by satellite television was positive or negative, group members clearly perceived the challenge as being important.

In contrast to audience opinions reflected in the focus groups, television network executives and television producers who we interviewed seemed to minimize the changing cultural landscape or saw it as a primarily positive outcome. The general manager at MTV India strongly argued that Western influences were not unusual for a country such as India to imbibe:

> I think that there is really no Westernization of Indian television. I believe there's a more broad-mindedness of Indian television. Okay? There is an adoption of influences. But there is no real major influence coming in. I can argue, you know, that long hair was worn by Lord Krishna. And earrings were worn by him. And I can win that argument very, very easily. (S. Lulla, MTV India, personal interview, July 16, 1998)

Most executives dismissed the concerns about "corrupting Western influences" that were repeatedly discussed in the media and among the focus group participants we interviewed. Instead, executives at MTV India, for example, referred to the changing cultural landscape as one that was hybrid rather than Westernized, arguing that for all of the Western dressing, the core still was Indian. According to S. Lulla,

> You should first look at the aspirations of young people in India. You must see where the aspirations are rooted. The aspirations are rooted in Indian psyche and Indian philosophy. So when they look at Western things, they look at it from an Indian perspective. (personal interview, July 16, 1998)

As a television network, MTV India provides the most revealing case for discussing the changing Indian cultural landscape with the notion of hybridity. After failing to attract viewership with primarily Western fare, MTV Networks launched the Indian channel, MTV India. Fully 70% of the programming on the new India-specific MTV channel was Hindi based after August 1997 (M. Varma, MTV India, personal interview, July 16, 1998). The strategy paid off, and MTV India rapidly gained advertiser support. It would be deceptive, however, to consider MTV India to be an "Indian" channel; it remains part of MTV Networks and maintains the programming format and symbolic baggage of the MTV corporate brand. Therefore, MTV India combines a hybrid mixture of the international MTV Networks form and Indian content. Moreover, MTV India executives celebrated the notion of a hybrid Indian cultural identity and consciously generated images to reinforce it:

> I think that a woman in a nice pair of faded blue jeans and a *ghagra-choli* [traditional Indian blouse], a backless ghagra-choli, would look really cool. Is it Western or Indian? It's both. And that's the thing. It's about being *desi-cool.*[5] (M. Varma, personal interview, July 16, 1998)

As desi-cool becomes the order of the day and new hybrid identities are negotiated in India, there also is rising concern about the consumerist lifestyle valorized by the networks. The privatization of television in India coincides with the liberalization of the Indian economy (Mankekar, 1999). The reinforcement of a consumerist lifestyle through the television glut of glossy, Western consumer products in Indian stores has been one of the greatest changes in Indian society. Although popular Indian cinema traditionally has been escapist, the current linkage between that escapist fantasy and a new consumerism warrants concern. The Indian hero has changed from the poor, disenfranchised, angry young man of the 1970s Hindi films to the wealthy, globally educated romantic who drives a BMW sports car at the start of the 21st century. The link among emotional well-being, fulfillment, and the consumption of material goods is problematic for a country like India, where more than one third of the population lives in poverty, barely at a subsistence level (Ninan, 1995). Mehesh Praad, India's secretary of information and broadcasting in 1992, expressed concern that the private commercialized networks were giving poor people "dreams which cannot be fulfilled . . . [and that would] create social tensions" (quoted in Coll, 1992, p. A31).

Therefore, emerging hybrid cultural identities and the celebration of desi-cool must be interpreted within the larger economic context where rising consumerist fantasies imported from the West are highly problematic. As one focus group participant said, "The standard of judging people has just changed. You don't take a person for the beauty of their heart, you know, you take them for their outward appearance, how much money that person has, how many times you go to the pub, whether you've got a boyfriend" (Neha, Focus Group 2).

CONFUSING GENDER NORMS: HYBRIDITY AND AMBIVALENCE

Indian womanhood never has been a stable and monolithic category, despite attempts to fix it in particular ways that are beneficial to patriarchal and colonial interests (Mohanty, 1991; Moorti, 2000). However, the exaggerated fluctuations and confusion about what it means to be an Indian woman in 2000 is indicative of a society undergoing rapid transitions. We found competing and contradictory notions of Indian womanhood being generated by television networks in India, where Westernization, sexuality, and consumerism were being celebrated through Indian models and video jockeys at the same time as traditional Indian values of self-sacrifice and modesty also were being reinforced in Indian female characters. Two possible reasons for these contradictions are (a) a policy vacuum at the networks and, more broadly, (b) competing ideologies in India.

The television networks have a glaring lack of formal policies regarding broadcasting content. The only policies the networks used were the formal "codes" (e.g., the Standards and Practices Code) that already were instituted in the countries from which the satellite television networks up-linked their broadcast programs (S. Shastri, Zee TV, personal interview, July 11, 1997).[6] Networks are, therefore, dependent on individual television programmers to exercise their discretion. This often translated into either a concerted effort not to offend anybody's sensibilities—"religious, national, or otherwise" (N. Pantvaidya, SONY Entertainment Television, personal interview, July 1, 1997)—or into adopting arbitrary standards that fluctuated based on the level of comfort that a particular programmer might have about a particular program on a particular day (S. Shastri, personal interview, July 11, 1997).

There were very few programmers who were concerned about issues of gender in a proactive way. However, executives at certain networks, such as MTV and Star TV, claimed that their networks were consciously working to include more programming on gender issues. Executives at Star TV pointed to certain women-driven programs they were broadcasting as proof that they were reflective of current gender issues in India. Many of the programs that appear to be progressive at first glance, however, often are found to reinscribe the status quo when deconstructed (for a detailed discussion, see Malhotra & Rogers, 2000).[7]

Tara is a case in point. *Tara,* one of the highest rated Zee TV soaps (Indian Management Research Bureau, 1997; Ninan, 1995) had as the protagonist a strong-headed woman around whose life and friends the story revolved. It was a program that became controversial because of its portrayals of women. Whereas some hailed *Tara* as a progressive portrayal of Indian women, showing them as independent and strong, others decried the program for equating strength in a woman to her being manipulative and evil. The Zee TV executives defended the program, saying that it was loved by audiences who, they argued, were the best judges of whether a portrayal was appropriate or not:

> I mean, there is an Indian woman. Just because she's smoking and drinking doesn't mean that she's bad in any way. You know? So we were very clear on that. That an Indian woman doesn't only mean *sati savitri* [the pure, self-sacrificing Indian woman]. Or a woman who just wears a *saree* [traditional dress for Indian women], and that's Indian-ness. We feel the Indian woman is really growing. Frankly, it was our own viewpoint. (S. Shastri, personal interview, July 11, 1997)

In addition to the policy vacuum, the Western consumerist and capitalist ideologies are at odds with Indian patriarchal and nationalist norms, particularly in the conceptualization of the role of women in society, leading to seemingly paradoxical imagery. One example of the contradictory portrayals of women in Indian media is the construction of Indian women as sexual beings. This competes with portrayals of Indian women as pure, asexual, mother-like figures who are the keepers of Indian culture and tradition. These ideologies appear to be oppositional on the surface given roots in Western versus Eastern philosophies, even though both are based in patriarchy. Since the 1991 advent of satellite television in India, the ideologies of Western consumerism/sexual freedom and Indian nationalism/moral conservatism have revived the tension between the traditional and the modern (also prominent in the nationalist struggle of the 1900s). The contradictory portrayals of Indian women are symptomatic of competing hegemonic ideologies and of sudden social change.

Given the contradictory notions of Indian womanhood currently represented on television, it is not surprising that many of the female students in our focus groups expressed a great deal of confusion over normative gender behavior. Many students mentioned feeling that they were caught between two worlds and confused by the different expectations that were being placed on them. The catalyst for this confusion, according to interviewees, was decidedly the Western television programming being broadcast in India by way of Western networks such as MTV (one of the channels broadcast as part of the Star TV network in 1993). One participant said,

> I feel like, you know, I feel a little confused. I feel a little caught between two worlds. Because when I go back home [to a smaller town], I have to really act a little more decent and control my tongue a little more, control my ideas a little more. . . . And then when you come here [to the city], you're expected to behave completely different. You're supposed to dress up . . . [like they do on MTV]. (Neha, Focus Group 2)

Neha's statement exemplifies the competing expectations that many young Indian women who live in the larger Indian cities are supposed to satisfy. Although they may change the way in which they dress, their job and career expectations, the music they listen to, and the way they think, they still are expected to maintain and uphold Indian traditions that teach women to be selfless and self-sacrificing.

However, most focus group participants did not believe that the answer lay in completely denouncing Indian culture. Some of the female participants believed that reworking traditional norms ultimately would prove to be the most liberating alternative for them. Others in the focus groups saw the moment as an opportunity to include new and liberating traditions that could coexist with preexisting Indian traditions. The confusion that Neha referred to earlier signifies a moment of rupture in the traditional gender role construction for Indian women. It usually is at such moments that dominant (patriarchal) interests compete most fiercely with the interests of nondominant groups to enforce hegemonic ideologies. It also is at precisely such moments, however, that meanings can be renegotiated and envisioned in a new or different way. This may produce hybrid identities about which both Indian women and men seem deeply ambivalent.

Interviewees frequently stated that satellite television created a more open society where women were more aware and where previously taboo subjects, particularly those that dealt with gender and sexuality, could be discussed. Many female students spoke positively about Star TV, for example, "It makes the woman more aware, you know. The woman of India, she's now more aware about things" (Priya, Focus Group 2). However, when it came to discussions of openness for Indian women, some male participants seemed concerned that women might interpret the new open atmosphere in Indian society as permission for promiscuity. When one male participant said that "girls are taking more liberties than they used to take" (Kirti, Focus Group 1), he was challenged by a female participant who argued, "Oh! And girls are not allowed to take liberties?" (Vimal, Focus Group 1). Another male respondent backed up Kirti's statement by saying, "The bra-burning attitude is coming now. . . . After 3,000 years [of] suppression, you cannot expect a bird to fly, okay? It needs to see the world outside, take a few faltering steps, before it takes off" (Kunal, Focus Group 1).

There was also a consensus that India was moving toward a more open society due to Western programming. One woman described her mother-in-law talking to her about the promiscuous behavior on Western soap operas, a previously taboo subject, and said that the conversation fostered closeness between them (Aarti, Focus Group 2). Although most respondents saw an open society as a positive trend, some participants (primarily males) were concerned that the openness was occurring too rapidly, particularly with regard to women.

The shifting ideas around gender and the hybridized identities that were emerging in India during the late 1990s ultimately might have liberatory potential as they allow flexibility in envisioning new possibilities. An individual who has internalized a hybrid identity may be able to imagine new gender role constructions in a manner that another individual who is operating out of a monocultural paradigm cannot. But the power differential between India and First World nations that export television programming (e.g., the United States, Great Britain), the one-way flow of programming, and the capitalist and materialist ideology of the West may combine to overshadow and subsume any disruptive and liberatory effects of hybridity in ever-changing gender roles.

NATIONAL TRANSITIONS: HYBRIDITY AND APPROPRIATION

Perhaps one of the most prominent trends we found was that of "Indianization" among private television networks.[8] Many of the networks that were foreign owned were consciously Indianizing their programming content and personnel to become more relevant to the Indian audiences of the late 1990s. Indeed, by 1998, interviewees articulated no real distinction between many of the Indian television networks and their Western counterparts.[9]

Although the trend in content definitely has been toward Indianization, when network executives talk about Indianization, they actually are referring to a hybrid form of programming. For example, when MTV first began broadcasting in Asia, MTV Networks clearly stated that MTV Asia would not broadcast programs that were based on Hindi film songs. However, as noted previously, the lack of viewership and a concern for the bottom line eventually led MTV Networks to reexamine its strategy and launch the Indian channel, MTV India (N. Malhotra, MTV India, personal interview, July 16, 1998). The new India-specific MTV channel used the colors of the Indian flag in the MTV logo and switched to a 70% Hindi programming mix in August 1997 (M. Varma, personal interview, July 16, 1998). Becoming a channel driven primarily by Hindi film music increased its viewership by 750% and expanded its advertising base from a handful of clients to more than 120 by 1998 (N. Hiro, MTV India, personal interview, July 16, 1998). Other Western networks such as Star TV have followed suit.

MTV India appears to have succeeded in its strategy of Indianizing a primarily Western product so as to make it relevant to young people in India. As mentioned earlier, MTV India cannot be considered a purely Indian channel due to its hybridity. MTV India's success, in fact, may be in its ability to create a hybrid television culture that appears to be local, even as it upholds Western values of consumerism and an almost universal sexism. The primary impact of this appearance of "going local" is that it deflates criticisms of cultural imperialism and transfers the blame for sexist and consumerist attitudes to the culture in which it operates. Thus, although it appears to grant agency to local audiences, MTV actually co-opts local cultures and perpetuates culturally destructive and sexist hegemonic practices.

Many of the Indian television network executives we interviewed said that it was acceptable to "mimic" Western television programs if they were successful. Although it may be argued that mimicry is de rigueur in Western media industries (Gitlin, 1983) and is a natural feature of the postcolonial condition currently being experienced in India, there is an ever-present danger that mimicking the West will not subvert Western influences but rather re-create Western problems in India:

> There's a lot of stuff on there [on Indian television] that's very derivative, just transplanted from Western things and it's said that, "Alright, this is our thing." That is very problematic! So, unless and until it finds its own voice from within, you know it might be . . . it's exactly like *[The] Bold and [the] Beautiful.* White trash has now become brown trash! (F. Samar, independent producer, personal interview, July 14, 1997)

Hybrid programming strategies and the emergence of hybridized identities seem to be popular with Indian audiences. This could be explained by the internalized Orientalism resulting from a history of colonization in India (Said, 1978) leading to an adoption of Western norms and beliefs, which combine with Indian norms and beliefs to produce a hybrid identity.

Another reaction to hybridization is rejection, motivated by the fear of losing one's "pure" culture (which actually cannot be pure within a postcolonial context). This fear may generate a reactionary resurgence of nationalist trends and a call to return to the roots of Indian cultures and traditions (Chatterjee, 1993). Indeed, the nationalist trend has been strong since the late 1990s in India. It is a trend that plays on Indian fears of neocolonization by the West and calls for the rediscovery of a national identity. Both of these reactions to the hybridization of Indian television programming and Indian identities are operating within the Indian context at the present time.

Focus group participants expressed similar ambivalence toward the colonizing influences of Western television programming. On the one hand, they appeared to valorize the freedom that they associated with Western cultural norms. On the other hand, they sometimes were critical of the Western-influenced television networks for their perceived arrogance toward Indian audiences. The following excerpt from an exchange is illustrative:

Kesar: What right do they have to give us those third-rate serials . . . , their castaways?

Mary: I think we've become a rubbish dump, you know. Even the culture. Imagine, even the culture that is dumped over there comes over here.

Jyoti: The problem is, we [Indians] are receptive to the shit they're dishing out.

Neha: Exactly. (Focus Group 2)

In this exchange, there is a clear resentment of the "colonizer" that seems to be at odds with the previously expressed admiration for and imitation of the same colonizer. There seem to be competing sentiments: a valorization of Western culture and progress as exemplified in the participants' desire to be more like the West in terms of its perceived freedom (as seen in previous focus group excerpts) versus a critique and repudiation of the West for its perceived arrogance and attitude toward India. The preceding exchange also demonstrates an internalization of the Orientalist discourse. The female participant, while critiquing the Western networks for their program "dumping" strategy in India, ultimately blames Indian audiences who accept such television programming.

The rising feelings of nationalism among Indian audiences and the success of the present ruling political party (the BJP) are important trends that have been bolstered by the privatization of television in India. The sudden changes facilitated by the liberalization of the economic policies and the Westernized television images being broadcast have created an atmosphere of uncertainty and a fear of neocolonization. The BJP and other conservative political parties seem to welcome and capitalize on the fear of colonization by fostering an atmosphere of fundamentalism and calling for a return to the "golden age" of Hindu self-rule.

Implications of the new nationalism for women in India are not positive. The BJP and its allies have constructed the Indian woman as the keeper of Indian culture without examining the sexism or oppression inherent in that construction (Moorti, 1998). Furthermore, the surge in nationalist and religious sentiments (wherein being Indian is becoming increasingly conflated with being Hindu) may be one of the most lamentable trends fostered by the Westernization of television in India and the accompanying fears of neocolonization.

The tendency of the BJP to frame the ideological debate in binary terms also is extremely problematic. In other words, disagreeing with the ideologies of the BJP is tantamount to being in favor of neocolonization. It is imperative to disrupt this binary. Neither the Hindutva conceptualized by the BJP political party nor the Western consumerist forces of neocolonization will advance the project of Indian women's liberation from traditional gender role constructions. Framing the debate as a false dichotomy between Hindutva and Western consumerism also impedes the project of secular Indian subjects.

CONCLUSIONS

Our research foregrounds the hybridity generated by the intersections of gender, nation, and culture in television programming and audience readings of such programming. We have highlighted not only some ways in which Western programming is appropriated by Indian television executives and audiences but also the ambivalence generated by such appropriations. The process of cultural hegemony is evident in the philosophies articulated by network executives and by Indian television audiences. Finally, we found that the contradictory constructions of gender roles for Indian women can be understood through an exploration of the competing ideologies of Western consumerism and Indian nationalism that emerged in India during the 1990s concurrently with the privatization of television.

It is possible that the presence of competing ideologies creates a rupture, allowing potential alternative constructions to be envisioned and articulated by Indian television producers and audiences. Nevertheless, we have only just begun to contemplate the political implications of these potentialities. Hegemony, after all, is not domination by force but rather "manufactured consent" (Herman & Chomsky, 1988). The process of Indianization that we have discussed in this chapter may actually be one mechanism of hegemony through which consent is manufactured. Thus, the Indianization of Western recombinant media forms and texts need not be inherently counter-hegemonic while it provides new manifestations of genre, character, context, and so on. Although there is the dissemination of a new kind of Indian programming, it also reflects an appropriation of Western frames for those messages. In the same way, it is presumptive to imply that audience members' resistant readings of television texts necessarily liberate them from constrictive or oppressive notions of gender or nation. Therefore, although hybridity can be a site of subversion, it is not always or necessarily so.

Our research has produced snapshots of the privatization of Indian television from various angles and at different moments in time (during the 1990s). There is a great need, however, for future research to develop the points suggested by these snapshots. For example, further research is needed on audience reception of the programming in different regions and social classes of India. Perhaps such research could increase our understanding of how different Indian audiences are negotiating their hybrid cultural identity within the context of increasingly dominant global capital.

Commercial television and globalization both are in the early stages of development in India. Therefore, many patterns, norms, and gender role constructions are being negotiated. It is hoped that the findings of our study and future studies, as well as the cultural manifestations of a nation in flux, will highlight alternative spaces in which ideologies can be transformed by "articulating the elements differently" (Hall, 1995, p. 19). At present, the transnational media corporations in India with their global consumerist ideologies appear to be clashing with the moralizing, patriarchal nationalist ideologies that are on the rise. Both are problematic. There always is the hope that future television programming in India, which is rapidly changing and experimenting with different possibilities, will disrupt both of these binary forces: the capitalist ideology being imported from the West and the reactionary nationalist ideology being fostered in India. This might not be a very realistic hope, however, when we consider the history of global transnational corporations operating for profit in colonial and postcolonial contexts. Such conditions usually work to crush transgressive disruptions rather than encourage them.

NOTES

1. The danger of essentializing the "Indian woman" is difficult to avoid in a chapter such as this. Dealing with imagery being generated about Indian women during the late 1990s makes it difficult to do so without essentializing the experience of women in India ourselves. But we would like to note the fact that the term is indeed an essentializing one and that it does not capture the experience of many Indian women. We also acknowledge the varied hybrid identities that are being produced during recent years in India and that we are trying to map in our research.

2. There have been two definitive works on Indian "womanhood" and its construction in the images produced by the National Network (*Doordarshan*) in India. Krishnan and Dinghe (1990) present a discussion of the construction of gender roles in India before 1990, and Mankekar (1999) presents a detailed critical feminist ethnography that explores the notion of nationhood and "Indian Womanhood" as it was constructed by Doordarshan and read by particular Indian audiences during the 1990s.

3. Names of focus group participants and media executives have been changed for purposes of confidentiality.

4. Although there was a brief discussion about what Indian culture was and how it might be difficult to categorize, in conversations we had with focus group participants and interviewees, there was a general monolithic construction of Indian culture that many of the students seemed comfortable in using for the purpose of our discussion.

5. *Desi-cool* may be roughly translated as being "cool" in the Western colloquial sense of the term but on Indian terms. *Desi* means "local" or "Indian."

6. The Standard and Practices Code deals primarily with commercial aspects of television programming rather than with programming content. The guidance on content was minimal and comparable with standards in the United States. For example, the code prohibits the use of particular swear words and frontal nudity (personal interviews with N. Pantvaidya, July 1, 1997, and S. Shastri, July 11, 1997). However, the code does not provide guidance on issues such as how women will be portrayed.

7. We are not suggesting that "positive" portrayals of gender roles in the media have a direct one-to-one correlation with gender role constructions in Indian society. But media constructions of gender can be one site where women struggle over notions of Indian womanhood in ways that disrupt the status quo.

8. "Indianization" is a term used by many of the current interviewees to connote a trend toward programming that is produced in India by Indians and for Indian audiences.

9. In terms of ownership, many private networks operating in India have a combination of both Indian and non-Indian financing. In addition, many networks have Indian executives in charge of their Indian offices. Therefore, it is not meaningful to delineate between most Indian and non-Indian networks in terms of their ownership and everyday operations in the Indian context given that these networks have Indian network executives and producers generating programming in India for Indian audiences. Perhaps the only network that still may be considered primarily "Western" in its programming mix and personnel is Star TV. Although Star TV has been steadily increasing its Hindi programming for its Indian broadcasts (achieving a 40%-60% mix of Indian and Western programs in 1997), its general entertainment channels continue to broadcast a large number of Western series such as *The Bold and the Beautiful, Baywatch,* and *The X-Files.* Also, the Star TV network has headquarters in Hong Kong and is managed by non-Indian personnel.

REFERENCES

Ashcroft, B., Griffiths, G., & Tiffin, H. (1998). *Key concepts in post-colonial studies.* London: Routledge.

Basham, A. L. (Ed.). (1975). *A cultural history of India.* Oxford, UK: Clarendon.

Bhabha, H. K. (1994). *The location of culture.* London: Routledge.

BJP Manifesto. (1998). [Online]. Available: www.bjp.org/manifes/chap2.htm

Bumiller, E. (1990). *May you be the mother of a hundred sons: A journey among the women of India.* New York: Random House.

Chatterjee, P. (1993). *The nation and its fragments: Colonial and postcolonial histories.* Princeton, NJ: Princeton University Press.

Chopra, A., & Baria, F. (1996, November 15). The beauty craze. *India Today,* pp. 20-29.

Coll, S. (1992, March 5). MTV age dawning in India. *Washington Post,* pp. A31, A38.

Crabtree, R. D., & Malhotra, S. (1996). On the ground and in the air: The commercialization of television in India. *International Communication Bulletin, 31,* 4-6.

Crabtree, R. D., & Malhotra, S. (2000). A case study of commercial television in India: Assessing the organizational mechanisms of cultural imperialism. *Journal of Broadcasting and Electronic Media, 44,* 364-385.

Crabtree, R. D., & Malhotra, S. (in press). Media hegemony, social class, and the commercialization of television in India. In B. L. Artz & Y. R. Kamilipour (Eds.), *Media hegemony and social class.*

Denzin, N. K., & Lincoln, Y. S. (Eds.). (1994). Introduction. In N. K. Denzin & Y. S. Lincoln (Eds.), *Handbook of qualitative research* (pp. 1-17). Thousand Oaks, CA: Sage.

During, S. (Ed.). (1993). *The cultural studies reader.* London: Routledge.

Embree, A. T. (Ed.). (1988). *Sources of Indian tradition: From the beginning to 1800* (2nd ed., Vol. 1). New York: Columbia University Press.

Gandhi, L. (1998). *Postcolonial theory: A critical introduction.* New York: Columbia University Press.

Gerbner, G. (1996). The hidden side of television violence. In G. Gerbner, H. Mowlana, & H. Schiller (Eds.), *Invisible crises: What conglomerate control of media means for America and the world* (pp. 27-34). Boulder, CO: Westview.

Gitlin, T. (1983). *Inside prime time.* New York: Pantheon.

Grossberg, L. (1996). History, politics, and postmodernism: Stuart Hall and cultural studies. In D. Morley & K. H. Chen (Eds.), *Stuart Hall: Critical dialogues in cultural studies* (pp. 151-173). London: Routledge.

Grossberg, L., Wartella, E., & Whitney, D. C. (1998). *Mediamaking: Mass media in a popular culture.* Thousand Oaks, CA: Sage.

Hall, S. (1995). The whites of their eyes: Racist ideologies and the media. In G. Dines & J. M. Humez (Eds.), *Gender, race, and class in media: A text-reader* (pp. 18-22). Thousand Oaks, CA: Sage.

Hegde, R. S. (1998). A view from elsewhere: Locating difference and the politics of representation from a transnational feminist perspective. *Communication Theory, 8,* 271-297.

Hegde, R. S. (1999). Marking bodies, reproducing violence: A feminist reading of female infanticide in South India. *Violence Against Women, 5,* 507-525.

Herman, E., & Chomsky, N. (1988). *Manufacturing consent.* New York: Pantheon.

Indian Management Research Bureau. (1997, July 8). *Television Rating Points Report.* (Bombay, India)

Krishnan, P., & Dinghe, A. (1990). *Affirmation and denial: Construction of femininity on Indian television.* New Delhi, India: Sage.

Lindlof, T. R. (1995). *Qualitative communication research methods: Current communication—An advanced text series* (Vol. 3). Thousand Oaks, CA: Sage.

Malhotra, S. (1993). *Satellite television viewership and perception of women's gender roles in India.* Unpublished master's thesis, Pepperdine University.

Malhotra, S. (1999). *The privatization of television in India: Implications of new technologies for gender, nation, and culture.* Unpublished dissertation, University of New Mexico.

Malhotra, S., & Crabtree, R. D. (1994, April). *Assessing media/cultural imperialism: An audience response to gender issues and Star TV in India.* Paper presented at the Third Annual Conference on Console-ing Passions: Television, Video, and Feminism, Tucson, AZ.

Malhotra, S., & Rogers, E. M. (2000). Satellite television and the new Indian woman. *Gazette: The International Journal for Communication Studies, 62,* 407-429.

Mani, L. (1989). Contentious traditions: The debate on sati in colonial India. In K. Sangari & S. Vaid (Eds.), *Recasting women: Essays in colonial history* (pp. 88-126). New Delhi, India: Kali for Women.

Mankekar, P. (1999). *Screening culture, viewing politics: An ethnography of television, womanhood, and nation in postcolonial India.* Durham, NC: Duke University Press.

Melkote, S. R., Shields, P., & Agrawal, B. C. (Eds.). (1998). *International satellite broadcasting in South Asia: Political, economic, and cultural implications.* Lanham, MD: University Press of America.

Mohanty, C. T. (1991). Under Western eyes: Feminist scholarship and colonial discourse. In C. T. Mohanty, A. Russo, & L. Torres (Eds.), *Third World women and the politics of feminism* (pp. 51-80). Bloomington: Indiana University Press.

Moorti, S. (1998, November). *Tailored bodies: The female figure in discourses of national identity.* Paper presented at the meeting of the National Communication Association, New York.

Moorti, S. (2000). Inflamed passions: *Fire,* the woman question, and the policing of cultural borders. *Genders, 32* [Online]. Available: genders.org/g32/g32_moorti.html

Morgan, D. (1988). *Focus group as qualitative research* (Sage University Paper Series on Qualitative Research, Vol. 16). Newbury Park, CA: Sage.

Morgan, M., & Signorielli, N. (1990). Cultivation analysis: Conceptualization and methodology. In N. Signorielli & M. Morgan (Eds.), *Cultivation analysis: New directions in media effects research* (pp. 13-34). Newbury Park, CA: Sage.

Ninan, S. (1995). *Through the magic window: Television and change in India.* New Delhi, India: Penguin.

Penley, C. (1988). *Feminism and film theory.* New York: Routledge.

Rajagopal, A. (1993). The rise of national programming: The case of Indian television. *Media, Culture, and Society, 15,* 91-111.

Said, E. (1978). *Orientalism.* New York: Vintage.

Schiller, H. (1976). *Communication and cultural domination.* New York: Augustus M. Kelley.

Shah, A. (1997). *Hype, hypocrisy, and television in urban India.* New Delhi, India: Vikas.

Shome, R. (1999). Whiteness and the politics of location: Postcolonial reflections. In T. K. Nakayama & J. N. Martin (Eds.), *Whiteness: The communication of social identity.* Thousand Oaks, CA: Sage.

Singhal, D. P. (1983). *A history of the Indian people.* London: Methuen.

Strauss, A., & Corbin, J. (1990). Coding procedures. In A. Strauss & J. Corbin (Eds.), *Basics of qualitative research: Grounded theory procedures and techniques* (pp. 57-74). Newbury Park, CA: Sage.

Tanzer, A. (1991, November 11). The Asian village. *Forbes,* pp. 58-60.

Thomas, P. N. (1999). Trading the nation: Multilateral negotiations and the fate of communications in India. *Gazette: The International Journal for Communication Studies, 61,* 275-292.

van Zoonen, L. (1994). *Feminist media studies.* London: Sage.

White, M. (1987). Ideological analysis and television. In R. C. Allen (Ed.), *Channels of discourse reassembled: Television and contemporary criticism* (2nd ed., pp. 161-202). Chapel Hill: University of North Carolina Press.

4

Indian Press's Response to International Satellite Television in India

A Textual Analysis

ABHIK ROY • *Howard University*

With the emergence of globalization and its accompanying global economy and mass media, issues of local and national identity have become problematic. According to Appadurai (1990), a main problem of globalization is the dialectical tension between cultural homogenization (globalization) and heterogenization (localization). Hall (1991a) argues that the process of globalization should be viewed as contradictory forces moving in opposite directions: "It goes above the nation-state, and it goes below it. It goes global and local in the same moment," and the global and local create "two faces of the same movement from one epoch of globalization, the one which has been dominated by the nation-state, the national economies, the national cultural identities, to something new" (p. 27). Barber (1992) describes this dialectical tension as a competition between "Jihad versus McWorld" in which international relations and the future of humanity will be marked by a "struggle between contradictory forces toward tribalism and ethnic/religious local loyalty, on the one hand, and homogenized, capitalistic, mediated images and identities formed by Western corporations such as McDonald's, on the other" (cited in Collier, 2000, p. 219).

According to Hall (1991a), globalization is dominated by global mass media that cross and re-cross "linguistic frontiers more rapidly and more easily" (p. 27). For Hall, global mass culture is dominated by

---

AUTHOR'S NOTE: The author thanks Mary Jane Collier, Gwen Roy, William Starosta, Melbourne S. Cummings, and two anonymous reviewers for their valuable suggestions and comments on an earlier draft of this chapter. Appreciation also is expressed to Kaushik Roy, who helped with the data collection.

> all the ways in which the visual and the graphic arts have entered directly into the reconstitution of public life, of entertainment, and of leisure. It is dominated by film and by the image, imagery, and styles of mass advertising. Its epitome is in all those forms of mass communication of which one might think of satellite television as the prime example. Not because it is the only example but because you could not understand satellite television without understanding its grounding in a particular advanced national economy and culture, and yet its whole purpose is precisely that it cannot be limited any longer by national boundaries. (p. 27)

Hall (1991a) is of the opinion that global cultures originate in the West by means of the flow of capital and technology as well as the transmission of images and information from Western cultures. Hall (1991b) believes that globalization has hegemonic tendencies in which "a certain configuration of local particularities try to dominate the whole scene, to mobilize the technology, and to incorporate, in subaltern positions, a variety of more localized identities to construct the next historical project" (p. 67). For Hall (1991a, 1991b) and Appadurai (1990), a dialectical tension between the local and the global exists. While the forces of globalization blur the borders of the nation-state, counter-politics and resistance simultaneously take place against such globalization in several cultures.

Hall's and Appadurai's conception of the dialectical tension between the global and the local holds true in many nations. The tension between the global and the local often is evidenced by some nations (e.g., Singapore, Malaysia) trying to close their boundaries to Western satellite television. Both Singapore and Malaysia banned the reception of international satellite television (ISTV), namely Star TV, for reasons that are ideological, cultural, and political (Chan, 1994). The ban on Star TV stems from the fear that "uncontrolled information from outside may disrupt social, racial, and religious harmony" (p. 115). However, it is now almost impossible to resist international media completely, and in Singapore and Malaysia the privileged have created access to ISTV (Chan, 1994).

According to several scholars (Appadurai, 1990; Dirlik, 1990; Giddens, 1990; Hall, 1994; Said, 1993), it no longer is possible to perceive cultures as closed systems. Said (1993) explains that cultural intersections are evident today where

> new alignments made across borders, types, nations, and essences are rapidly coming into view, and it is those new alignments that now provoke and chal-

> lenge the fundamentally static notion of identity that has been the core of cultural thought during the era of imperialism. (pp. xxiv-xxv)

Although several scholars examine the theoretical issues surrounding the globalization versus localization debate (Appadurai, 1990; Featherstone, 1990, 1991; Featherstone & Lash, 1995; Hall, 1991a, 1991b; Hannerz, 1990; Robertson, 1990, 1991, 1992, 1995; Wallerstein, 1974, 1990), little attention is given to the counter-politics and resistance of some nations against such forces of globalization. Specifically, there seems to be a paucity of research in the communication discipline concerning how certain nations, such as India, have rhetorically challenged the forces of media globalization. The Indian media not only have tried to raise public consciousness about the negative effects of the Western media presence in India but also have sought to re-create and protect the borders of the nation-state discursively. However, despite such attempts on the part of the Indian media to resist the influence of Western globalization, there is increasing evidence showing that certain members of the Indian community are embracing Western media.

By using India as an example, this study demonstrates that as the boundaries of the nation-state begin to waver with globalization, one witnesses a regression to a very defensive form of national identity, on the one hand, and a growing interest and enthusiasm to accept globalization, on the other. The focus of this chapter, therefore, is how the Indian press attempts to restrict the flow of international satellite broadcasting across its borders. By examining the Indian press's coverage of ISTV, this study explains how resistance to globalization in one indigenous culture takes place discursively. In addition, the study identifies the alternative voices that challenge the dominant discourse of the Indian press that oppose ISTV.

The basic assumption behind this study is that nationalism and ideology work together and are present in the institutional discourse, political speeches, media discourse, and religious discourse, among others, in any given culture. According to Collier (2000), these discursive processes may embody what is regarded as "strongly valued, moral, normal, respectable, and sinful" in a culture (p. 218). Because media discourse reproduces and sustains ideological forms (Hall, 1977, 1980), one of the ways of examining the ideological thrust of news is to study the language through which the news stories are presented. While examining the language of the Indian press, this study gives metaphors special attention because metaphors help the readers to see the "facts" as perceived by the rhetor. Metaphor is a "device for seeing something *in terms of* something else. . . . [It] tells us something about one character as considered from the point of view of another character" (Burke, 1969, pp. 503-504). By associating complex ideas with common images or experiences, metaphors can influence public understanding and subsequent action on important issues.

Mumby and Spitzack (1983) underscore the nature of cultural hegemony as embodied in mass media, wherein the dominant ideology is the representational field for the reportage. Their study takes note of the special work that metaphors perform in such presentations:

> If, for example, it is shown that certain metaphors are used consistently, then it can be argued that viewers are asked to draw upon particular domains of experience to make sense of news stories. Such a structuring of language suggests a nonarbitrary framing of reality within a particular ideological meaning system. (p. 164)

In a context of contradictory forces between the global and the local in India, this study seeks to answer the following research questions:

1. What are the major themes, assumptions, and arguments of the Indian press regarding ISTV?
2. What are the key metaphors and catchphrases? What are the rhetorical implications of such metaphors and catchphrases?
3. Are there any alternative voices that challenge the discourse of the Indian press? If so, in what manner?

BACKGROUND: INDIAN MEDIA SCENE

In 1991, India experienced the sudden emergence of ISTV from a Hong Kong-based broadcasting network called Star TV (Kishore, 1994; Ninan, 1995). This company was later purchased by Rupert Murdoch's News-Corp during the summer of 1993. According to *Television Media Scene,* the following channels were offered to Indian viewers by Star TV in 1998: Star Plus (syndicated U.S. and British comedy, cartoons, drama, and entertainment), Star Movies (mostly Hollywood/British movies), Star Sports (European, Asian, and American events), Channel V (Music Television), and Zee TV (all-Hindi television network) ("SET Launched More Channels," 1998). In addition to these channels offered by Star TV, Indians can now view programs on BBC, CNN, Discovery, ESPN, Hallmark, HBO, Kermit, MTV Asia, NBC/CNBC, National Geographic, Nickelodeon, and TNT, among others.

The Indian Government controlled the broadcasting of television since it started commercial television broadcasting during the 1960s. By setting up a vast bureaucratic organization under the rubric of the Ministry of Information and Broadcasting, the Indian government enjoyed a virtual monopoly over the dissemination of broadcast news and entertainment on Indian television. The government officials in the Ministry of Information and Broadcasting controlled, regulated, and monitored television broadcasting in India (Mitra, 1994; Sen, 1995). The rationale behind the government's control of Indian television was to achieve social integration among the diverse peoples of India as well as to educate the masses at the grassroots level.

The Indian government was completely unprepared for this sudden emergence of satellite television and was unable to control the content of the broadcasts of Western satellite television networks (Dhawan, 1992, p. 12; Mozoomdar, 1992, p. 10). The Indian viewers, used to watching lackluster, sterile programs produced by the Indian government, became hooked on ISTV (Dhawan, 1992). The sudden popularity of the international satellite networks in India meant not only a major loss of viewership for the Indian government's television programs but also a significant drop in advertising revenues. At this juncture, the Indian government found itself losing the power and monopoly it had enjoyed over its television viewers for decades ("Stars in Their Eyes," 1993).

Although the broadcasting industry always has been under the control of the Indian government, the Indian press has enjoyed autonomy in its dissemination of news (Nair, 1978). The birth of the Indian press can be traced back to the 1860s and the intense and bitter opposition to the British colonialists. The strength and independence of the current Indian press stems directly from its stubborn resistance to attempts to suppress freedom of expression by the British regime (Reddi, 1990). Given the history of the Indian press's nationalist attitude, it is not surprising that the Indian newspapers and magazines are critical of the sudden influx of ISTV.

Although complete and accurate data of viewership of all foreign satellite networks often are unavailable, as of October 1993, Star TV surveys showed an increase of Star TV viewers from 1.28 million to 7.28 million in just 2 years (Bhatt, 1994). According to a report in the *Economic Times,* Indian government-operated Doordarshan television reached all Indian television households, followed by (Star TV-owned) Zee TV with 29%

and Star Plus with 28% ("Television to Rule," 1995). Although no current data are available on the combined total viewership of Star TV's channels (Channel V, Star Movies, Star Plus, Star Sports, and Zee TV), according to a 1997 report by the Indian Market Research Bureau (IMRB), out of a total viewership of 40 million people in nine Indian metropolitan cities, Star Plus was reported to enjoy a viewership of approximately 1.3 million. The 1997 IMRB report also indicated that Star Movies had a viewership of 519,000 and that Zee TV commanded a viewership of approximately 6 million. Based on these reports, it is evident that ISTV has secured a firm foothold in Indian culture.

METHOD

The method in this study is based on the assumption that news is dramatic, involving a text whose language gives meaning to the world it reports, and this meaning can be understood through an act of interpretation. Thus, a textual analysis is performed to examine the discourse of the Indian press so as to get behind the "broad distribution of manifest content" to the "latent implicit patterns and emphasis" (Hall, 1975, p. 16). In such a textual analysis, a text acts as a means to the study and not as an end to the study. The text holds "potentially infinite processes of signification" (Cheney & Tompkins, 1988, p. 460).

For the purpose of textual analysis, each news item (news report, commentary, or editorial) is closely examined to understand the arguments, assumptions, and beliefs behind the discourse of the Indian press. The second step involves identifying the dominant themes based on such assumptions, arguments, and beliefs. The third step looks for metaphors and other catchwords, both explicit and implicit, that are present in the news reports. The final step is completed through an act of interpretation, which explicates the meaning offered to readers by these various parts of the news item. In a textual analysis, then, the new item remains central to the whole process of interpretation.

The sample of Indian newspapers and magazines was collected from the database of IPAN, the largest public affairs and public relations firm in India. Because of the nature and diversity of clients that IPAN serves, IPAN maintains an extensive database of Indian newspapers and magazines published in English. A detailed search of subjects and key words identified 10 newspapers and 2 newsmagazines that covered this issue between 1991 and 1994. After 1994, coverage on this topic was not to be found.

According to a 1998 report of the Audit Bureau of Circulation in India, all 10 newspapers that were reviewed—the *Business and Political Observer,* the *Economic Times,* the *Financial Express,* the *Hindustan Times, The Independent,* the *Indian Express, The Pioneer, The Statesman,* the *Times of India,* and *The Telegraph*—command status and influence as well as some geographical diversity. *India Today* and *Sunday* are market leaders in the category of newsmagazines. Of the 27 news items in these 10 newspapers and 2 newsmagazines, there are 13 articles, 13 commentaries, and 1 editorial. All articles, commentaries, and editorials pertaining to the issue of ISTV in India are included because the study seeks to capture the extent of coverage of each publication as well as the tenor of such writings. There are two reasons for selecting English publications. First, English is the official language of India. Second, given India's literacy rates (which are as low as 51%), the reach of the Indian print media is confined to urban-educated readers who are from an upwardly mobile, middle class background with English being their primary language of communication (Sarma, 1998).

DOMINANT RHETORIC: RESISTANCE TO INTERNATIONAL SATELLITE TELEVISION

The following news items decry the advent of ISTV in India. They argue that ISTV is inimical to the national identity and integrity of India because it threatens not only the economic well-being of India but also the very existence of Indian culture. Thus, steps need to be taken to sustain and protect the national identity and Indian cultural values against such Western powers. An in-depth reading of the text identified the following themes.

ISTV Is a Threat to Indian Culture

The dominant theme in the following reports and columns accuses ISTV of being a new form of colonialism/cultural imperialism that is destroying India's rich tradition and heritage. The sentiment is that if international satellite programming is not checked, then it will break the cultural and financial backbone of the country. Given India's past experience with colonialism under the British, the issue of cultural imperialism and colonialism, or the threat to India's cultural tradition and values, is likely to have a special significance with some Indian readers, especially the ones who have experienced the British colonization of India.

A commentary in *The Independent* states that while "the post-colonial states of Asia strive to free themselves from the slave-consciousness contained in the colonial culture of imperialism, [the international television networks] revalidated and reconfirmed colonial discourse through [their various programs]" (Bharucha, 1992, p. 21). This particular columnist portrays Star TV as "seeking to recontrol and recolonize through cultural hegemony" (p. 21). The commentary also argues that cultural programming from the Western satellite television networks created stereotypical representations of the Orient in which the Orient usually was depicted as the "exotic East," whereas the other representation focuses on humans. The Oriental person on such Western programs often is depicted as being "impulsive, weak, sly, lazy, irrational, and childlike . . . , [someone who needed] the analytical, rational leadership provided by the Occident to get out of his own mess" (p. 21). For this columnist, this stereotypical depiction of the Orient is a new form of cultural colonialism.

A similar note is sounded in another commentary, "Combating Cultural Imperialism," which states that "imperialism has assumed different forms. The concentrated beaming or, in other words, footprints of alien satellites have taken the form of a warfare. The new craze called Music Television is a form of imperialism" (Morarka, 1992, p. 11). Similarly, an editorial in the *Times of India* states that if this new form of imperialism is not stopped, then the "country runs the risk of financial hemorrhage, cultural anarchy, and maybe even political subversion" ("National TV," 1992, p. 12).

An article in the *Financial Express* ("Violence, Vulgarity," 1994) covers news about a national symposium on current trends in Indian television. It reports that the participants in the symposium unanimously called for action on the part of the Indian government to "check the menace of the alien culture [ISTV]" (p. 13). The article also quotes one of the "Indian authorities on mass media" as saying that "the onslaught of satellite TV was directly related to human rights as it developed a contemptuous attitude towards a section of the society, namely, women" (p. 13). The members of the symposium also are reported as decrying violence and vulgarity on international television, which they say is instrumental in corrupting the society and undermining the importance of Indian cultural heritage (p. 13).

A columnist in the *Indian Express* voices serious misgivings about the goal and intent of international satellite television in India. He is of the opinion that the Western satellite corporations are owned and operated by global corporations with enormous financial clout and that their interests will not be "in tune with [India's] national interest" (Ananthamurthy, 1993, p. 23). The columnist also warns that foreign satellite television is likely to create a new set of hierarchies in India whereby Indian viewers' language and culture might not have any place.

ISTV Promotes Violence in Indian Children

The major theme of the following reports and commentaries appears to be that viewing a steady diet of violence and other forms of aggression on ISTV is making Indian children prone to violence. In a society such as India, where the Gandhian principle of nonviolence is respected in most families, the specter of Indian children becoming violent, antisocial elements probably is quite disturbing and distressing to Indian parents and teachers. In the following reports, the columnists, by relying mostly on Western research findings on the impact of television violence on children, warn that India soon will face a new set of social problems dealing with antisocial behavior among Indian youths and that this problem will need to be taken seriously.

A commentary in the *Hindustan Times* discusses how the gross and violent scenes depicted in the various ISTV programs "trigger deep set instincts of violence and encourage social misdemeanor" (Dixit, 1994, p. 1). The commentary argues that violent scenes on international television programs are responsible for antisocial behavior among children in India. The columnist highlights research findings on children and television violence indicating that "repeated exposure to television violence makes children more acceptable to the idea that violence can solve problems" (p. 1). The columnist argues that an Indian child, by watching violent shows on ISTV, might get overwhelmed by the forces of evil and feel inclined to become "hateful and destructive, spreading pain and death around" (p. 2).

Similarly, a news article in the *Indian Express* reports that "by acting as a psychic stimulant . . . , [international television programs] pose the threat of creating a copycat effect among children and the youth" (Jain, 1994, p. 19). The report contains several research findings regarding television violence and its impact on children—all from the West—to argue about how violence on ISTV will have a negative impact on Indian children. In view of the research findings, the article poses the question: "Are we pushing our children to a situation where they will be so desensitized to violence that they will resort to it increasingly in their own lives?" (p. 19). In conclusion, the article reminds the readers that ISTV has launched its "intense assault on the mental health of our children" and that this is a "threat that the nation can hardly afford to add to its ever-growing kitty of problems" (p. 19).

Another column in the *Times of India* notes that "on satellite TV . . . , the children are being overfed on a diet of violence and are being numbed to violence in real life" ("TV Changing Values," 1994, p. 5). The same column reports that "GI-Joes, Donald Ducks, and Mickeys are now selling a cult of aggression, guns, and violence as an unquestionable means of getting anything" (p. 5).

ISTV Destroys Moral Values in Indian Children

The overarching theme of the following articles and commentaries is that ISTV is corrupting the minds of Indian children. By relying so heavily on Western television, Indian children are losing their sense of tradition and cultural heritage. Based on these reports, Indian children not only are replacing their Indian cultural heroes with Western substitutes but also losing their sense of morals as well as discipline and dedication in pursuing academic work and extracurricular activities.

An article in the *Times of India* ("TV Changing Values," 1994, p. 5) reports that exposure to programs on ISTV has changed the value system of Indian middle class children. According to the article, there is now a greater need among Indian children "to win sans ethics," which often leads to adopting violent ways of achieving results. The same article reports that "with more and more international television being watched, there is a drastic reduction in peer interaction and even pursuance of hobbies, outdoor activities, and even concentration while studying among the kids" (p. 5). Another article in the *Business and Political Observer* ("Children Pose," 1994, p. 15) blames ISTV for the increase in the desire of children to ape the West. The article voices concern about the commercials on ISTV selling a "Western lifestyle, an aggressive go-getter attitude so that Indian children can maintain an image that is acceptable to their peers" (p. 15).

A commentary in the *Financial Express* states that "international satellite TV has spread its tentacles far and wide and has rocked a whole generation of impressionable youngsters. They cherish heavy metal, baseball hats, long tresses, and Coke" (Malik, 1994, p. 21). In short, Indian children's newly found pleasure seems to be watching bad television on ISTV and consuming material things. Similarly, a commentary in the newsmagazine *Sunday* criticizes ISTV for encouraging Indian children to replace their traditional mythic heroes with Western heroes such as "Garfield," "He Man," "Master of the Universe," and "Ninja Turtle" (Jain, 1993, p. 72). Based on the same commentary, ISTV exposes Indian children to a "diet of blood, lust, and greed, and as a consequence their 'taste buds' had changed" (p. 74). Indian children seem to discard the "good, if dull, protagonist" in favor of the "Satanic figure or villain" (p. 74).

In a similar vein, an article in *The Hindu* chastises ISTV for taking Indian children on a "cultural leap into an alien land where Indian children do not have to listen to tales from [the Indian epics] Ramayana and the Mahabharata from their parents anymore" (Chatterji, 1994, p. 1). ISTV also threatens the bond between parents and children by "taking over the functions of an absent parent" (p. 1). Furthermore, by watching international television programs on a regular basis, Indian children are "picking up strange language [and] behavior patterns and imbibing these in their interrelationships with others" (p. 1).

ISTV also is criticized for causing a lack of discipline among Indian children both at home and in school. A column in *The Independent* (Mathur, 1992) states that student behavior in schools in major Indian cities is poor because of the student's addiction to international television. Due to this "newfound addiction," Indian children are neglecting their homework and not coming to class on time. Irate parents are complaining about not being able to get their children to do any household work due to their preoccupation with television. The columnist further states that this addiction has caused "hyperactivism" among Indian children in several cities. These children apparently find it difficult to "relate to the slow pace of real life after the zippy things they are constantly exposed to on satellite television. The symptoms are characteristic: at home, [there is] an all pervasive lethargy, and in school, there is a general lack of concentration in the classroom" (p. 5). The columnist also writes about the teachers being hard-pressed to come up with innovative ways of getting the children to watch less television.

The Indian Government Has Failed to Deal With ISTV

The consistent theme of the following news items is that the menace of ISTV could have easily been eradicated if only the Indian government was not so deluded, bureaucratic, and shortsighted. According to an article in *The Pioneer,* the Indian government is "shaken out of its apathetic ambivalence towards the future of Doordarshan [Indian-operated television] by the arrival of international satellite TV" (Mozoomdar, 1992, p. 10). It is believed that the Indian government initially showed an "ostrich-like complacency or false bravado" but that "now there is an extreme case of panic" (p. 10). Another commentary in *The Telegraph* urges the Indian government to get out of its "Rip Van Winkelian slumber" and "deal with the threat" from ISTV (Rawla & De Sarkar, 1993, p. 22). Similarly, *India Today* exhorts the government to "wake up from its deep slumber" and tackle the "issue head-on" (Jain & Sidhu, 1992, p. 160).

The following two reports in the *India Today* newsmagazine and the *Times of India* newspaper clearly convey a strong element of distrust of the Indian administration. *India Today* accuses the Indian government of "spinning a convenient web of 'legal fiction' that the large number of satellite dishes that have been erected by India are to receive Indian television and not international satellite television" (Jain & Sidhu, 1992, p. 161). According to the report, this is a consequence of "self-delusion" on the part of the Indian government officials to deal with ISTV. Another report in the *Times of India* criticizes the government for "attempting to cover up by claiming that they [the Indian government] are facing no threat" ("The Growing Threat," 1993, p. 17).

The following two items, one newspaper editorial and one newspaper article, directly blame the Indian government for failing to deal with ISTV and for jeopardizing India's national security. The editorial in the *Times of India* belabors the Indian government for being

> unable or unwilling or both to face the new challenges in the television field. . . . [The Indian government] has opted for a reckless course of action: In the name of 'market friendliness,' it is now likely to allow foreign satellite companies to operate in the country. ("National TV," 1992, p. 12)

Similarly, an article in *The Hindu* condemns the Indian government for failing "in its duty to protect the interests of the people and its own as well" (Subramanian, 1992, p. 14).

India Can Meet the Challenge of ISTV From the West

The rhetoric of the following news items articulates what Dirlik (1990) describes as "native chauvinism" (p. 401) as a means to reject and resist ISTV. The following commentaries are quite patriotic in their tone, boasting about India's resources in dealing with the phenomenon of ISTV. For example, a columnist in the *Economic Times* argues that India has the technology and talent to produce and market innovative programming that will effectively compete with foreign extravaganzas on ISTV networks (Dhawan, June 24, 1992).

Another commentary in the *Times of India* (Khanna, 1992) emphasizes the high caliber of Indian media professionals. The columnist believes that with more up-to-date training, these professionals will succeed in helping India to edge out its competition from foreign television. Finally, in an emotional tone, another commentator in the *Indian Express* appeals to Indians to rally behind the Indian government to deal with ISTV effectively. The commentary, very nationalist in its approach, speaks of India's capabilities to deal with this threat. The columnist argues that because ISTV cannot be stopped from beaming its programs into India, Indians should

> beat them [the West] at their own game. . . . We have a reservoir of talents, and given a chance, our producers can do an excellent job. . . . Despite our poverty and resource crunch, we, in our wisdom, made allocations and gave a fillip [boost] to space research. Our scientists have successfully put this satellite into orbit. What we have not fully realized is that India has become a space power of significance. Americans are aware of this, and this explains their opposition to Russia's cooperation with India in the field of missile technology. . . . We have a very long and rich cultural heritage, and no foreign television network can take away that rich heritage from us. (Morarka, 1992, p. 11)

In sum, a close reading of the text has identified the five themes that are consistently repeated in most of the articles and commentaries: ISTV is a threat to Indian culture, ISTV promotes violence in Indian children, ISTV destroys moral values in Indian children, the Indian government has failed to deal with ISTV, and India can meet the challenge of ISTV from the West. Further examination of the texts also reveals that a common cluster of metaphors is associated with "war."

METAPHOR OF WAR

The metaphors recurring either in the headlines or texts are "The *Invasion* of the Skies Has Begun" (Khanna, 1992, p. 12); "*Invasion* From the Skies: World TV *Assault* on India" (Dhawan, 1992, p. 12); "*Combating* Cultural Imperialism" (Morarka, 1992, p. 11); "the concentrated beaming or, in other words, footprints of alien satellites have taken the form of a *warfare*" (p. 11); "this *battle* can be *fought* by giving a greater choice of good Indian programs" (Jain & Sidhu, 1992, p. 160); "the *onslaught* of foreign TV channels" ("Violence, Vulgarity," 1994, p. 13); "[the Indian government] is gearing up to *ward off* the cultural *invasion*" (Rawla & De Sarkar, 1993, p. 22); "children with an impressionable mind were the largest groups of victims of the cultural *invasion* of satellite TV" ("Violence, Vulgarity," 1994, p. 13); and "[Indian television is] *counter(ing)* the *threat* to our culture posed by CNN, Star TV, [and] BBC World Service TV" (Mozoomdar, 1992, p. 10). In addition to the metaphor of "war," the Indian publications contain highly emotive words such as "financial hemorrhage," "cultural anarchy," "imperialism," "political subversion," and "cultural hegemony." The use of such vivid language on the part of the Indian press reinforces the war metaphor.

The metaphor of war has major rhetorical implications. Burke (1954) asserts that naming is an "interpretive act" and thus guides us to act in a certain way toward the named thing (pp. 176-191). This is partly due to the magical quality "implicit in all language" (Burke, 1973, p. 4). "If you size up a situation in the name of regimentation," Burke points out, "you decree it an essence other than if you size it up in the name of planned economy" (p. 6). Thus, the "command" that a person should act in one way rather than another is "implicit in the name" (Burke, 1959, p. 339). For example, the war metaphor generates several entailments, as pointed out by Lakoff and Johnson (1980): War (a) involves enemies, (b) is a threat to national security, (c) involves setting targets, (d) involves reorganizing priorities, (e) involves establishing a chain of command, (f) involves plotting new strategies, (g) involves gathering intelligence, (h) involves marshaling forces, (i) involves imposing sanctions, and (j) involves sacrifices (p. 156).

Mumby and Spitzack (1983) provide an additional list of entailments for the metaphor of war: War (a) involves attacks, (b) involves the use of weapons, (c) has leaders, (d) involves conflict, (e) usually ends in a victory or a defeat, (f) involves violence, (g) involves a struggle for domination, and (h) is dangerous (p. 168).

Describing the operation of ISTV as an assault, a battle, an invasion, a combat, a fallout, a threat, and an onslaught conjures the ominous image of a "cultural war" being waged on Indian soil. According to Lakoff and Johnson (1980), the concept of war as one of the primary metaphorical constructs is common. As with all metaphoric choices, the selection of a frame spotlights one conceptual framework while it simultaneously obscures others. The metaphor of war emphasizes certain realities that might force the readers to view the situation in no other terms but within the perspective of war. Here, in the present context, if one accepts the war metaphor used by the Indian newspapers, then a few things have to be assumed: that there is an external foreign enemy, that this enemy is out to destroy the basic cultural values of Indians, and that this enemy needs to be stopped at all costs. If this threat is not addressed, then the country will lose its cultural identity.

From a rhetorical perspective, the purpose of using a war metaphor on the part of the Indian press is to unify the masses against a common enemy, namely, the foreign satellite television networks. At the same time, the goal is to persuade Indians to combat this evil force. The rhetoric of war creates unity through a strategy of congregation by segregation. The rhetors using the metaphor of war create an enemy either at home or abroad, and this common enemy acts as a catalyst for unifying the masses (Duncan, 1989). Through the use of war metaphors in the news items, the Indian newspapers reveal their perception of the problem of ISTV as one that requires all Indians to rise up in defense of their cultural identity.

According to Lakoff and Johnson (1980), metaphors are grounded in the culture of the perceiver; thus, the metaphor of war is likely to trigger a different response from Indians than it would from someone in another group who has a different set of experiences. In the Indian context, the metaphor of war has major rhetorical implications in light of the fact that India has been embroiled in both internal and external conflicts for many years. Since its independence from Britain in 1947, India has fought several wars, one with China and two with Pakistan. The border hostilities between India and Pakistan still go on unabated. Furthermore, India is experiencing internal strife over language and religion in several parts of the country that have resulted in many deaths. This is why the use of the war metaphor may evoke vivid associations in some Indian readers.

OPPOSITIONAL VOICES: ISTV IS GOOD FOR INDIANS

Despite the fact that most of the news items in the Indian press place a negative spin on the issue of ISTV, the following newspaper articles and commentaries go against this grain. These articles and commentaries not only support the advent of international television in India but also accept this new phenomenon with alacrity. The following news items are oppositional voices given that they challenge the dominant rhetoric of the Indian press by accepting ISTV in India.

An article in *The Hindu* relates a story about a seminar concerning satellite television in India and quotes an academic as saying that a major benefit of having international television in India is that Indian youths can now "enjoy sports in a better manner than the youth[s] of yesteryears" ("Impact of Satellite TV," 1994, p. 1).

An article in *The Statesman* reports that Star TV is the "chief inspiration for major changes in Indian culture such as fashion and popular music, a spike in consumer demand for brand-name products, and vigorous new calls to liberate the Indian economy from once dominant state control" ("Star TV Electrifies," 1993, p. 9). Similarly, another report in the *Times of India* discusses how ISTV has changed the lifestyle of an Indian community, the *Gujratis,* who live in the western Indian city of Ahmedabad. According to this report, ISTV has Westernized the "social ethos and cultural outlook of average Ahmedabadi [residents of Ahmedabad]" (Vyas, 1992, p. 3). Like the characters on U.S. American soap operas and films, Gujratis in Ahmedabad spend their evenings at clubs, hotels, and kitty parties (i.e., luncheons usually organized by housewives where women put money in a kitty for the next person to take out to pay for the expenses of throwing a party for her friends). The report also states that foreign satellite television is instrumental in breaking certain social practices in this community. For example, "it was the practice that when the in-laws are sitting in the living room, the daughter-in-law is not supposed to sit in the same room. However, Star TV has lifted this barrier," and the daughter-in-law can now sit with the in-laws and watch TV with them (p. 3).

A columnist in *The Independent* criticizes Indian television programs for being "lackluster, mediocre, and trivial" (Masud, 1993, p. 10). He admits that he enjoys watching Western news shows and debates because they are well produced and well presented. The *Indian Express* contains a commentary in which the guest columnist describes viewing ISTV as an "enriching experience" (Karanth, 1993, p. 23). According to this columnist, foreign satellite television provides Indians with varied experiences and choices. This columnist argues that in a democratic country such as India, the viewers should have the choice to "accept or reject something. The advent of multichannel television offers this choice, and hence it is a positive development" (p. 23). This report also reminds the readers that people who are now criticizing the advent of ISTV in India as being a bad influence "did not even have the scope to judge and reject something as good or bad" before the advent of ISTV (p. 23).

A commentary in the *Hindustan Times* lists the pleasures of watching U.S. soap operas in India:

> There's nothing like a spattering of passion and deceit to perk you up at the end of the day. And it's good for you. It keeps your thirst for scandal and gossip satisfied without bringing you down to the level of thy neighbor's wife, keeps our voyeuristic instincts satiated without that sheepish feeling, keeps your daughter off the phone, and [keeps] your son off the streets after dark. For warmth and togetherness, for that wonderful feeling of family, get yourself hooked to Star TV. (Dev Sen, 1993, p. 4)

The columnist also appreciates the "sophisticated humor, subtle snides, [and] polite barbs" of U.S. soap operas. A viewer of U.S. soaps is quoted in the same commentary as saying that she watches them because they are "nice and glamorous and [solve] one problem at a time, unlike the hydra-like intrigues of the other soaps" (p. 4).

Similarly, an article in the *Hindustan Times* (Kumar, 1992) reports that Indian children in major cities enjoy watching MTV (p. 12). Whereas MTV is a popular phenomenon with Indian urban youths, entertainment programs, especially American soap operas, are popular in Saronda, a "sleepy" Indian village. According to a report in the *Times of India,* the residents of Saronda (mostly women) are mesmerized by shows such as *The Bold and the Beautiful* and *Santa Barbara.* Based on this article, women, both young and old, congregate with their neighbors and "avidly watch the bewildering world of American soaps" (Baria, 1993, p. 10).

Based on the preceding discussion, it is evident that some Indians are enjoying the new form of entertainment and information from ISTV. According to these reports, Indian women, both in metropolitan cities and in remote villages, have enthusiastically admitted their pleasure and admiration for U.S. soap operas. Another finding is that some Indians believe that ISTV has brought about several positive changes in the Indian culture.

CONCLUSION

Through a textual analysis of five major themes—ISTV is a threat to Indian culture, ISTV promotes violence in Indian children, ISTV destroys moral values in Indian children, the Indian government has failed to deal with ISTV, and India can meet the challenge of ISTV from the West—this chapter demonstrates how the Indian press seeks to resist the forces of

Western satellite television. In addition, by identifying the recurring metaphor of war, the chapter shows how the issue of ISTV is framed in the broader context of war against India's cultural values and identity. Finally, the chapter highlights the oppositional voices that often remain muted against the overwhelming anti-Western diatribe of the Indian press. These oppositional voices, few as they may be, forcefully challenge the dominant rhetoric of the Indian press that is so vehemently opposed to ISTV.

The significance of this study lies in demonstrating that a bipolar global-local dialectic, where the local always is compared against the global, is problematic. This study shows how two forms of globalization become juxtaposed. One form, perhaps having the loudest voice, is increasingly defensive and closed, and it speaks to protect Indian nationalism and cultural identity in a highly patriotic manner. The other form of globalization voices appreciation for the new phenomenon of global satellite television.

In addition, this study indicates how ISTV is responsible for bringing about changes in the Indian culture. More important, by explicating the oppositional voices against the dominant anti-Western rhetoric of the Indian press, the study reinforces the position of postcolonial critics that any totalizing attempt to resist globalization is unlikely to work. Against the forceful anti-Western rhetoric of the Indian press, the alternative voices send a strong message that relying on indigenous cultural and national identity as a rationale for rejecting and resisting media globalization is not going to be accepted by everyone in a democratic society such as India.

REFERENCES

Ananthamurthy, U. R. (1993, October 18). We're global consumers. *Indian Express,* p. 23.

Appadurai, A. (1990). Disjuncture and difference in the global cultural economy. In M. Featherstone (Ed.), *Global culture: Nationalism, globalization, and modernity* (pp. 295-310). Newbury Park, CA: Sage.

Audit Bureau of Circulation (ABC) Report. (1998). Bombay: Audit Bureau of Circulation.

Barber, B. R. (1992, March). Jihad vs. McWorld. *Atlantic Monthly.*

Baria, F. (1993, February 21). Follow that star. *Times of India,* p. 10.

Bharucha, N. E. (1992, October 29). Stereotyping the Orient. *The Independent,* p. 21.

Bhatt, S. C. (1994). *Satellite invasion of India.* New Delhi, India: Gyan Publishing.

Burke, K. (1954). *Permanence and change: An anatomy of purpose.* Berkeley: University of California Press.

Burke, K. (1959). *Attitudes toward history.* Los Altos, CA: Hermes Publications.

Burke, K. (1969). *A rhetoric of motives.* Berkeley: University of California Press.

Burke, K. (1973). *The philosophy of literary form: Studies in symbolic action.* Berkeley: University of California Press.

Chan, J. M. (1994). National responses and accessibility to Star TV in Asia. *Journal of Communication, 44,* 112-131.

Chatterji, S. (1994, April 26). Watch out for trouble. *The Hindu,* p. 1.

Cheney, G., & Tompkins, P. K. (1988). On the facts of the text as the basis of human communication research. In J. A. Anderson (Ed.), *Communication Yearbook 11* (pp. 455-481). Newbury Park, CA: Sage.

Children pose as targets of sales efforts. (1994, June 9). *Business and Political Observer,* p. 15.

Collier, M. J. (2000). Reconstructing cultural diversity in global relationships: Negotiating the borderlands. In G.-M. Chen & W. J. Starosta (Eds.), *Communication and global society* (pp. 215-236). New York: Peter Lang.

Dev Sen, A. (1993, April 18). Soap in the eye. *Hindustan Times,* p. 4.

Dhawan, V. (1992, June 24). Invasion from the skies: World TV assault on India. *Economic Times,* p. 12.

Dirlik, A. (1990). Culturalism as hegemonic ideology and liberating practice. In A. JanMohamed & D. Lloyd (Eds.), *The nature and context of minority discourse* (pp. 394-431). New York: Oxford University Press.

Dixit, R. C. (1994, June 25). Tele violence. *Hindustan Times,* pp. 1-2.

Duncan, H. D. (1989). *Communication and social order.* New Brunswick, NJ: Transaction Publishing.

Featherstone, M. (1990). Global culture: An introduction. In M. Featherstone (Ed.), *Global culture: Nationalism, globalization, and modernity* (pp. 1-14). Newbury Park, CA: Sage.

Featherstone, M. (1991). *Consumer culture and postmodernism.* Thousand Oaks, CA: Sage.

Featherstone, M., & Lash, S. (1995). Globalization, modernity, and the spatialization of social theory: An introduction. In M. Featherstone, S. Lash, & R. Robertson (Eds.), *Global modernities* (pp. 1-24). Thousand Oaks, CA: Sage.

Giddens, A. (1990). *The consequences of modernity.* Stanford, CA: Stanford University Press.

Hall, S. (1975). Introduction. In A. C. H. Smith (Ed.), *Paper voices: The popular press and social change, 1935-1965* (pp. 11-24). London: Chatto & Windus.

Hall, S. (1977). Culture, the media, and the "ideological effect." In J. Curran, M. Gurevitch, & J. Woollacott (Eds.), *Mass communication and society* (pp. 315-348). Beverly Hills, CA: Sage.

Hall, S. (1980). Encoding/decoding. In S. Hall, D. Hobson, A. Lowe, & P. Willis (Eds.), *Culture, media, language* (pp. 128-138). London: Hutchinson.

Hall, S. (1991a). The local and global: Globalization and ethnicity. In A. King (Ed.), *Culture, globalization, and world-system* (pp. 19-40). London: Macmillan (in association with Department of Art and Art History, State University of New York at Binghamton).

Hall, S. (1991b). Old and new identities, old and new ethnicities. In A. King (Ed.), *Culture, globalization, and world-system* (pp. 41-68). London: Macmillan (in association with Department of Art and Art History, State University of New York at Binghamton).

Hall, S. (1994). Cultural identity and diaspora. In P. Williams & L. Chrisman (Eds.), *Colonial discourse and postcolonial theory: A reader* (pp. 392-403). New York: Columbia University Press.

Hannerz, U. (1990). Cosmopolitans and locals in world culture. In M. Featherstone (Ed.), *Global culture: Nationalism, globalization, and modernity* (pp. 237-252). Newbury Park, CA: Sage.

Impact of satellite TV: Leave it to the people. (1994, October 1). *The Hindu,* p. 1.

IMRB Report. (1997, March). Bombay: Indian Market Research Bureau.

Jain, M. (1993, October 3). Goodbye, good guys. *Sunday Indian Express,* pp. 72-74.

Jain, P. (1994, September 23). Globalizing violence through TV. *Indian Express,* p. 19.

Jain, M., & Sidhu, W. P. S. (1992, March 31). Battle for the box. *India Today,* pp. 160-161.

Karanth, B. V. (1993, October 18). An enriching experience. *Indian Express,* p. 23.

Khanna, A. (1992, September 13). Tuning into the sky. *Sunday Times of India,* p. 12.

Kishore, K. (1994). The advent of Star TV in India: Emerging policy issues. *Media Asia, 21,* 96-103.

Kumar, S. (1992, October 10). The "cable" mania. *Hindustan Times,* p. 12.

Lakoff, G., & Johnson, M. (1980). *Metaphors we live by.* Chicago: University of Chicago Press.

Malik, B. P. S. (1994, October 2). Flickering role models. *Financial Express,* p. 21.

Masud, I. (1993, June 3). Middle-class culture. *The Independent,* p. 10.

Mathur, R. (1992, October 17). Are we turning into couch potatoes? *The Independent,* p. 5.

Mitra, A. (1994). An Indian religious soap opera and the Hindu image. *Media, Culture, and Society, 16,* 149-155.

Morarka, K. (1992, September 27). Combating cultural imperialism. *Indian Express,* p. 11.

Mozoomdar, M. (1992, May 18). Last gamble for Doordarshan and AIR. *The Pioneer,* p. 10.

Mumby, D. K., & Spitzack, C. (1983). Ideology and television news: A metaphoric analysis for political stories. *Central States Speech Journal, 34,* 162-171.

Nair, K. (1978). Forms and functions of mass media: The press. In M. L. Apte (Ed.), *Mass culture, language, and arts in India* (pp. 45-60). Bombay, India: Popular Prakashan.

National TV comes first. (1992, April 24). *Times of India,* p. 12.

Ninan, S. (1995). Transforming television in India. *Media Studies Journal, 9,* 43-51.

Rawla, S., & De Sarkar, B. (1993, April 4). Prime time all the time. *The Telegraph,* p. 22.

Reddi, U. (1990). Media and culture in Indian society: Conflict or cooperation? *Media, Culture, and Society, 11,* 395-413.

Robertson, R. (1990). Mapping the global condition: Globalization as the central concept. In M. Featherstone (Ed.), *Global culture: Nationalism, globalization, and modernity* (pp. 15-30). Newbury Park, CA: Sage.

Robertson, R. (1991). Social theory, cultural relativity, and the problem of globality. In A. King (Ed.), *Culture, globalization, and the world-system* (pp. 69-90). Albany: State University of New York Press.

Robertson, R. (1992). *Globalization: Social theory and global culture.* Newbury Park, CA: Sage.

Robertson, R. (1995). Glocalization: Time-space and homogeneity-heterogeneity. In M. Featherstone, S. Lash, & R. Robertson (Eds.), *Global modernities* (pp. 25-44). Thousand Oaks, CA: Sage.

Said, E. (1993). *Culture and imperialism.* New York: Knopf.

Sarma, N. (1998). *The changing face of Indian media.* [Online]. Available: www.comminit.com/review_indianmedia.html

Sen, A. (1995, November). *Impact of foreign programming on the youth of India.* Paper presented at the annual meeting of the Speech Communication Association, San Antonio, TX.

SET launched more channels. (1998). *Television: Media scene* [Online]. Available: www.indiaworld.co.in/home/nfdc/media.html

Stars in their eyes. (1993, July 10). *The Economist,* p. 30.

Star TV electrifies India while challenging cultural norms. (1993, February 6). *The Statesman,* p. 9.

Subramanian, N. (1992, May 3). Broadcasting truths. *The Hindu,* p. 14.

Television to rule the future. (1995, November 29-December 5). *Economic Times* (Perspectives).

The growing threat to Indian television. (1993, October 4). *Times of India,* p. 17.

TV changing values of kids. (1994, June 2). *Times of India,* p. 5.

Violence, vulgarity in mass media decried. (1994, September 24). *Financial Express,* p. 13.

Vyas, S. (1992, September 14). Gujratis take a new look at leisure. *Times of India,* p. 3.

Wallerstein, I. (1974). *The modern world system.* New York: Academic Press.

Wallerstein, I. (1990). Culture as ideological battleground of the modern world-system. In M. Featherstone (Ed.), *Global culture: Nationalism, globalization, and modernity* (pp. 31-56). Newbury Park, CA: Sage.

5

The Language of Honor (*izzat*) and Shame (*sharm*)

National and Gender Identities in Apna Ghar (Our Home)

KARUDAPURAM E. SUPRIYA • *University of Wisconsin–Milwaukee*

> Central to the creation of immigrant worlds is the idea of nation—not the nation as a bounded geographical unit but nation as an ideological force. In working with domestic violence, I have come to appreciate how the question of women is inextricably linked to nation-ness.
>
> —A. Bhattacharjee (1992, p. 19)

> We stipulate that intercultural communication is a transactional, symbolic process involving the attribution of meaning between people from different cultures. . . . If intercultural communication refers to communication between people from different cultures, then intracultural communication refers to communication between people from the same culture.
>
> — W. B. Gudykunst & Y. Y. Kim (1997, p. 19)

The study of the relationships between communication and culture is moving toward the inquiry of site-specific identity formation (Collier, 1998; Tanno & Gonzalez, 1998). The particular intersections among nationhood, gender, and discourses of identity in sites of migrancy is a crucial site for contestation and negotiation of power relations (Hegde, 1998; Lindsley, 1999). The focus of this chapter is a critical analysis of the relationships between discourses of members of the Indian immigrant community and national and gender identities. The particular context is domestic violence in the form of spousal abuse. The particular ethnographic site is *Apna Ghar* (Our Home), an Asian women's shelter founded in Chicago in 1989 (Levinsohn, 1991).

This chapter particularly examines how the language of honor (or *izzat*) and shame (or *sharm*) reproduces power relations, particularly the social control of women's speech, bodies, and everyday practices. The same language also is a means through which Indian immigrants construct national and gender identities in the particular context of violence against women. In relation to women's behavior, honor and shame have been documented in a sociological study of a particular group of women in the Indian subcontinent called *Pirzade* women by Jeffrey (1979). Jeffrey examines how the concepts of izzat and sharm organize gender relations within the family, particularly through prescriptions of women's speech and practice. Jeffrey observes,

> Two words were prevalent in conversations with the women—*izzat* and *sharm*. A woman who chatters too loudly will be criticized for being *sharm* or shameless; the woman who feels embarrassed when her son-in-law visiting will say that *sharm ata hai* or "shame comes"; a young girl who covers her head when her father enters the room will be praised for being *sharmanda* or *sharm-wali,* for being modest and ashamed. (pp. 99-100)

Jeffrey also argues that these concepts are central to perceptions of the Pirzade community about observation of norms of propriety between the sexes by group members.

The analysis seeks to bring to light the social practices around honor and shame that are reflected in the discourses of members of the Indian community while taking a critical position in relation to the possible effects of these discourses on Indian women in the context of domestic violence. These arguments are based on my interpretive study of the communication practices of immigrant women in Apna Ghar. The interpretations are not universal claims about Indian women and the surrounding community as much as they are particular meanings that emerge from particular discursive instances that were collected and analyzed in the course of a 2-year ethnographic investigation of the site. But they do provide insight into some of the ways in which national and gender identities intersect with one another in a context that is layered with multiple power relations and power-laden discourses. The discursive instances that constitute the focus of the chapter were collected through ethnographic methods of participant observation and fieldwork as part of a larger ethnographic investigation of identity construction in the shelter and surrounding community.

I first elaborate on the disciplinary location of the research. This is followed by a methodological discussion of the ways in which the discourses of the women and members of the Indian community were elicited by me, coded for the tropes of honor and shame, and critically analyzed through sociocultural constructionist theories of identity. The chapter concludes with a discussion of the implications of the research findings for understanding the relations between culture and communication as well as future directions for research.

A CRITICAL INTERCULTURAL COMMUNICATION FRAMEWORK

This chapter argues for the significance of incorporating cultural studies frameworks and theories of power and identity in the research and analysis of intercultural and intracultural communication processes and practices. Although primarily a critical analysis of a particular configuration of discourses and identities within the Indian community, the analysis also seeks to contribute to the field of intercultural communication through a heuristic delineation of a critical intercultural communication approach (Ono, 1998). This entails the use of critical theories of power, language, and identity as sensitizing and conceptual tools to provide a holistic and sound understanding of the complexities and contradictions that attend intercultural processes such as sojourner experiences. Such an approach is principally justified in terms of the power relations that circumscribe and contain the discourses and practices of the Indian community and Indian women who constituted the research focus of my ethnography of Apna Ghar.

The observation that processes and discourses of immigrants are implicated in and saturated by power relations suggests the need for a systematic incorporation of theories of power and language and the ways in which these relationships intersect with identity construction. Furthermore, theories of the intersection of national and gender identity construction are important for illuminating a significant intercultural process, the reconstitution of prior identities, by seizing on culturally available discourses in contexts of migrancy. Immigrants are faced with the contingent quality of their prior national and gender identities and the exigencies that attend threats to both group and personal identities. Also, a critical intercultural communication approach may be specified in terms of the social actors engaged in the act of communication, the contexts of communication, and the effects of communication on the community. Indian immigrant communication in the context of spousal abuse may be understood as a discourse that is produced when two different cultures, the South Asian and U.S. cultures, encounter each other in ways that make differing language and meaning systems collide with one another, especially when the immigrant community is, to put it figuratively, at war with itself.

More specifically, the role of a shelter for Asian women constitutes a discursive terrain that is fraught with struggles and contestation over the very meanings of nation, community, and self. In a related manner, the language of honor and shame that is deployed by members of the community has to be contextually discerned as emergent when a cultural group faces identity crises and conflicts that are precipitated when cultural groups emigrate to a different cultural milieu. The communication practices and patterns also may be understood as the site of identity construction in ways that reproduce, resist, and transform power relations within and between cultural groups. Taken together, this study of how Indian immigrants construct their national and gender identities in the context of violence against women in the community may be seen as advancing the study of communication between and within cultural groups in the disciplinary direction of critical intercultural communication.

PRAXIS APPROACH TO ETHNOGRAPHY OF COMMUNICATION

In this study, a praxis approach to research (Lather, 1986) was meshed with critical ethnography of communication to formulate an interpretive practice that was attentive to power relations (Conquergood, 1991; Katriel, 1994; Lather, 1986; Sharoni, 1995; West, 1993). Such a methodological approach was necessitated by two sets of power relations that prevailed on the participants: the power relations between the community and the women who were clients of Apna Ghar and the power relations between the latter group and myself, a set of relations that was especially pronounced during fieldwork. The gulf between women in Apna Ghar and myself can be characterized as power relations enacted along axes of class, education, and life possibilities while recognizing that power relations cannot be reduced to these categories of experience. Women in

Apna Ghar, especially if they have not secured permanent residency status, are left with little more than their possessions when they leave home, and their hardships are compounded when they have children. The women who constitute the narrative focus of the research did not have more than a high school education, and they frequently expressed the bleakness of their lives as they confronted the seemingly insurmountable economic, legal, and cultural obstacles to realization of their selfhoods (Lu, 1993).

These experiences necessitated a research method that combined knowledge gathering with the imperative of being attuned to field-based power relations characterized as a praxis-centered approach (Lather, 1986). These methodological principles may be applied through engagement with concepts from a critical ethnography of communication framework, particularly concepts of relationality, reflexivity, and representation.

Conquergood (1991) addresses the principle of relationality by observing that the communicative economy of ethnography can facilitate negotiation and management of power relations in ethnographic sites when the relational space between "other" and ethnographer is imbued with communicative co-presence constitutive of a dialogic relation. Conquergood (1991) particularly calls attention to the affective dimensions of ethnography wherein the ethnographer is finely attuned to the other's feeling states through participation in the lived material context in which language is produced and identities are embodied by participants within shifting matrices of power relations.

I began to immerse myself in discourse communities in and around Apna Ghar during the summer of 1992 as preparation for the intense stage of my fieldwork a year later. Immersion involved spending nights at the shelter and involving myself in shelter-related events on an ongoing basis during weekends including a memorial service that is presented here as an ethnographic vignette. It also involved talking with shelter supervisors and staff to learn about the organizational history of the shelter. The intense phase of fieldwork was preceded by participation in a 4-week volunteer training program that prepared me for living in the shelter round-the-clock for a period of 2 months, during which time I was able to come into close contact with three women from three different Asian countries: India, Pakistan, and the Philippines. My stay in Apna Ghar coincided with theirs including timing my exit with theirs. My association with the shelter continued for a period of time after that to achieve closure.

During this stage, I was able to use the methods of participant observation, field notes, archives (e.g., shelter records), and life history interviews with the women to gather and produce verbatim and reconstructed discursive accounts. I accompanied them during walks to the lake, to the grocery store, and to neighborhood thrift stores, but mostly I was a confidante and companion in the shelter. I also participated in community-related events such as fund-raisers. These methods enabled me to fully participate in the women's lives including experiencing exigencies such as their ambivalence over leaving their homes, their spouses, and (to an extent) their lives in the larger Asian community in Chicago. Bodily immersion and participation in the lifeworlds of Apna Ghar respondents through communicative co-presence made it possible for me to discern particular and concrete power-saturated cultural, national, and gendered discourses of honor and shame.

Feminist researchers of nationhood and the intersections of nation and gender offer suggestions on how to attend to nationhood as a power-saturated discourse that often constrains liberatory possibilities (Katriel, 1994; Sharoni, 1995). Katriel's ethnography of the construction of cultural memory in Israeli heritage museums includes use of a reflexive ethnographic practice, especially when the researcher herself is implicated in the discourse of nationhood by virtue of being of a particular national origin, in this instance, a member of Israeli culture. Only through such a practice, Katriel observes, can the ethnographer produce a nuanced account of nationalist discourses that simultaneously highlight both its excesses and its enabling possibilities, especially in the context of loss of experience of nation-ness or threats to reconstruction of nationhood. Based on qualitative research on the Palestinian-Israeli conflict, Sharoni calls attention to the ways in which gender becomes the locus of contestation over national identity and nationhood in ways that disable women and the necessity for feminist researchers to take this into account while studying women's experiences and struggles.

The use of another approach that was not relational and reflexive would have run the dual risks of erasing and eliding the culturally specific discourses of the Indian community that mediate the experience of domestic violence. On the one hand, there is the risk of erasing the cultural specificity of the experiences of Indian immigrant women by representing them as "confused" women. On the other hand is the risk of eliding a culturally specific interpretation of the discourse and use of the circulating nationalist tropes of honor and shame to reconstruct their identities. Being attentive to these tropes is significant because they express the contradictions and ambiguities of the intersections of nationhood and gender that render impossible any unmediated experience of flight from abuse. In short, communicative co-presence and researcher reflexivity made me sensitive to abuse as a culturally specific experience that cannot be universalized across nation, religion, and immigration histories, to women as a unitary group, or as a site for contestation over national identity.

West (1993) issues the caveat that the ethnographer not occupy a moral high ground but rather be firmly planted on *terra firma* when detailing the ways in which power complicates the lives of others through ethnographic representation. According to West, this can be done through several interrelated moves. The ethnographer should realize the intertextuality that governs both participants and ethnographer by paying attention to the "fluid tides of political ideologies" (p. 212) that interpellate participants in multiple and contradictory ways. This ought to occasion denaturalizing the identities of participants. West observes, "Communication research needs to move beyond any suggestion that individual and organizational action occur 'naturally.' Individuals are not the rational and autonomous monologic entities suggested by Western culture's ideology of individualism" (p. 213). West offers a powerful and relevant illustration of the latter by presenting a narrative of a battered woman as evidence of "institutional pressures to stay in their [battered women's] violent relationships" rather than making an essentializing or totalizing claim about the woman or cultural group of which she is a part.

Yet another representational move to be made by ethnographers is to realize the emancipatory impulse that is embedded in discourses of otherness, a move that is consonant with a praxis approach that calls for encouraging self-reflection by others. I have endeavored to incorporate these principles of ethnographic representation by juxtaposing selected examples from the discourses of an Indian woman and the community. These examples were collected through ethnographic methods of participant observation and field notes. Their use in this chapter is meant to illustrate the conflictual and mutually consolidating ways in which the values of honor and shame are communicated through particular discourse segments and populations within the Asian community. Such an analysis serves as a sensitizing practice in future inquiry to tease out similar and dissimilar uses of cultural speech in various contexts of intercultural communication so as to arrive at a typology of such speech.

The open coding methods of Corbin and Strauss (1990) were employed to extract the key categories of honor and shame. Corbin and Strauss emphasize the importance of generating categories or codes that are consonant with both in vivo use of language and academically driven categories of interpretation (pp. 68-69). Not only does the word *shame* appear in both

English and Hindi in the discourse of clients and community, but during fieldwork in Apna Ghar, staff enabled me to interpret the actions of the women through these concepts while explaining why women are resistant to change or when providing reasons for some of the women returning to their spouses. Incorporating the vernacular categories of honor and shame can be justified as valid categories of interpretation because they also appear in scholarly research and writings on the Indian and Pakistani community (Chaachhi, 1991; Jeffrey, 1979).

In investigating the construction of identity through language by Indian immigrants in the context of wife abuse, two discursive excerpts emerge from the corpus of discourse that illuminates the context of Apna Ghar.[1] The first was produced by an Indian woman in the shelter and the second by the larger Indian community in Chicago. Both of these discourses were selected because they are concrete and participant-generated "thick descriptions" of the discourse and practices of the intersecting languages of honor and shame.[2] The first pertains to that of an Indian woman who left home to seek assistance from Apna Ghar for the third time, having returned home after the first two occasions. The second pertains to the discourse of the larger South Asian community produced by members as they came to terms with the publicity generated by a prominent Indian woman client of Apna Ghar who had committed suicide. These two cultural scenarios are presented in relation to one another to demonstrate the intersections between gender and nationhood.

CULTURAL DISCOURSES OF IDENTITY

Cultural Discourses of Sunita

Sunita was an older Indian woman client of Apna Ghar. One of my informants, Mumtaz,[3] who was a shelter supervisor, informed me that Sunita had been a client on two previous occasions. Sunita returned to her home and husband because she could not come to terms with the meanings attached by her national and religious community to her act of leaving her spouse. The shelter supervisor also suggested that Sunita seemed unable to cope with the shelter facilities because she viewed herself as someone who was of a higher station.

During our initial encounters, Sunita appeared to demonstrate a range of emotions from exhaustion, to caution, to moments of composure. Following this, she seemed to want to emerge from a more reclusive state by engaging in conversation with another Pakistani client, meeting prospective job recruiters through Apna Ghar, and showing interest in my research project. During our first encounter, I informed Sunita about the purpose of my stay at Apna Ghar. When I approached her with the issue of participating in my research, she consented with much willingness, although she did request some time. I explicitly asked Sunita if I could write down what she said as she said it. She appeared both surprised and almost excited that someone would show interest in what she had to communicate, and she expressed her appreciation of the research. (In a later interview, Sunita did not consent to being tape-recorded and insisted that I write notes as she spoke. The note taking was facilitated by the presence of another student researcher.)

At the time the discursive segment presented in what follows was elicited, Sunita seemed to show nervous anxiety because of a scheduled court appointment during which she was to encounter her husband for the first time since she had left him a few weeks ago. The court appearance was related to seeking legal remedies from her spouse. Prior to her court appointment, Sunita asked me in a rather nervous voice (when I went to visit her in her room) whether I was going to be around at about 6 p.m. the following day. I distinctly recall her saying, "If you are, drop by the apartment. I'll tell you how it went."[4] When I informed her that I would like to document her experience, she readily consented to my request.

The following evening, I found Sunita sitting in her apartment in a chair near the window. The only light that seemed to be cast in the room was from the streetlights in the alley flanking the building. Sunita almost seemed to crouch in the chair. I was not sure how long Sunita had been in this position, but judging by her text and tone, it appeared that she had been reduced to a state of petrified immobility on her return from court.

What I would call a very somber and sullen dialogue ensued when Sunita took note of my presence. Sunita initiated the dialogue by observing,

> They were all there—my husband, his sister and brother. I could not look at him or them the whole time in court. I began to feel like the other two times. I felt shame deep inside me, and I wanted to run to him and to just fall at his feet and their feet and ask him to take me back.

When I protested, she spoke slowly but surely, "But you must understand. It's not right for me to be here." And then when I asked her why, she continued to talk at a rapid pace: "My duty as a wife is to be with him whatever happens." She continued by observing,

To be a good wife, you must be with your husband and do things for him. I must be at his side during "religious gatherings" and for those "community events" because he has a big name in the community. I must be there to give him a hot "Indian" meal after he gets back from work and to look after him when he is sick. He works hard and often falls sick, you know he's getting old. And now I have failed again. I left him again. And all these people know again. Here everyone knows—the staff, the guests who come to the shelter. Because here we have to speak to people all the time.

Communal Discourses About Shvetha

The suicide of an Indian woman, Shvetha Jethmalini, following her act of murdering her Pakistani husband, Khalid Quadri, was one of the first public events where I encountered the communal and cultural politics that surrounded Apna Ghar. On the very first day that I visited the administrative offices of Apna Ghar, the executive director, who was a woman of Indian descent with whom I had arranged to meet, looked very downcast and nervous as she greeted me. I recall her saying to me in a murmur that a tragedy had occurred as she pushed a photocopied newspaper clipping into my hands. She continued and said that a murder-suicide involving a former client of Apna Ghar had occurred and that news of the event had spread through the community press.

The executive director quietly requested that I attend the memorial service that was to be held at the Indo-American Center in the Indian commercial district of Chicago. She also informed me that one of Apna Ghar's staff members, Arshiya, would attend the memorial service. When I asked her who else would attend the service, she said that members of both the Indian and Pakistani community would attend the event because the incident involved both of the national communities. At that moment, Arshiya stepped into the room, and the director apprised her about me. As Arshiya and I stepped out of the office, she recounted to me that the murder-suicide involved an Indian woman named Shvetha and her paramour from Pakistan, Khalid. She mentioned that the woman had been both a client and a volunteer at Apna Ghar and that the couple had been very active in promoting the Indo-Pakistani culture through dance shows in the community. A shelter supervisor provided further background to me in the course of my fieldwork. The supervisor revealed that Shvetha and Khalid did marry each other, even though both had been previously married and parents when they became involved. The supervisor also informed me that at the time of the murder-suicide, their relationship was unstable.

That evening, I attended the memorial service, which lasted for about 1 hour. I chose to sit in a relatively unoccupied location toward the back of the dimly lit room so that I could take down field notes of the service in an unobtrusive manner. There were about 30 men and women, all of whom appeared to be either Indian or Pakistani in origin including Arshiya from Apna Ghar. The service began with a solemn announcement about the reason for the gathering made by one of the men who introduced himself as an officer of the Indo-American Center. Following the announcement, a few men stood up and expressed their condolences. One woman began to say a few words and began shedding tears. A man who appeared to be her companion escorted her back to her chair. One man then began to recite what is called a *doha* or a verse that typically is written by a famous poet. Everyone shook their heads, raised their voices, and said "wah, wah, wah" in a customary fashion. The man recited the verse in a somber yet mellifluous tone. The room resonated with his mournful voice, and the rest of the party joined in an incantation at regular intervals. The whole room was filled with a somber vibration that was broken occasionally by a sniff or a sob. After the man completed the recitation, the room seemed to be filled with a sepulchral and heavy silence. All were huddled over the chairs as if the weight of what appeared to be a national tragedy bore down on those who some day would live to bear witness to this violence to the nation, this national violence.

All of a sudden, the silence was disrupted by the noise of a chair being drawn with force across the floor. Then a man spoke in what sounded like a loud and angry voice as many heads suddenly turned: "Let's stop this. Let's not pretend anymore."[5] (Arshiya later identified the man as being of Indian descent.) At this juncture, the man who was seated next to me seemed startled. I looked toward Arshiya, and she looked visibly shaken. The man continued, "Let's not pretend. We all are saying something we don't mean. This should never have happened." At this juncture, another man got up from his chair and interrupted him and said, "Now, what are you talking about? We are here to pay respects to this couple that did so much for Indo-Pakistani unity—through the dances and the dramas and the different cultural festivals they organized." The first man continued, "Now come on. That is not the entire story." He then pointed to Arshiya and said, "This is about Apna Ghar. You know what I am talking about." Before Arshiya could reply, he continued,

> Why did you all let this happen? You all started this. This woman came there first. Then she was out on the roads sleeping in the car. All of this happened af-

> ter she left and came there. She has brought such a bad name to the Indian and Pakistani community. Everybody knows about what she did. Where are her Indian values? This woman had no shame, had no values. We are here paying respect to a woman who left her husband and told everyone about how bad he was. This should never have happened. Why was something not done to prevent this? Tell me, all of you in the room? Why was something not done to stop this? Why did we not tell her that what she did is wrong? Why did Apna Ghar not tell her to go back?

The room seemed to take on the aspect of a tense melodrama as members of the community were muttering to themselves and shaking their heads. At this point, Arshiya responded, in a very shaky voice, something to the effect that Apna Ghar cannot be blamed for this because its staff were just trying to provide shelter to Shvetha when she needed it. A man in front of me was telling another man in a hushed voice that Apna Ghar had forced a lot of issues in the community to come out into the open. He expressed regret that women could leave their homes in the manner of Shvetha and take matters into their own hands. I distinctly recall hearing him use the term *sharm* and what I took to be a commentary on why there was such tension within the community over the tragedy of the deceased couple.

Having noticed that the gathering had been audiotaped, at the end of the event, I approached an official of the Indo-American Center and asked him for a copy of the audiotape. He appeared to not know who had possession of the tape and said that this was not a good time and that I should call the center later. (I tried several times to procure the tape, but it was a futile endeavor as the center staff repeatedly denied knowledge of it on the phone.) As I was leaving, Arshiya, still appearing shaken by the incident, whispered to me not to repeat the incident to the director. She then asked me to write down her words:

> It is all about shame for the community. They want to protect the name and do not want anyone to know. But Shvetha was an abused woman, and she needed help. Apna Ghar opened the doors for her. Apna Ghar did not make her take the gun to his house and shoot him. Please take this down and tell people.

The Discourse of Shame and Honor

The linguistic and cultural symbol of shame and its implied or expressed twin symbol, honor, invoked by both Sunita and the Indo-Pakistani immigrant community during the memorial service function to construct gender and national identities in ways that reproduce power relations. A critical analysis of the use of cultured symbols of shame and honor is grounded in theories of the sociocultural construction of identity (Collier, 1998; Hall, 1990; Kondo, 1990). These cultural symbols underlie Sunita's construction of her gender identity as a shameless woman and are strategically deployed by the Indian community to construct Apna Ghar and its clients from the South Asian community as women who have betrayed their nation by bringing a "bad name" to the community in the United States.

Interpretation of these identity constructions and how these function as a form of social control of women's speech, bodies, and practices is grounded in anti-essentialist reformulations of identity in the works of French poststructuralists including Derrida, Lacan, and Foucault, who provide a philosophical foundation for a notion of identity as constructed through social and cultural languages (Alcoff, 1988; Hall, 1990; Kondo, 1990; Weedon, 1987). A sociocultural constructionist framework rejects a static essentialist notion of group and personal identities for a dynamic conceptualization of identity as both a communication phenomenon and a communication construct. As a phenomenon, identity is to be understood as a function and effect of language practices of a culture within a matrix of power relations.

This approach is consistent with that of Hall (1990). In the particular context of diaspora of postcolonial peoples in the West, Hall finds an essentialist model of identity that conceptualizes metaphysical essences as the locus and guarantor of cultural identity to be inadequate to understand the complexities that attend the experience of migrancy. Instead, Hall argues that identity is the shifting effect of particular languages and discourses, particularly of cultural membership, that are seized on by migrant persons to give meanings to themselves in different cultural contexts. Identity also is theorized as a linguistic construction that is implicated within and reproductive of power relations.

Based on an ethnographic study of the ways in which Japanese women construct their gender identities in a *sato* or confectionary factory, Kondo (1990) argues for the critical importance of theorizing identity as implicated in power relations of a culture. Kondo cites the works of poststructuralist scholars of gender identity, observing that such critiques by poststructuralists "would argue that a 'concept of self' is inevitably implicated in relations of power and, indeed, that the construction of identities cannot be discussed in the abstract, separately from power relations" (p. 43). According to Collier (1998), identity may be understood in terms of the tenets of cultural identity theory (CIT): "one of the major premises held by CIT scholars is that cultural identities are historical, contextual, and relational constructions" (p. 131).

The particular relationships between national and gender identities have been the object of both empirical and theoretical investigations in the study of identity and discourse (Bhattacharjee, 1992; Chaachhi, 1991; Kandiyoti, 1994; Lee, 1998; Mani, 1987; Pathak & Sunderrajan, 1989). The exploration of this relationship in different texts and contexts has led to the theoretical claim that national and gender identities operate in a paradoxical system. National and gender identities consolidate each other in ways that reproduce and maintain power relations at the juncture when they appear to destabilize each other.

Lee (1998) provides a powerful illustration of the communication formations within which Chinese women's bodies become a fetishized locus for staking out Western imperialism and Chinese patriarchy. Lee observes, "Footbinding was a 'woman's question,' *not for* Chinese women but [rather] as a means serving other ends. Within China, it was an argument serving chauvinistic-nationalistic ends" (p. 22). In Japan, China, and the United States, women's identities become the discursive ground on which ideas of nationhood are worked out and articulated in culture so as to preserve a dominant ideology of nationhood, especially when there is a perceived threat to national identity by women who construct their gender identities in ways that disrupt a unified ideology around nationhood. The effect of such a discourse is a reinscription of nationalism by rewriting gender identity so that women who position themselves outside or against the nation are constructed as the nation's others, a discourse that may function as a powerful form of social control of women who offer resistance to power relations such as patriarchy and communal-based nationalism.

Culture is central to this theory of identity as a sociocultural construction inscribed by power relations. A complex notion of culture emerges from juxtaposing two seemingly contradictory approaches: those of Grossberg (1993) and Williams (1961). Grossberg (1993) treats culture within a theory of contexts. Culture refers to the domain of contexts and relations among contexts within which individuals are positioned by social practices. Grossberg observes, "Culture itself cannot be defined autonomously of the context any more than theory can" (p. 2). In delineating three different senses of contextuality, Grossberg claims, "First, the concept of culture in cultural studies is caught between community (social formations), totality (the whole way of life), and aesthetics (representational practice)—to use the more common notion" (p. 2). Grossberg also conceptualizes culture in material terms so that it is not reduced to discursivity or textuality. This particular notion of culture is crucial for understanding the practices of identity construction of Indian women and the community surrounding Apna Ghar because this orientation to culture enables a contextual and material understanding of the community's practice of identity rather than treating culture and identity as decontextualized textual forms.

Williams (1961) explains culture as "the meanings and values implicit and explicit in a particular way of life" (p. 41). This is a more expansive conceptualization of culture as a whole way of life that appears to be constituted through specific expressive forms and norms for participation in quotidian life and attainment of the ideals of a group. This notion is significant because it can illuminate how the cultural values of honor and shame not only structure a way of Indian life but also become constitutive norms for participation in the community.

Combining these two different emphases for the concept of culture, the construction of identity by Indian women in Apna Ghar and the Indian immigrant community may be understood as taking place within the intersecting material contexts of migrancy of postcolonial persons to the United States and domestic violence within the community. Further, these are inflected through the values and norms of honor and shame that govern the conduct of quotidian life.

Other intersections containing the vectors of nation, religion, and gender emerge in relation to the symbols of honor and shame in Indian society and culture. Honor and shame may be understood as "core cultural symbols" (Lindsley, 1999, p. 1) that constitute a "discursive code" (Carbaugh, 1988, p. 217) with religious overtones for members of Indian culture. Carbaugh (1988) defines a discursive code as "subsystems of symbols and meanings" (p. 217). According to both Lindsley (1999) and Philipsen (1975), core cultural symbols are centralizing clusters of forces that unify group members around norms of appropriateness of speech and behavior. Codes are the basis for conferring and withholding membership from members of the culture. The core linguistic cultural symbols of honor and shame of Indian society, and Hindu and Muslim religious traditions, prescribe and prohibit behavior through their constitution as a cluster of cultural codes qua feminine and masculine virtue and form a means of social control.

Chaachhi (1991) examines the relationships between communal and gender identities that are structured by the concept of honor. Chaachhi argues, "Recent studies of fundamentalism have shown that it constructs particular notions of femininity and masculinity as symbolic of the community" (p. 162). Elaborating on how these notions of gender are constructed in the context of cultural practices such as the practice of widow sacrifice (or *sati*) and strictures against the payment of alimony to women under Muslim personal law, Chaachhi observes that the concept of honor has been one of the structuring codes of the Hindu and Muslim religions. Chaachhi explains,

> In both incidents referred to earlier, *sati* and the agitation over Shah Bano, women became crucial symbols of communal identity and markers of "tradition" and culture. The traditions that are resurrected are often both invented and selective. A feature of contemporary Hindu, Muslim, and Sikh fundamentalism is a stress on martial tradition. Hindu fundamentalists have incorporated the notions of honor, militancy, virility, and manliness from the *Khatriyas* (warrior castes) as essential elements of Hinduism, as is also the case in the incorporation of Rajput customs in relation to *sati*. (p. 162)

Thus, shame and honor are two concepts that structure women's behavior and speech within the Hindu and Muslim religions and in the Indian nation, in particular by prescribing appropriate codes of behavior and speech for the Indian woman. But neither of these concepts can be understood without a notion of "threats to honor." This is evident when Chaachhi (1991) argues, "In the context of fear and concerns over downward mobility, the link between the honor of the family and the honor of the community leads to attempts to control their 'own' women" (p. 162). Threats to, or loss of, control over their women are seen as direct threats to manhood/family/community that are treated as extensions of each other. Therefore, it becomes critical for the community to ensure patriarchal, familial, and communal controls over labor, fertility, and sexuality of women.

The intertextual discourse of Sunita and those of the larger South Asian and Indian communities in the particular context of the memorial service articulate the symbols of honor and shame as code and virtue to the act of leaving the home for seeking shelter at Apna Ghar to produce power-laden meanings of nation, community, and gendered self. This produces the dual identities that include the Indian community as an "honorable" community that, ironically, maintains its sense of honor by protecting its "name" through the power-laden act of naming members, Shvetha and

Sunita, as dishonorable women for having seemingly betrayed the community and nation.

Sunita constructs her gender identity as a "shameless woman," or a woman without shame, through speech that is layered with ideologies of the virtuous or honorable wife. These include the tropes of service and duty to the husband in relation to practices of everyday life including cooking, nursing, and religious adherence. Sunita expresses a great amount of pain over having putatively violated the code of being a virtuous woman by transgressing the line between honor and shame because she perceives herself as a wife who has not served her husband and performed her wifely duties. Sunita speaks about not being beside her husband because she has left him for shelter. She particularly calls attention to proscribed behaviors such as not cooking for him, deserting him in his old age, and (perhaps most sacrilegious of all) violating the sacred code of performing religious rituals by his side. Furthermore, the very act of speaking about him seems to be interpreted by Sunita as a transgression of the virtuous code of silence that becomes a sign of honor.

Sunita's personal discourse parallels a national discourse in that language and discourse operate in a context that Bakhtin (1975/1981) terms "heteroglossia."[6] The seeming publicness of Sunita's action of leaving home and "speaking to people all of the time" suggests that what Bakhtin characterizes as the base conditioning, which here refers to a patriarchal construction of India and Indian-ness, governs her expression and the interpretation by others of her personal gender identity. This is evident in the exposition of the symbol of shame and its twin term, honor, as markers of Indian identity.

This line of reasoning, when juxtaposed with Sunita's acute self-consciousness over not being able to perform religious duties that behoove an honorable wife, demonstrates that religion also operates in the production of meanings of the self or personal identity.[7] This particularly shows the relational and contextual process of identity construction of Indian women that is characterized by Hegde (1998) as "moving in and out of two distinctly different relational contexts" (p. 48). The relationships may be understood as those between Sunita's husband and herself and between the Indian national community and herself with Apna Ghar as a potent and precarious pivot. The particular relational aspect of Sunita's identity may be understood as existing in consolidating tension with her husband and community. By constructing Sunita's identity as "dishonorable" or as a "shameless woman," the husband's and community's identities are constructed to produce the identity effects of "honorable" man and nation.

In the context of the memorial service of Shvetha, a woman who also left her husband and sought shelter at Apna Ghar, both the larger South Asian and Indian communities appear to construct the identity of Shvetha as a "shameless woman" through the metaphor of shame and metonyms of "woman without values" and "woman who has brought a bad name" to the Indian nation. This has the effect of consolidating the identity of the national community as "honorable Indians" through a cathartic act of naming the woman as "other" so that communication works in the service of the nation (Spivak, 1988; Supriya, 1995).

The principle of bipolarity, which operates in language in contexts of power (Dahlgren & Chakrapani, 1982), is useful to explain differential constructions of "dishonorable womanhood." Based on Levi-Strauss's structural anthropology, Dahlgren and Chakrapani (1982) argue that identity "resides in the tension between its actual and its implied negation or antithesis" (p. 48). This suggests that in the context of wife abuse, the construction of national identity is governed by the base conditions of gender and religion in that the South Asian and Indian communities construct their identities as honorable in opposition to the construction of women such as Shvetha as women without shame. Therefore, it can be argued that in this context, the cultural factors of nation and gender intersect through identity formation to reproduce power relations. More specifically, these two forms of cultural identity are intertwined and intersect to produce both national and gendered Indian identities in the context of wife abuse in ways that protect the name of the community while placing prohibitions on Indian women's speech and practices.[8] The prohibitions prevail on Indian women, and by speculation on Asian women, who leave their spouses and homes and speak in public about their experiences, to interpret themselves as dis- honorable or shameless others even while protecting the honor of the community.

Ting-Toomey's (1988) work on face work as a mechanism of conflict negotiation and management provides another useful explanatory framework for examining these examples of gender and national identities from an individual perspective. Face is defined as a location in the communication process, a psychological concept of image, and a public notion of self-image that assumes significance in contexts of intercultural uncertainty and threat. Ting-Toomey makes a direct link between face and shame in the context of high-context cultures when she observes that face in high-context cultures is a psychological-affective construct that ties closely with other concepts such as honor, shame, and obligation. The construction of identity through the symbols of honor and shame suggests that Indian women's symbolic practices of leaving their homes and speaking about and against their husbands are seen by the Indian women themselves as a threat to the face of their husbands and, by extension, the nation. Sunita spoke with great difficulty of her identity as "shameless" and as being a "dishonorable wife" because the transgressive practice of leaving the home and "side" of her husband, as well as speaking to the staff and guests of Apna Ghar, appears to be interpreted by her as betrayal of her husband, religion, and nation and, hence, a threat to the face of her husband and, by extension, the Indian community. The act of construction of identity as a shameless woman, ironically, may be interpreted as an attempt at face management in the context of threat and uncertainty.

Similarly, the larger Indian community appears to perceive this as posing a representational risk bordering on danger to its identity within the dominant culture. Bhattacharjee (1992), who has critically analyzed communication patterns of Indian immigrants in a similar context, provides a useful explanation for the discourse of the larger Indian community. Bhattacharjee argues,

> As a minority community in a foreign nation, the Indian immigrant bourgeoisie experiences the loss if its power of ex-nomination. Where once it had stood for the no-name universal in the nation of its origin, it now perceives itself (and is perceived) to be in a position defined by difference. It now risks being named. The immigrant bourgeoisie's desire to overcome this condition manifests itself through the grasping of familiar essentials in whose shadows it can regain the power of being un-named. (p. 22)

One possible intrepretation of the discursive turn of the memorial service to a ritual of placing blame is in terms of threat to face. As Bhattacharjee (1992) observes, the perceived risk of being represented as other by the dominant culture may be seen to be overcome by face work that takes the particular form of representing those women who are seen to embody this threat to face as "shameless wives" or "dishonorable wives" because they have left their husbands and spoken against them. Face work is both a discursive and an extra-discursive act in this particular instance because it involves the production of a context imbued with affect and emotions for naming the woman as other. This interpretation is corroborated by Bhattacharjee, who observes in the particular context of another Indian women's domestic violence organization that "confronting accusations of having betrayed one's national cultural heritage is not an uncommon experience" (p. 19).

Discursive instances supporting the observation about reparation in the face of potential threat to one's name were evident in that both Indian and Pakistani immigrants' discourses registered the perception of threat through discursive modes such as denial and dissociation in the context of Apna Ghar. For example, at a fund-raiser for Apna Ghar, I observed a confrontation between a man of Pakistani descent and one of the staff members of Apna Ghar. The man happened to be the spouse of one of the former clients of Apna Ghar who had since returned to her husband. In my encounters with her, the client described her husband and marital life as what I would call a romance, even while blaming her situation on undesirable elements in his life such as his former wife and children. She had invited her spouse to attend the event.

During the confrontation that I witnessed, I heard the staff member say, with her voice close to a yell, "Who invited you? We do not welcome abusers at fund-raisers." He angrily retorted, "I am not an abuser. Do not call me that." The tension seemed to linger, even though other people and other staff diffused the encounter: "Do not let him bother you. We are here for a good event. We can talk about this at the next staff meeting." (I later learned that a similar scene had transpired between the same man and a staff member at Apna Ghar on a previous occasion.) A volunteer at Apna Ghar commented, during a taped interview, about reactions of the community that one of her relatives suggested that particular religious communities in the Indian subcontinent were complicitous in perpetrating domestic violence when the topic of Apna Ghar came up. The volunteer said,

> Like one of the comments that my uncle made, "I am sure they are all Indian Muslims." And I just looked at him and said, "It doesn't make a difference, uncle," and my uncle said, "You know they are very strict with their wives."

Face work in this context is both a cultural and gendered concept and a process of cultural maintenance because it seeks to link discourses about the ideal woman to ideal nationhood through the actual production of a discourse of lack of honor that is saturated with the politics of betrayal and denial. The observation that the discourse of ideal womanhood underwrites the act of naming a woman as dishonorable in the face of a perceived threat to one's name gains support in the voices and observations of native women and researchers. One of the former executive directors, an Indian woman, described this ideal of Indian womanhood: "We are taught values and attitudes about the role of the women that are suppressive, not expressive." A younger woman volunteer at Apna Ghar wrote in an autobiographical essay that she showed me, "All the tales revolved around the devotion, fidelity, and self-sacrificing nature of wives, and they left the desired impact on me. The ideal woman is submissive, dutiful, chaste, loyal, and dependent on her husband." Another Asian woman researcher at Apna Ghar provided a contextual explanation of such a discourse of womanhood tied to nationhood and the consequent need to contain the discourse from exploding in the intercultural milieu: "Some men would find the independence and freedom Western women possess in comparison to their home countries threatening."

The perceived threat to face and the move to seize the act of naming as a means of protection may be explained in historical, economic, political, and interpersonal terms. The history of British colonialism is an important context for understanding these communication practices and patterns. Said's (1979) discursive history of Orientalism is a compelling reminder of the constructions of colonized people as the barbaric other of the West. Spivak (1988) also has examined the Manichean construction of the "brown man" as the white man's barbaric other in the discursive context of the British reform of sati. Spivak argues, "The abolition of this rite (*sati* or widow sacrifice) by the British has been generally understood as a case of 'white men saving brown women from brown men' " (p. 297). It is possible that colonial memory engenders both postcolonial anxiety and resistance from Indians to the possibility of being constructed as other in the United States. This observation gains support in Bhattacharjee's (1992) analysis of the political position of Indian immigrants in the United States. Bhattacharjee explains, "In particular, the Third World bourgeoisie, as an immigrant group in the First World, finds itself in a position of subordination to the native bourgeoisie: a position defined partly by the experiences of Western colonialism and imperialism" (p. 22).

Yet another reason for the reaction from the Asian Indian communities could be the risk of losing their status as a "model minority" given that Asians in general appear to be among the more economically and professionally successful immigrant groups in the United States (Bhattacharjee, 1992; Ganguly, 1992). Bhattacharjee (1992) argues, "The Indian bourgeoisie, which sees itself as the custodians of the model Indian community in the United States, seems to be drawn to a certain 'worldly' discourse of diplomacy, negotiation, and officialdom" (p. 34). Bhattacharjee here implies what she stresses elsewhere—that the community seeks to maintain its face within the mainstream culture as it is propelled by ideological discourses and forces of upward mobility and immigrant success.

An Anglo-American woman interlocutor whom I fortuitously encountered on a bus while returning from the field made the following remark in the midst of a conversation we had about Apna Ghar:[9]

> This happens all the time in those countries. In India and those other countries, men are really dominating, are they not? See, I was riding a taxi one day. And the cab driver was Iranian. And I asked him if his wife wore that cloth on her head. And he said "yes." And it made me so mad. And I wanted to tell him, "You men don't treat your wives right. Now you are in America. You better start liberating the women."

This suggests that the threat from being named is real. It also is consistent with the work of Hegde (1998), who includes numerous instances of discourses of otherness about Indians and Indian women that are circulating within U.S. mainstream culture in her analysis of Asian Indian immigrant women's experiences of marginality.

The social control of Indian women through the cultural discourses of honor and shame may be understood in terms of the layers of cultural communication that constitute the discursive fabric of a culture. Philipsen (1987) differentiates among three interrelated senses of cultural communication: code, conversation, and community. Whereas code refers to the ideals of a culture, conversation alludes to the patterned representations of everyday life such as work, play, and worship that emanate from community, which represents spaces of shared memory that bind members of a culture. The "cultural terms" of honor and shame in the Indian immigrant community in the context of domestic violence take the form of what Philipsen characterizes as a "social drama" because it puts to the symbolic test the virtue of a community that is in tension with itself (p. 252).

This social drama becomes the symbolic site for the reification of honor and its violation as a postmodern taboo within a community that is driven by the countervailing forces of desire for cohesion and tendency toward fragmentation. This social taboo is enacted within a ritual of purification from contamination of one's name and defilement of one's honor, whose sacredness and virtue is perverted through contexts of power and dominance both within the community and within U.S. culture and society at large. In this particular configuration of discourses and meanings, Indian women seek a home away from their own as a refuge from physical and representational violence in historical and current times and in geographical spaces that are violently marked and traversed by national, religious, racial, ethnic, gender, sexual, and class strife and tension. These women bear the representational burden of otherness even as they tragically become social and cultural martyrs in defense of honor.

SUMMARY

A praxis ethnography of communication framework was formulated and used to investigate the practices and patterns of a case study of Indian immigrants in the context of wife abuse. One of the key findings is the use of symbols of honor and shame within a discursive code that gives a culturally embedded meaning to women who seek shelter at Apna Ghar through the identity trope of woman without shame or dishonorable woman. The communication pattern that characterizes this group in this site may be understood as the intersection of the ideologies of ideal nationhood and womanhood in the production of Indian cultural identity in ways that reproduce power relations within both the South Asian community and the U.S. cultural context, particularly relations that take the form of social control of the speech and bodies of Indian women who experience abuse. Theories of sociocultural identity construction provide a useful analytic framework for critical examination of the constitution of communal and personal identities in contexts of migrancy. Also, interpretive methods are powerful methodological tools for research into cultural identity in contexts of migrancy because discourse is the site in which a community defines itself within a different cultural milieu.

The research findings demonstrate the need for research into the interrelationships among language as communication, culture, and identity and the various ways in which these play out in the context of the encounter among different cultural groups. Research on how these interrelationships govern communication within cultural groups in the context of practices of postmodern and postcolonial communities such as travel, displacement, and relocation is necessary to further our understanding of community and identity.

Furthermore, the identity and voice of the scholar/critic needs to be the object and subject of critical reflection. Faced with the vicissitudes and ethical dilemmas of fieldwork in "uncommon" places, researchers such as myself appear to move, dangerously, among the emotional states of communicating institutional authority in the form of the detached and disengaged observer, being overwhelmed by the politics of participation-as-attachment, and imposing interpretations due to knowledge of a broader political context. The discursive and ideological space of Apna Ghar and the surrounding South Asian community calls for ethnographic engagement of, not removal from, the codes of honor and shame. Such engagement should enable the women who seek shelter at Apna Ghar, as well as the community, to interpret their actions as embodiments of honorable Indian womanhood and ones that stand up to the test of communal virtue in the face of enormous cultural odds. This study also speaks to the need for serious practical and ethical engagement with the practices and politics of representation of cultural others in the United States.

NOTES

1. For a more elaborate discussion of the history of Apna Ghar, the Indian immigrant community in Chicago, and the ethnography, see Supriya (1996).
2. For a discussion of "thick description" in ethnography, see Geertz (1973).
3. The names of the respondents and Apna Ghar staff have been changed to protect confidentiality.
4. Sunita's comments that appear as quotations are taken verbatim from field notes because she did not consent to the use of a tape recorder.
5. The following comments are based on field notes including verbatim comments that were written during the service.
6. Bakhtin (1975/1981), in *The Dialogic Imagination,* conceptualizes heteroglossia as base conditions, a matrix of cultural and social forces that determine meanings of utterances.
7. Of particular relevance to this analysis is Bakhtin's (1975/1981) notion of national languages, which are conceptualized as linguistic and expressive forms that are stratified into social dialects, languages of generations, age groups, religions, and so on.
8. For an extended discussion of the concept of prohibition on the body, see Foucault (1979, pp. 135-169).
9. The following comments are based on field notes that were taken down during the encounter. The woman was informed about the research and gave her consent to my taking down field notes.

REFERENCES

Alcoff, L. (1988). Cultural feminism versus post-structuralism: The identity crisis in feminist theory. *Signs: Journal of Women and Culture, 13,* 405-436.

Bakhtin, M. M. (1981). *The dialogic imagination: Four essays* (C. Emerson & M. Holquist, Trans.). Austin: University of Texas Press. (Original work published 1975)

Bhattacharjee, A. (1992). The habit of ex-nomination: Nation, woman, and the Indian immigrant bourgeoisie. *Public Culture, 5,* 19-44.

Carbaugh, D. (1988). Cultural terms and tensions in the speech at television stations. *Western Journal of Speech Communication, 52,* 216-237.

Chaachhi, A. (1991). Forced identities: The state, communalism, fundamentalism, and women in India. In D. Kandiyoti (Ed.), *Women, Islam, and the state* (pp. 144-175). Philadelphia: Temple University Press.

Collier, M. J. (1998). Researching cultural identity: Reconciling interpretive and postcolonial perspectives. *International and Intercultural Communication Annual, 21,* 122-147.

Conquergood, D. (1991). Rethinking ethnography: Towards a critical cultural politics. *Communication Monographs, 58,* 179-194.

Corbin, J., & Strauss, A. (1990). *Basics of qualitative research: Grounded theory procedures and research.* Newbury Park, CA: Sage.

Dahlgren, P., & Chakrapani, S. (1982). The Third World on T.V. news: Western ways of seeing the other. In W. C. Adams (Ed.), *Television coverage of international affairs* (pp. 45-64). Norwood, NJ: Ablex.

Foucault, M. (1979). *Discipline and punish.* New York: Vintage.

Ganguly, K. (1992). Migrant identities: Personal memory and the construction of selfhood. *Cultural Studies, 6,* 27-50.

Geertz, C. (1973). *The interpretation of cultures.* New York: Basic Books.

Grossberg, L. (1993). Cultural studies and/in new worlds. *Critical Studies in Mass Communication, 10,* 1-22.

Gudykunst, W. B., & Kim, Y. Y. (1997). *Communicating with strangers: An approach to intercultural communication.* New York: McGraw-Hill.

Hall, S. (1990). Cultural Identity and diaspora. In J. Rutherford (Ed.), *Identity, community, culture, difference* (pp. 222-237). London: Lawrence & Wishart.

Hegde, R. (1998). Swinging the trapeze: The negotiation of identity among Asian Indian immigrant women in the United States. *International and Intercultural Communication Annual, 21,* 35-55.

Jeffrey, P. (1979). *Frogs in a well: Indian women in purdah.* London: Zed.

Kandiyoti, D. (1994). *Identity and its discontents: Women and the nation.* In P. Williams & L. Chrisman (Eds.), *Colonial discourse and post-colonial theory: A reader* (pp. 376-391). New York: Columbia University Press.

Katriel, T. (1994). Sites of memory: Discourses of the past in Israeli pioneering settlement museums. *Quarterly Journal of Speech, 80,* 1-20.

Kondo, D. (1990). *Crafting selves: Power, gender, and discourses of identity in a Japanese workplace.* Chicago: University of Chicago Press.

Lather, P. (1986). Research as praxis. *Harvard Educational Review, 56,* 257-277.

Lee, W. S. (1998). Patriotic breeders or colonized converts: A postcolonial feminist approach to anti-footbinding discourse in China. *International and Intercultural Communication Annual, 21,* 11-33.

Levinsohn, H. (1991, November 1). A woman of the world. *Chicago Reader,* pp. 8-20.

Lindsley, S. L. (1999). Communication and the "Mexican way": Stability and trust as core symbols in Maquiladoras. *Western Journal of Communication, 63,* 1-31.

Lu, K. (1993). *Domestic violence, battered women's shelters, and battered Asian women.* Unpublished manuscript, Grinell College.

Mani, L. (1987). Contentious traditions: The debate on SATI in colonial India. *Cultural Critique, 7,* 119-156.

Ono, K. A. (1998). Problematizing nation in intercultural communication research. *International and Intercultural Communication Research, 21,* 193-202.

Pathak, Z., & Sunderrajan, R. (1989). Shahbano. *Signs: Journal of Women in Culture and Society, 14,* 558-582.

Philipsen, G. (1975). Speaking like a man in Teamsterville: Culture patterns of role enactment in an urban neighborhood. *Quarterly Journal of Speech, 61,* 13-22.

Philipsen, G. (1987). The prospect for cultural communication. In D. L. Kincaid (Ed.), *Communication theory: Eastern and Western perspectives* (pp. 245-254). San Diego: Academic Press.

Said, E. (1979). *Orientalism.* New York: Vintage.

Sharoni, S. (1995). *Gender and the Israeli-Palestinian conflict: The politics of women's resistance.* Syracuse, NY: Syracuse University Press.

Spivak, G. C. (1988). Can the subaltern speak? In C. Nelson & L. Grossberg (Eds.), *Marxism and the interpretation of culture* (pp. 271-313). Urbana: University of Illinois Press.

Supriya, K. E. (1995). Speaking others, practicing selves: Representational practices of battered immigrant women in *Apna Ghar* ("Our Home"). *Women and Performance: A Journal of Feminist Theory, 7,* 241-266.

Supriya, K. E. (1996). *Speaking others, practicing selves: Power, identity, and communication in Apna Ghar* (Our Home). Unpublished doctoral dissertation, University of Illinois at Urbana-Champaign.

Tanno, D. V., & Gonzalez, A. (1998). Sites of identity in communication and culture. *International and Intercultural Communication Annual, 21,* 3-7.

Ting-Toomey, S. (1988). Intercultural conflict styles: A face-negotiation theory. In Y. Y. Kim & W. B. Gudykunst (Eds.), *Theories in intercultural communication* (pp. 213-235). Newbury Park, CA: Sage.

Weedon, C. (1987). *Feminist practice and poststructuralist theory.* Oxford, UK: Blackwell.

West, J. (1993). Ethnography and ideology: The politics of cultural representation. *Western Journal of Communication, 57,* 209-220.

Williams, R. (1961). *The long revolution.* New York: Columbia University Press.

6

Queering the Nation

Diasporic Cinema and Media Definitions of Indian Femininity

SUJATA MOORTI • *Old Dominion University*

In December 1998, a small group of protesters halted the screening of the internationally acclaimed movie *Fire* in two theaters in Bombay, India. The following day, a similar group attacked a theater in New Delhi. In both cities, the protesters were primarily women affiliated with the Shiv Sena, a Hindu fundamentalist organization with roots in Bombay. They wore saffron-colored scarves to mark their religious affiliation, bought tickets to the screening, and once inside the hall burned posters, destroyed furniture, and effectively banned a film that had gained an audience primarily among women. The protesters condemned the movie's portrayal of lesbian sexuality, claiming that it was alien to Indian culture and an affront to Hindu values. Furthermore, they asserted that the movie's story line would "spoil women" and lead to the collapse of marriage as an institution.

The protests spread to other parts of the country, where theater owners withdrew the film[1] rather than face the wrath of the religious right.[2] The violent responses evoked by the film were countered by civil rights groups, women's groups, and other organizations that rallied in support of the screening of the film. The ensuing debate foregrounded the film's representation of women and sexual desire, the role of cinema in the articulation of a national culture, and the limits of dissonance and debate within a liberal democratic framework.

Popular opposition to cinematic representations is not novel, nor is it limited to India. This particular debate reveals the multiple and contradictory ways in which gender, sexuality, and religion intersect to produce discourses of national identity. Made by Indian-born Canadian director Deepa Mehta, the film's reception in India and other countries with sizable populations of Indian origin also reveals the imbrication of gender in local resistances to globalization. In Singapore and Kenya, residents of Indian origin were successful in banning the film. Viewing the film's reception through newspaper reports and commentaries, in this chapter I explore the historically conditioned contexts within which discourses of nation are produced, circulated, and consumed.

Media products have increasingly become sites where issues pertaining to identity are worked out. In the United States, television products, ranging from talk shows and music videos to animated shows, have become central to political debates about family values. Similarly, outside the United States, debates pertaining to national identity have coalesced around the circulation of media products, particularly those that have been labeled "Western." In this chapter, I underscore the need for a nuanced and complex reading that would help us to apprehend the identity wars that are played out in the media. Although scholars in various disciplinary fields have used postcolonial theories to analyze the contestation and negotiation of identity, such an engagement is strikingly limited in the field of communication. In particular, I argue that postcolonial theories not only enrich the discipline but also enact key transformations that require a reconceptualization of taken-for-granted terms such as *culture* and, by extension, the domain of intercultural communication.

Hall (1992) points out that national cultures construct identities by producing meanings about the nation. These are contained in the stories that are told about the nation, memories that connect its present with its past, and images that are constructed of it. But the stories rarely are stable. In an age of transnational flows, these debates over national culture and identity have become exacerbated. The arguments over national identity, who or what belongs, and who or what does not belong reveal a crisis. According to Mercer (1990), "Identity only becomes an issue when it is in crisis, when something [that] is assumed to be fixed, coherent, and stable is displaced by the experience of doubt and uncertainty" (p. 43). Transnational flows of people, products, and ideas have made national and cultural borders appear porous and hence destabilizing for the concept of identity. In this chapter, I take up the example of a film produced in North America, *Fire,* and through its reception in India, I demonstrate the specific ways in which debates over national culture are conducted. Through the use of postcolonial theories, I point out the modalities through which these identity wars are mapped onto the body of woman and with what effects.

Scholars such as Hegde (1998) and Shome (1998) have cleared the theoretical space for introducing issues of postcoloniality in communication. I take up their insights pertaining to hybridity and diaspora to unravel the location of female sexuality in discourses of national identity. The terms *hybridity* and *diaspora* are themselves contested and carry multiple valences. One of the definitions that Clifford (1994) offers for these migrant circuits is expatriate minority communities that maintain a memory, vision, or myth about a real symbolic homeland. A diasporic sensibility reflects "the sense of being part of an ongoing transnational network that includes the homeland, not as something left behind but as a place of attachment" (p. 311). Rushdie (1991) characterizes hybridity as having access to two traditions: that of the homeland and that of the new home. Both terms refer to sensibilities of displacement and of being decentered, and they contain complex feelings of memory, multi-locale attachments, adaptation, and resistance. In this chapter, *Fire* emerges from and articulates these ambiguous identifications in part because within India it is seen primarily as a Western product.

I argue that contemporary debates over belongingness in the South Asian subcontinent need to be examined within the historical legacies of colonialism. These identity wars reveal the particular brand of woman that is incorporated within the dominant discourse of national identity. The analysis demonstrates the limited sexual location available for women within competing discourses of national and cultural identity. It reveals the centrality of the heterosexual individual in definitions of Indian-ness. In these imaginings of nation, lesbian sexuality is ignored and women appear firmly located within the heterosexual family, primarily in their maternal capacity. In the Indian context, these debates over identity politics underscore the resilience of colonial formations on contemporary everyday lives within the subcontinent, particularly on women. By examining a media product produced within a diasporic context, this chapter foregrounds the specific ways in which national identities are reconceptualized. It also reveals the historically conditioned contexts within which discourses of sexuality are contested and negotiated.

In what follows, I address the multiple definitions of Indian identity that were articulated around the screening of *Fire*. I highlight the consequences of these identity politics for the material and symbolic lives of Indian women. To provide background, I briefly examine the plot of the film and the sexual and cultural spaces it makes available, but my focus is on the social relations and global flows that shape its viewing in India. Underpinning this analysis is a discussion of the ways in which transnational flows force a reconfiguration of the field of intercultural communication and suggestions of the ways in which the field of communication would be enriched by an inclusion of postcolonial theories.

ANALYSIS OF MEDIA RESPONSE

Data Analysis

The data for the media analysis were collected from a systematic review of press reports, editorials, and commentaries published in English-language newspapers in India. All of the organizations maintain online versions that can be easily accessed in the United States. The analysis emerges primarily from press coverage during December 1998 and January 1999, the 2 months when the debates about the film were most intense. I nevertheless scrutinized all coverage on *Fire* prior to and after the film's informal ban; this included press service reports and online services such as Rediff India. The analysis in this chapter focuses on four newspapers—the *Times of India, Indian Express, The Hindu,* and *The Statesman*—all of which are regionally based but have national readerships. (These newspapers are analogous to the *New York Times* and the *Washington Post* and often are seen as setting the agenda for other press coverage.) The *Times of India* and *Indian Express* have numerous regional editions but are primarily associated with the cities of Bombay and New Delhi, respectively. *The Hindu,* based in Madras, similarly has a national audience but tends to provide news from a perspective shaped by South Indian concerns. *The Statesman,* based in Calcutta, also is informed by concerns specific to the eastern region of India. In addition, I examined the Bangalore-based *Deccan Herald,* the New Delhi-based *Hindustan Times,* and the Calcutta-based *Telegraph.*

English-language newspapers in India tend to solicit a limited national audience, one that is middle class and literate. The regional variations in their coverage of a national phenomenon such as the controversy over *Fire* are minimal. In their coverage of the events surrounding the protests against and support of *Fire,* all of these newspapers provided fairly uniform reports; all presented "both sides" of the controversy. It is in the arena of commentary and editorials that some differences emerged. *The Hindu* and *The Telegraph* tended to publish more commentary from writers who are labeled feminist or are associated with the women's movement.

In the arena of newsmagazines, my data emerged from sites that solicit primarily a national audience. I examined *India Today, Frontline, Outlook,* and *The Week.* All of the newspapers and newsmagazines maintain Web sites and are accessible for U.S. audiences; this factor determined my choices for sources. Because my concerns in this chapter are driven by a focus on the specific ways in which a national Indian identity is constructed by media reports, the analysis uses national outlets. Examining regional and Indian-language newspapers would provide different perspectives, those shaped by locally specific concerns about how the regional is located within the national imaginary. This no doubt would provide a fruitful avenue for further research.

Zone of Debate

The multivalent reception of *Fire* in India is most usefully seen as an arena in which a number of discourses around female chastity, modern nationalism, and (more broadly) morality intersect and feed on each other with significant political effects. The various articles and commentaries present radically polarized understandings of the function of cinema and of *Fire*'s representations of middle class Indian women. These responses can be understood only in the context of the difficult shifts and uneasy negotiations that mark the construction of modern India—the different valences accorded to gender, sexuality, and religion in competing definitions of Indian-ness. Above all, they expose the centrality of the female figure in imaginings of nation. The multi-accented media commentaries reveal the ideological investments that have accumulated around the articulation of the female and the location of sexuality in discourses of Indian identity.

An analysis of the para-texts surrounding *Fire* also reveals the position that diasporic cinema occupies in definitions of national identity or national culture. I use the term *para-text* to refer to media discourses on the movie; this concept emerges from the idea that cultural texts (e.g., film) do not contain a singular meaning but can be interpreted variously. Thomas (1989) suggests that the concept of the para-text highlights the "complex issues involved in the reading of texts across cultures . . . , assuming that the text is not an object that contains meaning in itself but [rather] that meanings arise in the process of reading and texts open continuously onto other texts" (p. 13). The implications of this broad notion of intertextuality for how we talk about any individual film is the focus of this chapter. Para-texts allow us to examine the parameters within which the movie is understood and viewed.

Gupta and Ferguson (1997) theorize that newspaper reports are a discursive form through which daily life is narrativized and collectivities are imagined. I examine English-language newspapers and newsmagazines published in India as constituting a "zone of public debate" in which journalists, politicians, women activists, and community leaders formulate specific discourses about homosexuality, gender, community, and nation. With regard to discourse about *Fire,* the print media responded to and reinforced emergent cultural and political perceptions of a threat to the existing social structure. The perspectives presented reveal crucial questions about national identity, who belongs, who does not belong, which characteristics are considered indigenous, and which characteristics are considered alien.

HISTORICAL BACKGROUND AND CONTEXT

The controversy over *Fire* occurred at a historical moment when Indian woman was being reconstituted as a diacritic of Hindu nationalism, a specific religious nationalism. When the Hindu fundamentalist party, the Bharatiya Janata Party (BJP), took over the national government, its members attempted to resituate women within the patriarchal structures of the hearth and the home through a series of failed measures.[3] At the same time, politicians attempted to institute an affirmative action program that would ensure that women comprised at least a third of all elected officials at all levels of representation.

The centrality of the woman symbol in narratives of Indian national identity has to be understood against a historical background. The nationalist movement of the early 20th century protesting British colonial rule sutured sexuality and culture in the political arena, and woman emerged as a contested symbol central to the articulation of Indian identity (Mani, 1989). Chatterjee (1993) and Sangari and Vaid (1989), among others, document the different strategies through which the policing and containment of female sexuality became central elements in colonial imaginations of nation and national identity. With the rise of Hindu fundamentalism over the past decade, woman has emerged once again as the terrain on which different definitions of Indian identity are worked over. Through an examination of the various debates that exploded around the screening of *Fire,* in this chapter I demonstrate the manner in which homosexuality and women's assertion of sexual desire come to signify the endangered purity of the nation in contemporary India.

In what follows, I first describe the film and the way it plays with notions of femininity and tradition. Through an examination of newspaper and print media reports, I then describe the positions taken by those who protested against and those who supported the screening of the film. I unravel the politics engendered by their arguments, their conception of the Indian state, and their incorporation of a specific brand of woman within the body politic. I juxtapose these commentaries against the silence that invariably accompanies the objectification of women that has become an essential trope of mainstream Indian cinema. Finally, I point out the spaces made available by the debates presented in the print media and the discourses that were marginalized.

Rejecting Tradition

Fire is the first part of a trilogy offering a gendered view of the social transformations effected in India during the 20th century; the second part, *Earth,* already has been released and engages with the partition that followed British withdrawal from the South Asian subcontinent; the third part, *Water,* was under production in 2000 but subsequently was halted after Mehta's crew members were attacked by those protesting the story line. *Fire* is about middle-class arranged marriages and the persistence of joint family establishments in cramped urban apartments. Set in contemporary New Delhi, its protagonist, Radha, is married to Ashok. When the story begins, the childless couple has been married for more than 15 years. Radha runs the family takeout business, is the primary caregiver of her stroke-ridden mother-in-law, and stoically bears the stigma of her infertility. Ashok has shifted his attention from his family to his spiritual guru, attends to him, and practices celibacy. In a move reminiscent of Mahatma Gandhi's experiments with celibacy, Ashok insists that Radha share his bed so that he can test his capacity for sexual restraint.

Into this unhappy family enters Sita, the new bride of Ashok's younger brother, Jatin. It becomes clear very early in the film that although Jatin has agreed to the arranged marriage with Sita, he still is in love with his Chinese girlfriend. Jatin abandons his bride for his girlfriend and leaves Sita to negotiate her position within the joint family setup. Gradually, the two women, who have been abandoned by their husbands for different reasons, forge a deep emotional bond. This bond grows into a sexual relationship. Ashok stumbles on the two women in bed after he learns of their relationship from a disgruntled servant. The movie ends with the two women opting to leave the home, but not before Radha chooses to explain her choice to Ashok. While the husband and wife conduct a heated discussion, a fire erupts in the kitchen and Ashok decides to rescue his invalid mother rather than to help Radha, who is caught in the flames. She saves herself and leaves the house to join her lover, Sita.

Thomas (1989) has pointed out that the trial by fire is a convention that often is deployed uncritically by Indian filmmakers. The concept of this chastity test for females, *agniparikṣha,* is derived from the epic *Ramayana,* where Rama rescues his wife, Sita, from the clutches of the monstrous Ravana, the wicked king of Lanka. Ravana may have abducted Rama's wife, but he does not "defile" her. When the reunited couple returns to its kingdom, however, some of Rama's subjects challenge Sita's purity and consequent worthiness to remain queen. Rama accedes to his subjects' wishes, and Sita is made to undergo a test by fire. She emerges unscathed, proving her innocence. The citizenry remains skeptical, however, and Rama banishes her from his kingdom. In contemporary India, many women believe that they are subjected to a figurative chastity test, and *Fire* underscores this structure of feeling. The film tests Radha's devotion to duty and traditional Hindu values in an idiom that echoes Rama's testing his wife's chastity.

Fire can best be described as a melodrama. It draws on popular religious epics to highlight the troubled location that women occupy in a modernizing society that continues to structure domestic life within the parameters prescribed by "tradition." At three different moments (twice theatrically and once performatively), the film draws attention to the chastity test—the trial by fire—that Indian women are expected to meet. Religion and religious epics function here as heuristic devices for the modes through which the concept of tradition is mobilized in everyday life and shapes quotidian experiences.

What is unusual about the film is its focus on the female protagonists and its explicit articulation of lesbian sexuality. *Fire* points out that a bad marriage no longer needs to be a tragic event for women; they have other options. It also foregrounds questions of female desire outside patriarchal scaffolding. The narrative structure elaborates on the thematics of love as a relation of mutuality, which is in conflict with the compulsions of arranged marriages. With these themes, Mehta joins several Indian women filmmakers (e.g., Aparna Sen) who have redrawn the field of the visible by addressing the subject of female sexual desire. Bose (1997) and Arora (1994) point out that in alternative cinema, women filmmakers have solicited the female spectator and initiated a dialogue that points toward the articulation of a postcolonial sexual identity for Indian women.

At first glance, *Fire* is a flawed but compelling movie that draws attention to the oppressive conditions of women's lives in arranged marriages. It poignantly reveals the woman's point of view of being caught between desire and an oppressive tradition, and it delineates the everyday struggles women face when they try to work within the structures of the joint family. It offers its female protagonists a sense of individual agency, and the narrative permits them the expression of sexual desire. Mehta's film also captures the anxieties that accompany the changes occurring in the bourgeois Indian family as middle class women are interpellated within the flows of a global market economy. Foregrounding the gendered processes of modernity, the movie presents middle class mundane life as both stifling and marked with possibilities.

Fire attempts to reenvision Hindu culture and identity by positing the family, the domestic space, and various religious rituals as possible sites for a transgressive sexuality and a desiring female. Nevertheless, I characterize the movie as flawed because it offers a simple "happily ever after" ending for its protagonists and does not call into question the limits to expressing lesbian sexuality in contemporary India.[4] Parameswaran (1999) believes that the film uses religious devices to incite a reaction but ignores the political reality in which such gestures would be read. Similarly, Kishwar (1998) and Ramesh (1999) argue that the movie is heavy-handed in its critique of Indian traditions. They indicate that the final trial by fire is contrived to prove that the protagonists are worthy of their newfound lesbian love. Furthermore, the Indian tradition on which Mehta draws, particularly her reliance on the *Ramayana,* ignores the powerful female role models of Durga, Kali, and others.

My criticisms of the movie emanate from a different angle. I argue that the movie valorizes women's sexual desires but undermines this difficult gesture by offering a vision of lesbian sexuality that is problematic. *Fire* presents female same-sex desire as emerging primarily as an alternative to troubled marriages; lesbianism in this worldview is an option forced by conjugal neglect. Furthermore, the romantic ending does not call into question the limits to the expression of lesbian sexuality in contemporary India and the institutional structures that render it invisible.

Throughout this chapter, I use the term *lesbian* cautiously to refer to same-sex desire. Blackwood and Wieringa (1999) acknowledge the misrecognition and (Western) ethnocentrism that the use of the term *lesbianism* occasions: "Making lesbian a global category is problematic because it imposes the Eurocentric term 'lesbian,' a term usually used to refer to a fixed sexual identity, on practices and relationships that may have very different meanings and expectations in other cultures" (p. 19). Nevertheless, they suggest the use of the term to signify female/women's same-sex eroticism as distinctly different from men's and because it inherently demands a recognition of women's differences. These assumptions are implicit in my use of the term *lesbian.*

A winner of 14 international awards, *Fire* was first screened in India in 1997 at two international film festivals. It was hailed by diverse responses; whereas some were enraged by its portrayal of lesbian sexuality, others praised its presentation of a woman-centered narrative (Lak, 1998; Sidhwa, 1997). Before its theatrical release in November 1998, *Fire* was approved by the Central Board of Film Certification, commonly known as the censor board. No film can be publicly screened in India unless it carries a certificate issued by the censor board, an organization instituted during British colonial rule. Officially, the board can ban scenes because approval requires that a film "slurs no religious organizations, customs, and rituals" (Barnouw & Krishnaswamy, 1980, p. 75). *Fire* received an "A" (adults-only) certificate; the board did not require any cuts but recommended that one of the female protagonist's names be changed from Sita to Nita.

The film originally was made in English, but in India the English version was supplemented with a dubbed Hindi version. With the name change suggested by the censor board, both versions were screened in major metropolitan cities for 3 weeks before protesters halted the screenings. Theater owners averred that the film ran to full houses and was patronized primarily by young urban women before they were forced to withdraw it. Before the unofficial ban, some women's groups organized "women-only" screenings to facilitate female viewership of the movie because the traditional movie-going audience in India is predominantly male (Jain & Raval, 1998).

NARRATIVE FEATURES

Domestic Desires

The film replicates narrative strategies that are commonplace in mainstream Indian cinema and reworks them; its unique feature is its explicit portrayal of lesbian desire. In this section, I first address the narrative features that *Fire* shares with mainstream Hindi cinema as well as those that set it apart. Mainstream Hindi movies are referred to in common parlance as "Bollywood" products. Although film production centers are prevalent in many Indian cities and outnumber those produced in Hollywood, historically Bombay has dominated the production of films. Today, Bollywood functions as a metonym to signify mainstream Bombay-based productions, the Indian version of Hollywood cinema (Dayal, 1983; Prasad, 1998).

Kakar (1983) points out that in mainstream Indian cinema, "family relationships, their ramifications and consequences, are central to the plot" (p. 82). Similarly, the narrative in *Fire* centers on the (in)stability of the family. Through a focus on issues pertaining to the domestic arena and kinship relations, the narrative unravels the crisis within the middle class family and offers a tenuous resolution. According to Das Gupta (1983), mainstream Indian cinema upholds the status quo: "Pray to God, love your parents, live for your husband . . . , and everything will be perfect" (p. 40). The figure of woman often is cast as posing a threat to the unity of the middle class family. In *Fire,* the character of Sita is presented as introducing alien values that lead to an unresolvable crisis. These themes are addressed in *Fire* only to be cast aside decisively by its female protagonists. According to a writer in *The Hindu,*

> The loud message that comes through in the film is the loneliness of women within the institution of marriage, the inequality of patriarchy that gives men the right to seek their salvation in another woman or in God, and the impotence of men when women decide to take hold of their lives and look for love, compassion, and companionship elsewhere. (Kapur, 1998, p. 26)

Rather than uphold the institution of arranged marriage, the film configures it as a central site of women's oppression.

The conflict of values between tradition and modernity is another well-visited theme in mainstream cinema. According to Prasad (1998),

> The binary modernity/tradition, whether it is employed to indicate conflict or complementarity, amounts to an explanation, "a conceptual or belief system" which regulates thinking about the modern Indian social formation. This binary also figures centrally, both thematically and as an ongoing device, in popular film narratives. . . . The explanatory scheme in question functions as a disavowal of modernity. (pp. 7-8)

Fire also thematizes this issue with a converse effect. It reveals the tug-of-war between family affiliations and the individual's desire for freedom and independence, validating the latter. The repeated references to the *Ramayana* and other religious rituals function as signifiers of the traditional order, while modernity is manifested in women's assertion of desire and agency. It is important to note that within the logic of the traditional order, the husbands' behaviors are not cast as disruptive or as destabilizing the family order. With the presentation of the female point of view, *Fire* reveals an Indian society caught between the competing forces of tradition and modernity and the limited options available to women. It rejects traditional values to embrace the modern concept of foregrounding the desire of the individual over the well-being of the community.

The evocation and inscription of national identity through the figure of the woman is a common Bollywood device (Thomas, 1989). In mainstream films such as *Mother India,* the heroine as representative of the nation is cast as powerful because she respects traditional values and remains chaste and virtuous. *Fire* uses the figure of the woman to signify the changing social structures and the effects of the global economy on Indian family structures. Here, the heroine(s) gains agency by renouncing traditional values and the ideals of chastity and obedience.

The focus on female protagonists and the presentation of a social problem resonate with characteristics thematized in alternative Indian cinema. The women may destabilize the family and the traditional order, but they are not presented as villains. Instead, they are presented as heroic for affirming sexual and social relations based on individual happiness. In mainstream cinema, the Indian woman has a very clearly delineated role to perform within a marriage. If she deviates from it for any reason, she is seen as betraying her biological role and is expected to pay the price in humiliation and defeat. Suicide or a conveniently accidental death always has been the solution for uncomfortable situations of all kinds, particularly those involving women (Vasudev, 1983). *Fire* rejects this story line and offers a tentative "happy ending." Furthermore, women in mainstream cinema seldom are depicted as understanding or supporting of each other: "They are, in fact, the preservers of tradition and each other's worst persecutors, while male camaraderie has always been strong and is emphasised in most films" (p. 103). In *Fire,* not only do the female protagonists fall in love with each other, their relationship from the beginning is depicted as supportive.

Creating New Cultural Spaces

Fire might develop themes that have already been explored elsewhere, but it presents a narrative that transgresses on many levels. It foregrounds the economy of female libidinal desire and the limited space for its expression within the patriarchal structure of arranged marriages. Through its explicit articulation of female sexual desire, it opens the space for a cultural and social assessment of the institution of arranged marriage. The film configures a libidinal public space through a series of narrative devices that I discuss in what follows.

Mehta has deliberately selected the names of her protagonists as Radha and Sita. In mainstream cinema, these names are invoked to connote wifely chastity and subordination; they refer to a spectrum of archetypes of ideal femininity in Indian culture. Both names encode numerous cultural values inscribed in ancient texts and scriptures. They represent all that is ostensibly pure, chaste, and self-sacrificing about Indian wives. In particular, Sita is used to represent the "perfect woman, the perfect wife, acquiescing unquestioningly to her husband's rejection of her" (Vasudev, 1983, p. 98). The film constructs the two figures of Radha and Sita through a number of partial and conflicting representations that refer to a spectrum of archetypes of ideal femininity in Indian culture, and the figures operate as terrains on which notions of the ideal Indian woman are negotiated.[5]

Fire deploys conventional signifiers but in a subversive manner to "transgress nearly every sexual, cultural, and familial norm that constitutes India as it is imagined," according to a writer in *The Hindu* (Kapur, 1998, p. 26). The two women do not acquiesce to their husbands' abandonment; they seek affective relations elsewhere. Nevertheless, the presence of these names reveals the weight of tradition that continues to shape everyday women's lives. Furthermore, in Mehta's presentation of the trial by fire, it is the figure of Radha rather than Sita who has to undergo the ordeal, signaling that every woman in India is expected to conform to this ideal. By offering women options outside of marriage, the film overturns the celebration of female chastity.

In a contrived ending, *Fire* ends with the two lovers exiled from home seeking refuge in a Muslim shrine. Mehta's critique of the Hindu middle class family offers a tentative critique of patriarchy. The denouement is contrived because the protagonists do not seek a secular sanctuary when they leave home; their agency is limited to seeking shelter within another religious space. With this ending, the movie ignores the particular ways in which religious structures intersect with patriarchal institutions to limit the expression of female sexual desire. The ending suggests that Islam, as practiced in India, would be more receptive to lesbians than would Hinduism. Indeed, it is unlikely that any religious organization in India would offer these women refuge. In its desire to produce a future of possibilities for the protagonists, the narrative elides the particular structures that render lesbianism invisible in India. Nevertheless, this movie is unique because of its presentation of female sexual desire. In depicting the topography and vicissitudes of desire, the movie offers female same-sex relations as a viable alternative. But it is this same gesture that also highlights the limits of the narrative.

The expression of female same-sex desire initially was the central target of the various protests directed at *Fire*. Ironically, Mehta has repeatedly refused to characterize her film as one about lesbianism. Instead, she claims that it is about female characters "needing to be alive." She has asserted before and after the protests that her film is about desire and control, the choices people make, and the oppressive nature of religious and cultural traditions in India (Sharma, 1998).

> I really thought that this work was about choices. It also tries to define the place of women in a patriarchal society, which is caught between a seemingly modern and economically thriving existence, on the one hand, and traditional outdated values, on the other hand. There is a real conflict here. The people who zip around in fancy cars and have access to all that is current find that this lifestyle contradicts age-old customs, which has fewer takers even within their society, let alone the larger one. . . . Most specifically, I wanted to explore the place of women in Indian society. It is undoubtedly male dominated, where a woman is a mother, a daughter, a sister, or a wife but never a woman (for herself). (Bhaskaran, 1998, p. 10)

Mehta describes love between the two women as a metaphor for the transitions occurring in India: "Self-sacrifice and absolute devotion are characteristics difficult to maintain in the context of attenuating family ties and the erosion of the male figure as the source of wisdom, strength, and financial power" (Melwani, 1996). Indeed, once the protests started, Mehta herself characterized the film's portrayal of lesbian sexuality as simplistic. It is not "fair to lesbians because it shows that perhaps women turn to each other only if their marriages are bad" (Haidar, 1998). She also was insistent that her film not be "hijacked" by lesbian organizations, such as Sakhi and Sangini, to make visible their presence within Indian society. Even within the context of the protests, Mehta reiterated that her film was "about loneliness, about choices," and not about lesbianism (Jain & Raval, 1998).

I believe that Azmi's presence in the film, in addition to its exploration of female sexual desire, was a contributory factor to the virulent attacks. Azmi currently is a nominated member to the upper house of parliament, the Rajya Sabha. She is 1 of 12 nominated members selected for her contributions to Indian cinema and the arts and for her activism on behalf of Bombay's slum dwellers. She has acted in more than 110 films including 9 international projects. During her 25-year career, Azmi has emerged as an actor who is representative of the changing image of the heroine on the Hindi screen (Somaaya, 1999). She has acted in both commercial and alternative cinema and is associated with portraying a woman's point of view in her films. In addition to films, she has worked in regional theater companies and participated in hunger strikes to facilitate better living conditions for Bombay's slum dwellers. The BBC refers to her as the Vanessa Redgrave of India—an intelligent, articulate actor-activist (Ninan, 1998a). Her image on- and off-screen has increasingly become that of a person who transgresses female gender norms and yet has gained social and political power. Above all, she is a Muslim, and this feature stimulated particular criticism during the protests.

Opposers of the film sought Azmi's ouster from parliament, claiming that she had besmirched the dignity of Indian women. Specifically, they attributed her Muslim identity to her participation in this "insult to Indian women" ("Furor Over Sena," 1998). In these attacks, Indian identity is conflated with Hindu identity, eliding the multiplicity of religions that comprise the population. Furthermore, Muslims are specifically cast as un-Indian and as marking the limit point of Indian female identity.

A Rejection of the West

It is important to note that the movie did not ignite spontaneous opposition when it was screened in India. That the first protests were aired only 3 weeks after its release is significant. It indicates that the protests against the movie were well orchestrated to mobilize a political constituency. Media columnists pointed out that in both Bombay and New Delhi, protesters informed news media of their intentions and waited until the arrival of television camera crews before vandalizing the theaters (Berak, 1998; Jain & Raval, 1998; Ninan, 1998b). Their arguments against the movie were multifaceted and cannot be reduced to one single cause, but the protests were coherent within the logic of the Hindu right's desire for nation building. It is significant that few of the protesters or politicians who objected to the screening had themselves seen the film.

Initially, the protesters focused on *Fire*'s depiction of female sexual desire and women's exercise of choice. They asserted that these portrayals would "spoil women" by introducing them to ideas alien to Indian culture.

For example, Meena Kambli, the leader of the protesters in Bombay, claims that the "majority of women in our society do not even know about lesbianism. Why expose them to it?" (Swami, 1998). These arguments beg the question of why the nonexistent must be prohibited. The religious right's arguments reveal the anxieties that coalesce around the assertion of a desire that cannot be integrated within the national and/or cultural identities its members envisage.

Some sources elaborated on the specific nature of these anxieties. For example, the Shiv Sena chief, Bal Thackeray, objected to the portrayal of lesbian sexuality because its representation "will corrupt tender minds. Tomorrow it might start in all-ladies hostels. It is a sort of social AIDS" (Raval, 1998). Similarly, a leader of the BJP stated, "Any rational being will concede that homosexuality is unnatural. . . . All this is part of the current trend for 'modernization,' 'globalization,' and 'emancipation' " (Ansari, 1998).

This presentation of homosexuality as a Western phenomenon is neither novel nor unique to India. The ex-presidents of Malaysia, Singapore, and Indonesia have asserted that their countries are characterized by "Asian" values in which the patriarchal (heterosexual) family and state have priority over individual rights (Blackwood & Wieringa, 1999).

During the debate on *Fire,* protesters collapsed arguments supporting the institution of the heterosexual family with the continued well-being of the nation-state. In a hyperbolic statement, Kambli asserted, "If women's physical needs get fulfilled through lesbian acts, the institution of marriage will collapse [and] reproduction of human beings will collapse" (quoted in "We'll Resume," 1998, p. 11). These declarations reveal the central role assigned to women in conceptions of the Indian state; they are reduced to their biological function of reproducers of the nation. Furthermore, homophobia itself is cast as a patriotic stance, one that rejects Western values.

During the days following the protests, people who opposed the film developed a broader base for their objections, primarily by raising the issue of Western imperialism. They argued that the protesters were responding to a public outcry against moral degeneration and the "growing influence of Western culture" ("*Fire* Generates Heat," 1998). Everything that is considered objectionable in society is labeled Western and antithetical to indigenous culture. Mehta's status as a Canadian resident and the film's disavowal of traditional norms are used to mark the product as Western. Implicitly, "Indian culture" is evoked as a sign of resistance to the hegemonic ambitions of the West invading and polluting the Indian middle-class mind. This is not a new trend and has been codified in mainstream Indian cinema very crudely. For example, according to Thomas (1989), this strategy is routinely deployed in Hindi cinema where a chaste and pristine India is constructed by opposing it to a decadent and exotic "other," the licentious and immoral West, with the film's villains invariably sporting a cluster of signifiers of Westernization—whiskey bottles, bikini-clad escorts, or foreign limousines. The protesters deploy a similar logic in their arguments. The religious right has employed this strategy in several other instances as well. For example, religious right activists banned fashion shows in some regional centers, protested the staging of the 1996 Miss Universe beauty pageant in India, and objected to the broadcast of the Miss World and Miss Universe pageants (Nair, 1996; Saksena & Thomas, 1998).

The protesters' arguments collapse the differences that comprise India into a unitary "Indian" culture that must be defended from the incursions of the West. As Nandy (1998) points out, the West is an ideological construct and does not refer to a geographical or temporal entity; it signifies a psychological, economic, and cultural space. "The West appears in the Indian imagination as a transnational category capable of extending beyond geographical determinations and creating new and specific loci of power and knowledge through the manifold processes of Westernization" (p. 22). The anti-Western arguments promulgated by the protesters underscore the anxieties that coalesce around the economic and cultural transformations that have occurred as India has engaged more rigorously in global trade. Global economic flows are characterized as a one-way process, with India being inundated by a behemoth, ill-defined West.

This line of "isolationist" policy reflects the religious right's fears that India's national and cultural borders are porous. The religious right casts the Hindu population as being under siege both from within (from the minority Muslim population) and from without (from the West). Ironically, in the second week of the protests, Bombay labor unions and Muslim groups joined those who were protesting the film; Muslim groups objected to Azmi, a Muslim, portraying a lesbian.

Different religious and national interpretations of Indian-ness came to bear on the film. These two strands of arguments—the objections to *Fire*'s "vulgar and obscene" portrayal of women and the incursion of Western values—are reminiscent of themes developed during the nationalist struggle against British colonial rule (Chatterjee, 1993). Once again, woman is presented as the signifier of a pure authentic India and the repository of cultural values. She has to be shored against threats from evil forces of internal and external origins. This perceived threat explains the anxieties expressed by the protesters of *Fire*. If Indian women are contaminated by non-Hindu ideas, then they will become reluctant to fulfill their traditional duties of wife and mother. Here we can see enacted the elision between woman as a discursively constituted symbol and women as material subjects. Discourses of nation and belonging move out of the symbolic realm to a gendered space of identity politics, and these debates reveal the power of representational practices to be morally offensive.

Based on the objections raised by the protesters, the national government resubmitted the film to the Central Board of Film Certification for reappraisal. At this time, the arguments made against *Fire* shifted dramatically. Where once protesters objected to its presentation of alien values, the grounds for objection shifted to the terrain of religion. Now the religious right asserted that the film could be screened if the female protagonists' names were altered to reflect a Muslim identity, Shabana and Saira (Vijapurkar, 1998). The debate about homosexuality and its location within India were marginalized to a focus on religion; protesters now pointed out that the film was an affront to Hindu values (Jain & Raval, 1998). The film's use of the names Radha and Sita offended the religious sentiments of Indians. The protesters demanded Azmi's ouster from parliament; as a Muslim, her participation in the film reflects her anti-Hindu, and hence anti-Indian, values. These arguments that emphasize religious affiliations articulate a national identity in which only Hindus are recognized. The arguments make clear the religious codes embedded in imaginings of the Indian nation—who the protesters think is Indian, who they believe can represent India, and the role of religion in the secular national project. Hindu identity in these arguments is inextricably linked to conceptions of national identity. The protesters produced a totalizing discourse in which a "native" person is recast as alien. In their definitions, the borders of the imagined community of India expand to include all Hindus, scattered in the diaspora, and yet shrink to keep out everyone not Hindu, especially Muslims.

Subsequently, the censor board reapproved the film, and it was released again in major cities without much ado in December 1998. Although the board did not demand any changes, in Bombay, where the protests started and the Shiv Sena dominate, the names of both female protagonists were changed.

A "Secular" Vision

Objections to the protests against *Fire* were immediate, vigorous, and numerous. Civil rights organizations, cultural bodies, and women's organizations united to offer a range of arguments for the continued screening of the film. While the protesters against the film presented their arguments primarily from the streets, the supporters aired their voices in institutionalized sites of democratic processes. Some launched a legal action against the informal ban, others wrote columns in newspapers and newsmagazines, and still others held "speak out" rallies on various college campuses. These arguments can broadly be classified as threefold: demanding freedom of expression as an integral component of a democratic civil society, asserting homosexuality as an Indian phenomenon, and reiterating the secular impulses of Indian nationalism.

Whereas those who protest the film presented the West and forces of Westernization as problematic features, those who supported its screening resorted to a language of universal rights, a language that has been developed primarily in the geographic West and is associated with it. *Fire*'s supporters distanced themselves from the rhetoric of the religious right that conflates Indian-ness with Hinduism, but their language was replete with references to fascism and specified different uses of religion to assert a secular Indian national identity. It is noteworthy that the arguments for and against the screening of the film gain coherence from very specific interpretations of the role of religion in articulating national culture.

The majority of supporters framed their arguments broadly within the demand for freedom of expression. They asserted that because the censor board approved the film, it should be screened without hindrance. They accused the religious right of adopting a paternalistic attitude in determining what Indians may view, and the street protests served to deny Indians the right to choose. They cast the protesters deprecatingly as "thought police"—the self-appointed gendarmes of cultural values and saviors of Hindu dharma—and accused the religious right of conducting a cultural inquisition. For example, the *Deccan Herald* positioned the violent responses to *Fire* within a larger trend where "cricket players and singers are barred entry because of their nationality and artistes have been roughed up because their work has caused offence" ("Primitive Response," 1998). Similarly, others depicted the protests as another attempt by the religious right to assert their brand of cultural hegemony over India —a "terror raj" (Nambiar, 1998). These arguments assert the need for an open civil society in democratic states. As one writer proclaims, "After all, freedom of expression is the heartbeat of a democratic society" (Tharpar, 1998). Similarly, politicians eager to gain electoral mileage from the issue claimed that "no civilised society would gag freedom of expression" ("Sena Fanning," 1998, p. 11). They accused the religious right of practicing censorship through terror and instead demanded a "space for a rational debate on contentious points of view" ("Line of Fire," 1998). In these discussions, parallels are drawn between Hitler's Germany and an India governed by the religious right. Supporters contested the religious right's attempt to position the majority Hindu population as a beleaguered group. Instead, they deployed this instance to mark the outer limits of religion's presence in democracy; they insisted that religious affiliations could be permitted only so long as they are presented as secular and contribute to the maintenance of a multicultural society. Interestingly, amid this rhetoric of the marketplace of ideas, none of the writers challenged the paternalistic role of the censor board or its relevance. Their demands were primarily for a modulated freedom of expression; once the Central Board of Film Certification approved a film, Indians should be free to watch it.

The majority of these arguments were made in the pages of national newspapers. The only exceptions to this were a candlelight vigil organized in New Delhi and a poster campaign mobilized in Bombay by a group of citizens. The Bombay-based protests were conducted covertly with anonymous posters pasted up late at night to avoid the might of the local Shiv Sena. These protests moved beyond *Fire* to address issues pertaining to individual rights and freedom. These supporters repeatedly made links with broader notions of universal rights. The posters read, "Can Mumbai [Bombay] merely look on when rights and freedoms are throttled?" (Vijapurkar, 1999). The list of violations referenced a range of instances in which the religious right had trampled basic civil rights: the destruction of the Ayodhya mosque, the halting of the Pakistan-India cricket match in Bombay, the destruction of paintings by a renowned Muslim artist, the cancellation of a concert by a Muslim singer, and so on. *Fire* was just one more instance in a series of violations. The protesters were portrayed in *The Hindu* as "characters in a C-grade formula film in which local toughs, backed by strong political interests, terrorise people into submission" (Devidayal, 1998).

Feminists were the most vocal in pointing out the hypocrisy of the religious right's actions. They pointed out that the objectification of women in mainstream Indian cinema was routinely overlooked but that the depiction of women making choices was deemed unacceptable. One writer in *The Hindu* proclaimed,

> If the dignity of Indian womanhood had really concerned the Sena's roughnecks who protested against *Fire,* their attention would have been drawn first to the macho, gender-biased drivel that is often churned out by Bollywood and other Indian commercial cinema centres. However, this would mean taking on considerable business interests and a powerful film establishment. (Sharma, 1998, p. 27)

An editorial in the *Times of India* similarly pointed out that the religious right was not perturbed by the everyday oppression of Indian women; indeed, its members sanctioned it. Feminists asserted that Indian men, and not "alien values," were the implacable predators of women ("Preying on Draupadi," 1998). In these arguments, discourses of nation and belonging are returned to the symbolic realm to articulate a broad definition of identity politics.

Finally, a large proportion of those who supported the film pointed out that the religious right was wrong in presenting homosexuality as a Western phenomenon. They referred to the *Kama Sutra,* and the sculptures and friezes at Khajuraho and Konarak, to validate their claim that same-sex relations had existed in the South Asian subcontinent. These writers tapped into history to present a golden age of sexual tolerance in India, and they attempted to recover a past in which they could secure and fix homosexual identity as indigenous to India. Shah (1993) cautions against this strategy and instead suggests a more self-conscious use of the past to buttress claims and identities in the present: "The project of reclaiming and reconstructing the past is critical for present political and cultural struggles; let us not read too much of us today into the past. We may trap ourselves in the need of a history to sanction our existence" (p. 123). Nevertheless, feminists objected to Mehta's presentation of lesbian sexuality. They pointed out that depicting female same-sex desire as "an option forced by conjugal neglect" reinforces stereotypes (Swami, 1998).

Culture as Artifact

Hall (1996) offers at least two different ways of thinking about cultural identity. One position suggests that cultural identity consists of "one shared culture, a sort of collective 'one true self,' hiding inside the many other, more superficial and artificially imposed 'selves' within people with a shared history and ancestry held in common" (pp. 3-4). Cultural identity is based on a common historical experience. It is expected to remain stable, unchanging, and an essence that can be excavated.

The contested terrain of an authentic culture is the focus of the debates promoted by the two sets of discourses I have outlined here. Many of the concerns are developed precisely because *Fire* was made by a nonresident Indian. In all aspects of its production and reception, *Fire* represents a global film. Its actors and producers hail from different continents, and it is the specificity of Mehta's Western locus of enunciation that has invoked the ire of the religious right.[6] Rather than present a nostalgia for home, Mehta deployed her nonresident Indian status to raise issues that criticize tradition. It is likely that if she had recuperated the heterosexual family, *Fire* would not have drawn such criticism. Such a belief gains credence when we observe the response to *Bombay Boys,* a film that depicts gay male identity and was screened at the same time. Although there was some objection to the gay themes developed in *Bombay Boys,* it did not invoke the same kinds of protests. The different reception prompted by these movies that deal with transgressive subjects points out the anxious modes of regulation that come to bear on the figure of woman. It is not the presence of the queer subject that appears threatening to national identity formation. It is the decentering of the heterosexual family that is contested, not the presence of same-sex relationships. The discourses surrounding *Fire* reaffirm the centrality of woman to the heterosexual family. They effectively render to the margins the social, cultural, and political space available for the articulation of homosexual identity. According to Ratti (1993), the topic of homosexuality always has been rendered invisible in India. The debates surrounding *Fire* may have started with the topic of homosexuality, but they reenact a similar elision. They recenter the heterosexual family in definitions of Indian nationalism.

It is noteworthy that various media outlets devoted so much attention to the debates surrounding *Fire.* The airing of multiple viewpoints suggests that newspapers functioned in this instance as a "zone of public debate." Significantly, however, the discussions presented in media commentaries highlighted aspects of discord and dissonance. A glaring absence is the public response to the film. The majority of viewers expressed neither shock nor horror (Mehra & Menezes, 1998). The Indian viewing public did not recoil from the lesbian sexuality that was portrayed in *Fire.* In fact, when Mehta participated in an online chat room prior to the protests, the overwhelming response that she received was positive ("Deepa Mehta Chat," 1998).

Kishwar (1998) corroborates this point when she asserts that there exists no history of persecution of homosexuals: "In India, homosexuality has usually been treated as one of the many expressions of human sexuality" (p. 5). As editor of *Manushi,* a feminist magazine, she has repeatedly published authors such as Ismat Chugtai who deal with the theme of same-sex desire. "We faced no hostile criticism [or] upset readers. In fact, we received letters of appreciation from both male and female readers," she asserts (p. 6). Although one cannot extrapolate Kishwar's findings to the general population given that her magazine solicits feminist readers, it should not be forgotten that the Indian populace has in other instances also dealt calmly when the topic of homosexuality has been raised. For example, in 1987, two policewomen in the state of Madhya Pradesh got married in a public ceremony. The two women were supported by their respective families, and the national press rallied around their right to exercise sexual-marital choice (Anu & Giti, 1993).

To return to Hall's (1996) dual definition of culture, an alternative view to an authentic culture that can be excavated is one that recognizes the points of similarity, difference, discontinuity, and dispersal within a culture. He points out,

> We cannot speak about one identity, one story without acknowledging the ruptures and discontinuities of the story we tell or re-tell. We cannot speak for very long with any exactness about "one experience, one identity" without acknowledging its other side—differences and discontinuities. . . . Far from being grounded in a mere "recovery" of the past, which is waiting to be found and which, when found, will secure our sense of ourselves into eternity, identities are the names we give to the different ways we are positioned by, and position ourselves within, the narratives of the past. (p. 4)

Both protesters and supporters functioned within a definition of culture that needs to be excavated, whereas the majority response reveals cultural identity as shifting and fluid. The majority of the Indian viewing audience was willing to accept the expression of female same-sex desire as a facet of changing Indian culture.

CONCLUSION

The media commentaries that I outline in this chapter ignored preceding forms of same-sex desire in contemporary India; the zone of public debate that they made available was partial and fragmented. The most striking feature about the debate facilitated by the print media is its reliance on a discourse of compulsory heterosexuality. The unquestioned assumption that in all contexts women would choose heterosexual coupling and marriage is what Rich (1986) defines as compulsory heterosexuality. Although *Fire* addresses the queer subject, a discussion of the status of lesbians in India in the media commentaries is absent; instead, competing discourses try to fix lesbian identity as either native or alien. The character of Sita in the movie asserts that in Hindi "there exists no word to describe us." The social invisibility of gays and lesbians is not addressed in the media commentaries I examined, nor do the debates engage the issue of women's sexual desires. The media discourses instead reproduce the silencing; they emerge from and address a heterosexual perspective of national identity.

But the debates engendered by the screening of *Fire* were productive in mobilizing gays and lesbians. They have created a space in the political and social arena where gays and lesbians may assert their rights and make demands. Months after the furious debates ebbed, lesbian organizations began establishing civil rights campaigns around the country. They have formed coalitions with feminists and leftist organizations to establish the Campaign for Lesbian Rights with the express purpose of repealing sodomy laws (Bacchetta, 1999).

Fire functioned as a "coming out" narrative on other levels as well. The women's movement has had to confront its earlier silence on the issue of gay and lesbian rights. By highlighting the oppressive power of compulsory heterosexuality and patriarchal control over women's lives and female bodies, the debate has reenergized the women's movement. It also has helped to sensitize mainstream organizations to these issues; for example, leftist parties such as the two main Communist parties have had to modulate their assertions that homosexuality is alien to India.

In their presentation of only the radically polarized views of the film, media commentaries also failed to recognize the possibility that the protests represented local resistance to globalization. The arguments over national identity—who is Indian and who is not or which characteristics are Indian and which are not—reveal a crisis. *Fire,* in its authorship and conditions of production, could easily be identified as Western and hence representative of global cultural flows. A range of concerns and anxieties about the social and familial changes that have accompanied recent economic processes were displaced onto *Fire.* These responses are symptomatic of larger geopolitical processes and economic and cultural hangovers of the colonial era that have emerged as "new" sites of contestation in representational practices. The colonial hangover can be seen in two distinct areas: the role ascribed to religion in national identity and the centrality of the female figure in discourses of Indian nationalism.

The majority of the media commentaries presented the protests against *Fire* as a manifestation of the "saffronization" of the secular democratic nation and discussed the role of religion in democracy. The arguments presented by those who opposed and supported the screening of the film lay claim to specific interpretations of Hinduism and Indian-ness. Both sides invented tradition to bolster their claims of authentically representing national culture. Hobsbawm and Ranger (1983) argue that traditions, which appear ancient, are of quite recent origin. They are invented through a set of practices or rituals to inculcate certain values and norms by repetition. In the *Fire* debate, protesters claimed that the depiction of homosexuality affronted Hindus, whereas the film's supporters turned to a definition of Indian tradition that represented tolerance. The symbolic community that each group identified as nation generates a different interpretation of India and Hinduism. Those seeking the screening of the film presented the intolerant attitude of the protesters as being un-Indian, and the Indian identity they foregrounded was one that valued tolerance and assimilation of divergent views. Similarly, during colonial rule, nationalist leaders countered British definitions of primitive Hindus and barbaric Indian traditions by laying claim to a golden age of tolerance. These arguments reveal the religious discourses that underpin the secular democratic project in India and the limits of such a civil society.

The centrality of woman in these arguments underscores the gendered nature of the imaginings of nation. Woman becomes the repository of difference and carries the mark of the authentic India; her body is the terrain where contested definitions of national identity are worked out. The figure of woman is imbricated in the terrain between modernity and tradition, carefully treading their boundary lines. She never can be wholly located in the arena of tradition lest India's image be cast as primitive, nor can she be identified only with the modern lest she become un-Indian. The Indian female has to belong to both realms, carefully apportioning modern ideas with dollops of tradition. The responses to the movie underscore the colonial meanings of respectable sexuality and femininity that continue to shape women's everyday lives. They also highlight the problematic cultural construction of the female body as a gendered being. The discussion reveals that female bodies are assigned cultural meanings that affect the way in which females (heterosexual women, lesbians, and transgendered females) constitute their social relations. My discussion reveals that female sexuality in India continues to be addressed only within the immoral West versus authentic Indian paradigm established during colonialism.

Fire centers on the question of woman's position in an India with a liberalized economy, buffeted by transnational flows. It interrogates the price that women must pay when they transgress the codes of acceptable femininity—their exile from the institution of family. Ironically, the film itself was forced to undergo the test of public moral scrutiny and cultural validity: "It opened the seam lines of legitimate speech by pushing the boundaries of sexual speech and expression in and through the idiom of culture" (Kapur, 1999, p. 54). The responses to the film allow us to unravel the location of female sexuality in discourses of national identity. Opposers and supporters provided different valences to sexuality in articulating Indian identity, culture, and values. They offered normative solutions that reinforce the patriarchal family and simultaneously reference an authentic identity that can be excavated. The debates illustrate how communities are perceived and how public issues are framed.

The different conflicts that I describe in this chapter reveal the anxiety that accompanies the publicity of sex and sexuality. The entrance of the libidinal in the public arena creates the cultural space for a discussion of issues that seem to question tradition and culture. Both groups rely on an uncomplicated and static definition of culture, viewing Indian culture as a museum artifact. Neither position challenges the essentialist narrative of India or Indian identity.

As the debates solicited by *Fire* illustrate, there exists no stable Indian culture or identity that can be tapped. They also reveal the problematic location of the female body in constructions of cultural and national identities. The arguments tellingly point out that identities are constructed within representations. They reiterate the centrality of communication in any study of identity formation. Nevertheless, as this chapter demonstrates, scholarship in intercultural communication must engage with certain key questions about culture. This chapter illustrates that scholarship in international and intercultural communication should ask questions about culture and identity in new ways that recognize the fragmentary and contested nature of these key questions.

NOTES

1. The one exception to this trend was the city of Calcutta, where viewing audiences shouted out the protesters and forced them to leave cinema halls. In referring to Indian cities, I have used older, more familiar names rather than the revised names, such as Kolkata, that might be unfamiliar to readers in the United States.

2. The *religious right* and the *Hindu right* are umbrella terms that encompass groups that are committed to the creation of a Hindu state in India. This includes the Bharatiya Janata Party (BJP, the ruling political party), the Rashtriya Swayam Sevak (the group that provides the ideological component of the Hindu movement), and the Vishwa Hindu Parishad (which has a large base outside the subcontinent among populations of Indian origin in the diaspora). These are the primary exponents of the Hindu religious doctrine.

3. The BJP, like the Shiv Sena, espouses a Hindu-centered politics. Over the past 15 years, it has evolved from a regional political party into a national one. This change in stature has been accompanied by a rhetorical shift; the BJP has toned down the Hindu overtones of its platform. BJP members now seek to present themselves as "moderate" even as they continue to portray the 80% Hindu population of India as a beleaguered group under assault from religious minorities.

4. Kumar (2000) believes that the West is the ideal viewer of the film, and this explains some of its stereotypical depictions of women and India.

5. In Hindu mythology, Radha is a sexually desiring woman who abandons her marriage to pursue her lover, Krishna. Sita, on the other hand, is the chaste and submissive wife. The movie's characterization of the two protagonists reverses these narratives.

6. In Canada and the United States, the film has similarly defied easy labeling and national identification. In Canada, Mehta could not obtain public funds for her production because she is of Indian origin, yet the Toronto International Film Festival recognized it as a Canadian film. In the West, *Fire* has been characterized as too Western and not Indian enough, especially because the dialogue is in English.

REFERENCES

Ansari, R. (1998, November 24). Indian film with lesbian scene approved by censors. *Interpress Service* [Online]. Available: www.himalmag.com/98Nov/deepa.htm

Anu & Giti. (1993). Inventing tradition: The marriage of Lila and Urmila. In R. Ratti (Ed.), *A lotus of another color: An unfolding of the South Asian gay and lesbian experience* (pp. 81-84). Boston: Allyson.

Arora, P. (1994). The production of Third World subjects for First World consumption: *Salaam Bombay* and *Parama.* In D. Carson, L. Dittmar, & J. R. Welsch (Eds.), *Multiple voices in feminist film criticism* (pp. 293-304). Minneapolis: University of Minnesota Press.

Bacchetta, P. (1999, April). New campaign for lesbian rights in India. *Off Our Backs,* p. 6.

Barnouw, E., & Krishnaswamy, S. (1980). *Indian film* (2nd ed.). New York: Oxford University Press.

Berak, B. (1998, December 12). A lesbian idyll and movie theaters surrender. *New York Times,* p. A4.

Bhaskaran, G. (1998, December 20). *Fire* explores women's dilemma in modern world. *The Hindu,* p. 10.

Blackwood, E., & Wieringa, S. (1999). Introduction. In E. Blackwood & S. Wieringa (Eds.), *Female desires: Same-sex relations and transgender practices across cultures* (pp. 1-38). New York: Columbia University Press.

Bose, B. (1997). Transgressions: Female desire and postcolonial identity in contemporary Indian women's cinema. In B. Ghosh & B. Bose (Eds.), *Interventions: Feminist dialogues in Third World women's literature and film* (pp. 119-133). New York: Garland.

Chatterjee, P. (1993). *Nationalist thought and the colonial world: A derivative discourse.* Minneapolis: University of Minnesota Press.

Clifford, J. (1994). Diasporas. *Cultural Anthropology, 9,* 302-338.

Das Gupta, C. (1983). The "new cinema": A wave or a future? In A. Vasudev & P. Lenglet (Eds.), *Indian cinema superbazaar* (pp. 33-42). New Delhi, India: Vikas.

Dayal, J. (1983). The role of government: Story of an uneasy truce. In A. Vasudev & P. Lenglet (Eds.), *Indian cinema superbazaar* (pp. 87-92). New Delhi, India: Vikas.

Deepa Mehta chat. (1998). *Rediff India.* [Online]. Available: www.rediff.com/chat/firechat.com

Devidayal, N. (1998, December 28). Poster brigade draws unusual volunteers. *Times of India.* [Online]. Available: www.timesofindia.com/199812/28fp3.htm

Fire generates heat in Rajya Sabha. (1998, December 5). *Deccan Herald* [Online]. Available: www.fire.com/dhdec5th.html

Furor over Sena member's remarks on Dilip Kumar. (1998, December 15). *The Hindu,* p. 15.

Gupta, A., & Ferguson, J. (1997). Beyond "culture": Space, identity, and the politics of difference. In A. Gupta & J. Ferguson (Eds.), *Culture, power, place: Explorations in critical anthropology* (pp. 33-51). Durham, NC: Duke University Press.

Haidar, S. (1998). Deepa Mehta defends her film. *Rediff India* [Online]. Available: www.rediff.com/entertai/1998/dec/10fire.htm

Hall, S. (1992). The question of cultural identity. In S. Hall, D. Held, & T. McGrew (Eds.), *Modernity and its futures* (pp. 273-326). Cambridge, UK: Polity.

Hall, S. (1996). Who needs "identity"? In S. Hall & P. du Gay (Eds.), *Questions of cultural identity* (pp. 1-17). Thousand Oaks, CA: Sage.

Hegde, R. (1998). A view from elsewhere: Locating difference and the politics of representation from a transnational feminist perspective. *Communication Theory, 3,* 271-298.

Hobsbawm, E., & Ranger, T. (Eds.). (1983). *The invention of tradition.* Cambridge, UK: Cambridge University Press.

Jain, M., & Raval, S. (1998, December). Ire over *Fire. India Today* [Online]. Available: www.india-today.com/itoday/19981219/petrol.html

Kakar, S. (1983). The cinema as collective fantasy. In A. Vasudev & P. Lenglet (Eds.), *Indian cinema superbazaar* (pp. 78-86). New Delhi, India: Vikas.

Kapur, R. (1998, December 13). *Fire* goes up in smoke. *The Hindu,* p. 26.

Kapur, R. (1999). Too hot to handle: The cultural politics of *Fire. Feminist Review, 64,* 53-64.

Kishwar, M. (1998, November-December). Naïve outpourings of a self-hating Indian. *Manushi, 109,* 3-13.

Kumar, A. (2000). *Passport photos.* Berkeley: University of California Press.

Lak, D. (1998, November 13). Lesbian film sets India on fire. *BBC Online* [Online]. Available: news.bbc.co.uk/hi/english/world/south_asia/newsid_213000/213417.stm

Line of fire. (1998, December 5). *Times of India* [Online]. Available: www.timesofindia.com/199812/5edit.html

Mani, L. (1989). Contentious traditions: The debate on *sati* in colonial India. In K. Sangari & S. Vaid (Eds.), *Recasting women: Essays in Indian colonial history* (pp. 88-126). New Delhi, India: Kali.

Mehra, S., & Menezes, S. (1998, December 28). Shiv Sainiks go on a rampage in Bombay and Delhi cinema halls. *Outlook Online* [Online]. Available: www.outlookindia.com/19981228/fire.htm

Melwani, L. (1996, November). Trial by Fire. *Little India* [Online]. Available: 206.20.14.67/achal/archive/Nov96/trial.htm

Mercer, K. (1990). Welcome to the jungle. In J. Rutherford (Ed.), *Identity* (pp. 38-54). London: Lawrence & Wishart.

Nair, J. (1996, October 17). Bachchan and the battle for Bangalore. *The Hindu,* p. 12.

Nambiar, H. (1998, December 5). *Fire* put out after igniting Sena passions. *The Telegraph* [Online]. Available: www.telegraphindia.com/archive1001205/front_pa.htm

Nandy, A. (1998). *The secret politics of our desires: Innocence, culpability, and Indian popular cinema.* New Delhi, India: Oxford University Press.

Ninan, S. (1998a, December 20). Neena vs. Shabana. *The Hindu,* p. 27.

Ninan, S. (1998b, December 13). Newshounds or citizens? *The Hindu,* p. 27.

Parameswaran, U. (1999, Spring). Disjunction of sensibility? *Toronto Review,* pp. 99-106.

Prasad, M. M. (1998). *Ideology of the Hindi film: A historical construction.* New Delhi, India: Oxford University Press.

Preying on Draupadi. (1998, December 13). *Times of India* [Online]. Available: www.timesofindia.com/199812/13edit4.htm

Primitive response. (1998, December 6). *Deccan Herald* [Online]. Available: www.firemovie.com/dhdec6th.html

Ramesh, K. K. (1999, January 17). Under *Fire. The Hindu,* p. 29.

Ratti, R. (1993). Introduction. In R. Ratti (Ed.), *A lotus of another color: An unfolding of the South Asian gay and lesbian experience* (pp. 11-17). Boston: Allyson.

Raval, S. (1998, December). I added petrol. *India Today.* [Online]. Available: www.india-today.com/itoday/19981219/petrol.html

Rich, A. (1986). *Blood, bread, and poetry.* New York: Norton.

Rushdie, S. (1991). *Imaginary homelands.* London: Granta.

Saksena, R., & Thomas, K. S. (1998, May 17). Cleansing culture. *The Week* [Online]. Available: www.the-week.com/98may17/cleanse.htm

Sangari, K., & Vaid, S. (1989). Recasting women. In K. Sangari & S. Vaid (Eds.), *Recasting women: Essays in colonial history* (pp. 1-26). New Delhi, India: Kali.

Sena fanning the flames of hatred. (1998, December 13). *The Hindu,* p. 11.

Shah, N. (1993). Sexuality, identity, and the uses of history. In R. Ratti (Ed.), *A lotus of another color: An unfolding of the South Asian gay and lesbian experience* (pp. 113-132). Boston: Allyson.

Sharma, K. (1998, December 20). Fighting the moral police. *The Hindu,* p. 27.

Shome, R. (1998). Caught in the term "post-colonial": Why the "post-colonial" still matters. *Critical Studies in Mass Communication, 15,* 203-212.

Sidhwa, B. (1997, November-December). Playing with *Fire. Ms.,* pp. 76-78.

Somaaya, B. (1999, January 15). Symbol of the changing heroine. *The Hindu,* p. 25.

Swami, P. (1998, December). Furor over film. *Frontline* [Online]. Available: www.frontlineonline.com/fl1526/15260430.htm

Tharpar, V. (1998, December 6). *Fire* scripts Delhi's tryst with "social terrorism." *Hindustan Times* [Online]. Available: 64.225.143.242/nonfram/061298/detFR007.htm

Thomas, R. (1989). Sanctity and scandal: The mythologization of *Mother India. Quarterly Review of Film and Video, 11*(3), 11-30.

Vasudev, A. (1983). The woman: Vamp or victim. In A. Vasudev & P. Lenglet (Eds.), *Indian cinema superbazaar* (pp. 97-104). New Delhi, India: Vikas.

Vijapurkar, M. (1998, December 14). Thackeray's terms for screening of *Fire. The Hindu,* p. 13.

Vijapurkar, M. (1999, January 5). Poster campaign against intolerance. *The Hindu,* p. 13.

We'll resume stir if *Fire* is shown. (1998, December 5). *Indian Express,* p. 11.

7

Targeting the Latino Vote in 2000

Part I: The Construction of Latinos and Latino Issues

MARYANNE SCHIFFMAN • *University of California, Santa Cruz*
FEDERICO A. SUBERVI-VÉLEZ • *University of Texas at Austin*

> I hope we have put to rest this notion of Latinos as the "sleeping giant." . . . We are very much awake.
>
> —Guillermo Rodríguez (quoted in Goodno, 1998, p. 4)

> We have been sort of like a stealth bomber that has gone undetected and has now exploded onto the political scene.
>
> —Juan Andrade (quoted in Meserve & Woodruff, 1999, p. 6)

> What we are seeing is the *salsafication* . . . of American politics. . . . The "Latinization" of American politics, as well as American culture, is under way.
>
> —William Schneider (quoted in Crowley, Schneider, & Meserve, 1999, p. 2)

Whether the "sleeping giant" was ever really asleep is subject to inconclusive debate.[1] What is certain, however, is that sometime during the past few years, the giant got up and began to *mambo, tango,* and *salsa* its way across the U.S. political dance floor. Coast to coast, as numbers of U.S. Latinos grow faster than those of any other ethnic group, Latinos are transforming the country through their food, music, language, and (most recently) growing political participation. As the power of this Latino[2] population becomes increasingly apparent, political parties and the mass media are beginning to sit up and take notice. It is this budding relationship between the media and the U.S. Latino population that is the focus of this chapter.

Although in some respects a media "brownout" continues (Carveth & Alverio, 1996, 1997, 1998, 1999, 2000), and as such, Latinos remain virtually absent from U.S. media in proportion to their representation in the general population, signs of an increasing visibility of Latinos and "things Hispanic" were apparent in 1999. It was during the first half of that year, for example, that *Time, Newsweek,* and *People* magazines ran cover stories on top box office stars Jennifer Lopez and Ricky Martin. At the same time in Hollywood, one litmus test for music video jockey chic was pronunciation of phrases such as *La Vida Loca.* Nor should we consider it any small detail that in 1999, "Dinky," the Taco Bell Chihuahua, made the taco more popular than the hamburger and earned millions of dollars taping the fast-food restaurant's television commercials *in Spanish.*

More important in 1999, the media paid attention to people who were paying attention to Hispanics. For example, in California, site of the anti-immigrant Proposition 187, the media reported that Republican presidential candidate George W. Bush was peppering his stump speeches with phrases such as "Legal immigrants should have the same rights as everybody else" and "Every child ought to be educated, regardless of the status of their parents" (quoted in Crowley & Shaw, 1999, p. 2). Meanwhile, CNN anchor Bernard Shaw was heard posing the following question to his guest, columnist María Teresa Arce of the Spanish-language newspaper *El Diario-La Prensa:* "The line on Bush [is that] his accent is good, and he speaks the language more naturally than Gore . . . , [whereas] Spanish speakers say that Gore is grammatically correct but that his accent and delivery are stilted. . . . What do you think of their [Spanish]?" (Shaw, 1999, p. 2).[3]

Latino fairy tales? Political science fiction? *Al contrario.* Whereas 10 years ago these scenes might have been unthinkable, today they are part and parcel of a new American political landscape. As the United States crosses the threshold of the new millennium, we are witnessing the emergence of a nation less culturally monolithic than ever before. And as we enter this new era, it is Latinos more than any other social group who are putting the flexibility and fortitude of this nation's pluralistic democracy to the test. The study described in this chapter argues that one of the many repercussions of these demographic and political changes is the challenge they have created for media reporting on Latinos and political issues. The findings of this study suggest that the subsequent result of these difficulties has been the presentation of overgeneralizations and contradictory images of Latino voters and citizens.

Therefore, this chapter aims to describe and assess, through an interpretive perspective, media discussions of the emergent participation and influence of Latino voters in U.S. political processes. To this end, the study presents an exploratory analysis of media portrayals of "the Latino/Hispanic vote" and its anticipated influence on the year 2000 elections. It should be noted that the focus of this study is on the *media* and how they have identified and portrayed Latinos rather than on how Latinos identify and portray themselves. The latter subject is an important one and, admittedly, a topic with significant implications for understanding media comprehension of this political constituency. The specific goal of this study, however, is solely to examine media presentation of the Latino vote and to identify the patterns that emerged in the construction of Latinos/Hispanics as a cultural group and Latino/Hispanic issues during preelection campaign coverage.

Therefore, this study focuses on the character of media portrayals of the Latino vote during the first 8 months of 1999. Specifically, we analyze how the media constructed, through journalists and their political perspectives and through the voices of the politicians, civic leaders, and academics cited in the articles, the portrait of Latinos and Latino political power that was presented to readers and listeners. What concerns us is the substance of and contradictions within the information presented by the media about the Latino vote. We also examine the possible reasons why these contradictions emerged and the possible impacts of these discrepancies on media reporting.

Rationale

After surveying 8 months of reporting on the Latino vote, two key patterns emerged in presentations of the story. The first is the attempt to answer the question "Who are the Latinos?" The second demonstrates efforts to answer the question "What are Latino issues?" These questions, and the media's answers to them, formed the basis of media portrayals to the public of the Latino vote. In addition, these characterizations of Latinos and their concerns provided the foundation on which subsequent discussions of Latino political matters were constructed. These assessments are noteworthy because they inform and become the basis for community organizing tactics, political campaign strategies, and media outreach efforts of political candidates and parties seeking the Latino vote. For these reasons, this study focuses on the media's presentation of these two central issues.

The increasing importance of Latinos in the realm of political communication has been pointed out by political analysts such as William Schneider, who stated in a CNN interview that "the 'Latinization' of American politics, as well as American culture, is under way" (quoted in Crowley, Schneider, & Meserve, 1999, p. 2). The attention that candidates paid to Latino constituencies in 1999 and the flurry of media coverage surrounding this group at such an early stage in the campaign suggest that Schneider's claim is true; the importance of the Latino vote has grown beyond the arena of local electoral politics and is now part of a national political discourse.

What is less clear, however, is how the candidates and the media recognize and address the complexities of this growing Latino electorate. In the lengthy prelude to the 2000 elections, thousands of words were written about the expected influence of Latino voters. Yet, as is illustrated in this study, much of the media's coverage was built on simplistic discussions of Latino voter numbers and references to a homogeneous "Latino/Hispanic voter." As a result, this constituency rarely was discussed in terms of the political divisions that often fragment it by economic class, educational level, and issues of ethnic and regional identity. It is our intention to scrutinize media coverage of the Latino vote so as to document these varied presentations of the Latino voter and to examine, in future studies, whether these constructions remain stagnant or evolved. Scholars seeking to assess potential media effects may find that our analysis reveals important frameworks related to political mobilization of this ethnic group. For example, research building on media agenda-setting theories (McCombs & Shaw, 1972; McCombs, Shaw, & Weaver, 1997) may refer to this study to better understand the construction of Latino issues and how the presentation of these issues may play some role in Latino voting patterns.[4]

Media Coverage of the Hispanic Vote

Latinos have a long history of participation in U.S. electoral politics. But although Latino voter participation in various elections has received increasing academic attention, it was not until the 1996 presidential campaign that the U.S. public began to hear references to the Hispanic vote on major television networks.

Building on personal interviews and the works of historians, Santillan and Subervi-Vélez (1991) assessed the role of Hispanic elected officials and Latino political involvement in New Mexico and Colorado as far back as the 1860s. In addition, the intricacies of Latino political participation and activism since this time have been well documented by many other authors.[5] Although Latino perspectives on political communication were not the central focus in any of these earlier works, the subject has received attention since the mid-1980s in the research of Santillan and Subervi-Vélez and others.[6]

What emerges from these academic studies is a complex picture of Latino political activities and perspectives on political issues. At times, Latinos have made significant gains in political arenas and agendas, but these have occurred mostly at local levels. Only recently has it been possible to speak of a Latino vote in terms of national politics and presidential elections (de la Garza & DeSipio, 1999). As de la Garza and DeSipio (1999) demonstrate, the 1988, 1992, and 1996 elections provide evidence of the growth and maturity of Latino involvement in U.S. politics.

Nonetheless, in the aftermath of the 1996 presidential election, many analysts were quick to declare that the Latino vote had not packed the political punch that many had promised. Citing Latino voter registration rates disproportionately low for Latino presence in the general population, de la Garza and DeSipio (1999) speculated that the Latino vote would not develop into a decisive political force. These authors went on to describe Latinos as "awash in the mainstream," stating that "some have had more opportunities, but the majority have been informally excluded from political engagement" (p. 3). They further stated that "when the [last] election was over, it became evident that the expectations for a newly important role for Latino electorates were not met; the Latino voice in the presidential election was muted" (p. 4).

Just 2 short years later, however, the alleged phantom Hispanic vote materialized in 1998 as a nightmare for California Republicans as they were swept from power by a massive Latino turnout throughout the state (Van Slambrouck, 1998). During this same electoral period, Latino votes also proved decisive in elections in Texas and made notable inroads in other regions of the country (Garcia, 1998).

Political communication studies by Subervi-Vélez and others cited earlier found that these events, in turn, have proven to be influential for Democratic and Republican party outreach efforts. Providing evidence from past presidential campaigns, these studies demonstrate considerable contrast between the two parties in their strategies for attracting the Latino vote. In general, Republican party communication efforts aimed at Latino voters have been better funded and often more organized and more sophisticated in style than have those of the Democratic party, which has put less effort into research and development of political advertisements or free media.[7] Democratic National Committee operatives have pointed to a shortage of financial resources as a major hurdle in launching large-scale paid media campaigns directed at Latinos and in the past have indicated the lack of need for such campaigns due to the perception that most Latinos vote for their candidates anyway. As Subervi-Vélez and Connaughton (1999) document, the one major exception to this pattern emerged in the 1996 presidential campaign when budgets and human resources for Latino communication outreach efforts were multiplied exponentially. Afterward, Bill Clinton's reelection with the solid support among most Latinos, including an unprecedented number of votes from Cubans, was noted by people from all sides of the political spectrum and thus set a tone for the 2000 presidential contest.

It is in these contexts that the political clout of Latinos and their votes reemerged as issues in the 2000 elections. Converging with the increasing popularity of Latin music and Latino celebrities, the media soon began to focus their attention on this cultural group and its increasing impact on larger U.S. culture and politics. The object of analysis for this research endeavor is the nature and consequences of this coverage of Latinos and politics in the United States.

METHODOLOGY

The time frame of this study encompasses the early phase of the 2000 presidential campaign, spanning the period beginning January 1, 1999, and ending with the weekend following the Iowa straw polls of August 14, 1999. It should be recalled that during this period, candidates investigated the feasibility of their runs for the presidency, declared their candidacies, and conducted initial fund-raising endeavors. It also was within this period that several national Hispanic organizations, such as the National Council of La Raza (NCLR), the League of United Latin American Citizens (LULAC), and the National Association of Latino Elected and Appointed Officials (NALEO), held their conventions and invited presidential candidates to address them.

It is noteworthy to mention that candidate presence at or absence from these events generated even more media discussions of Latino vote issues. In the end, it was Senator John McCain, Vice President Al Gore, and Bill Bradley who attended many Latino organization conventions, whereas Governor Bush declined to attend even the most important of those (i.e., the NCLR, NALEO, and LULAC gatherings). In early July, additional press was generated by the Unity '99 Journalists of Color convention in Seattle, Washington, when Gore and McCain accepted invitations but Bush, who already was scheduled to be in Seattle at the time, declined to formally attend. Instead, Bush opted for an impromptu photo opportunity session and a 15-minute walk-through of the convention, where he refused to answer journalists' questions (Olivo, 1999b).[8]

To survey the extensive coverage of the Latino vote, we employed the Lexis/Nexis search engine to examine print, visual, and audio media sources with both local and national distribution. Using the study range dates of January 1, 1999, to August 15, 1999, we scanned each database twice, once for the key words "Latino" and "vote" and then again for "Hispanic" and "vote." For newspapers, the following databases were searched: under General News, the archives for "major newspapers"; under U.S. News, the archives for "western regional," "midwest regional," "northeast regional," and "southeast regional." In total, these searches scanned 262 different U.S. English-language newspapers. In addition, we searched the Magazine archives under "general news," which scanned 304 periodical databases. Under Television and Radio News Broadcasts, we searched the individual archives of CNN and National Public Radio.

Altogether, these searches yielded 232 distinct newspaper articles, 9 distinct magazine articles, and 9 distinct audio transcripts. We then briefly skimmed over these articles to determine whether or not they discussed the Latino vote or whether both of the search terms merely showed up in the text coincidentally. Those with only fleeting reference to Latinos or Hispanics and a voting matter were eliminated. (For example, many of the eliminated articles were related to school board elections in school districts with large Hispanic populations. For our selection process, if the articles did not relate the discussions to larger voting issues, then they were excluded from the study.) The articles that did focus on the Latino vote were then selected for analysis. This selection process resulted in a total of 141 newspaper articles, 9 audio transcripts, and 9 magazine articles for the study. The articles were then thoroughly read, after which we discussed the general themes and patterns that had emerged. The articles were then reread and coded for incidence of these themes to create a quantitative analysis as well as a qualitative one.

It should be noted that in relying on searchable Internet databases, this study was not able to incorporate Spanish-language news sources, few of which were online at the time of the study. Although we suspect that there might be significant differences between Spanish- and English-language media, the small number of Spanish-language sources available online would not have provided a balanced comparison to the hundreds of newspapers and magazines that were searchable in English. In addition, it is questionable whether such a small number of sources would have produced a representative sample of the larger Spanish-language media. For these reasons, Spanish-language coverage of the campaign will be addressed in a later study when more Spanish-language news sources can be accessed electronically or through standard archives.

INITIAL FINDINGS

The findings of this study are divided into two parts. The first presents media constructions of "Who are the Latinos?" The second discusses media constructions of "What are Latino issues?" In each, we examine the rationale presented for these images, the patterns encountered, and the consequences of these often contradictory media portraits of Latinos.

The Construction of "Who Are the Latinos?"

One of the biggest challenges for assessing media coverage of the Latino vote in the 2000 elections was winding our way through the maze of broad and often conflicting portrayals of the Latino voter. For example, James Goodno, writing for *In These Times,* stated that "the Latino vote is a significant vote, it's a working class vote, and it's a strong progressive vote" (Goodno, 1998, p. 8). Yet, John Leo reported in *U.S. News and World Report* that "immigrants from Latin America [are] the most socially conservative and family-oriented people in America—a natural Republican constituency" (Leo, 1998, p. 16).[9]

News reports published during this period not only made contradictory generalizations about Latino political affiliations but also clashed in their portrayals of who Latinos are in their private lives. We found that Latinos were presented as conservative, religious, family oriented, and frugal while—at the same time—they also were depicted as socially liberal, open-minded big spenders. In the end, we identified six themes that appeared consistently in media presentations of the Latino voter: Latinos speak Spanish, Latinos are conservative and a Republican constituency, Latinos are liberal and a Democratic constituency, Latinos are underprivileged and poor, Latinos are a powerful economic force, and Latinos have "culture." The following sections present examples of how these generalizations were constructed and presented.

Latinos Speak Spanish

According to CNN correspondent Jeanne Meserve, "If politics has its own language, it might be Spanish." Meserve made this observation in a CNN report on the Latino vote in which she described how Congressman Nicholas Lampson, a Texas Democrat, "communes with his computer everyday to conquer everything from 'hola' to 'adiós.' " From Meserve's perspective, "He's hoping to connect with a vital constituency[:] Spanish-speaking voters" (Meserve & Woodruff, 1999, p. 6).

Spanish was by far the most popular subject in media discussions of the Latino vote. Nearly half (46%) of the articles reviewed stated either that a candidate had spoken Spanish or was able to speak Spanish or that a campaign had issued election materials in Spanish for Latino voters to access. The degree of attention given to language seems to indicate an assumption on the part of journalists (and politicians) that most Latinos speak Spanish. Furthermore, one wonders whether it might even reflect an implicit belief that Latinos speak Spanish *only.* Just how accurate are these attitudes about Latinos and language, and just how important is speaking Spanish to winning Latino votes?

One perspective for the purposes of answering these questions comes from survey data gathered on Latino television viewers by the Tomás Rivera Policy Institute (1999). According to results of that study, 95% of Latinos interviewed said that they receive their political information from television and/or radio. In addition, 62% indicated that they listen to this information in English, whereas only 32% answered that they listen in Spanish. Further questioning revealed that 53% of U.S.-born Hispanic television viewers speak English primarily or exclusively, indicating a predominance of English-language skills among this segment of the voter-eligible Hispanic population. In addition, 60% of foreign-born Hispanics indicated that they speak English and Spanish equally well, suggesting that naturalized citizen voters would have an English-language propensity as well. The study also found that among English-limited study participants, only 11% of native-born Hispanics and 29% of foreign-born Hispanics speak Spanish primarily or exclusively. Based on the data at hand, we can argue that it would not be *necessary* for politicians to speak Spanish to access U.S. voters who are Latinos.[10] The issue then becomes a matter of strategy. Do Latino voters *prefer* a candidate who can speak Spanish? Is this true even if the voters themselves do not speak Spanish?

Despite these statistics and these as yet unanswered questions, fully 88% of the articles surveyed not only discussed a candidate's or a campaign's use of Spanish but also stated or implied that this strategy would help the candidate to win votes. Only 5% of these articles asked how many U.S. Latinos actually do speak Spanish or how a candidate's use of Spanish could influence Latino voters. Among these was a *San Francisco Chronicle* article by Carla Marinucci noting that whereas California Hispanic communities receive new Spanish-speaking immigrants every year, presumably keeping the language alive in many areas of California, in Texas "three quarters of Hispanic voters were born in the U.S. and have third- or fourth-generation American roots" (Marinucci, 1999, p. A7). The clear suggestion here is that in regions of the United States where Hispanics have deep roots and see lower rates of immigration, smaller percentages of Latinos will be found to speak Spanish. Census data from 1990 support this assertion, showing that among the population age 5 years or over who identified themselves as Hispanic in Texas, only 24% said that they did not speak English well or very well, whereas for the same population cohort in California, 44% said that they did not speak English well or very well (U.S. Bureau of the Census, 1990).

Other articles that debated the importance of language were more critical. An editorial in *The Weekly Standard* (Mujica, 1999) accused candidates of political pandering. Tim Chavez, a syndicated columnist who writes for the Nashville *Tennessean,* pondered the irony of Gore speaking Spanish to crowds in rural Tennessee. He observed that normally when Spanish is spoken in the area, "local folks yell at [speakers] to 'learn English before coming over here!' " (Chavez, 1999b, p. B9). Chavez went further to warn candidates against underestimating Latino voters, advising that they are "smart enough to realize that candidates can make promises they won't keep in any language." He also cautioned against the danger "for all voters of whatever ethnicity . . . that the candidates won't know when to stop with their new campaign gimmick . . . and will only turn this campaign silly and of less substance than previous ones" (p. B9).

Latinos Are Conservative and a Republican Constituency

Following closely behind the generalization that Latinos speak Spanish, the second most popular stereotype encountered in media reports was that Latinos are Catholic and that, as Catholics, they are social conservatives. *The Economist,* for example, reported without question the assertion by California Republican political adviser Mike Madrid that Latinos are "natural supporters of his party's 'family values' agenda, a support that is grounded in [their] Roman Catholicism" ("Enter the Garcias' Own Party," 1998, p. 21). This statement also illustrates the most frequent political generalization made in media reports during the period—that Catholicism is one and the same with conservatism. For example, during a broadcast of CNN's *Inside Politics,* anchor Judy Woodruff did not question the following statement made by former California Republican Representative Robert Dornan:

> Most Latinos are Roman Catholics. . . . [They are focused on] religious values, on the hard work ethic, on the love of the community, and on their battle cry that family, *familia,* is everything. . . . [Republicans] can overcome this siren song that the Democrats [sing to] them: "Betray your Catholic faith. Vote for abortion. Forget about pornography and family values." (quoted in Meserve & Woodruff, 1999, p. 4)

Recent California election results, however, suggest that it might be quite a while before Latinos will be swooning to any Republican serenades either. In fact, Latino rejection of California's Republican party during the late 1990s was consistent and *resounding.* In 1998 statewide midterm elections, as well as in state races accompanying the February 2000 primary elections, Latinos voted for Democrats over Republicans at a rate of six to one.[11] If Hispanics are Catholic, and if Catholics are conservative, then why do Republicans in California continue to get the cold shoulder from the state's "conservative" Latinos?

One factor that must be taken into consideration is the persistent anti-immigrant image that continues to plague California Republicans. The Republican image is so negative in California, in fact, that according to party organizer Bob Larkin, the Republican party is commonly seen as "anti-women, anti-minority, anti-gay, anti-just about everything but white males" (quoted in Meserve & Woodruff, 1999, p. 5). Republicans have found it difficult to transform this identity into a more inclusive one, and analysts agree that this has continued to cost them elections in a state where no one ethnic or racial group comprises a majority any longer. If assumptions about Latinos, Catholicism, and conservatism were true, however, then one would think that a kindred conservatism could have overcome at least some of the anti-Republican sentiment in California. How accurate, then, are these assumptions about Latinos?

First, although a majority of Hispanics do identify themselves as Catholic, survey data indicate that this figure hovers at only around 66% rather than the nearly 100% that is implied by media generalizations.[12] Second, the association by politicians and the media of Catholicism with social conservativism is misinformed. As O'Brien (1999) points out, "In the United States, there is an identifiable public Catholicism of [not only] the right [but also] the center and the left" (p. 257). Furthermore, he adds, "There are Catholics . . . whose politics in practice [is] 'left' but whose theology and ecclesiastical opinions are often quite conservative. In the same way, political conservatives might be rather progressive in their views on the governance of the Church" (p. 257).

In addition, the character of U.S. Catholicism is further complicated by its continual metamorphosis as an immigrant church. McGreevy (1999) discusses how immigrant parishioners bring to the church their views of "public Catholicism" and doctrinal perspectives that often conflict with current church practices and policies. According to McGreevy, although Irish, German, and Italian immigrants also reformulated the character of the American Catholic Church during the past century, "the situation with Mexican American Catholics presents the sharpest break [yet] with American Catholic history" (p. 199). McGreevy notes that "Mexican Catholicism has been closer to that of Italian Catholicism, with its anti-clerical heritage, a nationalism often juxtaposed against the church, . . . and a religious belief in both cultures [that] has (at times) depended only indirectly on the efforts of the 'institutional' church" (p. 200).[13] In addition, as many authors point out, Latin American Catholics have been profoundly influenced by the more left-leaning liberation theology (e.g., McGreevy, 1999; Matovina, 1999; O'Brien, 1999; Riebe-Estrella, 1999). And the Catholic Church's relationship with Chicanos has been influenced by its pro-union support of Cesar Chávez and the struggle of the United Farm Workers.[14]

Anthony York, writing for the *California Journal,* captured the complexity of American and Latino American Catholicism in his interview with David Hayes-Bautista, professor of public health at the University of California, Los Angeles, School of Public Policy. As Hayes-Bautista explained, "Latino Catholicism is . . . an entirely different kettle of fish. It's a very individual kind of Catholicism" (quoted in York, 1999, p. 4). He added, "Culturally, [Latinos] . . . may be kind of conservative, but [they are] conservative in private, . . . generally . . . very live-and-let-live" (p. 4).

Clearly, the claim that Latinos and their Catholicism are a "natural" conservative constituency is a misinterpretation of data and an oversimplification of what are very complex personal and political identities.

Latinos Are Liberal and a Democratic Constituency

The next most popular media characterization of Latinos was as a solidly working class and Democratic constituency. For example, during a broadcast of CNN's *Inside Politics,* Meserve asserted, "[Al]though Cuban Americans have historically voted Republican, the rest of the Hispanic vote has been reliably Democratic" (Meserve & Woodruff, 1999, p. 6). In a similar manner, Chavez (1999a) commented that although political pundits might have been impressed by Republican presidential candidate Bush's

> know[ing] his way around a tamale, . . . Hispanic voters are not that easily bamboozled. Their issues, particularly for this nation's Mexican Americans, are . . . closely tied to the Democratic party's agenda that makes fair and increased compensation in the workplace its chief calling card. (p. H3)

Of the few in the media that ventured to probe this apparent contradiction, the *California Journal* was one of those that engaged in a more in-depth discussion of the issue. York (1999) again deferred to the insights of Hayes-Bautista, who stated, "[Latinos] don't fall into the nifty liberal/conservative paradigm. We are very issue-driven voters and don't identify strongly with any political party. . . . I [even] start asking myself if 'Latinos' really exist because we generally don't agree on anything" (p. 4).

Latinos Are Underprivileged and Poor

This generalization was consistent in media coverage. The following exchange from CNN's *Inside Politics* illustrates the way in which this portrayal typically was constructed:

> **Jeanne Meserve,** CNN: The Hispanic community wants more than a nod [to] its culture and language. It wants attention to its problems.
>
> **Raul Yzaguirre,** president, NCLR: [Yes.] We are the most impoverished in this country. We have the lowest education rate. We spend less on Hispanic kids than we spend on other kids. We have more civil rights issues. (Meserve & Woodruff, 1999, p. 6)

As was common with the majority of media, the *Los Angeles Times* developed this theme through the discussion of statistical data. In the following example, Olivo (1999a) cited a report from the William C. Velázquez Institute detailing the status of California Latinos: "In every category, the report finds [that] Latinos lag behind other groups, with higher dropout rates, lower homeowner percentages, poorer access to health care, and greater unemployment" (p. B1).[15] Chavez (1999a) also linked Latino voting preferences (and party affiliations) to economic indicators:

> [Mexican Americans'] household budgets are not conducive to the exclusionary GOP [Republican] platform and the party's record of opposing minimum wage hikes. Even if Republicans nominated Speedy Gonzalez to run with Bush, most Mexican Americans still would [find it] difficult to [become] elephant lovers. (p. H3)

Latinos Are a Powerful Economic Force

In complete contradiction to the previous characterization of Latinos, this popular portrayal of Latinos as "the hot new market" got almost as much media play. *The Economist,* for example, reported that more than half of the households of American-born Latinos and about one third of those of foreign-born Latinos are middle class. That publication also noted that one third of Latinos now live in the suburbs and that the most common surname of new home buyers in Los Angeles County during the 1990s was Garcia ("Enter the Garcias' Own Party," 1998, p. 21). Likewise, a recent report on the influence of Latino youths in the American marketplace (Stapinski, 1999) revealed that marketers are salivating over research findings showing that Hispanic girls spend 60% more on personal purchases than do all other female teens and that, since 1990, projected Hispanic buying power has increased by 67% to $365 billion.

The economic power of Latinos was discussed by media sources not only in terms of consumer influence but also in terms of its political influence. In an article detailing the influence of Hispanic political campaign contributions, Mark Murray of *The National Journal* quoted José Villarreal, national treasurer for the Gore campaign, as stating, "[Although] in 1988 Latinos were an invisible factor, . . . all of that has changed with the explosive growth in numbers and economic power" (Murray, 1999, p. 1254).

This apparent contradictory "economic identity" of Latinos as both poor and a powerful market force also was the subject of a National Public Radio broadcast by John Burnett. Reporting for the *Morning Edition* from the July 1999 NCLR convention, Burnett (1999) noted that the event

> well illustrate[d] the contradiction within America's fastest growing minority. It was possible to attend workshops all day targeting problems that plague the Latino community—high school dropouts, uninsured children, lack of credit, unemployment, and poverty. But one could ride escalators down two floors to the Latino Expo, where corporate America was swooning over Hispanic buying power. (p. 2)

The *California Journal* presented an insightful discussion of this subject. Quoting Gregory Rodríguez of the Pepperdine School of Public Policy, York (1999) suggested the following perspective on the causes for these contradictory portrayals: "The perverse nature of the political spoils system has encouraged non-white politicians and activists to present their communities as profoundly disadvantaged" (p. 4). But one result of this tactic, he continued, is that "the political class . . . as well as the print and electronic media often confuse the most marginalized parts of the Latino population for the whole" (p. 4). This point was well made in an *American Demographics* interview with *Latina* magazine publisher Christy Haubegger. She described her frustrations in trying to convince advertisers of the purchasing power of Latinos: "I've had great information on [Latino] buying power for years, but when people close their eyes and picture [a] Hispanic wom[a]n, they picture someone who cleans up their office at night. We don't get to do a sales job in this market, we do an education job" (quoted in Weissman, 1999, p. 37).

Latinos Have "Culture"

One of the most interesting themes that emerged in this study was the continual reference to stereotypes of Latino "culture" in the midst of what were ostensibly political discussions. Allusions to a sort of intangible *je ne sais quoi Latino* ranged from the romantic ("Part of being Hispanic is being authentic and real"[16]) to the more gushing ("Latino music is a music of passion" [Stapinski, 1999, p. 63]). In the same fashion, many of these discussions also revolved around food. Take, for example, the tongue-in-cheek assertion of Chavez (1999a) that Bush "knows his way around a tamale" (p. H3) or the comment by *Crain's Chicago Business* that "[Chicago] City Council races in Latino wards [were] as hot and tangy as a good salsa" ("Vying for Hot Hispanic Votes," 1999, p. 3).

But putting these lighthearted references aside, when we consider more closely other examples such as the title of the *Crain's Chicago Business* article, "Vying for Hot Hispanic Votes" (1999), and *The Economist*'s assertion that "California's Republicans [are wooing] the state's *multiplying* Latinos" ("Enter the Garcias' Own Party," 1998, p. 21), we begin to ask what exactly is the message being communicated in these phrases. After all, the same media sources do not include discussions of Asian American politics in terms of soy sauce and rice. Nor do references to collard greens appear in coverage of the National Association for the Advancement of Colored People. Are Jewish voter turnout rates couched in discussions of bar mitzvahs and bris milah? The answer is *no.* Why, then, is this exception made for politics and Latinos? As the United States becomes increasingly Hispanic, one prediction might be that these characterizations will become noted and criticized.

The Construction of "What Are Latino Issues?"

In contrast to the stereotyping and generalizations that characterize media portrayals of Latinos themselves, the media's discussions of Latino issues were less contradictory and, to the extent that they coincided with the opinions of civic leaders and policy analysts, were more accurate. For example, Antonio González, president of the Southwest Voter Registration Education Project, stated in a *Los Angeles Times* interview that Latino concerns encompass issues such as "housing, education, employment, health, and business" (Olivo, 1999b, p. B1). And we found that the media very consistently referred to these issues in discussions of the subject. The following sections provide a review of the most common "Latino issues" cited by the media: economics, education, health care, immigration, affirmative action, discrimination, and police brutality.

Economics

Chavez (1999b), the syndicated columnist for the *Tennessean,* put it most succinctly:

> The workplace and the pocketbook are where this election will be decided, not in Spanish-language commercials. It's still the economy, stupid. This time, however, it will include a twist concerning economic fairness. The best lan-

> guage through which to reach these voters is not Spanish or English but [rather] America's economic tongue and its axiom that "money talks." (p. H3)

Another excellent example came from Burnett (1999), reporting from the NCLR convention for National Public Radio and quoting a young man whose comment was particularly pertinent: "Economic development is everything because if you have your own money, you can pay for your own bilingual education" (p. 2).

Education

The media also concurred in their assertions that education was one of the main campaign issues for Latino voters. Media coverage generally indicated that Latinos were concerned about the quality of education available to their children but also included discussions on bilingual education debates and "English-only" initiatives. In discussing education, the media often cited research findings. The *Los Angeles Times,* for example, referred to a William C. Velázquez Institute study that reported the following: "While three fourths of white high school students graduate, only half of Latino students receive diplomas" (Olivo, 1999a, p. B1). The media also relied on interviews with Hispanic leaders to support their claims. The *Sacramento Bee* asserted that "improvements in education and tighter gun control" are issues that "Latino leaders say play well among [Latinos]" (Mecoy, 1999, p. A4). Likewise, The *Los Angeles Times* reported on panel discussions from a Southwest Voter conference at which Los Angeles County Supervisor Gloria Molina "expressed frustration with low standardized test scores and high dropout rates" and claimed that "[Latino] kids are getting 'dumbed-up' by the system" (quoted in Olivo, 1999a, p. B1).

Health Care

Much of the media argued the importance of health care to Latinos by referencing campaign speeches by the candidates, and in particular those of Gore, who made the issue a central topic. The *Washington Post,* for example, reported on Gore stump speeches in which the candidate pledged his unwavering support for Medicare, "which provides health insurance to two million elderly and disabled Latinos" (quoted in Fletcher, 1999, p. A1). The *Washington Post* also noted that Gore's speeches criticized Bush for his record in "a state where a quarter of the children have no health insurance coverage and more than half of the uninsured are Latino"

(p. A1). Research findings also were used to support claims that health care was important to Latinos. For example, the *Los Angeles Times* reported, "Whereas 80% of whites, African Americans, and Asian Americans have health insurance, roughly [only] two thirds of Latinos [have medical coverage]" (Olivo, 1999a, p. B1).

Immigration

Discussions of immigration and the access of immigrant noncitizens to social services appeared in many news articles on the Latino vote. Coverage generally focused on the about-face of Republicans on these issues during the past year and on all candidates' efforts to assure Latinos that they were not "anti-immigrant." Thus, more often than reporting immigration as a "Hispanic issue," media discussions tended to report candidate references to these issues and then conclude from the discussions that, therefore, these issues were important to Latinos. One of the best examples we can offer on the coverage of this topic stems from Ronald Brownstein of the *Los Angeles Times,* who quoted Frank Sharry, executive director of the National Immigration Forum, explaining candidate preoccupation with this issue: "It's gone from being a race to the bottom to get tough on immigrants to who can be more pro-immigrant without appearing to be soft on uncontrolled immigration" (Brownstein, 1999, p. A5).

Affirmative Action, Discrimination, and Police Brutality

These issues were mentioned periodically in press coverage, although they were not often discussed at length. Lori Rodríguez of the *Houston Chronicle,* in an interview with NCLR President Raul Yzaguirre, reported the concern that all Hispanic issues be given time by the candidates. Yzaguirre stated,

> This is an interesting time for us. We're being recognized for our voting power, purchasing power, and cultural contributions. But on the other hand, it's very hard to get policy makers to focus on our issues. I recently met with the president and the attorney general. . . . The Department of Justice was conducting a study on attitudes towards police abuse. But it didn't include Hispanics. They ignored the largest minority in this country. It was egregious. (Rodríguez, 1999, p. 19)

DISCUSSION

As is evidenced by the preceding summary of news media coverage on Latino voters, the construction of "Who are the Latinos?" at this early stage of the campaign often was contradictory, and its development often was superficial. According to these recent media portrayals, Latinos are conservative and favor a Republican platform, yet their interests also coincide with a progressive Democratic agenda. They are wealthy political donors and middle class home buyers, yet they comprise a militant working class and are among the most destitute of America's poor. They are one of the most disadvantaged sectors of our society, yet their economic power is so strong that Latinos alone are transforming American marketing and business culture. Moreover, Latinos are a traditional and reserved Catholic constituency, yet their spicy food, passionate music, and gyrating hips have mesmerized the nation.

This is a lot of baggage for one demographic group to carry or, better said, to have thrust on it. It probably is safe to say that individual members of the U.S. media are alternatively unaware of, uninterested in, or perplexed by the complexities of the Latino voter. It also is clear that at least some of these contradictions arise from the diversity of the U.S. Hispanic population, an issue that the media simply failed to recognize and address. But much of the inconsistency in reporting also seems to stem from a tendency among journalists to reproduce statistics and quote "experts" without first analyzing more thoroughly the information at hand.

Demographers and scholars of Latino studies (e.g., Delgado & Stefancic, 1998; Fox, 1996; Moore & Pachon, 1985) acknowledge that this is a very heterogeneous group—so diverse, in fact, that Latinos almost defy categorization. Furthermore, these authors note that even while many Latinos share similar perspectives on American politics, significant differences abound (e.g., de la Garza, DeSipio, García, García, & Falcón, 1992). But researchers and scholars take care to acknowledge and reference these differences. So, why is it that the media do *not*? Why were the media able to identify Latino voter issues such as economics, education, health care, immigration, and discrimination and to discuss them consistently and evenly across the board, yet when it came to telling us *who Latino voters are,* their reporting was contradictory and laced with generalizations and stereotypes?

A partial explanation for the media's inability to navigate the complexities of this voter constituency may be found in something that Gregory Rodríguez referred to as "brokerage politics" (quoted in Woodruff, 1999, pp. 5-6). According to Rodríguez, this practice "[treats] non-white groups in this country as centralized, hierarchical organizations [even though] they are not" (p. 6). The effect of brokerage politics is that we believe that "we can somehow speak to the [leaders] of these groups, and [in so doing, we speak] to all members of that group" (p. 6). Rodríguez suggests that what is needed is a reorientation of the discussion of Latino politics to another level—a level at which we can "[communicate with] people, . . . people who actually go to the ballot boxes." This can be accomplished simply by treating Latino voters the same way as Anglo voters are treated in this country, that is, "by [going] out and trying to reach the broadest number of people" (p. 6).

This suggestion is particularly resonant as we examine the differences between the construction of "Who are the Latinos?" and the construction of "What are Latino issues?" Whereas the "what" of Latino issues seemed to comprise a fairly consistent reporting of matters of concern to Latinos, the "who" construction of Latinos left the "awakening giant" appearing schizophrenic. The reason for these differences might lie precisely in the methodological quandary that Rodríguez posed. Reviewing the sources cited by journalists for the articles during the period of study, we found that the majority of information for their news stories came from statistical reports, interviews with Hispanic leaders, and the campaign speeches of candidates. It was only in rare instances that Latino voters themselves were interviewed for any of the stories. Thus, *who the journalists talked to* and *how they generalized from these sources* might be two of the most important factors contributing to the overgeneralizations and contradictions encountered in media coverage of the Latino vote.

Another factor that might have proven critical to the quality and accuracy of the media coverage relates to who the journalists and media gatekeepers *themselves* are. If we accept the assertion that journalists should talk to Latinos when discussing politics and Latinos, then we need to consider what kind of imagined or real barriers might exist for the majority of journalists—who are Anglos—to access this group.[17] Are the journalists assigned to the task well versed in the history and diversity of the various Hispanic groups in the United States? Can they speak Spanish if necessary or code switch to keep pace with the flow of a bilingual speaker? Do they feel comfortable mingling in crowds with people who do not look like themselves or who do not come from their same backgrounds? Could the effect of barriers such as these help to explain why the portrait of the Latino voter was left so confused and incomplete?

The study found that journalists did interview Latino community leaders to learn about issues of their concern. But when it came to reporting on who Latinos were as a demographic group, the media more often deferred to generalizations and statistics. Ironically, this information often was obtained from the very same community leaders who seemed to find it expedient to paint a picture of Latino communities with very broad strokes. Could these images of Latinos have been constructed more clearly if the journalists had stepped back and asked themselves, "Would we make statements like this about a generalized 'white vote'?" Or, could the picture have been different if, as Rodríguez suggested, the media had taken their questions "to the people who actually go to the ballot boxes"? (quoted in Woodruff, 1999, p. 6). As the outcome of the 2000 election is analyzed, and as the impact of the Latino vote is assessed, we hope that the political importance of Latinos in this country will prompt a closer look and more careful media treatment of this voting constituency in future election campaigns.

THEORETICAL IMPLICATIONS

Martin and Nakayama (1999) outline trends in the research of scholars of culture and communication (including those adopting an interpretive approach) toward incorporating issues of broader macro contexts, power differentials, and relevance to lived experience. The results show that all three issues are important to interpretations of media texts about Latinos. The current study began with an interpretive approach to building understanding about "Who are the Latinos?" and "What are Latino issues?" What emerged from the analysis is the necessity of considering the broader historical, political, and social contexts (Martin & Nakayama, 1999) in the interpretation of the media texts—the history of Latinos as an ethnic group in the United States, general media coverage of Latinos and Latino issues in previous elections, the role of institutional influences of religion and education, and continuing socioeconomic discrimination. In addition, we focused on media portrayals of Latino identity and political issues in the 2000 presidential election. Politics and identity are two themes that often are addressed by scholars whose approaches can be categorized under the critical humanist paradigm (Martin & Nakayama, 1999).

Martin and Nakayama (1999) argue that studies incorporating issues reflecting a critical stance often "explore how media and other messages are presented and interpreted (and resisted) in often conflicting ways" (p. 9). Media institutions often function to perpetuate stereotypes that are "collective abstractions of persons or groups asserting that members lack individuality and conform to a pattern or type" (Johnson, 1999, p. 417). As Subervi-Vélez (1984), among others, points out, individuals rely on various media forms for impressions of others with whom they have little or no contact, and such stereotypes do have an impact on and are influenced by public policy. What we found in this campaign is that when Latinos were the spokespersons for their own groups, they pointed to multiple and diverse voices within their groups. They held common views, however, about areas in need of political change. These political issues pertained to interrelated institutions (e.g., education, health care), governmental policies about immigration and affirmative action, and social practices that have become the "norm" (e.g., discrimination, police brutality). Finally, our study demonstrates, as do others (e.g., Rios, 2000), that journalists' positions and privilege may constrain what is reported and what audiences take away from the articles about Latinos. All of these practices reflect the means through which power is exerted and through which resources are distributed or withheld. They are examples of the negative consequences of such political policies and practices on Latinos' everyday lives.

NOTES

1. The term "sleeping giant" originally was coined by Edward R. Roybal, the first Mexican American elected to the Los Angeles City Council in the 20th century (in 1951). Roybal used the phrase to refer to the untapped political potential of Latinos that he saw in Los Angeles at the time. Roybal went on to become California's first Mexican American congressman (in 1961), an office that he held for 30 years. As congressman, he co-founded the National Association of Latino Elected and Appointed Officials (NALEO) and the Congressional Hispanic Caucus. He also has been a lifelong activist for community health issues and was a pioneering advocate of AIDS research during the early 1980s. See Olivo (1999b).

2. The term "Latino" is preferred by the authors and is the main one used in this chapter. For a justification of the use of this term, see Hero (1992). The term "Hispanic" also is acceptable to refer to this ethnic group, and it is the most common term used by the media. Thus, we use these two terms interchangeably in this chapter. In fact, based on a recent poll, "Hispanic" may be the most preferred term by members of this group (Granado, 2000).

3. Arce's response to the question was as follows: "Both of them need to brush up on their Spanish, but their choice of words is very standard in Spanish. They know the issues that they're trying to push. So, [for example, when Bush] talks about immigration, . . . I think

the fact that he's talking about immigration helps him even more than the fact that he is saying it in Spanish" (quoted in Shaw, 1999, p. 2).

4. The first study to explore agenda-setting theories with Latino media was conducted recently by Rojas (2000).

5. See Castro (1974); de la Garza and DeSipio (1992, 1999); de la Garza, Menchaca, and DeSipio (1994); DeSipio (1998); Guzmán (1976); Hero (1992); Montejano (1999); Valdes y Tapia (1976); Vigil (1987); and Villareal, Hernández, and Neighbor (1988).

6. See also Subervi-Vélez (1984, 1988, 1992); Subervi-Vélez and Connaughton (1999); and Subervi-Vélez, Herrera, and Begay (1987).

7. Republican National Committee and party outreach efforts were based on extensive polling of Latinos on their views, opinions, and even media habits so as to better design and disseminate messages specifically directed to the various Latino voters or potential voters. With one major exception—that of Bob Dole's presidential bid in 1996—Republican media campaigns have included extensive paid and free media in Spanish as well as in English specifically directed at Latinos. See Subervi-Vélez and Connaughton (1999).

8. The *Los Angeles Times* went on to report, in Olivo's (1999b) interview with Antonio González, president of the Southwest Voter Registration Education Project, that in the aftermath of this event, Bush's staff unsuccessfully tried to rearrange the governor's schedule so that he could attend the Southwest Voter Silver Anniversary Conference. Bush had been invited 6 months earlier but originally had turned down the invitation.

9. Although this article was published just before the period of the study began, the quote is used to illustrate perceptions of Latino voters at the very beginning of the campaign.

10. The issue of Latinos and language proved to be a sticky subject to tackle. For example, although U.S. census data reveal that 7% of the U.S. voting-age population (13,177,411 people) spoke Spanish in 1990, census data for that same year show that only 8% (14,596,559 people) of this population age 18 years or over identified themselves as Latino or Hispanic (U.S. Bureau of the Census, 1990). Thus, if we were to accept these data at face value, then we could conclude either that, as a uniform cross section of the American public, 7% of Hispanics speak Spanish or that, assuming that most of the U.S. Spanish-speaking population is in fact Hispanic, all or most Latinos speak Spanish as their primary language at home, as does at least 1% of the non-Hispanic American populace. It is likely that this confusing picture of this country's Spanish-speaking population has resulted from the now well-documented underreporting of Hispanic residents that was produced by the structure of the ethnic/racial identity section of the 1990 census. It is useful to note, however, that of the people age 18 years or over who did identify themselves as Hispanic, 56% said that they spoke English well or very well. This figure increased to 78% of those between 5 and 17 years of age. It is noteworthy that the majority (77%) of this population would have been of age to vote in the 2000 elections.

11. Latino voting results were reported as follows. Democratic candidate for governor Gray Davis received 82% of the Latino vote, whereas his opponent, Republican Dan Lungren, received only 17%; Democratic candidate for lieutenant governor Cruz Bustamante received 85% of the Latino vote, whereas his opponent, Republican Tim Leslie, received only 13%; and Democratic Senator Barbara Boxer received 78% of the Latino vote for her reelection to that seat, whereas her Republican challenger, Matt Fong, received only 20% (Cabrera, 1999).

12. See Vega (2000), citing U.S. census data from Andrade and Hernández's (1999) *The Almanac of Latino Politics 2000* and surveys by the Gallup Organization cited by the Princeton Religion Research Center. Findings from the latter study show that the total

Catholic population in the United States comprises only 26% of the population, compared to 58% who are Protestants, 2% who are Jewish, 6% who identify as "other," and 8% who state no religious affiliation (U.S. Bureau of the Census, 1990). McGreevy (1999) notes that of the total U.S. Catholic population, 12 U.S. archdioceses are now predominantly Latino. He also cites projections that within 30 years, half of the U.S. Catholic population will be Hispanic (p. 200).

13. McGreevy (1999) notes, "The surge of Asian and Latin American immigration after the alteration of American immigration laws in 1965 [also] has produced the most powerful echo of the past. Vietnamese, Puerto Rican, Haitian, Cuban, and Mexican Catholic immigrants . . . ensure the persistence of old debates about representation and integration. . . . [And although] Vietnamese and Cuban Catholics are generally conservative, . . . the intuitive sense that Catholics primarily concerned with racial matters and social justice are theologically liberal remains accurate" (p. 199).

14. For a discussion of the history of Mexican Americans and the Catholic Church, see Dolan and Hinajosa (1994). For a discussion of the relationship between the Catholic Church and Cesar Chávez's struggle for the United Farm Workers, see Mosqueda (1986).

15. The report was released July 17, 1999, by the William C. Velázquez Institute, the research arm of the Southwest Voter Registration Education Project, and detailed the status of California Latinos in housing, education, employment, health, and business (cited in Olivo, 1999a).

16. This quote is from Juan Faura of Cheskin Research (cited in Stapinski, 1999, p. 63).

17. For details about the status of minority employment in the news media, check the "diversity" section of the American Society of Newspaper Editors' website (http://www.asne.org/kiosk/diversity/index.htm), especially annual newsroom employment census reports. See also the diversity information on the Radio & Television News Director's Association website at http://www.rtnda.org/research/womin.shtml.

REFERENCES

Andrade, J., & Hernández, A. (1999). *The almanac of Latino politics 2000.* Chicago: Hispanic Leadership Council.

Brownstein, R. (1999, July 19). Latino clout, improved economy soften GOP stance on immigration. *Los Angeles Times,* p. A5.

Burnett, J. (1999, July 29). Capturing the Latino vote. *Morning Edition* [National Public Radio broadcast].

Cabrera, Y. (1999, November 5). Latino candidates savoring historic election victories. *Los Angeles Daily News* [Online].

Carveth, R., & Alverio, D. (1996). *Network brownout 1996: The portrayals of Latinos in network television news.* Washington, DC: National Association of Hispanic Journalists and National Council of La Raza.

Carveth, R., & Alverio, D. (1997). *Network brownout 1997: The portrayals of Latinos in network television news.* Washington, DC: National Association of Hispanic Journalists and National Council of La Raza.

Carveth, R., & Alverio, D. (1998). *Network brownout 1998: The portrayals of Latinos in network television news.* Washington, DC: National Association of Hispanic Journalists and National Council of La Raza.

Carveth, R., & Alverio, D. (1999). *Network brownout 1999: The portrayals of Latinos in network television news.* Washington, DC: National Association of Hispanic Journalists and National Council of La Raza.

Carveth, R., & Alverio, D. (2000). *Network brownout 2000: The portrayals of Latinos in network television news.* Washington, DC: National Association of Hispanic Journalists and National Council of La Raza.

Castro, T. (1974). *Chicano power: The emergence of Mexican America.* New York: Saturday Review Press.

Chavez, T. (1999a, April 18). Don't underestimate the Hispanic vote. *Denver Post,* p. H3.

Chavez, T. (1999b, June 29). Playing politics in Spanish. *Denver Post,* p. B9.

Crowley, C. (Correspondent), & Shaw, B. (Anchor). (1999, June 29). George W. Bush courts Latino votes in California. *Inside Politics* [television program]. (CNN Transcript 99062905V15)

Crowley, C. (Correspondent), Schneider, W. (Political Analyst), & Meserve, J. (Anchor). (1999, June 24). Politicians court Hispanic voters. *Inside Politics* [television program]. (CNN Transcript 99062402V15)

de la Garza, R. O., & DeSipio, L. (Eds.). (1992). *From rhetoric to reality: Latinos in the 1988 elections.* Boulder, CO: Westview.

de la Garza, R. O., & DeSipio, L. (1999). *Awash in the mainstream: Latino politics in the 1996 elections.* Boulder, CO: Westview.

de la Garza, R., DeSipio, L., García, F. C., García, J., & Falcón, A. (1992). *Latino voices: Mexican, Puerto Rican, and Cuban perspectives on American politics.* Boulder, CO: Westview.

de la Garza, R. O., Menchaca, M., & DeSipio, L. (Eds.). (1994). *Barrio ballots: Latino politics in the 1990 elections.* Boulder, CO: Westview.

Delgado, R., & Stefancic, J. (Eds.). (1998). *The Latino/a condition: A critical reader.* New York: New York University Press.

DeSipio, L. (1998). *Making Americans/Remaking America: Immigration and immigrant policy.* Boulder, CO: Westview.

Dolan, J. P., & Hinajosa, G. (Eds.). (1994). *Mexican Americans and the Catholic Church, 1900-1965.* Notre Dame, IN: University of Notre Dame Press.

Enter the Garcias' own party. (1998, August 15). *The Economist,* p. 21.

Fletcher, M. A. (1999, July 29). Gore chases Hispanic vote on Bush turf: Texas governor's absence at conference is noted. *Washington Post,* p. A1.

Fox, G. (1996). *Hispanic nation: Culture, politics, and the constructing of identity.* Secaucus, NJ: Birch Lane Press.

Garcia, J. (1998). Bush led GOP inroads among Latinos. *Politico: The Magazine for Latino Politics and Culture* [Online]. Available: www.politicomagazine.com/garcia110900.html

Goodno, J. B. (1998, July 12). Awakening the giant. *In These Times,* p. 4.

Granado, C. (2000, December). A new poll finds that the term "Hispanic" is preferred. *Hispanic Magazine,* pp. 40-42.

Guzmán, R. C. (1976). *The political socialization of the Mexican American people.* New York: Arno Press.

Hero, R. E. (1992). *Latinos and the U.S. political system: Two-tiered pluralism.* Philadelphia: Temple University Press.

Johnson, M. (1999). Pre-television stereotypes: Mexicans in newsreels, 1919-1932. *Critical Studies in Mass Communication, 16,* 417-435.

Leo, J. (1998, November 16). Free advice for the GOP. *U.S. News and World Report,* p. 16.

Marinucci, C. (1999, September 1). State's Latinos a quandary for Bush: They're younger, poorer, more likely to vote Democratic than in Texas. *San Francisco Chronicle,* pp. A1, A7.

Martin, J., & Nakayama, T. (1999). Thinking dialectically about culture and communication. *Communication Theory, 9,* 1-25.

Matovina, T. M. (1999). Representation and the reconstruction of power: The rise of PADRES and Las Hermanas. In M. J. Weaver (Ed.), *What's left? Liberal American Catholics* (pp. 220-237). Bloomington: Indiana University Press.

McCombs, M., & Shaw, D. (1972). The agenda setting function of the press. *Public Opinion Quarterly, 36,* 176-187.

McCombs, M., Shaw, D., & Weaver, D. (1997). Communication and democracy: Exploring the intellectual frontiers in agenda-setting theory. Mahwah, NJ: Lawrence Erlbaum.

McGreevy, J. T. (1999). The problem of diversity. In M. J. Weaver (Ed.), *What's left? Liberal American Catholics* (pp. 191-204). Bloomington: Indiana University Press.

Mecoy, L. (1999, July 18). Gore pursues Latino votes in south state appearance. *Sacramento Bee,* p. A4.

Meserve, J. (Correspondent), & Woodruff, J. (Anchor). (1999, February 26). Latino vote could be surprise weapon in presidential primaries. *Inside Politics* [television program]. (CNN Transcript 99022600V15)

Montejano, D. (1999). *Chicano politics and society in the twentieth century.* Austin: University of Texas Press.

Moore, J., & Pachon, H. (1985). *Hispanics in the United States.* Englewood Cliffs, NJ: Prentice Hall.

Mosqueda, L. J. (1986). *Chicanos, Catholicism, and political ideology.* Lanham, MD: University Press of America.

Mujica, M. (1999, May 3). Ay caramaba! *The Weekly Standard,* p. 7.

Murray, M. (1999, May 8). Blacks and Hispanics: A lock for Democrats? *The National Journal,* p. 1254.

O'Brien, D. J. (1999). What happened to the Catholic left? In M. J. Weaver (Ed.), *What's left? Liberal American Catholics* (pp. 255-282). Bloomington: Indiana University Press.

Olivo, A. (1999a, July 18). Expansion of Latino voter roles celebrated. *Los Angeles Times,* p. B1.

Olivo, A. (1999b, July 27). Grandfather of Latino politics faults new leaders. *Los Angeles Times,* p. B1.

Riebe-Estrella, G. (1999). Strategies on the left. In M. J. Weaver (Ed.), *What's left? Liberal American Catholics* (pp. 205-219). Bloomington: Indiana University Press.

Rios, D. (2000). Latina/o experiences with mediated communication. In A. Gonzalez, M. Houston, & V. Chen (Eds.), *Our voices: Essays in culture, ethnicity, and communication* (pp. 105-112). Los Angeles: Roxbury.

Rodríguez, L. (1999, July 2). Gore courts Hispanic vote on swing through Houston. *Houston Chronicle,* p. A1.

Rojas, V. (2000). *Latino media coverage of the 2000 electoral campaign: Issue framing and candidate images.* Unpublished manuscript, University of Texas at Austin.

Santillan, R., & Subervi-Vélez, F. (1991). Latino participation in Republican party politics in California. In B. O. Jackson & M. B. Preston (Eds.), *Racial and ethnic politics in California* (pp. 285-319). Berkeley, CA: Institute of Governmental Studies.

Shaw, B. (Anchor). (1999, July 15). The war of words over Hispanic votes. *Inside Politics* [television program]. (CNN Transcript 99071503V15)

Stapinski, H. (1999, July). Generación Latino. *American Demographics,* p. 63.

Subervi-Vélez, F. A. (1984). *Hispanics, the mass media, and politics: Assimilation vs. pluralism.* Unpublished doctoral dissertation, University of Wisconsin–Madison.

Subervi-Vélez, F. A. (1988). Spanish-language daily newspapers and the 1984 elections. *Journalism Quarterly, 65,* 678-685.

Subervi-Vélez, F. A. (1992). Republican and Democratic mass communication strategies: Targeting the Latino vote. In R. O. de la Garza & L. DeSipio (Eds.), *From rhetoric to reality: Latinos in the 1988 elections* (pp. 23-40). Boulder, CO: Westview.

Subervi-Vélez, F. A., & Connaughton, S. (1999). Targeting the Latino vote: The Democratic party's 1996 mass communication strategy. In R. O. de la Garza & L. DeSipio (Eds.), *Awash in the mainstream: Latino politics in the 1996 elections* (pp. 47-71). Boulder, CO: Westview.

Subervi-Vélez, F. A., Herrera, R., & Begay, M. (1987). Toward an understanding of the role of the mass media in Latino political life. *Social Science Quarterly, 68,* 185-196.

Tomás Rivera Policy Institute. (1999). *Latinos and entertainment* [Online]. Available: www.trpi.org/entertain.html

U.S. Bureau of the Census. (1990). [Online]. Available: www.census.gov

Valdes y Tapia, D. (1976). *Hispanos and American politics.* New York: Arno Press.

Van Slambrouck, P. (1998, November 5). California sends message of change and power of Latino vote. *Christian Science Monitor* [Online]. Available: www.csmonitor.com/durable/1998/11/05/p5s1.htm

Vega, D. (2000, February 14). Bush demonstrates a lack of compassion for the Latino community. *Democratic National Committee* [Online]. Available: www.democrats.org/archive/rel2000/rel021400.html

Vigil, M. (1987). *Hispanics in American politics: In search for political power.* Lanham, MD: University Press of America.

Villareal, R. E., Hernández, N. G., & Neighbor, H. D. (1988). *Latino empowerment: Progress, problems, and prospects.* New York: Greenwood.

Vying for hot Hispanic votes. (1999, February 15). *Crain's Chicago Business,* p. 3.

Weissman, R. X. (1999, May). Los niños go shopping. *American Demographics,* p. 37.

Woodruff, J. (Anchor). (1999, July 28). Al Gore woos Latino voters. *Inside Politics* [television program]. (CNN Transcript 99072800V15)

York, A. (1999, April 1). Latino politics. *California Journal,* p. 4.

8

Traveling Identities in Joking Performances

Peril and Play in an Arab-American Community

KELLIE D. HAY • *Oakland State University*
SUSAN L. KLINE • *Ohio State University*

> Almost anything can happen in the fictional world of joking, and thus it happens that members of Western Apache communities sometimes step back from the less malleable realm of everyday life and transform themselves into Anglo-Americans through the performance of carefully crafted imitations.
>
> —K. H. Basso (1979, p. 6)

> Meaning in any face-to-face encounter is always negotiable; it is discovering the grounds for negotiation that requires the participants' skill.
>
> —J. Gumperz (1982, p. 14)

Arab-Americans living in urban centers in the United States travel in and through several worlds with at least two sets of cultural practices, economic realities, and historical possibilities. Some have first traveled from their home country to Europe, whereas others have relocated directly to the United States. The cultural collisions that shape the daily lives of these U.S. Arab-Americans produce worldly yet unsettled identities that shift betwixt and between a myriad of national spaces. That is, the political boundaries that shape national identities for U.S. Arab-Americans are not fixed; they shift as people absorb new cultural practices and registers of knowledge while they resituate themselves in locations that are not yet home.

A number of postcolonial theorists and cultural critics are articulating the ways in which the decolonization of the Third World has affected migration patterns across the globe, patterns that call into question what once were imagined as binary oppositions between local and global cultures and industries (Appadurai, 1996; Bhabha, 1994; Hall, 1991, 1995, 1996; Morley & Robins, 1995). Arab-American communities continue to grow rapidly in the United States as a result of many, often hostile conditions that have resulted from colonialism, the emergence of postcolonial nationalism, independence, and the geopolitics of late capitalism. As part of the scholarship that explores migration, exile, displacement, and diaspora, we provide a case study of some aspects of the new and rich transnational identities that are produced when Arabs relocate in the United States.

The first author (hereafter referred to as K) has been working with the Arab-Americans of Mid-America (AAMA)[1] for the past 5 years. K has worked with the organization in a number of capacities—as a participant observer, as an active member, as the organization's secretary, and as one who opened her house for dinner parties and subcommittee meetings. K also opened the organization's cultural center every day during the summer of 1995, when many families and individuals came by to enjoy the center's resources including games for children, a social space for mingling, and (on occasion) a place where they gathered to host guest lecturers, artists, and activists. K and members of the organization also have worked together in organizing picnics, the international festival, and *haflehs* (the annual dance parties/award banquets that the organization hosts for the community-at-large).

K gained entrée into this organization quite serendipitously in 1995 when a former adviser gave her the business card of a Palestinian man (Sami) taking her feminist cultural studies seminar. K made contact with Sami, and after a long first visit, K learned that Sami was the president of the AAMA at the time. Sami invited K to attend the organization's monthly board meetings, which she did, and this interaction led to a 5-year engagement with the AAMA. Before AAMA members were willing to open up on any level, it was important for K to demonstrate that she had traveled and lived in the Arab world, was learning Arabic, and understood many of the issues that were salient to this community. After 1 year of service and participant observation, members began to open up in joking performances and more traditional narrative forms of conversation, leading to interactions in which the politics and pleasures of identities in the making were at once constructed, lived, struggled over, and performed.

AAMA members come from all corners of the Arab world—the Gulf states in the Arabian Peninsula, the Levant (those countries bordering the

Eastern Mediterranean) and Fertile Crescent region (the Levant plus Iraq and Egypt), and North Africa (Morocco, Sudan, Tunisia, Algeria, Egypt, and Libya). AAMA members define themselves as a cultural and educational organization, yet they also advocate Arab-American interests and resist media attempts to cast Arabs into terrorist stereotypes. In response to being altercast by the media in such one-dimensional positions, the AAMA takes a proactive stance toward the media so as to reconstruct Arab-American identities. They also host cultural and social events, although the political always is present in their social activities.

AAMA members bring with them memories of their former homelands, and this makes their histories and cultural practices a diverse mix. On many occasions, members told K that being Arab-American means having one foot here and one foot back home. Often, the way in which issues of location and displacement are narrated involves joking, as when a member remarked that the maps must be wrong because "there is no place on the map to point to that says Palestine, my homeland." In fact, it is in joking performances that some of the most provocative, painful, and explicit stories about loss and exile have been communicated in formal meetings. K recorded several of these jokes, humorous narratives, and joking performances, and she talked about them with their tellers and their audiences. More than a coping strategy, these enactments serve as one way in which U.S. Arab-Americans are interpellated into the discourses of citizenship while also coding their memories and discontent in the discourse itself.

Joking and humorous stories, then, are the communication practice through which we examine the enactment of transnational identities in this chapter. We contend that many cultural struggles are embedded within political jokes, narratives of displacement, and broadly defined joking performances about perceived erasure; joking is a site in which history is remembered and performed.

Our approach to discourse analysis is informed generally by work in ethnography of performance, linguistics, and ethnomethodology (as represented by scholars such as Bauman, 1986; Clark, 1996; Conquergood, 1991; Gumperz, 1982; Katriel, 1994, 1997; Kline & Kuper, 1994; Tracy & Naughton, 1994; Webber, 1991). The conceptual and empirical base that both postcolonial theory and communication theory contribute to the study of identities provides a lexicon for understanding how joking operates in U.S. Arab-American exile and diasporic communities. We pose, then, the following research questions. First, how do joking performances by and about exile communities illuminate the ambivalence of hybrid national identities? Second, how do joking performances enact transnational identities?

Our analysis proceeds through several stages. We begin by reviewing the objectives of postcolonial analysis and lines of work within postcolonial scholarship pertinent to our analysis of exile liminality. Our review of cultural analyses of political jokes is preparation for a case study of political joking in this U.S. Arab-American community.

It is important to clarify what we mean when we use the concepts of Arab and Arab-American. Following Suleiman (1999), we conceive of Arab-Americans as

> immigrants to North America from the Arabic-speaking countries of the Middle East and their descendents. The Arabic-speaking countries today include Algeria, Bahrain, Egypt, Iraq, Jordan, Kuwait, Lebanon, Libya, Mauritania, Morocco, Oman, pre-1948 Palestine and the Palestinians, Qatar, Saudi Arabia, Sudan, Syria, Tunisia, United Arab Emirates, and Yemen. Somalia and Djibouti are also members of the League of Arab States and have some Arabic-speaking populations. (p. 1)

However, we choose not to use the concept of North American because it includes Canada and Mexico. Suleiman does consider Canadian Arabs, yet his historiography of Arab-American immigration applies to the U.S. context exclusively. Because our study took place within the midwestern region of the United States, when we use the term "Arab-American" we are referring to U.S. citizens unless we indicate otherwise. We also refer to the community with which K studied as Arab-American because this mode of identification is important to the organization and community-at-large. They have named themselves as such, and we think that it is important to respect the ways in which ethnic groups name themselves.

The majority of AAMA members are U.S. citizens who identify as immigrants while also stating that they live diasporic lives. Other members identify as exiles, students, and refugees, and although many of them are pursuing U.S. citizenship or green cards, the majority of this group self-identifies as Arab. In many contexts such as formal interviews, casual conversations, and even public protests, this latter group has explained to K that being Arab means coming from the Arab world, speaking Arabic, and not letting go of indigenous cultural practices—resisting a quick and furious process of assimilation while being located in the unavoidable situation of absorbing many registers of U.S. cultural practices and politics.

This particular conception of Arab and U.S. Arab-American does not assume an exclusive racial emphasis precisely because many different ethnic groups live in the Arab world and participate in it culturally, economically, and religiously. For example, Egyptian Copts, Iraqi Chaldeans, Armenians, Jews living in Israel and in Arab countries, and North African Berbers are some of the groups who live in the Arab world and maintain a distinctive ethnic history. Often, many of these groups also speak indigenous languages (e.g., Berbers, Armenians, Jews), yet their cultural practices and languages can be mixed into Arabic, and Arabs likewise can be equally culturally hybrid.

Particularly in the U.S. context, Arabness often elides racial/ethnic categories. Arabs are considered Caucasian, yet they are not treated as such. Some scholars argue that Arabs are "not quite white and not quite colored" (Samhan, 1999, p. 209; see also Majaj, 1999). Although U.S. Arabs do not live with the privileges of whiteness, their olive complexions do not grant them minority status either. Even the U.S. census forms for the year 2000 did not include a place for U.S. Arab-Americans to state their ethnicity unless they chose to specify it in the "other" area of the form.

In addition to questions of racial/ethnic difference, U.S. Arab-Americans struggle against multiple cultural and religious conflations such as the notion that all Arabs are Muslim; in fact, many are Christian, particularly those who came in the first wave of immigration during the late 19th century. Another misconception that we have heard in conversations is that Arabs come from the most sexist part of the world, an area that is the origin of practices such as clitorectomy. This practice, however, is associated more predominantly with the African subcontinent.[2]

Although the U.S. Arab-Americans with whom K worked maintain that ethnicity is part of what it means to be an Arab, they also insist that the concept of Arab also connotes national and pan-national struggles. On the one hand, Arab nationalism stems from colonialism; on the other, Arabs look forward to an imagined Pan-Arab source of solidarity (Joseph, 1999; Mohanty, 1997).

POSTCOLONIAL THEORY AND TRANSNATIONAL IDENTITIES

Since the late 1970s and early 1980s, the concept of the postcolonial and the emergence of postcolonial studies have figured prominently in contemporary social theory, particularly in cultural studies and comparative literature (Behdad, 1994; McClintock, 1992; Mufti & Shohat, 1997; Said, 1978, 1994; Shohat, 1992; Trinh, 1989). Of late, several scholars in the discipline of communication have contributed to the burgeoning literature of postcolonial theory, stressing the role of communication practices, the politics of race, and transnational feminism (Collier, 1998; Grossberg, 1995; Hegde, 1998; Shome, 1996). These theorists make visible the ways in which the conventional national boundaries of identities and cultures have been destabilized by global changes in economic structures and the transnationalization of capital. Hence, an overall objective of postcolonial scholarship is the study of "cultural productions in the field of transnational economic relations and diasporic identity constructions" (Grewal & Kaplan, 1994, p. 1). Because economic formations "produce possibilities for some and obstruct opportunities for others," critics "query" locations and positions and deconstruct the images of colonial discourses including forms of tradition, patriarchal nationalism, local structures of domination, and legal oppression (Kaplan, 1996, p. 155). Then postcolonial scholars attempt to "represent the experience of living in diasporic locations," with a specificity "greater than only being spoken of in terms of oppression or subordination" (Grewal, 1994, p. 238). This involves disrupting binary oppositions such as home-abroad, power-exploitation, and center-margin so as to show how subjectivities are multiply placed and multiply linked. In Grewal and Kaplan's (1994) view, postcolonial critics explore how identities are constituted in specific locations and positions and also are shaped by local opportunity and social relationships.

Local analyses of identity facilitate yet another objective in postcolonial analysis, which is to enact a "politics of location" by identifying the grounds for "creating alternative histories and possibilities for alliances" (Kaplan, 1996, p. 138). Material conditions in a world of diasporic populations and multinational corporations require coalitions of people of different cultural backgrounds, races, classes, sexualities, and nations. Grewal and Kaplan (1994) argue further that if theorizing postmodern subjectivities is going to make a difference, then it cannot be conceptualized as simply being fragmented, playful, or removed from politics.

A postcolonial theory of identity emphasizes the processes through which national and transnational identities are constituted. Analysts examine the multiplicities, contradictions, and specificities of language that enable people to create new forms of consciousness and being (Bhabha, 1994). Following Grewal and Kaplan (1994), we believe that it is in communicative performances that people negotiate between their homelands and new host nations. It is in communication that displacement produces hybrid identities and diasporic discourses.

EXILE COMMUNITIES AND EXILE DISCOURSE

Displacement and Exile Communities

As colonialism pulls back and new Third World nation-states become an independent part of the world's economy, new cultural spaces are crafted. Hybridity is that process of becoming in a new location for Third World peoples resituating themselves, travelers, and immigrants. Relocation also mixes up the First World host's structure of social relations, and populations become more diverse, complex, and ambiguous.

Naficy's (1994) study of Iranian television in Los Angeles demonstrates cogently the new geopolitical effects of exile and immigration. He argues,

> The Third World is no longer "out there" in some far-off land; it is "here" and located within the so-called First World. In fact, every large-scale metropolitan city in America harbors several small Third Worlds whose relations of power within the metropolis appear to duplicate in large measure the previous relations between the Third and First World[s]. (p. 4)

Kaplan (1996) echoes Naficy's argument:

> Differences in origins entail difference[s] in power relations in exile. The colonial, neocolonial, and imperialistic history that characterizes much of the exchanges between the originating Third World countries and the United States provides a tumultuous context against which cultural, ideological, and religious differences in exile are played out, contested, and negotiated by the new immigrants. (p. 3)

Exile Discourse

Beyond these general contours, the concepts of travel, diaspora, exile, and displacement organize much of the work in postcolonial scholarship. For our specific purposes, we rely on and extend the works of Kaplan (1996), Gilroy (1993), and Naficy (1994) because their studies of travel writing, music, and television can help us to analyze joke telling and joking performances as sites for identity negotiations.

Exile is the consequence of the phenomenon that Kaplan (1996) calls the condition of "translation," that Naficy (1994) maps as the "slipzone," and that Gilroy (1993) illustrates in his "traveling ship of double-consciousness." Kaplan (1996) finds in modernist literary theory a model of aesthetic gain in which the solitary writer, driven by cultural curiosity or nostalgia, travels to another land to author unique observations of the exotic. Kaplan argues that the term *exile* best signifies all of these versions of displacement, which Kaplan and Naficy end up defining as those disaffected who either "voluntarily or involuntarily relocate to another country" (Naficy, 1994, p. 2). Exile is the specific space for studying the relationship among identity, location, and politics. Wanderlust is a related concept here because it is threaded through with the pleasures of travel; it is both an imagination of a more exotic, utopic social space and a site of multiple cultural collisions.

Gilroy (1993) explores hybridity and exile discourse in his study of black popular music. He argues that we should move beyond Afrocentric readings of racial identity to see "Black English" as a blending of traditions. To understand Black English, Gilroy proposes studying the way in which cultural forms intermix and create an explicitly transnational perspective that he calls the "black Atlantic." For Gilroy, the black Atlantic is "the stereophonic, bilingual, or bifocal cultural forms originated by, but no longer the exclusive property of, blacks, dispersed within the structures of feeling, producing, communicating, and remembering" (p. 6).

Gilroy (1993) advances DuBois's concept of "double consciousness" to describe the practices of striving to be both European and black. Double consciousness refers to the identity negotiations whereby the boundaries of national and ethnic identities are unhinged, the Occidental privilege over the Oriental breaks down, and new grounds are then reimagined. It includes the formation of polysemic cultural forms and rhythms, as well as strategies of opposition, as "blacks" weigh contrasting varieties of subjectivity.

For Naficy (1994), an exile is in a continual process of becoming, involving separation from home, a period of liminality, and potential incorporation into the dominant host society. Liminality is that real or imagined space of in-betweenness that was echoed earlier when an Arab-American man described the experience of "having one foot here and the other back home." At once, liminality is an imagined space of becoming, a discursive site of identity production, and a site where material relations are struggled over and rearticulated.

Whereas exiles are defined by utopian possibilities, exile cosmopolitanism also involves doubt about the self, home traditions, and taken-for-granted values. So, exile cosmopolitans discursively construct multiple identities and oscillate among them. They focus on representing their particular histories and articulating their specific positionalities between their "home" and "host" societies. By not remaining fixed in any one identity, exiles face a continual paradox: Although they do not return to their homeland, they refuse to become totally assimilated; instead, they dream of an unrealizable return to an imagined construction of home.

In the slipzone, exile groups haggle over their subordinate status, resist colonized representation, and articulate similarities and differences while taking cultural forms from the host society to guide their ethnic transformation. Because exiles are in a constant process of becoming, they are incessantly defining and explaining themselves to others and continually restating their similarities and differences in an aesthetics of repetition. Exile discourse also may involve mimicry, in which the exile uses cultural forms to critique the host society while at the same time idealizing it.

POLITICAL JOKING AS SITUATED COMMUNICATION

The joke is a multifaceted speech event, and so too are the narratives of displacement and erasure by which U.S. Arab-Americans structure their comedic perspectives and framings of painful experiences. In this section, we review studies of joking that display the cultural dimensions of these performances. We review work only on political and ethnic jokes, with a sidelong glance at sexual jokes. But we recognize that political, ethnic, and sexual jokes are not mutually exclusive; rather, they are a lamination of cultural collisions in which the political cannot be understood outside of a particular cultural or ethnic context, and what is sexual is similarly culturally bound.

Many scholars have studied the popularity of political, ethnic, and sexual jokes by analyzing how they perform the general functions that joking serves (Basso, 1979; Fine, 1976; Oring, 1987; Sacks, 1978; Silberman-Federman, 1995). Joke telling often is seen as a means of popular entertainment and a mechanism for coping with the "demands and hardships of everyday life" (Draister, 1989, p. 119). Most agree that the joke works through a geometry of incongruities. The basic structures of jokes "revolve around the conflict between norms and the incongruous union of two distant ideas or meanings" (Stein, 1989, p. 91). For political jokes, the structure of incongruity usually is between what leaders or governments are supposed to be and what they actually are like (Draister, 1989; Stein, 1989; Stokker, 1991). The greater the distance between such normative spheres and the greater the significance of these spheres, the better the joke.

Working in the context of East and West Germany after the fall of the Berlin Wall, Stein (1989) shows that political and ethnic jokes can create and express resistance in response to repressive political conditions. Stokker (1991) makes a similar move in her analysis of Norwegian resistance to Nazi invaders. In a theoretical overview of political and ethnic jokes, Goldstein (1976) demonstrates that jokes also are used to derogate oneself, helping those feeling helpless to transcend their predicaments by seeing their weaknesses within a larger frame.

La Fave and Mannell (1976) argue that joking incongruities are processed differently by groups that are both ethnically and nationally different from one another. They reflect on two of their earlier studies in which they compared "black African" college students with "Caucasian Canadian" citizens living in a large Canadian city. They studied 44 people from each group, giving each group the same set of representations to examine. In one cartoon,

> a man with a baby on his back is shaking hands with an older woman while two younger women stand by. The caption reads: "A man was carrying a baby on his back when he met his mother-in-law. He shook hands with her, hugged her, then went dancing with his sisters." (p. 232)

From this example, La Fave and Mannell explain the "perceived" incongruity at work in the cartoon:

> The above item is at odds with black African culture because a black African male (a) is supposed to avoid physical contact with his mother-in-law, (b) should not do women's work such as baby-carrying, and (c) is not allowed an incestuous relationship with his sisters such as dancing with them. Note, however, that this item violates no Caucasian Canadian norms. (p. 233)

La Fave and Mannell (1976) expected that the black Africans would find this depiction more strange and amusing because of the cultural incongruities, yet it was the Caucasian Canadian senior citizens who were most amused and who found the picture most strange. Based on this example, which is the only one that they pull out of this particular study, La Fave and Mannell contend that incongruities are culturally relative; political jokes might not convey prejudice but instead indicate "the ethnocentrism of the amused rather than anything absurd about the ethnic's behavior" (p. 231).

La Fave and Mannell (1976) never make clear what part of Africa they are considering (e.g., West Africa, Sub-Saharan Africa, East Africa, North Africa) or whether they assume a Pan-African sense of Africa. Likewise, they do not problematize how they are juxtaposing the label *black* to the label *Africa.* In one sweeping paragraph, without providing evidence, they assume that it is common knowledge that black Africans observe the aforementioned taboos. This is a homogenizing move. The way in which they imply that Caucasian Canadians always find such actions acceptable is equally reductionistic.

Other scholars conclude that political joke telling can be an act of civil disobedience eliciting a response from heads of government. Draister (1989) traces the ways in which the Soviet government censored jokes about its administration, and Shehata (1992) examines Nasser's decision to banish political jokes when he led Egypt's government.

Similar meaning patterns in political jokes are emerging in the literature about the Arab world. Shehata (1992) shows how Egyptians satirized Mubarek:

> They asked the presidents of Egypt what was the most difficult year in their lives. Jamal Abdel Nasser thought a little bit and said, "The year of the *naksa* (setback), 1967." Sadat thought a little and said, "The year of the Ramadan War, 1973." Mubarek immediately said, "My second year in high school." (p. 87)

Similarly, Dundes and Pagter (1991) show how jokes and cartoons produced during the Gulf War sought to humiliate Saddam Hussein and glorify Allied military superiority. Often, the humor attacked Hussein's masculinity in crude sexual terms: "Do you know what Saddam Hussein and his father have in common? Neither of them pulled out in time" (p. 309). Allied jokes also displayed Iraqi stupidity: "How may Iraqis does it take to launch a SCUD missile? Three. One to aim, the second to fire the missile, and the third to watch CNN to see where it landed" (p. 318). From their analysis, Dundes and Pagter conclude that "jokes are veritable fictional bullets firing a constant barrage at a repressive system and its leadership" (p. 14).

Kanaana (1995) suggests the other side of what Dundes and Pagter (1991) uncover. Working from the perspective of Palestinians, Kanaana (1995) also examined political jokes during the Gulf War. She found that an important balance principle at work in political jokes was that "one's enemy's enemy is one's friend" (p. 66). Iraq's enemies were the United States, Saudi Arabia, Kuwait, and Qatar; thus, the jokes all were targeted toward the weaknesses of these nation-states and their leaders. Hussein was profiled as a strong witty protector of Islam and all things truly Arab: "Someone asked Saddam how many hours it took him to occupy Kuwait. He answered, 'Four hours.' And how many hours would you need to take Saudi Arabia? 'Eight hours.' And Bahrain? 'That, we can take by fax' " (p. 70). The open hostility expressed toward the Allies served as a means of solidarity, relief, and resistance in the face of oppression. As the prewar, wartime, and postwar stages proceeded, the jokes changed from demonstrating pride and excitement, to demonstrating joy and revenge, to demonstrating lament—but always with Hussein remaining the hero.

Sexual jokes, like political and ethnic jokes, occur in most cultures and serve to stress ties among group members, draw the lines between in- and out-groups, and reinforce norms for behavior. When sexually explicit jokes show up in the Arab world, we see similar discursive patterns. Shehata's (1992) study of jokes about Nasser, Sadat, and Mubarek reveal implicit and explicit norms about sexuality and gender in Egypt and the larger Arab world. Because Sadat's wife, Jihan, is a vocal feminist and urged Egypt to address equality for women, she was the subject of many jokes that equated her feminism with promiscuity. The jokes about Sadat often implicated Mubarek as Jihan's lover and kept Jihan harnessed while Sadat traveled away from home.

Scholars examining cross-cultural joking performances are aware of the limits of functional approaches. Studies of humor that employ a general functional framework are necessarily limited because the meanings of joke texts never are fixed. Rather, the functional meaning and use of a joke is deeply dependent on the specific cultural, political, and social context of the joke as well as on the interpersonal nuances of its performance. Fine (1976), Stein (1989), and others note that cultural and social norms have a radical effect on political jokes and on the strict contexts for the safe performance of them and that the meaning of any particular joke telling is constructed in its performance. Performance meanings are "the specific meanings in relation to particular tellers, audiences, settings, and interactions" (Oring, 1987, p. 278). By grounding themselves in the specifics of the context and attending to shifts in performance, some discourse analysts have offered rich detailed interpretations for particular joke tellings that have enabled these analysts to show how humor is used subversively to invert and change social identities and political relationships.

For example, in her study of "Native Eskimo" writing, Atwood (1990) suggests that Natives usually are depicted in Canadian literature as "humorless savages or victims." Yet her analysis of two short stories by Thomas King, an indigenous Eskimo, reveals the Natives' sense of humor. In these stories, Native humor is created at the "white man's" expense.[3] One of King's stories involves the production of a local pageant in a Canadian town. By appropriating the linguistic practices and narrative forms of what he constructs as "white," King's stories incorporate an array of role reversals.

Joe is a local white man who is not well respected; he is constructed as the village idiot. But he enters the town's pageant with a skit titled "The Native Suns." Thinking that Joe has come up with something clever, local officials welcome his contribution. His skit, however, is a massacre scene in which white people sneak up on Native Eskimos and massacre them. Performing whiteness, the Natives pull out cap guns and ketchup flows from their guns as they shout, "protect the women and children" (Atwood, 1990, p. 245). Natives poke fun at white people and their barbarian practices, and readers see a construction of history where there are no virtuous white heroes, only a massacre. Atwood concludes that it is in the shifts of viewpoint and twists of narrative that humor becomes a subversive form of resistance, teaching, and identity negotiation.

Basso (1979) traces similar patterns in his analysis of Western Apache joking. Basso notes that the Western Apache engage in elaborate imitations and mimicry of "white" U.S. citizens, but in jokes that usually are told only among themselves. Their joking performances are social critiques of the white man's attitudes and behavior, conveyed in the ways in which verbal and nonverbal behaviors are distorted and orchestrated in delivery. Increased speech volume and tempo, exaggerated pitch and movements, and repetition of phrases and movements all are combined in performance to enact the white man's ineptness and Western Apache superiority.

Finally, Battaglia (1992) shows how joking performances subversively alter political identities and relationships. Battaglia analyzes the jokes that Trobriand Islanders in Papua New Guinea tell about lower-class Bau commoners, particularly those concerning the rise of a Bau politician who casts himself as an "urban cowboy," reforming the local city by sponsoring an urban yam/garden festival. Sponsoring the festival enables the politician to link the traditional values ridiculed in Bau jokes to his acts of leadership and reform. Battaglia concludes that culture is not a closed system of meanings about incongruities; rather, joking performances use deferral and displacement of meaning to alter the political relationships among the teller, target, and audiences.

Given our emphasis on understanding how performance meanings in joking alter national identities and political relationships, we now turn to several examples of political jokes, humorous narratives, and comedic allegories in one Arab-American community to explore how the specific moves in the joking performances illuminate exile liminality and produce transnational identities. We also bring to bear Gilroy's conception of double-consciousness as well as Naficy's interpretation of exile liminality and the slipzones to the joking performances that we analyze. Each joking and narrative encounter points to moments of diasporic yearnings and practices, liminal and hybrid identity negotiations, and the national imaginary.

POLITICAL JOKES AND ARAB-AMERICAN IDENTITIES

Because of the collaborative nature of joking performances, it is important that readers have a clearer sense of the first author's positionality because she was part of the audience for these jokes. K is a Native American and Portuguese U.S. citizen. Before she earned entrée into the AAMA, K was aware of only two common experiences that she shared with its members: traveling and living in Jerusalem and an interest in Arab/U.S. Arab-American politics. K has traveled and lived in Jerusalem, a city that both Israeli Jews and Palestinians consider as their capital. K speaks more Hebrew than Arabic, yet she is neither Jewish nor Arab. K's lack of fluency in Arabic positions her at the edge of the interpretive community of Arabic-speaking members, yet her familiarity with issues in the Arab world helps to balance the differences. Over time, K learned that she and the Arab world have other mutual interests such as support for a Palestinian state, support for unveiling terrorist stereotypes that fix Arabs into dangerous subjectivities, and enjoyment of cultural practices including dancing, food, and storytelling.

During the period from 1995 to 1997, K met regularly with AAMA members for monthly board meetings and small working dinner parties. Other gatherings included formal subcommittee meetings, local festivals, and cultural events such as annual parties and banquets (haflehs), picnics, and potlucks. The first joke analyzed was recorded at a monthly board meeting. When K recorded the first joke, she had known Sami, the narrator, for 6 months. He was the president of AAMA at the time. Sami (hereafter referred to as S) is a Palestinian U.S. citizen, and he narrated the first two jokes.

Performance of Joke 1

During the announcement portion of the board meeting, the president notes that a famous Palestinian poet is performing in a nearby city. Then he launches into a story about this poet:

The narrator addresses K:

001 **S:** Oh, *habibti* [sweetie], you have to hear this story. For a while, Muzaffar Al Nuwab, the *best,* the absolute most *beautiful,* of Palestinian romantic poets, lived in Jordan. When Hussein read his work, Hussein threatened to kill him. (Looking at K, the narrator makes a flat hand and places it under his throat.) *Do* you *know* what *I mean*?

(pause)

002 **K:** (smiling and nodding) Um hmm.

003 **S:** Hussein was *really* going to kill him. So then he moved to Egypt. (pause) Mubarak got ahold of some of his work *and he* wanted to *kill him.* So he moved *again,* this time to Syria. (pause) He only lasted in Syria 1 week, and Assad wanted to kill him. *Now* do you know where he is? (pause) (S looks at K as if she might know)

004 **K:** (shakes her head)

005 **S:** He is living in *New York* with *Salman Rushdie*!

(general laughter)

The first reference to King Hussein (Turn 001) sets up the spatial temporal alignment. We begin with the clue that Al Nuwab is not in Palestine; he is in exile and must negotiate a Palestinian-in-Jordan subject position. Jordan, in terms of Palestinian interests, is a liminal site because Jordan has taken in many exiled Palestinians and has granted many of them citizenship. That Hussein has acted as representative of the Palestinian people in the past, particularly after the Six Day War, shapes the interpellation at work in this joke.

It is important to recognize that in Turn 001 the narrator (S) addresses three different audiences. K is the primary audience in that she is singled out and addressed as habibti (a term of address that assumes closeness and familiarity). The second audience consists of those AAMA members who are Arab-Americans native to Jordan, Lebanon, Sudan, Palestine, Algeria, and Saudi Arabia; they have the inside knowledge about the work of Al Nuwab, and they are aware of his actual present exiled location. The third audience is U.S. Arab-Americans who are born and raised in the United States as well as U.S. citizens who are not Arabs but are married to Arab-Americans. Within the third audience, very few speak Arabic. This audience neither knows the work of Al Nuwab nor knows about the details of his exile. Yet all three audiences know about Hussein's ruffled relationship with Palestinians.

In the next move of the joke (Turn 003), Al Nuwab moves to Egypt and we are introduced to another Arab leader who, after Sadat's assassination, represents Palestinians in international peace talks. Sadat is much more famous for speaking for Palestinians; the image of Sadat, Begin, and Carter embracing at the end of the Camp David accords left an indelible mark on Arabs, Israelis, and U.S. citizens. Yet the mark also is tainted with deep-seated ideological struggles and pain. For whom did this limited peace serve? Palestinians were not the immediate benefactors; in fact, after Camp David, Libya, the Saudi government, and Iraq expelled Palestinian migrant laborers. With peace, then, came more exile as well as more ambivalence, hope, and fear. The audiences know that Palestinians have not forgotten their troubled relationships with the leaders of these states.

In Turn 003, the performance of S becomes more dramatic as Al Nuwab moves to Syria. A sense of certain fatality is explicit in this move of the joke. Assad, leader of Syria, had a seat at the "Middle Eastern" peace table. All three leaders had lost land to Israel. However, only Assad did not recover land, so Syria's relationship with Israel remained very hostile, and Assad's allegiance to Palestinians was slippery at best.

Thus far, the information explicitly stated in this joke is quite meager. A well-known Palestinian poet, already living outside of Palestine, is threatened with death and flees each time the ruler of the state reads his work. Although he is an Arab, none of these three Arab nation-states will claim him. This rejection and Al Nuwab's repeated flights recapitulate in a poignant way the Palestinian experience of exile, danger, and displacement.

The incongruities of this joke lie in the unstated information and context, and to the extent that different cultural groups in the immediate audience can fill in this information, they respond more enthusiastically to the joke. S maximizes the disparity and significance of these incongruous spheres through superlatives (Al Nuwab is "the best" and the "absolute most beautiful") and nonverbal emphasis. Al Nuwab's poetry is actually quite political given that it is highly critical of the Arab regimes that he believes lost Jerusalem and Palestine. S identifies Al Nuwab only as a poet, not a political agitator or dissenter. Al Nuwab is, in fact, all three, thus further heightening the incongruity. Moreover, Al Nuwab is threatened not with censorship but rather with death, a point that S highlights by pausing, addressing K directly, making a hand gesture, and waiting for her to give a response of understanding. Like the Palestinians, Al Nuwab is threatened with death by the very states that one might expect to be most hospitable —the Arab states—and repeated relocations bring no safety.

Jokes, like any joint project, require coordination and joint commitment by both the narrator and the audience. Coordinating a hearer's interpretation always is a function of the speaker's actions in two communication "tracks." Track 1 is that in which the content of the joke unfolds, and Track 2 is that in which matters of communicative understanding are worked out among the participants (Clark, 1996, p. 154). Much of S's performance works both communication tracks to ensure K's comprehension of the joke, using many different signals to coordinate K's understanding. For example, he signifies who Al Nuwab is by using a contextualizing frame (i.e., the "best" and the "absolute most beautiful") that both describes and indicates emphasis with superlative intensifiers (e.g., "best") and vocal indicators (e.g., "*best*"). S also signifies the danger of Hussein's intent to kill Al Nuwab by both asserting and demonstrating Hussein's intent with a hand chop and following it by repeating the assertion ("Hussein was really going to kill him") and using another intensifier and vocal indicator ("*really*"). S then checks K's understanding ("Do you know what I mean?") and underscores the importance of the comprehension check with vocal indicators (e.g., "*Do* you *know*") and by waiting for K to acknowledge her understanding in Turn 002 before continuing. Finally, S invites K to test her understanding again in turn 003 with a direct glance and question ("*Now* do you know where he is?").

With K's head shake, she becomes a full participant in the joking event, soon to realize that she is caught in her acknowledgment of being unaware that her own country would be a likely site for Al Nuwab. The incongruity between the safety of New York, a site within K's national home, and the dangers of Jordan, Egypt, and Syria is clear. It is heightened by the balance principle that Al Nuwab's enemies should be K's enemies as well given that Al Nuwab is now a New Yorker. As we are led by S to appreciate Al Nuwab as the best poet and to detest the dangers created by Hussein, Mubarek, and Assad, so too do we appreciate the solution to Al Nuwab's dilemma—that he takes refuge in New York. S's performance cues, therefore, help K to understand the joke and help other audience members to become more amused by the incongruities.

The performance by S does something more powerful; he commits K to become a participant in a joint project that involves her own country and hence involves her as a citizen of the safe location for Al Nuwab and for Arab-Americans. This move also calls into question K's position as a transnational ethnographer. Having traveled in Jordan, Egypt, and Syria, K can appreciate the stakes in Al Nuwab's migration. That she works within postcolonial theories and literatures also casts her in a transnational intellectual space that is reflected through K's relationship with S. If K is not aware of Rushdie's exile status—that he lives in London rather than in New York—then the ultimate location of Al Nuwab is not funny. The punch line is a test of colonial history.

The incongruities that create the humor of the joke, then, are connected to the problem-solution structure posed in the joke. This structure is discussed in detail by Sacks (1978), who describes sexual jokes as creating puzzles for their audiences to solve, with punch lines as the answers to the puzzles posed by the jokes. In this case, by pausing after each new place name and then pausing after the final question, S emphasizes that locational issues are central to this joke, and the leading question becomes the following: Where is Al Nuwab now? But the question for the audience posed by the joke actually is much deeper: Where are we now, the Palestinian people, the Arabs abandoned and exiled by other Arabs?

The answer on the surface, New York, resonates on several cultural levels. New York is the well-known disembarkation point for refugees and immigrants to the United States. But it also is the Third World city par excellence, in the view of Naficy (1994) and other postcolonial critics, who point to its heterogeneity, multizones of identity, and political and economic maze. Rushdie's position also echoes that of the Palestinian people; like them, he has been attacked by other Muslims and forced to flee.

But in fact, Al Nuwab is not in New York, he is in France, and Rushdie is in England, as S himself knows. This punch line is a subtle historical move. Invoking Britain and France introduces the layers of colonialism that also are part of the joke's articulation, producing the ambivalence and liminality of postcolonial exile identities. India no longer is safe for Rushdie; he takes asylum in England, former colonizer of his homeland. Al Nuwab is taken in by France, the imperial power that colonized Algeria and Tunisia. That England and France have embraced Third World exiles has many ambiguous dimensions. These ambiguities signal an answer to the question: Where are we Palestinians now? Both Al Nuwab's and Rushdie's positions closely approximate that of the immediate audience for this joke. They inhabit a slipzone, taking refuge in a country they see as colonial and imperialist, immersed in Western culture while struggling to maintain their own, always seeing out of several perspectives. Hence, the content of the joke illustrates the ambivalence and liminality of Palestinian identities.

The joke is a joint project organized by layers of action, and it is in the correspondences between layers that identities can be negotiated in performance (Clark, 1996). Clark (1996) points out that in a joint action, each layer has its own deictic frame. These are frames of reference often communicated through pronouns such as I, you, here, and now that specify persons, time, and space (p. 358) and thus characterize situational features with layers of action present at the same time. In analyzing the performance by S, the bottom layer of action is the domain of "serious" action, organized by conventionalized understandings of who S, K, and the other audience members are and how they came to be involved in a joking relationship at an AAMA meeting. Another layer of action is the nonserious fictional frame of Al Nuwab and Rushdie occupying the liminality of exile. Participants typically employ a principle in which they imagine and appreciate the contrasts between layers of action or between the hypothetical situation of the joke and the actual situation of the participants. The audience also may employ a correspondence principle linking features across layers of action. Given their shared political and cultural knowledge, as well as the plausible similarities among S, the Arab audience, and Al Nuwab, K can legitimately draw inferences about S and the Arab audience similar to those of Al Nuwab and Rushdie who become New Yorkers, the inference being that they too have transnational identities.

The joke, then, leads the hearers to infer from the characters in the joke that the identity of S and the Arab audience can be reconfigured from Arabs to Arab-Americans. Hence, the joke in performance constitutes the location of Arabs in closer political and social relationship to K and situates Arab-Americans as transnational. By virtue of her joint participation in the joke, K helps to create the moment that enables S and the Arab audience to position themselves with Rushdie and Al Nuwab as exile cosmopolitans with transnational identities that reconfigure the political relationship they have with K. Thus, as Battaglia (1992) observes, it is the act of constructing meaning in joking performances through substitution and displacement that alters the political relationships among the participants.

Performance of Joke 2

The second joke analyzed occurred when S came to a dinner party at K's house after working together for a year. It exemplifies multiple layers of action and registers of narration. It was framed by the prior statement, "When you learn more Arabic, these jokes will be funnier." The narrator and K were upstairs in her study smoking cigarettes. He put out his cigarette, and the following exchange occurred:

001 **S:** Do you remember when Arafat married Suha *Taweel*?

002 **K:** Yes, but the timing of it is fuzzy in my head.

003 **S:** Well, after their marriage, Arafat told people that when there is a *Palestinian state* he was going to establish a Palestinian airline. He wanted to call it *Air Arafat.* You know what "*air*" means in Arabic?

004 **K:** No.

005 **S:** It means *dick.*

006 **K:** (laughter)

007 **S:** Do you know what Taweel means in Arabic?

008 **K:** No.

009 **S:** It means *long.* When Suha heard that Arafat wanted to call the airline *Air Arafat,* she insisted that her name had to be a part of it too. So we're going to have the name *Air Arafat Taweel* [long dick Arafat].

010 (laughter)

In terms of the joke's structure, K's knowing what Taweel meant in Arabic is crucial to its temporal-spatial alignment. Once that is established, the movement toward a Palestinian state with an official state airline locates the heart of the joke. S announces his awareness of the need to monitor K's understanding in Turn 001 and does so, checking her understanding of Arabic terms three times (Turns 001, 003, and 007). The code switching in and of itself serves as a primary part of the humor in this performance. Once Taweel is translated, the content is clear to K before S performs the punch line.

In telling the joke, S expresses to K, for the first time, a humorous yet critical perspective of the leadership in the Palestinian national struggle.

He also communicates his own degree of Westernization and in-betweenness, not so much through the telling of a "dirty joke" to a woman as through the telling of an ever-so-slightly politically resistant joke to a non-Palestinian. Although he could have communicated the substance of the joke without the last sentence, he carefully completes the joke, uttering the sexually and politically risqué combination of words together.

Because this is a political joke, it creates instances of identity that call into question the relationship between culture and power. These elements and the slippages between them construct identities, in this case transnational ones. Although the structures of spatial and temporal alignment shape each discursive move, it is the participants who translate structure into lived experience. That is, the sensual and emotive power of this performance punctuates the linguistic structures at work in the narration; both an aesthetic of pleasure and one of pain are embodied in narration.

The seriousness of the issues in political joking is what distinguishes political jokes from other types. In the first joke, Al Nuwab's life is at risk in each turn of phrase; his political dissent throws him from state to state in the Arab world, and he becomes a cultural nomad. In the second joke, what is assumed before any utterance can make sense is that the Palestinian state that Arafat imagines is one that gives him the power to create a national airline named after the head of state.

These two jokes illuminate liminality, hybridity, and transnational identities. Although the narrator of these political jokes is not speaking about himself per se, he is making claims about the state of Palestinian traveling identities. In the first joke, the audience laughs at the repetition, at the running from one nation to another, as S's pitch and tone encourage such a reading. It is funny that Al Nuwab is thrown from nation to nation because everyone knows exactly why each nation's leader would be outraged by Al Nuwab's work. He is a cultural dissident, sympathetic to Marxism and also to aesthetics that run counter to those of Islam.

An especially appreciative audience for the first joke would be Arabs and Palestinians who have family displaced by colonial dissolution, by the extremism rampant in the postcolonial Arab world, or by the threat of political and cultural resistance. That Al Nuwab is introduced as the most beautiful writer among the Palestinian romantic poets signifies that S and most of his audience have a political allegiance to him and an awareness of the volatile nature of his work; the story would offend pious observers of Islam or Christianity. Clearly, they do not see him as the threat; rather, it is the heads of state who are the threat, rekindling the pains they associate with themselves. The first joke, then, employs characters correspondent with the experiences of the audience, which in turn helps to constitute their own status as liminal exiles. Both jokes also illuminate transnational identities for the narrator, the participating Arab audience, and K. These are constituted by S and ratified by K's participation in the performance of the joke.

S demonstrates in the flesh what Basso (1979) explains in his analysis of political joking performances. For example, in both jokes the metanarrative elements of the narration include a quickening tempo in S's speech. S asks questions more loudly and rapidly in certain moments of his performance, and nonverbally his body speaks with its own intensity. When S asks in the second joke, "Do you know what 'air' means in Arabic?," he moves away from K. After K replies, "No," he translates, "It means dick." By the time he asks K whether she knows what Taweel means in Arabic, he draws much closer to her and is even more animated. This shifting around allows S to occupy a hybrid space of identity, a slipzone in which multiple identities are negotiated. The intimacy of the performance creates a closer, more personal identity for S and his relationship with K while simultaneously reasserting his Palestinian identity.

In the performance of both of these jokes, therefore, liminal and hybrid identities are negotiated. Al Nuwab has no fixed identity as a Palestinian because in the absence of a Palestinian state he becomes a nomad, vulnerable to hostile borders. Still, he moves to Jordan as an Arab, albeit a non-Jordanian one. Thus, he walks in between shared identity and difference; his location is constantly shifting, producing a constant set of new slipzones. In the second joke, a Palestinian identity is attached to a national airline. What tempers this imagined identity is the lack of a recognized territory. The "Long Dick Airlines" signals Palestinian envy; the imagined phallus becomes the state. In addition to the new, transnational U.S. American identity that S constructs for himself, the jokes remind the audience what is at stake for Arabs and the possibilities for Palestine. The second joke brings up issues of representation and otherness in as much as it is tinged with desire. Still, by taking a mocking stance toward Arafat's arrogant desires, S configures his identity as closer to K, occupying a transnational space. Thus, both jokes display hybrid identities, and in displaying them, they construct the joke teller as hybrid as well.

Joking performances by others also illustrate the transnational location of U.S. Arab-Americans. After working with the AAMA for 1 year, K attended a retreat/planning session in the spring of 1996. A group of 12 board members and members active in the organization attended. At the beginning of the meeting, Jami (hereafter referred to as J), vice president of governmental affairs for the AAMA, said, "So, [K], you're getting to know us now. Did you know that for every three Arabs, there are four political parties?"

We were still laughing when the phone rang. Eddie (hereafter referred to as E), the organization's treasurer and the host of our retreat, picked up the phone and said,

"Hello. Who is this?" After a short pause, he said in exasperation, "It's Mohammed. That's like calling an Italian's house and asking for Pauli. *Which* Mohammed?" After another pause, he announced to us,

"Oh, it's Mohammed Sadi, and he is running on Arab time [is late]."

In the first joke, J makes a relational claim that positions K as being closer to the community, not as an insider but rather as one who knows the community. Then J touches on an issue to which many U.S. Arab-American communities and those in the Arab world are sensitive—that of solidarity. Although they share a language (Arabic), Arabs differ ethnically, nationally, in terms of cultural practices, religion and religious piety, political affiliation, and so on. Here, J plays with this diversity that constitutes Arab identities, drawing it out into a joke that takes an outsider's perspective to the point that the joke might even have been construed as derogatory if uttered by a non-Arab.

Even though K is singled out as J's interlocutor in this joking performance, there also is a larger, more diverse audience participating. Six of the audience members were born in the Arab world and are recent immigrants to the United States. They laugh the hardest at this joke because they know of the Syrian comedian who is famous for telling this joke. They also have lived through many different facets of national struggles and nationalist movements in Palestine, Egypt, Iraq, and Lebanon. Four other audience members were U.S. Arab-Americans who were born in the United States, speak little or no Arabic, but are immersed in Arab political advocacy in the United States. They have experienced the challenges to solidarity in the United States through their work with national and local Arab-American organizations. They also enjoy and appreciate the joke.

Having lived in Jerusalem during the mid-1980s, just 6 months prior to the *Intifada* (the Palestinian uprising against Israeli occupation), K witnessed the production of underground leaflets that different nationalist groups in Palestine disseminated to their communities, the tensions among the groups, and the Israeli response to Palestinian resistance. The irony is that K lived with Israelis as an overseas student at the Hebrew University of Jerusalem yet immediately behind an Arab village where she was closely connected to three families who afforded her access to the production of leaflets. At the same time, one of K's Israeli roommates had just finished 2 years of intelligence work in the army and was very suspicious of Palestinian resistance.

J knows of K's experiences and thus targets her as an insider/outsider listener. Without the experiences of living in the heart of Jerusalem and traveling across the Fertile Crescent, K would not have been able to understand the humor and/or appreciate the pain associated with the joke.

E's joking performance also assumes a transnational in-between position. Once the phone rings, he notes the ubiquity of the name Mohammed by reference to another non-Arab ethnic group, Italians. Then he locates himself again both inside and outside Arab identity by referring to "Arab time," a concept that only takes on meaning through contrast with non-Arab time. While on the phone, he performs his part of the conversation for everyone attending the retreat. The moment he declares that Mohammad was running on Arab time, the liminal space that many members occupy becomes quite visible. E runs on what he and others, such as Yasmeen (AAMA social/cultural director), explain as "American time"—"you know, the R.S.V.P., have an agenda, and be on time" schedule. Yet the internal joke within this particular U.S. Arab-American community is that Arab time runs more slowly, for example, "people get here when they get here." Both Eddie and Yasmeen have communicated to K that being Arab-American is like living in between two worlds. The first-generation newer immigrants feel the pressure of adapting to U.S. time, but they do not worry about it enough to actually live up to its expectations in contexts such as volunteer organizations. They often turn the joke back on its teller, suggesting that if people really want to recover an "Arab identity," then they should live like Arabs and change the clock of their hectic lives. Each move makes the push and pull between Arab and non-Arab time a liminal issue.

Several years later, when K knew E much better, K found herself driving with him back to his house. In that relaxed context, E told K a story about an experience that he had with his father. E's father and grandfather both were Syrian Lebanese Arabs who immigrated to this country during the early 1900s. Unlike 95% of the first-wave Arab immigrants, they are Muslim.

> **E:** One day my dad says to me, "Come on, let's go to the city." So, I asked him, "Why?" He says, "I've got some business there." So, we went. He had me drive him to the cemetery where my grandfather is buried. My dad told me to watch guard. It turns out there was a Star of David on my

> grandfather's grave, and my dad was hard at work, with a hammer and chisel, pounding it off. (E laughs as he remembers the scene.) It had to be on my dad's mind because he had talked with his *Imam* [Muslim religious authority] about it, and the Imam said, "You've got to get that off of there."

Both K and E burst out laughing at that point. When K asked E to explain how this could have happened in a midwestern city with such a large Arab population, he explained, "People knew so little about Islam at the time [early 1970s] that they assumed that if you were not Christian, you must be Jewish." For pious Muslims, this story might not seem funny. This is particularly true for Palestinians who already feel oppressed by Israeli practices of religious and political Judaism. Yet it was funny to E because, as he explained, "This is just another example of the American way. Lump everyone together and ignore real differences; if one is not Christian, he must be the recognized 'other'—Jewish."

Through this story, E also hinted at the limits of assimilation. E's father lived with the inappropriate gravestone for nearly 20 years before he spoke to his Imam about this matter. As he neared the end of his own life, he could not bear the thought of leaving his father's gravestone marked as Jewish. This story pinpoints a diasporic condition that was articulated earlier when those Arabs who consider themselves exiles and refugees told K that being Arab means maintaining indigenous cultural practices and refusing to assimilate into the melting pot of culture in those spaces that are not yet home. E's father was not willing to fully assimilate, nor was he ready to let his father's grave be mismarked, to the extent that he was willing to "desecrate" a grave and break a law. Yet in this act of undoing, he left the gravestone unmarked, erasing difference. He could not sculpt in a crescent and a star; he could only commit an act of erasure of the Star of David.

Although E did not necessarily articulate this situation as being diasporic or transnational, it does indeed reflect both conditions. That his father and grandfather immigrated to the United States because they could not survive economically in the south of Lebanon points to global conditions of migration. E and his father drove from one medium-sized midwestern city with a considerable population of Arabs to another large midwestern city with one of the largest Arab populations in the country, where they both have lived. This speaks to another diasporic condition. Arabs build little Syrias, Palestines, Egypts, Yemens, Lebanons, and so on in those cities where they have either migrated or first landed when they arrived in this country. Yet despite the large numbers of Arabs, E's father and grandfather could not escape institutional powers that mark ethnicities and religious differences. It is in this spirit and fight to recover and maintain differences that another one of the AAMA's members told K, "Diaspora means that my granddaughter's granddaughter will go to haflehs."

CONCLUSION

Our analysis illuminates some of the ways in which transnational identities are produced and lived through communicative practices. The narrators skillfully invite hearers to make correspondent inferences between the characters in the joking performances and the political identities of their Arab audiences. Understanding and appreciating these performances means learning the political stances of the characters in relation to the participants in the performance context. This results in the identities of the narrators and their Arab audience members being reconstituted not as Arab but rather as transnational Arab-Americans, betwixt and between the seemingly fixed Third World and First World.

Perhaps most important, our analysis also shows that the identities constituted in these joke tellings are shaped by all of the audience members. The audience includes K, the U.S. citizen who is at once outside of this community yet inside it as an ethnographer, not speaking Arabic yet being one who lived and traveled in the Arab world. By listening to the joking encounters, K becomes a multiple-role player and participant in the performances. With K's participation in and appreciation of the jokes, her lines of action ratify the transnational identities claimed and performatively enunciated by all of the narrators.

Finally, each joke illustrates different aspects of the themes elaborated by Gilroy (1993) and Naficy (1994)—displacement, exile, liminality, double consciousness, and possessing multiple homes and subjectivities. The first joke about Al Nuwab engages the issues and politics of exile, liminality, and Wanderlust. The second joke about the Palestinian airline plays with an imagination of the state-to-be, yet its humor cuts against the grain as the phallus becomes the absent state. In the third joke, the narrator's liminality allows what could be construed as an ethnic slur about Arab factionalism to instead function as in-group humor. And the last story highlights the diasporic conditions of so many U.S. Arab-Americans who struggle against assimilation.

In her ethnography of Tunisian folklore, Webber (1991) draws in her readers to consider a simple yet profound idea. Pulling from an old Tunisian saying that "every story suggests another," she opens up the interdependent relationship between storytelling, with its traces of preceding narratives, and the shifting historical conditions to which the narration responds in performance. Once performed, the story becomes a moment in history, a temporary ground that holds the possibilities for the next performative iteration. Clearly, stories, like jokes, take many forms that stretch the immediate context of a single performance beyond itself and toward a plethora of other practices.

Our analysis opens up the ways in which differential sets of power relations are reinscribed when exiles relocate; it is in discourse that binary oppositions gain their authority, and it is through such moves that identities seemingly have been "fixed" in the first place. Postcolonial theory alone, however, does not show readers how global practices and cultural forms are translated into the daily speaking practices of postcolonial exiles. Our analysis of political joking suggests that until each move in the discourse is tapped, one might not see the roles that metanarration, the coordination of meaning, performance cues, and moves of the body play in the construction of social identities. Transnational identities are produced in cultural forms and situated communication practices.

NOTES

1. AAMA is a pseudonym, as are all of the individuals' names in this chapter.
2. For transnational feminist treatments of these conflations, see Joseph (1999) and Mohanty (1997).
3. Labels of "Natives" and "white men" are those used in the original text by Atwood (1990).

REFERENCES

Appadurai, A. (1996). *Modernity at large: Cultural dimensions of globalization.* Minneapolis: University of Minnesota Press.

Atwood, M. (1990). A double-bladed knife: Subversive laughter in two stories by Thomas King. *Canadian Literature, 124,* 243-251.

Basso, K. H. (1979). *Portraits of "the Whiteman": Linguistic play and cultural symbols among the Western Apache.* Cambridge, UK: Cambridge University Press.

Battaglia, D. (1992). Displacing culture: A joke of significance in urban Papua New Guinea. *New Literary History, 22,* 1003-1017.

Bauman, R. (1986). *Story, performance, and event: Contextual studies of oral narrative.* Cambridge, UK: Cambridge University Press.

Behdad, A. (1994). *Belated travelers: Orientalism in the age of colonial dissolution.* Durham, NC: Duke University Press.

Bhabha, H. (1994). *The location of culture.* New York: Routledge.

Clark, H. (1996). *Using language.* Cambridge, UK: Cambridge University Press.

Collier, M. J. (1998). Researching cultural identity: Reconciling interpretive and postcolonial perspectives. In D. Tanno & A. Gonzalez (Eds.), *Communication and identity across cultures* (pp. 122-147). Thousand Oaks, CA: Sage.

Conquergood, D. (1991). Rethinking ethnography: Towards a critical cultural politics. *Communication Monographs, 58,* 179-194.

Draister, E. (1989). Soviet underground jokes as a means of popular entertainment. *Journal of Popular Culture, 23,* 117-125.

Dundes, A., & Pagter, C. (1991). The mobile SCUD missile launcher and other Persian Gulf warlore: An American folk image of Saddam Hussein's Iraq. *Western Folklore, 50,* 303-322.

Fine, G. (1976). Obscene joking across cultures. *Journal of Communication, 26*(3), 134-140.

Gilroy, P. (1993). *The black Atlantic: Modernity and double consciousness.* Cambridge: Harvard University Press.

Goldstein, J. (1976). Theoretical notes on humor. *Journal of Communication, 26*(3), 104-112.

Grewal, I. (1994). Autobiographic subjects and diasporic locations: *Meatless Days* and *Borderlands.* In I. Grewal & C. Kaplan (Eds.), *Scattered hegemonies: Postmodernity and transnational feminist practices* (pp. 231-254). Minneapolis: University of Minnesota Press.

Grewal, I., & Kaplan, C. (1994). Introduction: Transnational feminist practices and questions of postmodernity. In I. Grewal & C. Kaplan (Eds.), *Scattered hegemonies: Postmodernity and transnational feminist practices* (pp. 1-33). Minneapolis: University of Minnesota Press.

Grossberg, L. (1995). The space of culture, the power of space. In I. Chambers & L. Curti (Eds.), *The postcolonial question: Common skies, divided horizons* (pp. 169-188). London: Routledge.

Gumperz, J. (1982). Introduction: Language and the communication of social identity. In J. Gumperz (Ed.), *Language and social identity* (pp. 1-21). Cambridge, UK: Cambridge University Press.

Hall, S. (1991). The local and the global: Globalization and ethnicity. In A. D. King (Ed.), *Culture, globalization, and the world system: Contemporary conditions for the representation of identity* (pp. 19-40). London: Macmillan.

Hall, S. (1995). From Eurocentrism to polycentrism. In I. Chambers & L. Curti (Eds.), *The postcolonial question: Common skies, divided horizons* (pp. 13-54). London: Routledge.

Hall, S. (1996). Cultural identity and diaspora. In P. Mongia (Ed.), *Contemporary postcolonial theory: A reader* (pp. 110-121). New York: Arnold.

Hegde, R. S. (1998). A view from elsewhere: Locating difference and the politics of representation from a transnational feminist perspective. *Communication Theory, 8,* 271-297.

Joseph, S. (1999). Against the grain of the nation: The Arab. In M. Suleiman (Ed.), *Arabs in America: Building a new future* (pp. 257-271). Philadelphia: Temple University Press.

Kanaana, S. (1995). Encounters with folklore: Palestinian humor during the Gulf War. *Journal of Folklore Research, 32,* 65-75.

Kaplan, C. (1996). *Questions of travel: Postmodern discourses of displacement.* Durham, NC: Duke University Press.

Katriel, T. (1994). Sites of memory: Discourses of the past in Israeli pioneering settlement museums. *Quarterly Journal of Speech, 88,* 1-20.

Katriel, T. (1997). *Performing the past: A study of Israeli settlement museums.* Mahwah, NJ: Lawrence Erlbaum.

Kline, S. L., & Kuper, G. (1994). Self-presentation practices in government discourse: The case of U.S. Lt. Col. Oliver North. *Text, 14,* 23-43.

La Fave, L., & Mannell, R. (1976). Does ethnic humor serve prejudice? *Journal of Communication, 36,* 231-244.

Majaj, L. (1999). Arab-American ethnicity: Location, coalitions, and cultural negotiations. In M. Suleiman (Ed.), *Arabs in America: Building a new future* (pp. 320-336). Philadelphia: Temple University Press.

McClintock, A. (1992). The angel of progress: Pitfalls of the term "post-colonialism." *Social Text, 31/32,* 84-98.

Mohanty, C. T. (1997). Under Western eyes: Feminist scholarship and colonial discourses. In A. McClintock, A. Mufti, & E. Shohat (Eds.), *Dangerous liaisons: Gender, nation, and postcolonial perspectives* (pp. 255-277). Minneapolis: University of Minnesota Press.

Morley, D., & Robins, K. (1995). *Spaces of identity: Global media, electronic landscapes, and cultural boundaries.* London: Routledge.

Mufti, A., & Shohat, E. (1997). Introduction. In A. McClintock, A. Mufti, & E. Shohat (Eds.), *Dangerous liaisons: Gender, nation, and postcolonial perspectives* (pp. 1-14). Minneapolis: University of Minnesota Press.

Naficy, H. (1994). *The making of exile cultures: Iranian television in Los Angeles.* Minneapolis: University of Minnesota Press.

Oring, E. (1987). Jokes and the discourse of disaster. *Journal of American Folklore, 100,* 276-287.

Sacks, H. (1978). Some technical considerations of a dirty joke. In J. Schenkein (Ed.), *Studies in the organization of conversational interaction* (pp. 249-271). New York: Academic Press.

Said, E. W. (1978). *Orientalism.* New York: Vintage.

Said, E. (1994). Notes on exile. *Boundary, 2*(1), 153-176.

Samhan, H. (1999). Not quite white: Race classification and the Arab-American experience. In M. Suleiman (Ed.), *Arabs in America: Building a new future* (pp. 209-226). Philadelphia: Temple University Press.

Shehata, S. S. (1992). The politics of laughter: Nasser, Sadat, and Mubarek in Egyptian political jokes. *Folklore, 103,* 75-91.

Shohat, E. (1992). Notes on the postcolonial. *Social Text, 31/32,* 99-113.

Shome, R. (1996). Postcolonial interventions in the rhetorical canon: An "other" view. *Communication Theory, 6,* 40-59.

Silberman-Federman, N. J. (1995). Jewish humor, self-hatred, or anti-Semitism: The sociology of cards in America. *Journal of Popular Culture, 28,* 211-229.

Stein, M. B. (1989). The politics of humor: The Berlin Wall in jokes and graffiti. *Western Folklore, 48,* 85-108.

Stokker, K. (1991). Heil Hitler—God save the king: Jokes and the Norwegian resistance. *Western Folklore, 50,* 171-190.

Suleiman, M. W. (1999). The Arab immigrant experience. In M. W. Suleiman (Ed.), *Arabs in American: Building a new future* (pp. 1-21). Philadelphia: Temple University Press.

Tracy, K., & Naughton, J. (1994). The identity work of questioning in intellectual discussion. *Communication Monographs, 61,* 281-302.

Trinh, M. (1989). *Woman, native, other: Writing postcoloniality and feminism.* Bloomington: Indiana University Press.

Webber, S. J. (1991). *Romancing the real: Ethnographic representation in North Africa.* Philadelphia: University of Pennsylvania Press.

9

Dialogue on the Edges

Ferment in Communication and Culture

MARY JANE COLLIER • *University of Denver*
RADHA S. HEGDE • *New York University*
WENSHU LEE • *San Jose State University*
THOMAS K. NAKAYAMA • *Arizona State University*
GUST A. YEP • *San Francisco State University*

During the past few years, dialogue has become a topic of interest for communication scholars. Building on the foundations established by philosophers such as Bakhtin (1981) and Buber (1970), personal relationship scholars such as Baxter and Montgomery (1996) have explored dialogue in relationships; Shotter (1995) and Stewart (1995) have expanded social constructionism as an orientation to interaction as dialogue; Altman and Nakayama (1991) have written about dialogue and a critical perspective; Gajjala and Mamidipudi (1999) have cyber-dialogued with each other about the uses and barriers of technology to empower women within both First World and Third World contexts; Houston (1997) has written about dialogues across race, gender, and class; and two communication journals, *Communication Quarterly* and *Southern Communication Journal,* have devoted special issues and sections to dialogue and to practical theory and dialogue, respectively. In addition, international conflict resolution scholars have been applying models of intercultural dialogue in work with Palestinians and Israelis, in Northern Ireland, and in South Africa, and organizations such as the Public Conversations Project and Public Dialogue Consortium have sponsored hundreds of community dialogues across the United States.

Our lives as citizens in an increasingly interdependent global community, as well as in culturally diverse local communities, call out for the need for new models of dialogue. There is a demand for new models that move beyond those that privilege specific types of advocates and speakers and that reinforce already unbalanced hierarchies. Examples of actual dialogue among scholars in communication journals, however, are few, and still fewer are exemplars of dialogue in which the scholars address the complexities of culture, let alone deal with intersecting forces of race, class, gender, and sexuality and incorporate discussions of structural forces such as histories, institutions, and ideologies.

After observing the lack of such published scholarly dialogues among scholars of culture and communication in communication journals, and wanting to expand the format of the "forum" sections used in some previous volumes of the International and Intercultural Communication Annual, I developed the idea of devoting a closing chapter in Volume 24 to such an interchange. I value reading published dialogues such as that between bell hooks and Cornel West (hooks & West, 1995). It occurred to me how the opportunity to participate in such a dialogue, with an opportunity to reflect, respond, challenge, and clarify positions over time, could produce a different form of knowledge. In addition, the emerging and undeniable ferment in the study of culture and communication that is increasingly evident among academics and practitioners of inter/trans/national/cultural communication seems to call out for new forms of academic engagement and scholarly inquiry. For these reasons, I invited Radha Hegde, Wenshu Lee, Tom Nakayama, and Gust Yep to participate in this dialogue because I know and respect their work and have high regard for who they are and what they each bring to the being/doing of their work on culture and communication.

The dialogue primarily took place over e-mail through the creation of our e-group (iicadialogue.yahoogroups.com). We began in October 2000 and finished in April 2001. As we began the dialogue, Lee suggested the following:

> I would like to have the group generate a list of issues (theoretical and methodological) that we in intercultural/international/transnational studies need to pay attention to at the turn of a new millennium, suggest possible solutions or new ways of asking questions, and think about the purposes of our scholarship, for whom, and for what social/political causes.

The five of us did meet in person in November 2000 at the National Communication Association (NCA) conference in Seattle, Washington, to discuss our progress and possible formats for proceeding. We agreed to have what Yep summarized as "current conversations at the edge of the field . . . , issues of metatheory, theory, and method" and to discuss what Hegde described as "possible paradigm shifts, a ferment . . . , the panopticon *gaze* . . . , alternative views of how do we read the field." Nakayama added the need for attention to "consequences such as social justice," and this was echoed by Lee and the rest of the group. When talking about form, Yep suggested, "This is experimental writing. We don't necessarily want closure." Nakayama added, "We don't have to come to hard [consensus-based] conclusions." Lee suggested that what we may be striving for is to create a conversation similar to the following: "When I read Spivak or hooks, I basically just enjoy the conversation, and then when I'm finished, I feel a new spirit or I feel encouraged, something that is heightened."[1]

We also discussed different options for a title that would capture our cyber-dialogic experience. We easily agreed on *ferment* as a theme that was appropriate in the title. Hegde reinforced the need to focus on transformative directions in theory, culture, and communication. Lee summarized "our turn to contextualized, critical, and politicized scholarship and the need to be specific and situated. In addition, there is a shared commitment to justice and challenging power." She captured our goals for the dialogue in the following way: "We hope this essay can help legitimize graduate students' and scholars' choices to do a new kind of scholarship. They can travel with us along our critical itineraries in intercultural and transnational communication."

We considered using the term *fringe* in the title because, as Lee noted, it is "a bit different from margin. . . . Margin comes with a clear sense of center, whereas fringe simply makes the limits/boundaries unclear . . . and identifies the place where boundaries are blurred. . . . Fringe includes the unease, tension, and hope" that we bring to and seek to engage in this dialogue. However, as Hegde and Yep noted, fringe could problematically connote a marginalized or "minority" perspective. When Nakayama suggested "on the edge," I expanded the term *edge* to the plural *edges* to move away from connotations of "sharpness" or organizational currency as in "cutting edge" or anxiety as in "being on edge." "Dialogue on the edges" connotes to us a liminal space of keenness, an intensity, a pointed but fluid border in which we are "on the brink." It features moving in from out, out from in, down from above and beyond. It points to voices and positions that are unfolding, are contested, and call us to question who we are and what we do. Edges paradoxically function to limit and define what is current as well as help us to create new boundaries and angles from which to view culture and communication.

As you read, you will see that several things are being accomplished in the dialogue that make this format much different from most of our current published work in communication. The first is that each of us not only take the opportunity to advocate for particular ideas but also respond to one another and build on each other's ideas. A second accomplishment of this dialogue is the co-construction of a relationship of respect for each other. There are many examples in which one of us begins his or her remarks with a polite greeting and ends with a reminder to others to feel free to "tear it up" and disagree. Each one of us recognizes the value of our colleagues' contributions by referring back to specific ideas shared by someone else.

In addition, each scholar shares personal narratives about his or her own graduate school experiences, current classrooms, and everyday life. They recognize their humanity, acknowledge that who they are affects what they study, and are reflexive. Their voices demonstrate that this exchange is an embodied dialogue and one that has been enacted with an invitational and open-ended tone as well as clear claims, critiques, and questions. These scholars co-create an unfolding and unfinished conversation about issues that are central to all of us, a conversation that I am sure will spark more dialogue among scholars/teachers/students/practitioners. I am very grateful to all of them for their participation and investment of time, energy, heart, and spirit.

QUESTION FROM MARY JANE COLLIER

What is the nature of international/cultural communication scholarship? What are key issues that scholars/teachers/practitioners need to engage in their work?

Tom Nakayama

Here is something to get us started on our intercultural communication dialogue. Feel free to "tear it up," but more important, let's discuss. I am not sure if this is where we want to go, so please feel free to post something that leads us in other directions as well.

The study of intercultural communication treads into risky terrain. It deals with other cultures and peoples and has the potential to have tremendous impact on how people might think about, understand, deal with, and make policy regarding these other cultural groups. Because of this risky venture and its potential impact, we (as intercultural communication scholars) need to be particularly attentive to the project of intercultural communication.

My concern is that the project of intercultural communication be attentive to issues of social justice. This sensitivity entails the following concerns that intercultural communication scholars should take into account when doing their research.

1. We should be attentive to the ways in which intercultural communication has, in some ways, served the interests of white U.S. Americans. We should be sensitive to the ways in which some studies have focused on ways that "Americans" can communicate with "others" without pointing out that "Americans" means white U.S. Americans. For example, if I hand out a survey in our basic communication course, then the respondents who are white will far overwhelm the other respondents—even if I do not report that my respondents are white. If we do not bring this sensitivity to the project of intercultural communication, then we risk serving a more traditional strand in (social) scientific research that—unwittingly or not—services the needs of imperialism, colonialism, and sometimes white racial politics. If the project of intercultural communication becomes one of helping white U.S. Americans better communicate, succeed, and dominate "others" domestically and overseas, then do we engage in a different project of disempowering other cultural groups in the United States and abroad? In short, we need to take a postcolonial turn in intercultural communication so that we are not complicit in serving the unstated, invisible whiteness interests in intercultural communication. See, for example, works on whiteness that connect whiteness to invisibility to power (Delgado & Stefancic, 1997; Dyer, 1997; Nakayama & Martin, 1999).

2. We need to be reflexive about the ways in which our methodologies fall into the trap of serving colonialist/imperialist interests (Harding, 1993, 1998). There probably is no method that is free from this problem. What method could take into account all of the ways of knowing, in all of the cultures around the world, in all time periods? By interrogating our own approach to knowing and understanding, we are better positioned to challenge our own methods and the claims we make.

3. We need to be attentive to the various interests that drive intercultural communication research, whether these are from the private sector or the public sector. Ignoring these pressures on intercultural com-

munication studies, as well as the uses to which our writing may be put, does not serve us well. It does not change the environment in which we work. We need to be aware of these pressures that impinge on our work and the ways in which our writing may be used.

Gust Yep

Hi, everyone. Thank you for getting us started. I agree with Tom. As intercultural communication scholars, we need to be mindful of the ethical responsibilities and dilemmas in our work. Regardless of whether we acknowledge the politics in our work, the project of intercultural communication is highly political. We are dealing with power, representation, visibility/invisibility, celebration, and marginalization. It also is highly practical; our work can be used to understand individuals and communities—to make decisions and (re)shape policy.

I also would like to add other issues to our discussion. I propose that intercultural communication scholars need to engage in conversations regarding assumptions that undergird the project of intercultural communication. For purposes of discussion, I am artificially placing them into three categories: basic or foundational, (meta)theoretical, and methodological (Yep, in press).

Basic Issues

1. *Conceptualizations of culture.* Although there are numerous ways of conceptualizing culture, current hegemonic definitions tend to view culture as "nation-state" and fairly stable (as opposed to fluid and constantly shifting) entities.
2. *Centrality of culture.* Borrowing from Shuter's (1998) work, culture has not been central in a lot of work in intercultural communication.
3. *Role of communication.* Is communication viewed as the foundation for creating and maintaining cultural and social harmony? To create change? Is communication the site of power struggles to fix and naturalize cultural meanings?
4. *Power.* Power needs to be (re)incorporated into intercultural communication theory and research.
5. *Ideology.* Ideology (e.g., capitalist, Eurocentric, racist, classist, sexist, heterosexist, heteronormative) needs to be recognized and made explicit in our work.
6. *History.* History needs to be brought up to the study of intercultural interactions.

(Meta)Theoretical Issues

1. *Nature of knowledge.* Do we assume that knowledge about intercultural communication is objective and generalizable? Do we assume that knowledge is ideologically saturated and historically situated?
2. *Values.* What is the role of values in our work? Should they be excluded and "kept out" of the research process (i.e., made invisible)? Should they be included and privileged in our analysis (i.e., made explicit and visible)?
3. *Voice.* How is voice represented in our research? What are the politics of speaking (e.g., "speaking for," "speaking as")? Should research present a singular voice (e.g., the researcher's articulation of events)? Multiple but concordant voices? Multiple but discordant voices?
4. *Inquiry aim.* Is the primary goal of our work to explain and predict? To critique and transform? To emancipate? To understand?

Methodological Issues

I am concerned that a number of our current methodological debates are grounded in different (and at times contradictory) paradigmatic assumptions, not unlike asking Hindu questions directed at a Muslim audience or raising Catholic issues with a Methodist group. One of such issues is related to criteria of quality. Do we judge the quality of intercultural communication research based on notions of internal and external validity, reliability, and objectivity? Or do we judge this research based on trustworthiness, historical situatedness, and potential for social change?

Radha Hegde

I decided to write down a few of my thoughts before I react to the others' comments. So, here they are. This is a very interesting historical moment to be engaged in discussion about theorizing in the field of intercultural communication. Self-reflexivity is a good and humbling exercise at all times; right now, the moment seems to call for it urgently. At a time when it seems like everyone has a stake in defining and seizing terms such as *culture, globalization,* and *identity,* it seems only right that we engage in stock-taking activity about our own intellectual labor in the field of intercultural communication.

I think that we need to address how the field, as it is being produced today, reflects and responds to the social issues that surround us. In the context of changing geopolitical scenarios and the complex social fallout, we absolutely need to revisit the assumptions and theoretical reach of the field. The issues that we need to dialogue about concerning the patterns of intercultural knowledge to a large extent depend on how we situate the work we do in the larger context of our academic vocation and vision.

First, I think we need to rethink the ways in which we talk about culture. The fact is that much water has flowed under the bridge here and everywhere in the world for us to conceptualize culture in theoretically sealed ways. Twenty minutes of interacting with my very diverse student body in an intercultural communication class is enough to blow up the myth of finding definitional closure to the concept of culture. This is an area that we need to continually revisit and historicize for the precise reason that it is a site of struggle and contestation.

This leads into the second pressing issue—power. We do need to think about culture and power in interrelated ways because culture cannot be abstracted from structures of power. With the changes in the world political scene and postcolonial global developments, we cannot afford to perpetuate an apolitical reading of intercultural communication. The notion of neutrality that is so prized in our approaches denies history, denies structure, and denies the subject positions of those involved (drawing, of course, on Spivak, 1990, here).

If we begin from the fact that we do need to complicate our problematization of culture, power, and intercultural communication in general, then we certainly need to both expand and enrich the theoretical vocabulary of our enterprise. The issues that we raise almost demand an interdisciplinary outlook. Considering the fact that globalization is being played out in such uneven ways, the point is not to push for defined disciplinary spaces. This is where the larger picture of why we are doing scholarship comes into play. What are we producing as intercultural knowledge today? Is this production consistent with our view of social transformation? Issues of culture in this diverse and multiply connected world are too complex to be studied in terms of clean and clear authenticity.

Wenshu Lee

Hi, all. After reading the messages from Tom, Gust, and Radha, I sense that there are two important issues. First is the theme that intercultural communication scholarship is, through and through, "political." Second, there is a need to center "culture" and its definitions in our scholarship.

Is Intercultural Communication Scholarship "Political"?

Gust is unambiguous in saying *yes:* "Regardless of whether we acknowledge the politics in our work, the project of intercultural communication is highly political." Radha says, "With the changes in the world political scene and postcolonial global developments, we cannot afford to perpetuate an apolitical reading of intercultural communication." Finally, in Tom's e-mail, he urges "a postcolonial turn in intercultural communication," asking us to be attentive to the purposes of intercultural communication scholarship and not to be complicit in serving "the needs of imperialism, colonialism, and sometimes white racial politics."

This consensus that intercultural communication is political sensitizes us to politically charged vocabulary, interests, purpose, issues of power, ideology, voice, identity, visibility/invisibility, marginalization, self-reflexivity, and so on. It also contextualizes our scholarship through the time (e.g., importance of history), space (e.g., private/public sectors, transnational, interdisciplinary), and agents (e.g., race, gender, sexuality, nationality, education, religion) on which we focus and through the time, space, and agents that we exclude.

But if scholarship can only be political, then how can researchers claim the irrelevance of politics and argue for the paradigm of "neutrality" and "objectivity"? Gust raises a similar issue in the end of his comments regarding "criteria of quality." This is a big question frequently contested in our classrooms, journal reviews, and publications. So, I would like to spend some time here thinking it through.

What differences are marked by the expression "political"? To answer this question, I propose two differences (or binaries, if you will) marked by "political" as a sign:

Difference 1: *political versus scientific/scholarly.* Political here reads "unscientific, unscholarly work done by partisans, politicians, and people 'on the street.' " "Political" thus becomes a "scientific other or scholarly other." It is "othered" or judged as different from and inferior to something labeled as "scientific/scholarly," which reads "real scholarship—rigorous, scientific, generalizable, and done by people in the 'academy.' "

Difference 2: *political versus acontextualized.* Political here reads "engaged, contextualized scholarship acknowledging interests served and limits/exclusions practiced." It is different from and superior to "acontextualized scholarship that does not or refuses to acknowledge interests served/promoted and interests left out/excluded."

Rendering explicit these two (and more if you can suggest them) differences (or binaries) is one of the most important ways of articulating the taken-for-granted assumptions in intercultural communication theory and research. A paradigmatic shift in intercultural communication, in my view, occurs when Difference 2 becomes persuasive to students and scholars whose professional goals and personal ethics and aspirations cannot be actualized by the hegemony of Difference 1.

Assuming the standard valorized by Difference 1 (i.e., scientific as rigorous and real scholarship) puts those of us who subscribe to Difference 2 on the defensive, obliging us to prove that we are "real scholars" as well and that our research is "rigorous" as well. Difference 2 affirms that all scholarship is political, whether you acknowledge it or not (Gust also mentions this). For example, earlier in the dialogue, Tom does an excellent job of contextualizing the political nature of "social scientific" intercultural communication research. Another fine example is Leeds-Hurwitz's (1990) "Notes in the History of Intercultural Communication," connecting the early intercultural communication field to the Foreign Service Institute of the U.S. Department of State. I personally made a politicized shift in "A Sociohistorical Approach to Intercultural Communication" (Lee, Chung, Wang, & Hertel, 1995). I broke my multiple silences. I spoke against the dis-reality constructed by the high/low-context theoretical regime on "the Chinese" as uniformly docile, inscrutable, and nonconfrontational. I also spoke against the nationalist, class-based, and paternalistic hegemonies in Chinese traditions.

Affirming Difference 2, those who write "scientific" articles also have in mind the audiences they are trying to persuade (i.e., journal editors and reviewers who often fail to acknowledge their time/space/agent-specific identities). So, a logical conclusion is not to abandon social scientific intercultural research. Rather, it is important to contextualize research (whether scientific, rhetorical, critical, ethnographic, or otherwise) and name its politics. The question then becomes, "What would contextualized, socially responsible scientific research look like?"

On a final note, my theoretical position is that human language is such that we cannot escape binaries or differences. So, binary thinking is *not* guilty. What is oppressive is the power to silence alternative binaries and to suppress debates among alternatives. What do you think?

Conceptualizing Culture/s

Both Radha and Gust raise the issue of culture. How do we conceptualize culture? How do we talk about culture? I think that all of you would agree with the view that the act of conceptualizing culture is itself political and should be contextualized/situated with an ethical/moral commitment. Hence, my political act here assumes at least five things:

1. "Culture," singular and with an uppercase C, should be replaced with "cultures," plural and with a lowercase c.
2. Among the plural "cultures," rank-ordering and hierarchy (assuming that some cultures are superior) are more prevalent than differences/diversities/pluralism (assuming that all cultures are equal) in practice. But given the power structure in the United States (i.e., a white, straight, male-dominated postsegregation and profit-driven society), scholarship and academic/social programs accept the talk of "cultural diversity," "cultural pluralism," and "cultural differences" more than they accept the talk of "cultural hierarchy."
3. Those who define "cultures" as "the Culture" tend to assume ahistorical stability and consensus in culture. That is, in their view, Culture is "shared" language, beliefs, values, and so on. They also use a nebulous collective voice (e.g., "society," "tradition," "people") to authorize their definition.
4. Those who reconceptualize "the Culture" as "cultures" tend to assume historical and local "instability" and "contest/struggle." That is, in their view, cultures are processual, unstable, and open for debate, struggle, and contest. They invoke history more, often bring alive "silenced" voices, and are more sensitive to differences in geography, class, gender, race, sexuality, and so on. There also is the issue of inequity, injustice, invisibility, and discursive erasure/amnesia.
5. Any act of defining culture should not forget political questions such as the following. Whose interest is served by this definition? What definitions are left out or unimagined?

As a result of going through the following list, I hope that readers will become vigilant. That is, whenever the word *culture* is used, ask yourself the following questions. What does culture mean here? Who stands to benefit from this definition? What other possible definitions are left out and why?

On the Definitions of Cultures

1. *Culture = uniquely human efforts (as different from nature and biology).* For example, "*Culture* is the bulwark against the ravages of nature."
2. *Culture = refinement, mannerism (as different from things that are crude, vulgar, and unrefined).* For example, "Look at the way in which he chows down his food. He has no *culture* at all."

3. *Culture = civilization (as different from backward barbaric people).* For example, "In countries where darkness reigns and people are wanting in *culture,* it is our mandate to civilize and Christianize those poor souls."
4. *Culture = shared language, beliefs, and values (as different from language, beliefs, and values that are not shared; dissenting voices; and voices of the "other").* For example, "We come from the same *culture,* we speak the same language, and we share the same tradition."
5. *Culture = dominant or hegemonic culture (as different from marginal cultures).* For example, "It is the *culture* of the ruling class that determines what is moral and what is deviant." This definition is a more charged version of Definitions 2, 3, and 4 through the addition of power consciousness.
6. *Culture = the shifting tensions between the shared and the unshared (as different from shared or unshared things).* For example, "American *culture* has changed from master/slave, to white only/black only, to anti-war and black power, to affirmative action/multiculturalism and political correctness, to transnational capital and anti-sweatshop campaigns."

Each of these definitions privileges certain interests. Definition 2 privileges high culture and leaves out popular culture and cultures that are deemed "low" (a very class-based, education-based, adult-based, straight-based understanding of culture that draws the critique launched by cultural studies scholars). Definition 3 privileges nations that are/were imperialistic, colonizing, or neocolonizing (e.g., Spain during the 16th to 19th centuries, Britain and France during the 19th century, Germany and Japan during World War II, the United States and the Soviet Union during the cold war period, the United States currently). Definition 4 privileges a "universal and representative" view of a society, but such a view often represents only a specific powerful group and silences other groups that do not readily share this view (e.g., groups that are marginalized due to race, class, gender, or sexuality).

Definition 5 privileges the interrogation of the culture authorized by the dominant group/sector/nation; this view is more charged—more politically explicit—than Definitions 2, 3, and 4. Definition 6 is the one that I like the most. It is more of a "meta" view of cultures. It focuses on the "links" between "the shared" and "the unshared." But the *sharedness,* the *unsharedness,* and their *links* remain not only situated but also unstable, shifting, and contested. This view of cultures holds a keen sensitivity to power, justice, history, and praxis. Johnson's (2001) recent challenge of queer studies through "quare studies" is an excellent example of cultures articulated along the line of Definition 6.

Definition 2 is prevalent in domestic discourse, and Definition 3 is prevalent in the center of empires. Definition 4 is more prevalent in intercultural essays and textbooks that are liberal, open-minded, descriptive, and scientific but uncritical and limited to the geography of single nations (e.g., within the United States, within Japan, within Mexico). Definition 5 is more prevalent in critical intercultural scholarship (e.g., postcolonial, cultural studies, transnational, feminist, queer studies, Marxist approaches) with an eye to intervention and social change. Definition 6 is uncommon but, in my view, is the direction in which politicized intercultural communication is shifting. What do you think? Using Tom's expression, "feel free to tear it up."

Gust Yep

Good afternoon, everyone. I am going to add two more definitions of culture to Wenshu's original list:

1. Culture is a contested conceptual, discursive, and material terrain of meanings, practices, and human activities within a particular social, political, and historical context.
2. Culture is an enabling fiction, characterized by the ongoing and shifting tension between the shared and the unshared, that creates, sustains, and renders meaning to the social world.

Both definitions assume that culture is a contested space and that power differences are recognized. They move beyond hegemonic definitions of culture as "shared and transmitted from generation to generation" that assume that we all experience a "common culture" and that it is passed down from one generation to the next in a linear and seemingly static fashion. As I mentioned in another posting, this is a dangerous myth. To endorse such conceptions, in my opinion, is to participate in a "pedagogy of the big lies" that works in invisible yet extremely powerful ways to suppress and erase marginalized voices and experiences. In Definition 2, I incorporate one of Wenshu's definitions and work with Anderson's (1991) concept of "imagined communities."

Mary Jane Collier

Hello everyone. I am so enjoying your ideas and find myself nodding in agreement. As I read Gust's two conceptualizations of culture and review

Wenshu's preferred conceptualization listed previously, I am struck by how much the field of intercultural scholarship has evolved during the past 20 years. The three conceptualizations focus on communicative and social practices and activities rather than on particular groups of "people," or people who are from/reside in a geopolitical "place," and move beyond ideas that culture can be defined as consensus-based/normalized "patterns" of behaviors or cognitive "schemata." In the three conceptualizations, I see attention given to what is accomplished through and by these communicative practices and activities—reification of institutional norms and policies, politics, ideologies, histories, and social meanings. In Gust's first conceptualization of culture as "a contested, conceptual, discursive, and material terrain of meanings, practices, and human activities within a particular social, political, and historical context," I see a range of forms that includes conceptual, discursive, material, and social (practices).

A question that does come up for me is reminiscent of Hall's (1976) question about what distinguishes culture from communication. I think that what I am looking for is a clearer sense of the parameters of culture and more specific distinguishing features than the communicative activities "within a particular social, political, and historical context." I acknowledge that conceptualizations of culture emerge within the framework of assumptions within theoretical perspectives (e.g., postcolonial, cultural studies, rhetorical, interpretive, functionalist). Regardless of theoretical positioning, however, perhaps what is missing for me is a discussion of who/what generates, produces, or constructs the communicative activities. I am inclined to ask how the concept of culture(s) can make sense without some attention to "groups" either in a membership/alignment sense or in the characterization of/by others sense. I am thinking of this idea of group as that which is accomplished through discursive practice, institutional policy, media imagery, and historical account. What do you think?

Wenshu Lee

Gust and Mary Jane's comments on the definitions of cultures enable me to make a clearer theoretical link between "cultures" and my earlier discussion of "the political." Definitions 2, 3, and 4 of cultures are linked to Difference 1. My Definitions 5 and 6 and Gust's elaboration of them belong to Difference 2. I think that Gust and I both find the latter persuasive.

In other words, this has signaled a paradigmatic shift in intercultural communication. Call it a "critical turn in intercultural communication."

Along with the shift to *political as contextualized scholarship* and *cultures as contested space in power relations,* I think that "a politics of location"—a line of theorizing alternative to identity politics—is useful to answer Mary Jane's concerns about "communication" and "groups." Mary Jane asks, "Perhaps what is missing for me is a discussion of who/what generates, produces, or constructs the communicative activities" and "how the concept of culture(s) can make sense without some attention to 'groups.' " Let me first explain what a politics of location is. Then I will use this perspective to suggest a reenvisioning of cultural groups and communication.

Location is not a static space or place. Rather, it is conceptualized as an *itinerary*[2] or "a *series* of locations and encounters, travel within diverse but limited spaces" (Clifford, 1989). Following the critical turn identified earlier to "scholarship as politicized" and cultures as "the shifting tensions between the shared and the unshared" (my Definition 6 and Gust's Definition 2), location should be expanded, in my view, to mean *itinerary of temporalities of struggles.*[3] This is nicely illustrated in the research on *sati* (the contested ritual of widow burning) by Mani (1989, 1998). Her itineraries during the late 20th century from India to Britain and the United States as a Marxist feminist complicated the way in which she documented and critiqued different sectors of discourses about sati during the 18th and 19th centuries and in contemporary India (the controversy surrounding Roop Kanwar's death in 1987).

Cultural "group," envisioned in terms of a politics of location, would mean the affiliation or alliance among people whose itineraries in temporalized struggles converge. The five of us involved in this dialogue are a good example. We come from very different traditions in race, gender, sexuality, and regions, yet we are forming a new cultural group. In our heterogeneous ways, we converge in our struggles for a more socially conscious and critical scholarship at the turn of a new millennium. But such a convergence takes hard work. It demands mutually critical consciousness. It also may be unstable; that is, there is no guarantee of its sustained status.

Along the same vein, one way of reenvisioning "communication" is to systematically unpack our current professional and pedagogical schemes (e.g., verbal communication, nonverbal communication, denotation, connotation, tropes, debates, social movements, naming systems, whiteness) by paying attention to "what itineraries of temporalized struggles are involved in this specific communication phenomenon." For example, we can unpack an intercultural communication claim, "Individuals from low-context cultures are confrontational and verbally explicit," by asking, "Along what route and in what historical period did such a claim travel? Did it receive hostility or hospitality? Where, when, and from whom? Any detours? Canceled trips? Unplanned routes? Any other fellow claims that traveled together and perhaps went separate ways?"

Mary Jane (and others), does this reenvisioning of "communication" and "groups" along the line of a politics of location work for you?

Gust Yep

I like Wenshu's "temporality of struggles." Groups, in my view, have fluid and constantly shifting boundaries and "real" and imagined memberships. I will modify Definition 2 to say that culture is an enabling fiction for individuals and groups, characterized by the ongoing and shifting tension between the shared and the unshared, that creates, sustains, and renders meaning to the social world.

Mary Jane Collier

Thank you, Wenshu and Gust. These additions are very helpful for me. Approaching culture as temporalized struggles and itineraries allows for culture to be located in an array of different spaces and times and "groupings." I can see great value in identifying cultural alignment as the itineraries and trajectories that are evident in situated discourse, community deliberations, social policies, institutionalized practice, and that which is constructed in liminal spaces for imagined communities. Adding attention to the questions of "Who/What is doing the producing/imposing/constructing/contesting of culture?" and "Across what times and spaces?" to questions such as "What is being accomplished?" and "For whose benefit?" keeps our view broad enough to encompass the "macro" structural influences and constraints and "micro" situated practices and communicative conduct.

QUESTION FROM MARY JANE COLLIER

What is/are the problems(s) that need to be addressed in this dialogue? How is the field of scholarship around internationalization, culture, and communication shifting? How can we characterize this current ferment in the field?

Gust Yep

Hi, everyone. I am going to respond to the first question here regarding problems/issues being addressed in our dialogue. Several seem to come to mind. Some of them are more reactive, and all of them seem reflective of the current intellectual shifts in our discipline.

Perhaps one of the most important reactions that many intercultural scholars experience today is how politically unconscious, ahistorical, disembodied, and Eurocentric the field has been in terms of theory, research, and praxis during the past two decades. A number of us have been trained to think of (inter/intra)cultural interactions as communication events devoid of power and politics. Power and politics are not the domain of "rigorous scientific research," we were told. This legacy continues today and, in many ways, undergirds the vigorous discussions and conflicts between researchers. At the bottom of this, I believe, are fundamental differences and (perhaps incompatible) worldviews about the knowledge production process in general and assumptions about culture and communication in particular.

During my graduate school years, I was trained to think of intercultural communication as "stand-alone" events that can be isolated, reduced, examined, and analyzed independently of the larger social, historical, and economic context. To include the larger context meant that there were "too many variables" in the research. We were taught that "good" research design meant maximizing differences between groups, minimizing variability within groups, and controlling for extraneous variables. This translated in many ways to research practices that involved the study of groups that are very distinct from each other. For example, we were taught to maximize intergroup differences (e.g., focusing on Japan and the United States, although business interests were clearly motivating this research as well), to homogenize "cultures" (e.g., assuming that U.S. Americans are fairly similar to each other, assuming that Japanese culture is assumed to be a "homogeneous" society), and to eliminate "extraneous factors" (e.g., personal and collective histories that we bring to our interactions, economic interests, and political ideologies).

As I read, practiced, and engaged in this research, I became increasingly dissatisfied with it. My work on HIV education for communities of color, for example, was being accepted and published in interdisciplinary journals. If publication meant that my research was appropriately designed and executed according to the standards of the academy, then it seemed to me that at least my research designs were sound. But I still felt dissatisfied with my work. I rationalized it by telling myself that my research might be saving people's lives and that the effectiveness of the work is not readily visible. (We see our "failures" much more easily, like people seroconverting; however, we do not see our "successes," the individuals who actually listened to the health protective messages and remained uninfected.) I walked around feeling a disconnectedness to my work for a long time.

One day, it occurred to me that the "cultures" that I was describing in my research (e.g., Asian Americans) were very distant from how I would describe myself. I came to realize that much of the research on culture was like that—distant and exotic. In the case of HIV research, culture also is pathologized. For example, researchers discuss "cultural barriers" to prevention (as if we need to teach cultural members to overcome some of their own "cultural traits" so that they can learn to live healthy lives). What would it be like for me to research and study cultures as experiences of people without pathologizing and marginalizing them? I came to the conclusion that not only did I need to learn new ways of thinking about theory and research, but I also needed to unlearn many of the "standard research practices" that I learned in graduate school.

Armed with new ways of thinking (influenced by critical theory, feminism and womanism, critical race theory, queer theory, postmodernism, and poststructuralism, among others), young scholars now come to study culture and communication and automatically react to the research in the field by questioning hegemonic definitions of culture and bringing up issues of ideology, power, and Eurocentrism. When traditionally trained and new scholars come together, interesting and lively exchanges occur. This is, in my opinion, the context for the current ferment in the field.

The field of scholarship around internationalization, culture, and communication is shifting in interesting ways. First, more traditional notions of communication and communication settings as well as disciplinary demarcations are blurring. Conceptualizations of communication as face-to-face contact, which is separate from mass media, and compartmentalization of settings (e.g., interpersonal, small group, organizational) are becoming less useful. For example, new communication technologies such as what we are doing here, an ongoing e-group dialogic exchange, challenges those traditional definitional boundaries. Likewise, international communities are brought together in new, interesting, and sometimes challenging ways.

Second, and closely related to the first way, is the shift from traditional (i.e., physical) ways of conceptualizing space, a physical geography, to a postmodern and virtual geography. New communication technologies obviously have contributed to this shift. International communication can occur on one's computer screen. Likewise, international and interpersonal communication can easily take place between individuals and groups regardless of physical proximity, geographical boundaries, and political systems. This shift has many implications for society (e.g., legal, economic, political) and for individuals. Communication has become "communication across differences" in very real, material, and discursive ways.

Third, internationalization has set the stage for new forms of domination through the expansion of corporate interests and cultural and media imperialism. For example, the "internationalization of the university" has become a coded phrase to bring affluent, middle to upper class, mostly English-speaking students to attend, pay tuition dollars, and get educated at U.S. American universities. Through education, these international students learn "the American way" and then return home to take on better jobs and secure their positions in their social hierarchies. In this process, the position of the social elite is secured and maintained while individuals from different social locations get further marginalized.

Finally, the process of internationalization might be shifting our discipline to become more vigilant of ethical concerns and issues of social justice as scholars reflect on the political nature of their work within the institutional and societal contexts that knowledge production occurs.

I stop for now and look forward to reading your reactions and responses to the first question. I hope your weekend is going well.

Radha Hegde

Every few years, we do have ferment brewing in the field, Kuhnian arguments about paradigmatic shifts (Kuhn, 1970). Ferments are good if they are about keeping the theoretical debate alive. Of course, the ferment reads very differently depending on the perspective from which you look at it. Issues of culture seem to rise to the forefront all around us. There is an ideological battle around the crisis of culture, common culture, nation, and identity that is being played out, and this certainly affects our role as scholars and educators. We have to take a stand on these issues and their political import. Our vocation as intellectuals makes it imperative that we address social issues and the changing structure of social and political relations. Theory and methodological practice have to be situated within the larger social sphere of ideas in order to be socially responsive. This, of course, is related to doing scholarship that is driven by a commitment to social transformation.

First, there are a lot of changes happening in the social landscape at an unprecedented pace. Yes, cultures have been in contact for centuries, but there is a radical revision of basic taken-for-granted categories that is explosive. Time, space, and culture all are in the process of revision and redefinition, and this is affecting the very meaning of identity, agency, and community. The moment certainly demands self-reflection, and moreover, I think that we need to assess the perspective we as communication scholars can provide in terms of making connections among theory, pedagogy, and social change.

Within our field, there has been and continues to be a wariness about turf and guarding of disciplinary domains. It is common across academe, as Hall (1996) points out, to assume that theory consists of a series of closed paradigms. Paradigms lose their explanatory reach or are so ideologically tilted that they fail to even name certain realities, with modernist Eurocentric worldviews being a case in point. We have to cross borders and boundaries to even begin to understand the complex practices of contemporary life. For example, how can we study intercultural meaning without addressing questions of representation, identity, media, global networks, political systems, colonial legacies, and global capital? So, the field needs to open out from the now anachronistic Person X meets the foreigner model. All is not well in that scenario when Person X, in all probability, is the "model" U.S. white male. Who is the "real" citizen, and who is the "foreigner," the "alien," or the "other"? We cannot afford to be rigid or provincial in our research outlook when the global world is fast passing by. It is like being in an Imax theater, with life zooming in super fast, and before we know it we are smacked up against the screen. That is the point we are at now in terms of historical/social contradictions in the social field that we are addressing.

I see our task as not sealing off an answer or signing off on a paradigm that is relevant to our times and our academic work. I believe that our task as scholars should go beyond providing pithy answers and solutions. Rather, I see the very format of this dialogue as a way of opening up the project of intercultural study.

Categories leak, assumptions run dry, and we need to get our field a little dirty in terms of deconstructing the neat categories—the sanitized divisions between categories and areas. In our theoretical activity and in this dialogue, we begin to read against the grain. My suggestion is that we get intellectually "impure."

Tom Nakayama

I am joining in this discussion, but I want to tag on to some things that Gust and Radha said and push the dialogue further. Radha and Gust note the internationalization of the university. I think that they make important points here, but let's not overlook the historical foundations that not only created cultural differences but also created different senses about how power has influenced the development of cultural groups. Power is the key to the development of critical intercultural communication studies.

I want to urge some caution before we rush headlong into embracing "internationalization" without discussing what internationalization means. For example, when immigrants came to the United States during the 19th century, they (and their children) did not have the kinds of access to their homelands that contemporary immigrants have. Today, immigrants can get on the Internet and pull up newspapers written in their native languages, e-mail people, and maintain connections with distant cultures (and languages) in ways that earlier immigrants could not. In addition, many people who spoke non-English languages felt tremendous pressure earlier in the 20th century to speak only English to demonstrate that they were "Americans." The current embracing of different languages and cultures, as problematic as it has been, is a very recent context in which post-1965 immigrants find themselves, but it is not the same context that earlier immigrants experienced.

The construction of various ethnic communities in the United States, then, is hardly homogeneous; earlier immigrants found different contexts that shaped their ethnic identities and communities. One of the issues that we need to confront is the dialectical tension between a more rigid notion of cultural groups and a more fluid one. Much of our intercultural research and everyday discourse assumes a more rigid notion of cultural categories. As Radha writes, "Categories leak, assumptions run dry, and we need to get our field a little dirty in terms of deconstructing the neat categories—the sanitized divisions between categories and areas."

In part, I wonder whose interests are served by the more rigid notions of cultural categories. Cultural categories are not universal; not only do they change over time, but the ways in which we categorize the world are not universal. Thus, to produce knowledge about a particular cultural group always is in context and from a cultural perspective. We often have focused on the cultural group that we are studying in intercultural research, but how often do we recognize the cultural perspective from which we are generating this "knowledge"? For example, when we do studies that tell us about the "Japanese," are we doing so in ways that serve certain cultural interests over others? Do we assume that the hypothetical intercultural communication interaction is between a white American and a Japanese? What do we know about how Japanese and Japanese Americans view each other? Or Japanese and Mexican Americans? When we do not mention "white," is it still the assumed purpose of intercultural research? If so, this has tremendous implications for the project of intercultural communication itself.

Also, when we speak of "internationalization," I think that it is important to think about what that means. People have moved, migrated, and so on for ages, but in very different contexts that led to very different cultural communities. So, when we say "internationalization," I worry that we are somehow forgetting that "Americans" are constructed from transnational migrations. If we mean something else by internationalization, then I think we need to discuss what that something else means.

Part of my concern is that I see "American" as having been defined (here and abroad) to largely mean white Americans. Although it might seem obvious to point this out, I am concerned about the ramifications of this definition for intercultural research as well as for how we conceptualize our project. In a certain sense, this hegemonic definition has ideologically shifted the terrain so that we do not see whites as having come from abroad. Have whites somehow usurped the position of being seen as the indigenous people, and does intercultural research, then, unwittingly end up serving certain interests?

My questions are troubling, but I would like us to look at the larger project of intercultural communication because I think that these questions are part of the ferment in the field. I have found that many of my students of color have been intensely unhappy with intercultural communication as it has been constituted.

Wenshu Lee

Hi, all. Here is my response to the question about problems that need to be addressed and characterizations of current ferment in the field: "fringe scholars and empire's heteropatriarchy." The past and current empire's heteropatriarchy has been the implicit reigning ideology of international and intercultural communication. In such a hegemonic system, the "problems" rest with the "strangers," that is, the foreign, non-man, non-straight, non-English speaking, not well to do, and so on. Scholarly efforts are designed to "domesticate" these generalized others, turn them into known quantities, and co-opt them into the mechanism serving nationalistic and corporate interests of the empire.

On the fringe of the empire are women and men of color.[4] They were once the object of imperialist gaze, but now scholars want to talk to them. From visual scrutiny to communicative domestication, they remain in the eyes of the empire and the scholars—nonconfrontational, indirect, and high context. The empire and the scholars cannot and will not see the subtleties and power of the fringe. What they do see and create in their representation of the fringe must conform to the logic of the empire—domination, control, erasure, and profit taking.

In my view, four of us are fringe scholars; three immigrated to the United States as young adults, and one was born and raised in the United States. We are racial minorities; all four are of Asian origins. In different ways, we also are gendered and sexual minorities. We remained erased, speechless, and unheard for a long time. But here and now, we are speaking, dialoguing with each other, and exercising our agency.

So, the problems are the hidden hand of the empire's heteropatriarchy. The symptoms are as follows:

1. Conventional intercultural and international research makes all four of us "unrealities." Gust says, "One day, it occurred to me that the 'cultures' I was describing in my research (e.g., Asian Americans) were so distant from how I would describe myself."
2. Conventional intercultural and international research is white-centric. Tom questions, "Do we assume that the hypothetical communication intercultural interaction is between a white American and a Japanese? What do we know about how Japanese and Japanese Americans view each other? Or Japanese and Mexican Americans? When we do not mention 'white,' is it still the assumed purpose of intercultural research?"
3. Conventional intercultural and international research is anachronistic. Radha notes the importance of "addressing questions of representation, identity, media, global networks, political systems, colonial legacies, and global capital." Gust and Radha both urge the blurring of disciplinary and setting-specific boundaries.

4. Conventional intercultural and international research neither acknowledges nor interrogates scholarship and its construction of knowledge as politicized and co-opted.
5. Conventional intercultural and international research makes "situatedness" an irrelevant scholarly criterion. It does not historicize and is not sensitive to differences (e.g., gays and lesbians, women working in sweatshops) within a broad and rigid category (e.g., Americans, Japanese).

It is not so much a scholarly ferment that we are naming here as a glimpse of the imminent power shift within and outside of the empire. Fringe scholars are not marching into the center and preaching to the already converted. There is a responsibility to remain on the fringe so that we can see and hear more clearly from "meta" perspectives and think and talk impurely to push issues unaddressed and unnamed.

Mary Jane Collier

First, I want to say that I am very glad that each of you agreed to participate in this dialogue. I am engaged, stimulated, and feeling undone and insecure given my own history and identity, and I thank you. What you are creating here seems incredibly important to me.

One thing I noticed during my process of writing this iteration is that I am struggling with my own voice and role in this dialogue. Naming and use of terms becomes particularly important. For example, if I use "we" to note some issues on which I think the five of us agree, then the "we" sounds presumptuous and as potential co-optation. It also sounds as if I can voluntarily choose to ignore my whiteness and class for the time being to align myself with what Wenshu describes as "fringe scholars, racial minorities, and gendered and sexual minorities" because I am moderating the dialogue. I also can go to a meeting on campus tomorrow where my white skin allows me to fit in with the "center" and "normalized" in ways that you four cannot. On the other hand, if I use "you" to point out what you have argued, followed up by a statement describing my agreement, then it sounds as if I am reinforcing a hierarchy and the difference between us and that I somehow have the "authority" to have the last word.

One issue that I am thinking about is how to define what/who makes up the fringe. Although I do not wish to align myself with early first-wave feminists who were seemingly oblivious to their race and class privilege, I do argue that how I have been treated as a woman in our discipline, for example, places me closer to the fringe than white heterosexual males. So, part of my struggle here has to do with interrogating my relationship in/to the fringe. On the one hand, I may claim and avow "membership" in the fringe and alignment with the struggle against oppression in multiple forms. On the other hand, it is not just up to me to "declare" a membership; my itinerary, location, and work should be open to interrogation. What I am concluding is that another part of being in the fringe is to have my itinerary and alignment with the struggle recognized as similar or aligned with others struggling to overcome oppression. Fringe, therefore, means attention to the discursive and nondiscursive forms of the struggle, the itinerary unfolding over time—in short, participation in the struggle, the embodied "doing" of struggle with others.

I will jump into my musings and attempt to talk as one who is endeavoring to recognize the privilege of being white, privileged, and European American. As I think about what my role should be, I realize that with new forms of intellectual engagement comes uncertainty, and with the uncertainty comes fear. So, I want to talk briefly about the affective dimension of what we are doing in this dialogue. As I read what you four have written so far, I am struck by the eloquence and importance of each of your scholarly voices, and I feel intimidated. During graduate school, one of my professors (all white males) told another female student and me, "If you can't speak up and make an argument for what you believe, you don't belong in this profession."

While one of my instincts says that I had better say something profound and say it soon, I think of my Zen Buddhist friend who would say that I need to quiet my ego self and simply be present. A Navaho medicine man I met years ago might advise me to listen and reflect and wait to speak until being invited into the conversation by those with more wisdom. My counseling psychology colleague might tell me that I need to share my feelings with you in the form of "I statements" about how I am feeling here and now. My point is that in the traditional forms of scholarship, individuals advocate, make arguments, seek to persuade others, and do not talk about personal emotions or experiences. That form does not allow for co-creation of ideas or for acknowledgment of fear, pain, or joy, nor does it encourage knowledge building as evolution. That form does not always serve who we are as complex humans with multiple cultural identities and voices, people with a range of relational and spiritual orientations and lives in very different historicized and politicized contexts.

In thinking about my own evolution as a person in the academy, I see links between "culture being pathologized," as Gust mentioned, and intercultural communication competence research/praxis and approaches to international training. The focus often has been (and is evident in my own earlier work) on prescriptive skills (which I now see were white/privileged/patriarchal/Eurocentric/"Americanist"). So, what we have been taught and what we have advocated as trainers and teachers of trainers is to try to identify "the Cure," a cultural communication style that is "Comfortable" as well as "Competent" (note the capitalization) and best manages "Difference" as "Disease."

You each discuss the intellectual shift that is occurring and the growing recognition of what Gust describes as how "politically unconscious, ahistorical, disembodied, and Eurocentric the field has been in terms of theory, research, and praxis during the past two decades." One of the things that occurred to me is that there has been a kind of *ontological erasure* about how humans do the being of who they are (loosely after Sacks, 1984) in the name of "objectivity." Group members' experiences of their identities include individual variations and responses, and as Trinh (1989) argues, we can be insiders and outsiders simultaneously. Using social science concepts, group "patterns" include responses that are "average" and responses that are "outliers."

I believe that our characterization of the traditional "dominant paradigm" is grounded not only in what we were taught in graduate school but also in our continuing experiences as faculty members, consultants, and community members with institutions and ideologies that reinforce that there is "a Truth" and that we can recognize what it looks and sounds like because it is "out there" waiting for us to discover it. As you each point out, there are not only multiple truths but also multiple ways of knowing, and we decide who "counts" as "expert" and construct what we know within institutional frameworks and paradigms that have ideologies and embodied hierarchies and histories. Recently in one of my seminars, a graduate student from our business school said, "You can talk all you like about needing to study interpretations of people's conversations or to critique corporate ideologies and media influences. I just want to be able to predict and explain people's general buying habits for international products." The dominant paradigm is alive and well.

Gust and others noted as problematic the traditional disciplinary boundaries that are based on physical space and proximity (interpersonal, group, organizational, and public/rhetorical communication) as rather distinct kinds of phenomena. International communication often is still defined as mediated messages and processes and/or policies or technologies that cross national borders. Therefore, international communication is supposedly different from intercultural communication, which typically is approached as interpersonal and face-to-face contact of small numbers of people from different places/spaces.

One implication of these conceptualizations and orientations is that we define what we study in an arbitrary and limiting way as if where we live or what means we use to communicate can be separated from each other. In addition, the assumption seems to be that where we live and what means we use to communicate are somehow more important than how we live, when we live, and who we are. An additional consequence of this kind of territoriality is that we end up presenting our work to/with those scholars who share an interest in the same contexts/topics. A complacency can emerge in which we end up seeking validation from those who also benefit from doing the validation. Because we are recognizing these consequences, a call for changing these boundaries and models is occurring inside/outside these existing structures and boundaries in our own departments, schools, and curricula and also is reflected in what we see in textbooks and major journals and what we hear being talked about at conferences.

The unfolding conversations within and sparked by this dialogue involve you, the readers, as well as critics who may write about the published dialogue and instructors and students who may discuss it in seminars and classes, among others. All of us bring educational, social, cultural, and personal histories, as well as implicit ideologies and standards of what constitutes "publishable" and high-quality scholarly writing and knowledge, into this unfolding conversation. Our dialogue is emerging as different from more familiar forms of academic writing such as empirical reports, theoretical pieces, rhetorical or discourse analyses, and critical arguments. I am grateful to you, the four scholars who have taken the time and energy to co-construct this dialogue, for being willing to take professional risks to challenge and begin to transform the dominant norms. You have chosen to not allow the indoctrinations (Anderson, 1996) of graduate school to define who you are and what you study. I add my voice to yours to celebrate and sing along with the Bob Dylan song, *The Times They Are A-Changin'*.

QUESTION FROM MARY JANE COLLIER

How does this shift and ferment affect us as scholars and affect people in our field? Why should we care about this ferment?

Gust Yep

Here is my response to the second question. I keep returning to Tom's earlier e-mail about issues of social justice in intercultural communication theory and praxis. All of us have identified social justice either implicitly or explicitly in our discussion. Wenshu is more explicit when she writes,

> The past and current empire's [Eurocentric] heteropatriarchy has been the implicit reigning ideology of international and intercultural communication. . . . The empire and the [mainstream] scholars cannot and will not see the subtleties and power of the fringe. What they do see and create in their representation of the fringe must conform to the logic of the empire—domination, control, erasure, and profit taking.

In short, the current reigning ideology of the field is domination of individuals and groups on the fringe as defined by the empire (e.g., women, people of color, gender and sexual minorities, the underclass) in the name of knowledge generation, production, and distribution. But this domination must remain invisible, naturalized, and taken for granted.

If we are to strive for the creation of a just society, then we must address issues of social oppression based on culture, race, ethnicity, language, gender, social class, and sexuality, among other vectors of difference and inequality. For me, a just society means an end to all forms of oppression. Although different individuals and groups experience various forms of oppression differently, we must be vigilant not to buy into the empire's "divide and conquer" mentality by creating and acting on a hierarchy of oppression and competitive victim status (e.g., an Asian transgender who is non-English speaking, immigrant, and poor is more oppressed than a Latino who is English speaking, U.S. born, and working class).

Hierarchies of oppression do not serve us well because they detract our attention from the larger structural and discursive inequalities of the social and political system. I think of Lorde's (1983) words here:

> As a black, lesbian, feminist, socialist, poet, mother of two including one boy, and a member of an interracial couple, I usually find myself part of some group in which the majority defines me as deviant, difficult, inferior, or just plain "wrong." From my membership in all of these groups, I have learned that oppression and the intolerance of differences comes in all shapes and sizes and colors and sexualities, and that among those of us who share the goals of libera-

> tion and a workable future for our children, there can be no hierarchies of oppression. (cited in Adams, 2000, p. 5)

Therefore, I am proposing that to strive for social justice, we must closely examine, analyze, and challenge social oppression based on differences that typically are manifested at the intersections of culture, race, class, gender, and sexuality. This focus on social justice is, in my view, an ethical imperative of communication scholars in general and of intercultural communication scholars and teachers in particular.

To address issues of inequality and injustice, we need to be multilayered and multidimensional. This is when scholarship, activism, and social change blur and inform each other. As scholars, I believe that "theory is a liberatory practice"—to invoke hooks's (1994) words. It is through our personal experiences of privilege (e.g., I am an educated middle-class male in the United States), marginality (e.g., I am a person of color actively questioning heteronormativity), and pain (e.g., I have experienced subtle and overt mistreatment based on my race and accent) that we theorize to make sense of current social relations and institutional and societal practices to heal ourselves, to become whole again, and to work with others to find our way home. This recovery of ourselves and our histories can help us to reclaim our agency and humanity.

I see our work as scholars as following two intersecting tracks. One is to interrogate and unpack current taken-for-granted assumptions and "wisdom" about culture and intercultural communication. For example, in our earlier e-mails we question current definitions in the field. Wenshu offers different ways of conceptualizing culture. Radha and Tom propose the need to examine what internationalization means. Tom and Wenshu urge us to make whiteness visible in current scholarship. Radha invites us to question the rigidity of current cultural categories.

I think that we need to look at how the term *culture* is used. Culture has been used in many ways to mark, objectify, contain, and scrutinize people of color and other individuals at the margins. For example, when I discussed self-reflexivity and the "researcher as a multicultural subject" in my field research seminar last semester, a graduate student from Europe immediately commented, "You mean more people of color are doing this kind of research?" People of color and individuals with accents are assumed to have "culture," whereas European Americans often claim their "lack of culture." Intercultural theory reinforces this process of marking nondominant groups by making them objects of the "imperial gaze," and research becomes a voyeuristic journey into "exotic communities." Another area of potentially productive interrogation is to examine the impulse and constitution of "sanitized" categories in research. For example, we talk about cultures as nation-state or national memberships. Although gender is somewhat addressed (typically as an essential and homogeneous category), social class and sexuality often are ignored. Gender and sexuality typically are viewed outside of the domain of "intercultural communication." Rarely do intercultural researchers immerse themselves in the messiness of the "busy intersections" of race, class, gender, and sexuality.

Along with questioning (meta)theoretical assumptions in current research, a second intersecting track is to produce alternative visions, voices, and options for ourselves that are situated in history, politics, and practices. This counterhegemonic knowledge is necessary and must exist, in my opinion, in an ongoing dialectical and productive tension with the center. The goal is not to replace one form of dominant discourse with another but rather to create new spaces for multiple voices and knowledges from individuals and groups yet named, recognized, and honored. I agree with Wenshu; I strongly believe that we must remain on the fringe to see new possibilities and develop new options.

Mary Jane, you asked who will be going to the WSCA (Western States Communication Association) conference. I will not be at WSCA. I will not be attending to protest the choice of location for the conference. This will be the first WSCA that I will not attend in over a decade. I really appreciate all of your summaries and your reflections. I have been thinking a lot about our dialogue, and I am artificially asking myself to put some of these thoughts on paper. I hope that all of you had a great holiday season.

Radha Hegde

Greetings. Here is my response to the second question. Why do we as scholars need to address this shift in the field? This second question directs us to articulate our motivations for academic engagement. Why do I do what I do? The academy is situated within the complexity of the real and material world. Scholarship is not about simply reducing the world to data and reducing people to subjects. There has to be a deeper passion and conviction that inspires the work we do. The desire to speak and write in the interest of truly democratic life is an integral part of progressive thought.

There is indeed a visible shift happening in terms of reconsidering our work as scholars and the meaning of the enterprise in which we are engaged. The reconceptualization that is happening in the academy is part of a larger scenario that is defined by economic and geopolitical changes. We have seen major political changes worldwide, migrations, global changes, and national borders being reconstituted, and all of this is happening in the context of technology. Clearly, this affects the kind of work we do and the questions we ask; change is happening, and we in the academy are implicated in it. I think it is our responsibility as scholars to be attuned to these changes and to respond to them in our academic endeavors.

For me, one of the reasons for being in the academy is to be able to stand for progressive social change. How do we relate what we do as scholars, our intellectual labor, with matters of social concern? All of our responses to the earlier questions make reference to issues of representation, social justice, and the highly problematic playing field out there. In his response to the first question, Gust discusses the accepted fact that power and politics are antithetical to scientific rigor. Problems have to be named, as Wenshu notes, in order to be exposed and critiqued. After all, this is the larger mission of a field such as intercultural communication. To be meaningful in these troubling global times, the field, as Tom rightfully reminds us, should not be just a field of study but a "project."

Of course, we are taking on the mantle of speaking for the oppressed, the need to stand in for the exploited, a task that has been sharply criticized and renamed by the right in various ways—chest beating, pretentious ideology and not scholarship, or what D'Souza (1992) calls a victims' revolution on campus. We need to be intellectually fortified to survive this attack. The political turn in scholarship is not about dueling positions, nor is it only about naming the bad guys and coming out moralistic and superior. I think that it is about doing sound scholarship that is incisive, is resistant, and provides dynamic critique of received views of common culture. It surely is not about a bunch of "bleeding heart liberals" wailing for their "pet cause," as our critics would characterize us. The issues are real and urgent, and so is the need for our commitment to democratic goals in the production of knowledge.

Having said that, the "why" question posed to us is still connected to that in which we are intervening. The exclusions and the canonization of certain views of communication are configurations of a modernist worldview that dominates our field. The intercultural canon never has "named," to draw on Wenshu's earlier comments, questions of race or racism except in clinical terms. In this context of naming, Mary Jane's example of skills-based training in intercultural communication is highly relevant. The training model always has reminded me of the manager who wants to make obedient subjects—docile bodies ever ready to serve corporate gods. The rationale for this model comes from the worldview of the sovereign subject in total control of *his* action. All of these conceptualizations emerge from a linear view of communication—the "innocent" conception whereby everything communicates and consensus will be reached if we just communicate effectively (a view that ignores all of the complexities of identity that we have referred to earlier in the dialogue). This we need to subject to relentless critique. So, why do we intervene? We intervene to complicate, name, and problematize the issues that have not ever come to the surface.

Tom and Gust made reference to the pedagogical imperatives associated with this ferment. The classroom is an absolutely important site in our work. Whether it is the Amadou Diallo shooting, the killing of Matthew Shephard, or Jerry Falwell's paranoia about TeleTubbies, we need to tackle the political complexity of these issues in the classroom. This is not at all easy. But this is where our contribution as cultural workers is most directly felt. A progressive pedagogical approach is intrinsically related to our commitment to a democratic vision. The theoretical project always is theory plus something more. Arguing against the finality of a finished paradigm, Hall (1996) writes, "I am not interested in theory, I am interested in going on theorizing" (p. 150). The dialogue to enable productive social transformation has to be kept alive.

The university is not the same place today in terms of sheer demographics. As a graduate teaching assistant in a public speaking class at a large midwestern university, there were many times when I was the only nonwhite person in class. My very first semester, I also remember being told that I could not teach as a graduate student because I was not a native speaker of English. To a postcolonial subject like myself who was taught English in India by Irish nuns who routinely smacked my knuckles as a 6- or 7-year-old for blurting a word of Tamil, the notion of not being qualified to teach in English in the United States was preposterous. I surely have learned English the hard way, wouldn't you say? Today, these experiences are grist for my teaching. My class in New Jersey is altogether different in terms of the diversity, the receptivity to discussion, and the experiences shared. This is a major factor contributing to the ferment in the field. The demographic changes should affect the kinds of questions we ask and the types of knowledge we produce and impart to our students. This is the point where we are today; we already are headlong into the scene. And to view knowledge as neutral and pedagogy as transparent transfer of the truth does not cut it in a world marked by inequalities of every kind.

I got a bit carried away but kept to the spirit of Mary Jane's idea of "let it flow."

Wenshu Lee

I am not sure so far that we have "dialogued" about the "problem/ferment." But I will go ahead in answering the second question. In my earlier e-mail, I talked about the tension and anxiety in the felt power shift that occurs once marginalized people have enough discursive apparatus to name the complicities and silences of the research establishment—a center and fringe reversal. This "rupture" has to be addressed because it gives some people pain and a sense of loss, while it is welcomed by others. In brief, it is contested in the journal publication process, classroom teaching, and conference organizing.

This rupture has to be addressed because it matters; it makes significant differences for some people. I can make a list of such differences.

This rupture makes possible the style shift from "variable-driven writing" (which often is impersonal, detached, and too nebulous to name an agency) to "narrative history-driven writing" (which is more personal, historicized, politicized, agency specific, and reflexive). This difference leads us from vacuum to contexts, depth, and voice.

This style shift also affirms the centrality of "ethics." It becomes acceptable and even obligatory for scholars to take a stand/position in relation to significant sociohistorical issues (e.g., immigrant rights, gay and lesbian rights, transnational workers' rights).

This rupture makes possible the metatheoretical shift from shared heritage and commonly accepted norms of behavior to differences, disagreements, confrontations, surveillance, insurgency, uprising, and hegemonic domination. What matters is, in a Foucaultian sense, breaks and shifts rather than "trans-historical" continuities (Foucault, 1999).

I reflect on why I have changed to endorse a position-specific and history-specific way of teaching and research. I feel more in touch with "my self" who had been silenced and erased in my earlier research paradigm. My teaching assignments place more emphasis on embodied performances than on textually based projects. I am more willing to take risks in disclosing myself, addressing touchy social issues (e.g., Vermont civil union law, sweatshops in Third World countries), and becoming more "drained and exhausted" emotionally in teaching and research. My students are more likely to describe me as "inspiring" because many of their selves had been denied and silenced by various discursive establishments (e.g., family, church, school). My research is described more as "giving meaning" and "making a difference."

This rupture, however, gives some people pain and loss of control. They are more likely to argue why we should not continue/endorse such a shift/ferment. As I noted in an earlier e-mail regarding "politicized scholarship," the arguments include the loss of neutrality, privacy, scientific rigor, replicability, and generalizability. In brief, this shift/ferment/rupture affects people differently and is still contested heavily in different realms of scholarly apparatus.

Tom Nakayama

As producers of "knowledge" about intercultural communication, other cultures, and certainly other peoples, it is very important that we recognize the implications of our studies. While we are situated in a privileged position, the history of academic knowledge has left many in our society feeling extremely suspicious of such knowledge. Scientific studies that "proved" the superiority of white people, for example, are well known (Harding, 1993). More recently, AIDS protesters often have made explicit connections to the Tuskegee Syphilis Project (Reverby, 2000; Solomon, 1985).

Intercultural communication is not immune from this suspicion about academic work. I have seen many students get angry and hurt over the ways in which some studies characterize particular groups. Although I am happy to see that these students feel empowered enough to speak out against such research, I also am saddened to see some of them reject pursuing the study of communication because of what they perceive to be an insensitive discipline. The work of critical pedagogy can be helpful in encountering these issues in the classroom (Giroux, 1993, 2001). When culture gets reduced to a variable, the historical and material contexts for cultural beliefs, attitudes, and values get erased. Wenshu's observation about the connection to ethics here is very significant in that our studies are historically situated and contribute to ongoing dialogues about various kinds of social change.

It is very important that we are attentive to this ferment in the field. If we are not, then we risk losing out on the richest resource available to us—future scholars with very different cultural backgrounds, experiences, and perspectives that can enrich the study of intercultural communication. Questions about how we characterize and study "others" certainly are not unique to communication studies. The issues raised here point toward many concerns raised by the ferment including the ways in which our studies (de)humanize others, the ethics of our work, and who these studies serve. By focusing our studies on others, do we risk assuming that the "norm" is the white American trying to communicate with these others?

Mary Jane Collier

Greetings, everyone. I would like to share with you an example from a recent speech by Rod Hart at the Rocky Mountain Communication Association conference in February 2001 to illustrate the nature of the "status quo," who is served by it, and its consequences in our research and teaching. I select this example because Professor Hart spoke about his research program addressing the question "Who are the American people?" that has resulted in several publications and sparked much dialogue.

Although I think that the question he asks is an important one, as the presentation unfolded I noted several claims that I found problematic. For example, to characterize the various ways in which politicians and their rhetoric exemplify "the American people," I could not help but notice that Professor Hart chose to show several television clips from white male presidents and presidential candidates, actors who were playing white male presidents in films, and one clip from a white female (Hillary Clinton). I would respectfully point out that the range of politicians who influence how people in the United States think of their national group is a little broader and more diverse than this selected sample who, with one exception, looked and sounded a lot like the professor addressing us at the conference.

Professor Hart also said, "We may not have a common ethnicity or history, but what we do have in common is the idea of freedom and democracy." I wondered who among the "we" he referred to would agree on the meaning or share experiences of "freedom" or "democracy" and if the "we" he was thinking of included those who were not white. Tom already has pointed out the need to uncover such unspoken assumptions. Hart noted that the "American" public may be identified by pointing to a common core of values evident in media advertising or in formula films in which he equated the formulas with values that have been reinforced throughout "our" history.

Professor Hart also argued that the American public is evident in every election by examining the voices of the "majority" of voters. To reinforce the value of studying the majority of voters as equivalent to what/who are Americans, he simply wrote down "51%" on an overhead as if that number was a definitive and equivalent sign of the voices of "American" people. Hart did not clarify that the 51% figure he quoted was based on those individuals who were eligible, able, and cast their ballots (and had their votes counted). He did not raise questions about who can and cannot vote. As we know from the U.S. presidential election of 2000, some African Americans and elderly residents of Florida, among other groups in other places, were not permitted to exercise their right to vote. Other questions that should have been asked include the following. What counts as a vote? Who decides? Who/What counts the votes? Who ultimately decides the results?

Furthermore, if we look to entertainment products disseminated by media corporations for economic profit to reveal the values of "American people," then we learn more about the elite who are controlling the industries than we do about the audiences. In addition, audiences are increasingly counterhegemonic and have diverse voices. Using these means to pinpoint what/who is "American" illustrates the dangers of erasing context and history, making assumptions without interrogating what is being taken for granted, and reifying ideologies that serve an elite privileged group. When people like Professor Hart and myself begin to recognize the unearned race and class privileges and uncover the systemic ways in which that privilege has been reified for our benefit, we can see a different world around us. This, in turn, should change the nature of the questions we ask and the way in which we ask and answer them.

Let me also add here that in an e-mail message to the four other participants in the dialogue (sent to the group in February 2001), I wondered aloud whether my comments regarding Professor Hart's presentation sounded like a somewhat angry personal attack rather than disagreement with the arguments being advanced. I also said, however, that I thought that my critique was important because one of my goals as a scholar is to invite readers who are like me—from privileged, white, middle/upper class locations—to question their taken-for-granted assumptions.

Wenshu Lee

Before I start reworking my sections in the dialogue, I would like to talk to you, Mary Jane, regarding your musings and the questions you raised in your e-mail. I think that your criticism of Professor Hart is right on. In an odd way, I do not sense "anger" in your writing. I feel "outrage" and I feel "solidarity." Welcome.

Who are the *real* Americans? How do we know when we see one, an *authentic* one? Those who share the idea of freedom and democracy? Whose freedom and whose democracy? Your encounter reminds me of the practices of "intersectional ghettoization" loudly accepted in our field. In rhetorical studies, in organizational studies, in interpersonal studies, in health communication, and so on, we see "women" (read straight-appearing white females), then "minorities" (read straight-appearing colored males), then "women of color" (read straight-appearing still), then sexual minorities (read white-appearing males), and so on, in a sequential order making it into appendices, then footnotes, then bibliographies, then a publication or two, and then promptly forgotten, falling into the *naturalized* state of absence and erasure.

Tom talked earlier about Americans = whiteness. This metonym is power. It also is a stereotype providing impoverished knowledge about complex and fluid phenomena. So, let us complicate this stereotype and make it possible for people like me, a "naturalized" U.S. citizen of the "correct" sexual orientation and "correct" class standing and education but of the "wrong" race, "wrong" gender, "wrong" skin tone, "wrong" size, and "wrong" accent to be American. Can people who are of everything "wrong" be Americans? Who has the authority to circulate a nebulous sense of "wrongness," and who gets to invoke the question of "authenticity"? I wonder.

What about the organizational insurgency at the NCA during the past 3 years? Each and every one of the African American Communication Studies division, Latino/Latina American Communication Studies division, Gay/Lesbian/Transgendered/Bisexual division, and Asian Pacific American Communication Studies division had to go through getting 300 signatures to initiate a new division, to be endorsed by the legislative assembly, and to continue having 300 members per division; otherwise, that division will be demoted and disenfranchised. The NCA also has its own "naturalization" surveillance procedure deciphering "What are the *real* NCA divisions?"

I have one final thought. Mary Jane, I noticed that you recognize your own *privileges* of being white, middle-class, and European American. I keep wanting to ask you: Why is it that other identities (e.g., gender identities, sexual identities) do not make it into your discursive persona and consciousness? I also want to ask you: Why do you put European American and white together? Do they signify different meanings for you? Finally, we all experience both privileges and oppressions at certain points in our lives. What are the oppressions you have experienced as a white woman/girl in politicized contexts (e.g., family, church, grade school, high school, graduate school, classrooms, academic departments, publication processes)? As you remark, "When people like Professor Hart and myself begin to recognize the unearned race and class privileges and uncover the systemic ways in which that privilege has been reified for our benefit, we can see a different world around us. This, in turn, should change the nature of the questions we ask and the way in which we ask and answer them." By acknowledging the *oppressions* you experienced, will you also ask different questions? If yes, what are they? And how would they change your view of your identities and your academic politics? I do not expect you to answer all of these questions, especially in a public forum. I just want to share some of my thoughts and questions. Good night.

Mary Jane Collier

These are excellent questions you raise, Wenshu. First, let me say thank you for calling my attention to the ways in which I choose to align myself. This is an excellent illustration of the individual agency, choices, and freedom I am exercising to claim or not claim identifications. I have been systematically taught to think of myself as an individual and to make these choices without thinking at all about consequences or contextual constraints. In addition, your questions illustrate the importance of a kind of dialogue in which we can ask each other to be more reflexive, and together we uncover and examine assumptions and interpretations. So, I do want to respond, at least briefly, to your very important questions.

You ask about my use of particular labels and groupings. At some points in our previous cyber-dialogue, I was problematizing my race and ethnicity because my whiteness and European American ethnic heritage provide me sources of unearned privilege and social/economic advantages to which you four do not have the same automatic access. I distinguish between race and ethnicity because these are identity categorizations that are widely circulated and used quite differently by different peoples socialized in different conditions. I find that when I emphasize how race or ethnic categorizations, for example, are socially constructed, my students sometimes revert to "Why can't we just treat everyone as individuals?," and some of my students then forget that we are biologically marked by each other in conversations, politicians' speeches, organizational policies, and media texts with powerful consequences.

I can give examples of how these categorizations are invoked differently by pointing to my experience in South Africa. Race is socially and economically constructed as a preeminent categorization on which apartheid was based and with which the "new" South Africa is struggling, whereas ethnically based markers (which are coded into linguistic markers of Afrikaans speaking or English speaking) are used to ascribe identifications of heritage and group membership among whites and by blacks. It is noteworthy that during my last visit to South Africa in the fall of 1999, many blacks told me that they definitely avowed their racial identity as blacks as often as possible. I spent a day with a young man, Mnadisi Fono, in Nyanga township outside Cape Town. Paraphrasing what he told me, he identified as black and Xhosa (and he spoke four languages fluently). When I asked him what he thought about race and affirmative action, he had to think about it awhile. He said that his people's black skins had made them suffer during apartheid. He also said that labor unions and mass actions (strikes) were not always good in that innocent people sometimes get hurt. (His grandmother lost her job because of a mass action.) Overall, he said, with blacks having the right to vote and with everyone working hard, there is reason to hope that things are going to get better. He pointed out that blacks, more than whites, did need basic things. The family (here meaning a grandmother, an aunt, a mother, and two small children) with whom we spent a good part of the day were on a local waiting list to eventually be put on a community waiting list for a 10-year development plan for a one-room wooden house to replace the part cardboard, part tin structure (without running water or electricity) in which they lived.

In the United States, whites who align themselves as Polish American, Cuban American, or Jewish American do not enjoy the same comfort and complacency that European Americans like me who are the center may enjoy. For reasons such as these, in the earlier part of the cyber-dialogue, I included my own race and ethnicity to mark interrelated locations of privilege and status. I distinguish between them because from whiteness comes an overarching form of privilege and from European American comes an overarching form of presumed entitlement. As you each point out, these markers are essentialist and are so common as to become transparent. (As one of my undergraduate students put it, "European American is really just normal, isn't it? Why do we need to call it anything?")

One example of the benefits I enjoy is that very few white colleagues or students over the years have asked me to explain my positionality and politics of location in my co-authoring (with Sidney Ribeau and Michael Hecht) a book on African American communication (Hecht, Collier, & Ribeau, 1993). When discussing intercultural communication training a few years ago, a corporate executive told me that he was much more comfortable with me being a facilitator than he was with the last diversity trainer, who had been confrontational and stirred up trouble; he thought that his employees could better relate to me. At hotels where we stay for our academic conferences, I have not once been asked whether I could fetch some extra towels or quickly clean a particular room, whereas several of my female colleagues of color do get asked such questions. When I joined the University of Denver, the first doctoral dissertation I directed was on the topic of lesbian cultural identity among administrators in higher education, in which the author, Betsy Metzger, described story after story about the agonizing identity and career decisions made by 55 courageous women (Metzger, 1998). I do not have to experience what my gay and lesbian friends throughout the nation go through as they watch heteronormativity and homophobia infuse voters and state legislators with fear and hostility and watch as those same voters and legislators create laws and policies regulating all of our private and public lives.

I also would like to point to instances in which I experienced what I define as oppression on the basis of gender and sexuality. Let me preface these examples by saying that I have been very lucky in that the intensity, frequency, and consequences of what I experience do not compare to those of women around the world who are physically, emotionally, socially, and spiritually abused. Having said that, I will share a story about my experience during graduate school. During my graduate coursework, one of my professors (who knew I was married and had met my husband) sexually harassed me one evening after class. Rather than keeping my description abstract and emotionally empty, let me add that he approached me as I was leaving his office, turned me around to face him, pushed me against the wall, and began to kiss me. I was able to push him away and rushed out of his office. At the time, I did not tell anyone else (not my husband or any other friend) about his behavior because I believed that I must have done something to "lead him on," and I assumed that his advances were my fault somehow.

After agonizing for several days and thinking about the fact that this professor had said in graduate seminars that "I know lots of folks in the discipline" and "It's a good idea to remember I can make or break your career," I decided to talk to him. He never repeated this behavior, but I was very careful to set up appointments in the middle of the day, and I avoided contact when I could. Years later, I got the nerve to talk to another woman graduate student who was in the program with me and learned that I was not the only one he had harassed.

My own experiences and extended conversations with colleagues (male and female) who are feminists have led me to recognize that systems of oppression are global and local. I am developing, I hope, different ways of hearing and then responding to comments from students, administrators, and faculty. For example, several years ago, during a university committee meeting in which I was the only female, I was considering whether to volunteer to chair the committee, and two of the men turned to me and asked me to take the minutes. I chose to point out that I was willing and able to chair the committee and said that because I was willing to take on that task, perhaps one of them could take the minutes. That is what ended up happening.

Wenshu, you ask whether these kinds of oppressions and recognized privileges lead me to ask different questions. My answer is that "I hope so." And I trust that the questions I ask now also are consistent with a critical turn in my own scholarship about culture and communication. I will give two examples about my research and my professional praxis. The kinds of questions I now ask about (inter)cultural alliances in South Africa relate to the ideologies, unearned privilege, and heterosexual gendered norms that emerge in discourse about topics such as the role of affirmative action today. I engage my research with people whom I hear identifying themselves and being defined by each other and institutions in intersecting ways as Afrikaans-speaking, English-speaking, and multilingual South Africans; as black, colored (mixed-race), white, and Asian Indian; as holding various socioeconomic class positions; and as having various genders and sexualities. I spend time in universities, urban settings, and townships. As one result of this dialogue, I will think about how to orient my research toward examination of itineraries and shared struggles.

My second example of how my experiences affect what I do involves my work for 3 years with a program focusing on bringing young women from Palestine, Israel, and the United States together at a camp in the Rocky Mountains. I began to uncover what I saw as elitist ethnocentric assumptions positioning the Palestinian young women's ways of being in the world as less "appropriate" than the Israelis' ways of being and the Middle Eastern young women's ways of being as less appropriate than the U.S. Americans' ways of being. Indeed, Wenshu, this relates to a politics of location on several levels. I first chose to share my observations in discussions with other staff members in the program, and later I included my observations in an evaluation report to the board of directors and offered to meet with them. Ultimately, I made the very difficult decision to leave the program when my role was redefined to very limited contact with the young women and I could see that reflexive examination about the hierarchies, power, and problematic ethical issues in the program was not welcomed.

Wenshu Lee

Mary Jane, when you first decided to "jump in" as a dialogical partner rather than a moderator on February 12, I responded with an earlier e-mail welcoming your shift—a difficult, self-reflexive, and courageous choice.

The section on "a politics of location" that I added a few days ago reflects an answer (an emerging and provisional one) to my long and ambivalent positions regarding "identity politics." The quest for new and assertive "identities" helped me (and other historically oppressed peoples) to gain increasingly complex consciousness as a human. Yet no matter how insistent we are that identities are provisional and in between and should not be essentialized as biological, we are in danger of falling into the trap of "social essentialism" or "constructivist essentialism." For example, "whiteness" or "gender" is *socially constructed* rather than biologically based; sexual minorities are *constructed* into "deviants" and so on. Okay, this makes sense. But whiteness = privilege/morality = maleness = straight = education = wealth = able-bodied . . . , these words seem so hollow, one-dimensional, and certain as I search for answers to "irregularities" in specific times and spaces. For example, white people are not equally privileged, women are not equally oppressed, and Asians are not all nonracists. "Identities" too often lead us into "social or constructivist essentialism." "Locations," in comparison, point to "political provisionality" and "itineraries of struggles"—specific people in a specific time/place working together toward articulated goals. Still, locations are not angelic places; they often are muddy, fuzzy, and leaking where struggles somehow have to occur. (I am still trying to formulate this.)

This shift from "identities" to "locations" has a profound implication for how I located you, Mary Jane, differently as our cyber-dialogue evolved. Without knowing much about your biographical itineraries, I had fallen easily into the trap of "social/constructivist essentialism." I realize that I viewed you as a "white" person who was conscious of your "class" standing. I asked for the other identities (i.e., gender and sexual identities) that had not made it into your writing. Note that I did not ask for your locations, your itineraries of struggles. It would have been far better for me to ask for "intersectional locations" rather than "intersectional identities" if my aim was to forge alliances and not to be trapped by my own essentializing acts.

Mary Jane, I appreciate your frank comments in the earlier part of the dialogue on the "affective dimension of what we are doing in this dialogue," especially the addition of your gendered consciousness growing out of the white male professor's harsh remarks that equated speaking up with belonging to the profession. This "belongingness" took a further turn in meaning when the (white male) professor who had sexually harassed you remarked, "It's a good idea to remember I can make or break your career." My stomach tightened as if I could envision myself in the room with you. I also cheered you on when you stopped this professor and, years later, you challenged the almost all-male committee's secretarial assumption of you and became the chair of the committee. Your "journey" from point to point involved an increasingly critical sense of gendered agency, which was richer than a one-liner "I am a woman."

When you mentioned that some of your female colleagues of color had the experiences of being treated as "maids" at conference hotels, I recall my frequent experiences in department offices where I taught/teach. When the secretary is away and regardless of whether I am alone or with other professors or graduate students (who are white and bigger than me), students who walk in usually single me out and say, "Could you put this in Professor X's box?" or "Can you give this to the secretary you work for?" I am not a tenured professor; I am a petite colored female = work-study student. This automatic link between social standing and race/gender/size is played out in my struggle here and now, which is richer than a one-liner "I am a woman of color."

Your academic routes evolved from a social scientist looking for the "cure" to a critical scholar reflecting on the politics of location in co-authoring a book on African American communication, becoming a trainer who the corporate executive felt "comfortable" with, doing a project on (inter)cultural alliances in South Africa, and leaving a program where you had challenged their politics against Palestinian young women vis-à-vis Israeli and U.S. American ones. The journey you chose to embark on and routes you took and rethought through are important for me (and the readers of this dialogue) to learn about.

This exchange has helped me to understand the power of "intersectional locations." It has marked a big step in my critical pursuit. I have learned to follow/ask about "intersectional locations" in this cyber-dialogue. I will practice it in my classrooms and daily encounters. I will more consistently suspend my constructivist-essentialist assumptions that my white students are automatically privileged, my Chinese female colleagues are automatically in alliance with me, my gay/lesbian friends are automatically nonracists, and so on. I am not advocating that every encounter is devoid of collective histories. Africans were forced into slavery, women could not vote in the United States until 1920, and same-sex marriage became legal in the Netherlands on April 1, 2001. We cannot forget these histories. But we also can create and relocate histories by allying more and more individuals in their/our critical itineraries for a more equitable world.

So, who are the "fringe" scholars? Biology or visually available markers of race, gender, sexuality, and class are too easy an answer. Our respectively complex and difficult itineraries and struggles embodied in this dialogue, in my view, point to a more persuasive answer.

Mary Jane, it is heartening to follow your itineraries of struggles both personally and academically. It also is heartening to witness the articulation of your privileges and oppressions and their implications for your paradigm shift. I have learned a great deal.

QUESTION FROM MARY JANE COLLIER

What can we do to address these concerns? What should be the agenda for scholars of international/intercultural communication?

Wenshu Lee

Scholars of international/intercultural communication need to become "co-performers" in the research process. As I discussed elsewhere (Lee, 1998), this involves an interrhetorical relearning process with co-equals across cultural boundaries. This means not only learning a new language if it is necessitated by the research project to gain proficiency but also learning rhetorically what persuades who in what context in both cultures.

Research questions and methodologies become processes of revision; we need to be open to interrogations of our naming the system, the ways in which research questions are framed, and how the purposes of the research are articulated. We can honestly confront the question, "Who benefits from the knowledge production process?" Our publications need not always present the polished, unruffled, and coherent surface. We may make false starts (Warren, 2001), stumble over our taken-for-granted blind spots, and learn to see new things from a different subject position.

In addition to interrhetorical proficiency and a processual research trajectory, scholars need to learn genealogical histories in situ with priorities given to subjugated knowledge in a given culture. For example, student protesters on the Tiananmen Square in China in 1989 came from a long, insurgent student tradition rooted in the May Fourth Movement in 1919. This tradition and these students cannot be contained in the general and hegemonic view of Chinese being collectivist and nonconfrontational.

We cannot do everything and correct all of the world's wrongs, misconduct, and exploitations. We need to preserve our energy; pick our fights given our personal, institutional, and political limits; and give each other support without relinquishing our critical sensibility.

Finally, we need to write and speak to multiple audiences. Can my mother understand my e-mail here? Can my sisters of color from different parts of the globe understand "interrhetorical proficiency, processual research trajectory, critical sensibility, and multiple audiences?" I guess *not*. So, I will stop here and begin thinking about writing in Mandarin Chinese to my mother, in plainer English to my neighborhood organizers, and in English/Spanish to my friends in Mexico on something important to make the world a better, more equitable place for them/us to inhabit.

Radha Hegde

With the increased levels of mobility we see today in conjunction with the unprecedented growth of technology, the repercussions for our scholarly agenda are serious. With the collapsing of space/time dimensions, we are witnessing new configurations of community and cultural groups. The changing social scenario is full of questions waiting to be asked and explored. The global dynamics that have been set into motion need to be articulated and theorized by scholars in communication. Recognizing the need, of course, is easier than a precise answer to the question: What should be done?

In trying to lay out an agenda of what we, as scholars, should be doing, I must clarify that my objective is not to create an authoritative version of what should now count as acceptable research and theory. As the question states, it is the agenda, the larger story, on which I want to focus. My intention certainly is not to define prescriptive norms about how to create an alternative intellectual bizarro world. To me, that would undermine the whole purpose of critical and resistant scholarship. My comments on what we should do are related to my larger concern for democratizing the reach of theory in the discipline.

If we get rigid, then we create a new theoretical canon, a new hegemonic underworld, which certainly is not how we open up spaces for new questions and more engaged readings of culture. Having said that, I am not advocating some funky, free-floating research that lacks rigor or purpose. Our questions and methods have to relate very clearly to the larger goals of the theoretical enterprise. Theory, to echo Hall (1996), is a detour to something else. It is our social and academic responsibility to define that something else. What is it that we want to achieve through our theoretical work?

Let me illustrate with the notion of difference. The understanding of difference as constituted in multiple ways is central to contemporary life and to our scholarly work. The mantra of race, class, and gender (to use Mercer's [1992] phrase) is recited everywhere for multiple reasons. The challenge for us is how to theorize more than one vector of difference without the incredulousness of the colonial gaze or the oversimplification of difference as distinct variables. The issue is more than recognizing difference in a benign way; it is to articulate how those differences have been represented and surface in particular societal formations. As Mohanty (1989) writes, "The central issue, then, is not one of merely acknowledging difference; rather, the more difficult question concerns the kind of difference that is acknowledged and engaged."

This, of course, leads to the question of voice and method. If our objective is to extend our representational possibilities, then how do we represent voices and whose voice is privileged? This is a continuing debate among critical scholars to which we need to pay close attention. The important point here is to problematize the notion of voice and positionality. How does the recovery of voices contribute to a body of alternative knowledge that challenges the dominant representations? Just the act of registering other voices does not make our research political. Mere spectating and marking the exotic or faraway is not the same as coming to an informed and critical understanding of the "other."

Let me turn to the part of the question that asks who is entitled to speak and who should be silenced. I would say that we should not resurrect identity politics around issues of silence and voice. Why silence anyone? Rather, let us encourage debate and dialogue. The goal is to extend the representational reach of our research endeavors. In turn, this should help us to deal with the question of insider and outsider. Plain old cultural markers or identity badges do not make you an insider. This is especially true in our global times when the notion of authentic identities has been thrown into crisis. As Wallace (1991) writes, "Women are not to be trusted just because they're women any more than blacks are to be trusted because they're black or gays because they're gays and so on" (p. 185).

We need to be very clear about the goals of our research and the motivations to do intellectual work. This is the serious metatheoretical issue that we need to grapple with to understand cultural practices and identities. Different theoretical perspectives need to be engaged in dialogue in order to see how their various trajectories determine patterns of research. I do believe that interdisciplinarity is an expected and essential turn in the study of culture, identity, and space. So, drawing on multiple vocabularies enriches our understanding. It allows us to question traditional categories and to work the tensions inherent in the conceptualizations. This is the dialogue that we need to encourage. The issue of relating theoretical perspectives is more related to how best we can sharpen our critique to be consistent with our larger objective of democratizing knowledge. After all, theory is not a template for replication; it is an outlook that shapes our questions about the issues that beset our globally (dis)connected world.

Mary Jane Collier

I want to echo Radha's call for "intertextual" dialogue and reflexive dialogic examination of our scholarly orientations with those who hold dissimilar views. At NCA 2000, when the five of us met, several of us wondered aloud how so many in our discipline could be ignorant of, or choose not to acknowledge, the ferment in our field, the critical turn, and the immediacy of the need for change. This makes me wonder how much our socialization of graduate students has changed over the years, if at all. We are caught in the following "in-between space" of evolution. Many of us recognize that the traditional contexts on which the communication discipline are organized are dated and no longer serve us, but the traditional groupings are still very much evident in our professional associations, journals and textbooks, and curricula. So, if we encourage graduate students to select a communicative phenomenon or "communication problem/issue" that crosses the traditional contexts such as cultural identity and voice, then the students are immediately placed on the "edges" of the discipline and are different from graduate students who choose an area of specialization such as intercultural *or* interpersonal communication. What we study is the key to who we are in the discipline.

Borrowing from Radha's excellent metaphor, our gaze as professionals often is trained to focus the camera lens and maintain the focus rather than learning how to operate the zoom, learning how to operate two cameras simultaneously with panoramas and close-ups, working with a host of people operating lots of cameras recording images to fill the IMAX screen, or even stopping all the cameras and taking a walk around the community. We certainly can approach our own projects and teach our students to start by questioning who, if anyone, has the right to use a camera at all and to talk about what it means to be "invited" and collaborate in a way that is more participative and action research based. As I think of how we organize our graduate curriculum, our departments could explore new configurations. For example, my department is creating graduate seminars about particular phenomena (i.e., dialogue) in which graduate students and faculty talk together and engage in diverse philosophical/theoretical/methodological perspectives about situated examples of dialogue.

Each of you refers to an epistemological narrowness and hegemony that can occur when one paradigm, such as the functionalist social science paradigm, is reinforced as the best and most respected paradigm in graduate programs and is regarded as the most scientific and trustworthy in academic publications and corporate settings across the globe. How humans are cultural beings; how power and privilege affect lives, relationships, and who we are; and how we live often are ignored or declared to be extraneous sources of variance. This is where we can engage in intertextual dialogue across perspectives. For example, scholars using functionalist social science paradigms and those speaking from critical standpoints could discuss additional forms of "validity" and "reliability," and we could name these ontological/engaged validity and reliability. In other words, the criteria of "useful" social science research may be expanded to include evaluating particular studies according to the extent to which the "results" resonate with the experiences of cultural group members or are "repeatable" for them/us as they/we live their/our lives in complex contexts.

Tom Nakayama

Scholars who are sensitive to this "turn" in intercultural communication scholarship need to be reflexive about the positions from which they write as well as about the kinds of "knowledge" they are generating. Although none of us can completely control the ways in which our writings will be used by others, in different contexts and for very different purposes than we originally wrote, we can be sensitive to the implications of what we are writing about.

Although intercultural communication scholars are unlikely to agree on many points, if we take social justice as a starting point for understanding why we want to know about other people, then we can begin to avoid the pitfalls of other scholars who have written about "others" in the past. Although we cannot guarantee that our writings never will be used for colonialist, imperialist, or other modes of domination, we also must be sensitive to that history of intellectual work. Theories about "race" and difference historically have been used to justify the domination and control of peoples around the world. Although much of this work occurred before the appearance of "intercultural communication" per se, we have inherited and use many of the research methods and theories from that past.

We must be reflexive about the ways in which we use these tools—how they can help serve different ends today as well as the pitfalls of unreflective use of them. Like Radha, I do not think that there is any point in advocating for a singular approach to understanding, studying, and knowing about other people. But we must be sensitive to the fact that we are studying other people. We must remember that we are not in a zoo and exoticizing other people. To be humane and to understand other people and other cultures requires sensitivity, reflexivity, and a multiplicity of methods and theories. All of these can be fraught with danger, but we can find these tools useful if we wield them judiciously.

Gust Yep

Regarding Mary Jane's question about how to acknowledge the WSCA boycott, public statements at various business meetings are good, although I am unsure about their effectiveness. What do the rest of you think we can do?

Here is my addition to the third question given that I started answering this question when I responded to the second. In that response, I argue that international and intercultural communication scholars have the "ethical imperative" to address issues of inequality and social justice in our work. I also see our work along two intersecting tracks. The first is the interrogation of current knowledge in the field, and the second is the creation of counterhegemonic knowledge and "naming silenced lives" (to invoke the words of McLaughlin & Tierney, 1993).

As international and intercultural communication scholars, we produce and disseminate knowledge about culture. This process of production and dissemination locates us in a privileged space in the academy and society and, at the same time, makes us accountable for our work. As members of the academy, I see that we are accountable for our research and pedagogy. All of us have observed the significance of reflexivity in our work. As Radha notes, "Self-reflexivity is a good and humbling exercise at all times; right now, the moment seems to call for it urgently." Although we do not have control over the mis/uses of our research, we do have control over—and responsibility for—the what, how, and why of our research (the research topics, the approach to these topics, and the personal and political motivations behind the work, respectively).

With accountability, privilege, and ethical imperative as our backdrop, I believe that our work is situated within the framework and challenges of what West (1990) calls the "new cultural politics of difference." This work is neither simply oppositional nor transgressive but rather committed to demystify the operations of power in society in order to empower and enable social action.

One area that I would like to focus on here is the demystification of the idea of a "common culture" in our teaching and research. This impulse is motivated by my own interrogations of this concept as well as past discussions in my graduate seminar in culture and communication and current discussions in my upper division undergraduate course in intercultural communication. It seems to me that in our field, as well as in others, we continue to reproduce dominant ideology through a series of normalized and widely accepted conceptualizations of the notion of culture itself. For example, I was troubled by how all of my graduate students (in my graduate seminar in culture and communication last year) had adopted the notion of a "common culture," the sharing of beliefs, values, attitudes, behaviors, and so on (i.e., a "typical textbook definition" of culture).

When I pointed out how remarkably similar their definitions were, one graduate student told us, "I guess we have all been good students and have learned the accepted definitions in the discipline." I felt uneasy with that comment. Are we reproducing dominant belief systems and producing disciplined bodies and uncritical minds? This incident is contrasted with my undergraduate students this semester. When defining culture, most students used variations of the widely accepted notion, but one student —not a communications major—almost indignantly jumped into our discussion and said, "Do we really have a common culture?" She then followed with the question, "Whose version of a shared and common culture are we talking about?"

To me, these two incidents foreground several things. First, I need to reflect on my own pedagogy—curricular choices, classroom practices, and so on. If my curricular choices are reproducing current taken-for-granted conceptualizations, then I am participating in the maintenance of current power relations and imbalances. If my classroom practices are providing spaces for other voices to emerge, then I (along with the students) need to listen to different perspectives and incorporate them into my teaching and research. Second, someone outside the field (as in the case of the undergraduate mentioned earlier) can provide us with crucial questions and critical insights about work in the field. I am in some ways invoking Kuhn's (1970) idea of a paradigm shift introduced and created by "outsiders."

Wenshu mentions that the four of us are "fringe scholars" with lived experiences of marginalization. In that sense, we are outsiders who can bring our own perspectives and experiences as the foundation for our work. This also underscores the importance of interdisciplinary engagement. We have a lot to learn about culture and communication by reading and examining the work done in other disciplines such as anthropology, sociology, psychology, ethnic studies, women's studies, and queer studies. These "outside" perspectives can enrich our work and provide us with important questions for self-reflexivity and interrogation.

Third, current conceptualizations of culture as shared are hegemonic in the intercultural communication literature and must be unpacked and interrogated. Calling the idea of a common shared culture a "poisonous pedagogy" or the "pedagogy of the big lies," Macedo (1994, 1999) notes that such a notion celebrates the supremacy of Western heritage and degrades and devalues other cultural narratives along the lines of race, ethnicity, gender, social class, sexuality, and language. Criticizing Hirsch, Kett, and Trefil's (1988) celebrated book, *The Dictionary of Cultural Literacy,* Macedo (1999) points out that the idea of "widely accepted cultural values often equates Western culture with civilization while leaving unnoted Western culture's role in 'civilizing' the 'primitive others' " (p. 120). He further writes, "To execute its civilizing tasks, Western culture resorted to barbarism so as to save the 'other' cultural subjects from their primitive selves. . . . [Western culture], in the name of civilization and religion, subjugated, enslaved, and plundered Africa, Asia, and the Americas"

(p. 120). Historical omissions are essential for the idea of a "shared and common culture" to work.

To return to the question that my undergraduate student posed about whose version of a shared and common culture we are talking about, we can see that this "sharing" is a lie that hides Eurocentric assumptions and historical truths. Therefore, the idea of U.S. America as a "common culture" also means what Tom noted in an earlier message, namely that "U.S. Americans = white." As scholars and teachers of intercultural communication, do we want to perpetuate this lie?

QUESTION FROM WENSHU LEE

I have read the entire dialogue. I feel energized. The exchanges are generative, compelling me to ask more questions.

Affirming the centrality of social justice or just society in intercultural work, can we talk more about it? Tom raises this issue on many occasions. Gust defines it as "an end of all forms of oppression" and "to heal ourselves, to become whole again." Radha raises the issue of "progressive social change," and I talk about "the centrality of ethics." If we have community organizers in different parts of the world, our relatives, and high school students in mind, what should we say to them about a justice/ethics/progressive social change-centered project of intercultural communication? What would it look like in real life, in contexts relevant to them and us?

Tom Nakayama

I would like to continue Wenshu's requests for discussion by responding to her first question. I sense that there is wide agreement here on the potential value (and potential harm) of the kind of inquiry we do into other cultures and peoples. Hence, the continual return to issues of social justice, ending oppression, social change, and so on reflects a real concern that we focus on and strive to produce "knowledge" that leads to positive intervention. But it also leads me to reflect on the broader assumption here that the "knowledge" that we are producing is a contingent contextual knowledge. That is, we do not seem to be engaged in a project of finding "covering laws" that govern culture's influence on communication (and vice versa).

The "knowledge" that we produce always is within particular contexts (e.g., social, economic, political) that are dynamic. Hence, the ways in which domination and resistance function also are dynamic. Some groups that were formerly in power (or disempowered) may find themselves in later years in a very different context. For example, when I was young, I remember that any products that were marked "made in Japan" were assumed to be junk; to say that something was "made in Japan" was a negative assessment. In a short period, "made in Japan" became something positive, completely the opposite. I sense a similar shift in the kinds of things written about Japan and the (rising and falling) interest in Japan and Japanese culture. So, what we "know" when we study dynamic issues such as culture and communication (which always is in contexts of all kinds) must be necessarily contingent and contextual. Although cultural patterns do continue through many changes, how these patterns are perceived and understood by other cultures is very much influenced by these contextual frames. I think we have to be sensitive to the dynamic nature of what we are studying and how we "know."

Gust Yep

Good morning, everyone. I read Tom's response to Wenshu's first question, and I am going to add to it. My immediate reaction to this question is about who we are and how we live our lives in the world. Let me explain. To me, social justice, progressive social change, and ethics are not simply concepts we discuss in our classes (although that always is a good start), but they must be embodied (and lived) by us to make a difference, regardless of the magnitude, in the world. In that sense, it becomes an attitude, a "way of being" in the social world.

At the risk of potentially sounding reductionist, what does this attitude look like? What is it comprised of? To me, it is the cultivation of an awareness of how power operates. I am reminded of Foucault's (1978/1990) words in *The History of Sexuality* (Vol. 1) about the hidden mechanisms of power when he notes that the "success [of power] is proportional to its ability to hide its own mechanisms" (p. 86). One of the goals of this justice/ethics/progressive social change-centered project of intercultural communication is demystification (Yep, 1998). The process starts within ourselves through an awareness of our own privileges based on a number of vectors of difference—race, class, gender, sexuality, nationality, education, profession, and so on—and an understanding of how we contribute to the (re)production and change of current power relations. It also is an awareness of our marginalities and how we negotiate (and resist) them in our everyday encounters.

But we must not stop there. I believe that the demystification process works from inside out through the creation of spaces to cultivate awareness with others. When I teach this in my classes, students usually get in touch with strong emotional responses—anger to protect themselves from guilt and shame or rage to express years of daily encounters with silencing and erasure. I call this the "pedagogy of pain." It is a difficult space to create and sustain. There is a lot of intense emotional labor here. But I believe that it is a necessary place to be before healing and transformation can take place. At the same time, I struggle with students who cannot seem to move beyond the guilt, shame, and rage. Critical pedagogy tells us that we teach to and respect people's experiences and where they find themselves. I am concerned, however, about the student who feels "stuck" in his or her emotional work, particularly when the term is over and the class no longer is there to continue processing these issues.

I am experiencing flashbacks to different classroom episodes and re-living some of those emotions at the moment, so I stop for now. I hope you are having a great weekend at WSCA (Wenshu and Mary Jane) and at home (Tom and Radha).

Mary Jane Collier

Hello, everyone. I want to thank Wenshu and describe for the rest of you an example of what we accomplished as a "justice/ethics/progressive social change-centered project of intercultural communication" that occurred at the WSCA conference in Coeur d'Alene, Idaho. Along with Gust, many of our colleagues who are members of this organization chose or felt forced to boycott the convention because of fears for their safety, not wanting to financially contribute to a community in which white supremacist headquarters were located and not wishing to stay at a hotel in which substantial investment interests were held by white supremacists. Wenshu and I obtained the endorsement of the Intercultural Communication Interest Group, with support from members including Lynda Dee Dixon, Michael Brydges, Melanie Bloom, Ron Lustig, and Kathryn Sorrells, to present a resolution asking the executive council to gather more detailed information in advance from the members of the professional organization prior to the choice of our convention sites. After presenting the resolution on behalf of the Intercultural Communication Interest Group to the legislative council, and after deliberation, the resolution passed.

ADDITIONAL QUESTIONS FROM WENSHU LEE

We have not taken Tom's issues of "visible" (and "invisible") internationalization very far. Are we proposing different kinds/forms of internationalization?

We talk about intersectionality and multiple dimensions of oppression. What will a concrete intercultural communication project look like if intersectionality is deeply integrated rather than given lip service? What are the dimensions usually left out? Silenced? I personally do not see a lot of issues regarding "sexuality" raised.

Gust Yep

I think that we already are working with intersections in self-reflexive and deeply contextualized scholarship. Intersections become lip service when we treat race, class, gender, sexuality, and so on as isolated (read "independent") variables or "main effects" without considering all of them together as constitutive of human experience. I agree with you, Wenshu, about how we closet sexuality, and when we do this, we fail to make heteronormativity visible and open to interrogation. I think of Richardson's (1996) words:

> Although [heterosexuality] is deeply embedded in accounts of social and political participation, and [in] our understandings of ourselves and the worlds we inhabit, heterosexuality is rarely acknowledged or, even less likely, problematised. Instead, most of the conceptual frameworks we use to theorise human relations rely implicitly upon a naturalized heterosexuality, where (hetero)sexuality tends either to be ignored in the analysis or is hidden from view, being treated as an unquestioned paradigm. (p. 1)

In this sense, aren't we contributing to the reification of a normative heterosexuality?

ADDITIONAL QUESTIONS FROM WENSHU LEE

Although the issues of "fluidity," "opening up issues," "democratizing knowledge" (using Radha's expression), and "dialectical tensions" (using Tom's expression) are important metatheoretical positions to take, I constantly want to ask, "Are we in a position to democratize research agendas when we still encounter people who blatantly dehumanize others in nativist impoverished terms without being conscious of it (e.g., Hart)? Do we want to urge phases in our political work (e.g., oppositional discourse, autonomy/sovereignty, strategic essentialism) in order to mobilize progressive changes and pave the way for truly egalitarian freedom and democracy?

Any questions or comments on my earlier thoughts regarding "culture/s"? I feel that, so far, we have expressed our views a lot but have not asked each other enough questions and engaged in enough dialogue. Some issues were raised and got dropped, and we moved onto other issues without taking them deeper. Can we move in this direction a bit more? Asking more critical questions? Taking each other's issues further?

Radha Hegde

I guess that our dialogue is coming to a close, and I would like to make a brief comment in response to Wenshu's call to address culture. It is interesting that just the other day (March 16, 2001), the front page of the *New York Times* had a story on the phenomenal diversity in New York City's population. As I read the article about the census data, I come across statements such as "neighborhoods that have been rapidly transformed in recent years by the arrival of unprecedented numbers of largely Hispanic and Asian immigrants"; "nearly one in ten New Yorkers is Asian"; and "whites . . . , many of whom have . . . moved away, have dwindled to just over a third" (Sachs, 2001, p. A1). Or here is another, once again from the *New York Times:* "The future middle class of the city is a foreign born population. It's really a dramatic change" (p. A1).

There seems to be a whole story being told here of change, resistance, and power. In this context, this ferment is inevitable. In fact, we need to be stewing over the directions of a field such as intercultural communication. To me, this is once again a reminder that our politics, scholarship, and pedagogy are intricately related. It is interesting to see in how many different ways we can read and write about the story of the changing census data. How do these multiple narratives relate to one another, and how have they related over time? I think that the bottom line is that we need to relate our work to the material realities of life outside. Out in the streets, culture is not always colorful and codifiable. The space of culture is about community and about incommensurable differences; it is about history and its erasure; it is about individual pride and defeat.

Wenshu Lee

When I first read through the provisional draft put together by Mary Jane, I wanted our cyber-dialogue to follow up on some important questions raised but did not get sufficient responses. Because we are running out of time, I will sketch some answers by referring to four books. Together, they point to a new kind of intercultural and international communication scholarship/project discussed in our cyber-dialogue.

In *Yours in Struggle* (Bulkin, Pratt, & Smith, 1984), Elly Bulkin (an Ashkenazi Jew), Minnie Bruce Pratt (a white Christian-raised southerner), and Barbara Smith (an African American), three U.S. lesbian women, try to work out their disagreements in order to overcome racism and anti-Semitism between and among themselves as means for suggesting possibilities for alliance building between and among their respective communities. In *Meatless Days* (Suleri, 1989), Sara Suleri, a Welsh Pakistani woman, reconstructs the personal and political tensions among her family members and the crossing from Pakistan to the United States. In *"Other Kinds of Dream"* (Sudbury, 1998), Julia Sudbury, a Nigerian British woman adopted by a British family at 6 months of age, documents and historicizes black[5] women's organizations in England to un-erase the voices of political activism by minority women. In *Scenes of Instruction* (Awkward, 1999), Michael Awkward, a U.S. black male scholar "traveling" from segregated elementary school in Philadelphia to his current position as professor of English at the University of Pennsylvania, draws on his life and important experiences in educational settings to answer the questions of black men's violence against black women, black separateness, and black men doing womanism.

These authors all are aware of their "itineraries of temporalized struggles" (referring back to my earlier discussion of "a politics of location") in their personal and political worlds. Each writes with multiple audiences in mind. Defying easy and biological categorization, they turn our attention to different possibilities of grouping and creating cultures that are more humane and more equitable in complex locations. Each pushes me fundamentally to become a transnational womanist. Each also reminds me of my impulse not to fall back on biological determinism and reductionist theorizing.

To end my part in this dialogue, I would like to echo Rich's (1986) expression "picking up new fire" (p. xiii). Running away from darkness, I feel darkness re-enveloping me if I ever stand still and stand alone as a person and scholar. This dialogue is important for me because Radha,

Tom, Gust, and Mary Jane in different ways make me feel that I am not standing alone and that together we can move forward, picking up new fire in our conversations, arguments, and struggles. Thank you all. Let us dialogue on. More questions are to follow in making a critical politicized turn in intercultural and international communication.

Gust Yep

I, too, very much appreciated our dialogue and the creation of our own cyber-community. Yes, we are not standing alone, but we must not forget that we are more than islands. We can be "bridges, drawbridges, and sandbars" (Anzaldúa, 1998, 2000) in our ongoing work toward greater cultural understanding, individual and community empowerment, and struggle for peace and social justice.[6]

Tom Nakayama

I have just come back from a conference at the University of Mississippi where I participated on a panel discussing the recent vote to retain the Mississippi state flag that included (among others) Reverend Dolphus Weary and Jack Reed, who both were on the state flag commission. It was an invigorating discussion that highlighted the complexities of dealing with the past—and consequently the future—and the democratic process. Although the vote has been counted and the majority voted to have the flag retain its Confederate canton, is the ballot box the best place to negotiate complex social issues and bring about social justice? Will it begin an important dialogue in Mississippi about contemporary social issues?

I mention this now because our discussion highlighted the complexities of living in a multiracial/multicultural world in which there are tremendous economic, historical, and political power differentials between and among groups. I hope that our dialogue can begin to open up more space to begin to address these larger social issues in the face of enormous challenges and social upheavals—from Cincinnati, to Bosnia, to South Africa, to Indonesia and elsewhere around the world. We live in a world where we cannot and should not assume that everyone seeks out intercultural contact. Thank you all for taking the time to dialogue. Let us continue the discussion in other venues at other times.

NOTES

1. For examples of such dialogue through interviews, see Foucault (1999), hooks and West (1995), Said and Barsamian (1994), and Spivak (1990).

2. Clifford (1989) proposes his definition of "location as itinerary" by building on the works of Rich (1986) and Said (1983).

3. I suggest this definition of "location" based on the critical works of Kaplan (1994), Mani (1989), and Mohanty (1987). Radhika Gajjala and Bettina Heinz (my colleagues at Bowling Green State University), after reading earlier portions of this cyber-dialogue, independently brought up the issue of location in the study of critical intercultural communication. I thank them for their insights and support.

4. For me, color does not mark the biological differences between white and nonwhite people. "Women and men of color" refers to individuals who are aware of and can unpack the arbitrary and unjust categorization of "race" and "color" in a transnational context.

5. "Black" in Sudbury's (1998) book acquires its contested meaning in a uniquely British context. Unlike its narrower meaning in the United States as referring to people of African descent, "Black" in England refers to "people of African, Asian, and Middle Eastern descent" (p. 20).

6. I dedicate my portions of this dialogue to Nancy G. McDermid, who will retire in the summer of 2001. She served as dean of the College of Humanities at San Francisco State University for more than two decades. Nancy, in my opinion, exemplifies and embodies the spirit of the humanities. I am inspired by her dedication to the cultivation of personhood through a democratic education and a commitment to social justice.

REFERENCES

Adams, M. (2000). Conceptual frameworks. In M. Adams, W. J. Blumenfeld, R. Castaneda, H. W. Hackman, M. L. Peters, & X. Zuniga (Eds.), *Readings for diversity and social justice: An anthology on racism, anti-Semitism, sexism, heterosexism, ableism, and classism* (pp. 5-9). New York: Routledge.

Altman, K., & Nakayama, T. (1991). Making a critical difference: A difficult dialogue. *Journal of Communication, 41*(4), 116-128.

Anderson, B. (1991). *Imagined communities: Reflection on the origin and spread of nationalism.* London: Verso.

Anderson, J. (1996). *Communication theory: Epistemological foundations.* New York: Guilford.

Anzaldúa, G. (1998). Bridge, drawbridge, sandbar, or island: Lesbians-of-color *haciendo alianzas.* In P. M. Nardi & B. E. Schneider (Eds.), *Social perspectives in lesbian and gay studies: A reader* (pp. 527-536). London: Routledge.

Anzaldúa, G. (2000). *Interviews/Entrevistas* (A. Keating, Ed.). New York: Routledge.

Awkward, M. (1999). *Scenes of instruction: A memoir.* Durham, NC: Duke University Press.

Bahktin, M. M. (1981). *The dialogic imagination: Four essays* by M. M. Bakhtin (M. Holquist, Ed., C. Emerson & M. Holquist, Trans.). Austin: University of Texas Press.

Baxter, L., & Montgomery, B. (1996). *Relating: Dialogues and dialectics.* New York: Guilford.

Buber, M. (1970). *I and thou* (W. Kaufmann, Trans). New York: Scribner.

Bulkin, E., Pratt, M. B., & Smith, B. (1984). *Yours in struggle: Three feminist perspectives on anti-Semitism and racism.* New York: Long Haul Press.

Clifford, J. (1989). Notes on travel and theory. *Inscriptions, 5* [Online.] Available: humwww.ucsc.edu/divweb/cultstudies/pubs/inscriptions/vol_5/clifford.html

Delgado, R., & Stefancic, J. (Eds.). (1997). *Critical white studies: Looking behind the mirror.* Philadelphia: Temple University Press.

D'Souza, D. (1992). *The end of racism.* New York: Free Press.

Dyer, R. (1997). *White.* New York: Routledge.

Foucault, M. (1990). *The history of sexuality: Vol. 1. An introduction.* New York: Vintage. (Original work published 1978)

Foucault, M. (1999). Space, power, and knowledge. In S. During (Ed.), *The cultural studies reader* (2nd ed., pp. 134-141). London: Routledge.

Gajjala, R., & Mamidipudi, A. (1999). Cyberfeminism, technology, and international "development." *Gender and Development, 7*(2), 8-16.

Giroux, H. A. (1993). *Living dangerously: Multiculturalism and the politics of difference.* New York: Peter Lang.

Giroux, H. A. (2001). *Theory and resistance in education: Towards a pedagogy for the opposition.* South Hadley, MA: Bergin & Garvey.

Hall, E. (1976). *Beyond culture.* Garden City, NY: Anchor.

Hall, S. (1996). On postmodernism and articulation: An interview with Hall, edited by L. Grossberg. In D. Morley & K. Chen (Eds.), *Stuart Hall: Critical dialogues in cultural studies* (pp. 131-150). New York: Routledge.

Harding, S. (Ed.). (1993). *The "racial" economy of science: Toward a democratic future.* Bloomington: Indiana University Press.

Harding, S. (1998). *Is science multicultural? Postcolonialisms, feminisms, and epistemologies.* Bloomington: Indiana University Press.

Hecht, M. L., Collier, M. J., & Ribeau, S. (1993). *African American communication.* Newbury Park, CA: Sage.

Hirsch, E. E., Jr., Kett, J. F., & Trefil, J. (1988). *The dictionary of cultural literacy.* Boston: Houghton Mifflin.

hooks, b. (1994). *Teaching to transgress: Education as the practice of freedom.* New York: Routledge.

hooks, b., & West, C. (1995). Breaking bread: A dialogue among communities in search of common ground. In G. Ruggiero & S. Sahulka (Eds.), *The new American crisis: Radical analysis of the problems facing America today* (pp. 224-241). New York: New Press.

Houston, M. (1997). When black women talk with white women: Why dialogues are difficult. In A. Gonzalez, M. Houston, & V. Chen (Eds.), *Our voices* (2nd ed., pp. 187-194). Los Angeles: Roxbury.

Johnson, E. P. (2001). "Quare" studies, or (almost) everything I know about queer studies I learned from my grandmother. *Text and Performance Quarterly, 21,* 1-25.

Kaplan, C. (1994). The politics of location as transnational feminist practice. In I. Grewal & C. Kaplan (Eds.), *Scattered hegemonies: Postmodernity and transnational feminist practices* (pp. 137-152). Minneapolis: University of Minnesota Press.

Kuhn, T. (1970). *The Structure of scientific revolutions.* Chicago: University of Chicago Press.

Lee, W. (1998). In the names of Chinese women. *Quarterly Journal of Speech, 84,* 283-302.

Lee, W., Chung, J., Wang, J., & Hertel, E. (1995). A sociohistorical approach to intercultural communication. *Howard Journal of Communications, 6,* 262-291.

Leeds-Hurwitz, W. (1990). Notes in the history of intercultural communication: The Foreign Service Institute and the mandate for intercultural training. *Quarterly Journal of Speech, 76,* 262-281.

Lorde, A. (1983). There is no hierarchy of oppressions. *International Books for Children Bulletin,* No. 14.

Macedo, D. (1994). *Literacies of power: What Americans are not allowed to know.* Boulder, CO: Westview.

Macedo, D. (1999). Our common culture: A poisonous pedagogy. In M. Castells, R. Flecha, P. Freire, H. A. Giroux, D. Macedo, & P. Willis (Eds.), *Critical education in the new information age* (pp. 117-137). Lanham, MD: Rowman & Littlefield.

Mani, L. (1989). Multiple mediations: Feminist scholarship in the age of multinational reception. *Inscriptions, 5* [Online]. Available: humwww.ucsc.edu/divweb/cultstudies/pubs/inscriptions/vol_5/latamani.html

Mani, L. (1998). *Contentious traditions.* Berkeley: University of California Press.

McLaughlin, D., & Tierney, W. G. (1993). *Naming silenced lives: Personal narratives and the process of educational change.* New York: Routledge.

Mercer, K. (1992). "1968": Periodizing politics and identity. In L. Grossberg, C. Nelson, & P. Treichler (Eds.), *Cultural studies* (pp. 424-449). New York: Routledge.

Metzger, B. (1998). *Negotiating the closet: Cultural identity enactment and communication practices of lesbian administrators in higher education.* Unpublished doctoral dissertation, University of Denver.

Mohanty, C. T. (1987). Feminist encounters: Locating the politics of experience. *Copyright, 1,* 30-44.

Mohanty, C. T. (1989). Race and voice: Challenges for liberal education. *Cultural Critique, 14,* 179-208.

Nakayama, T. K., & Martin, J. M. (Eds.). (1999). *Whiteness: The communication of social identity.* Thousand Oaks, CA: Sage.

Reverby, S. M. (2000). *Tuskeegee's truths: Rethinking the Tuskegee Syphilis Study.* Chapel Hill: University of North Carolina Press.

Rich, A. (1986). Notes toward a politics of location. In A. Rich (Ed.), *Blood, bread, and poetry* (pp. 210-231). New York: Norton.

Richardson, D. (1996). Heterosexuality and social theory. In D. Richardson (Ed.), *Theorising heterosexuality: Telling it straight* (pp. 1-20). Buckingham, UK: Open University Press.

Sachs, S. (2001, March 16). City population tops 8 million in census count for the first time. *New York Times,* p. A1.

Sacks, H. (1984). On doing "being ordinary." In J. M. Atkinson & J. Heritage (Eds.), *Structures of social action: Studies in conversation analysis* (pp. 413-429). Cambridge, UK: Cambridge University Press.

Said, E. W. (1983). Traveling theory. In E. W. Said (Ed.), *The world, the text, and the critic* (pp. 226-247). Cambridge, MA: Harvard University Press.

Said, E. W. (1993). *Culture and imperialism.* New York: Vintage.

Said, E. W., & Barsamian, D. (1994). *The pen and the sword.* Monroe, ME: Common Courage Press.

Shotter, J. (1995). In dialogue: Social constructionism and radical constructivism. In L. Steffe & J. Gale (Eds.), *Constructivism in education* (pp. 41-56). Hillsdale, NJ: Lawrence Erlbaum.

Shuter, R. M. (1998). Revisiting the centrality of culture. In J. N. Martin, T. K. Nakayama, & L. A. Flores (Eds.), *Readings in cultural contexts* (pp. 38-48). Mountain View, CA: Mayfield.

Solomon, M. (1985). The rhetoric of dehumanization: An analysis of the medical reports of the Tuskegee Syphilis Project. *Western Journal of Speech Communication, 49,* 233-247.

Spivak, G. C. (1990). *The post-colonial critic: Interviews, strategies, dialogues.* New York: Routledge.

Stewart, J. (1995). *Language as articulate contact: Toward a post-semiotic philosophy of communication.* Albany: State University of New York Press.

Sudbury, J. (1998). *"Other kinds of dream": Black women's organizations and the politics of transformation.* New York: Routledge.

Suleri, S. (1989). *Meatless days.* Chicago: University of Chicago Press.

Trinh, M. T. (1989). *Woman, native, other.* Bloomington: Indiana University Press.

Wallace, M. (1991) Multiculturalism and oppositionality. In H. A. Giroux & P. McLaren (Eds.), *Between borders: Pedagogy and the politics of cultural studies* (pp. 180-191). New York: Routledge.

Warren, J. (2001). Doing whiteness: On the performative dimensions of race in the classroom. *Communication Education, 50,* 91-108.

West, C. (1990). The new cultural politics of difference. In R. Ferguson, M. Gever, T. T. Minh-ha, & C. West (Eds.), *Out there: Marginalization and contemporary cultures* (pp. 19-36). Cambridge, MA: MIT Press.

Yep, G. A. (1998). Freire's conscientization, dialogue, and liberation: Personal reflections on classroom discussions of marginality. *Journal of Gay, Lesbian, and Bisexual Identity, 3,* 159-166.

Yep, G. A. (in press). Encounters with the "other": Personal notes for a reconceptualization of intercultural communication competence. *CATESOL Journal.*

Author Index

Subject Index

About the Editor

MARY JANE COLLIER (PhD, University of Southern California) teaches in the Department of Human Communication Studies, School of Communication, at the University of Denver. Her research focuses on the social construction of and structural constraints affecting the enactment of interrelated cultural identities and negotiation of intercultural relationships. Her work has appeared in *International Journal of Intercultural Relations, Communication Monographs, Communication Quarterly,* and *Howard Journal of Communications* as well as various scholarly texts and books. She is editor of Volumes 23 to 25 of the *International and Intercultural Communication Annual.*

About the Contributors

HUI-CHING CHANG (PhD, University of Illinois at Urbana-Champaign) is Associate Professor at the University of Illinois at Chicago. Her research interests lie in Chinese relationships and communication, cross-cultural communication, and critical ethnography. She has published in *Discourse Studies, Journal of Language and Social Psychology, Research on Language and Social Interaction, Intercultural and International Communication Annual, Communication Quarterly,* and *Critical Studies in Mass Communication,* among others.

ROBBIN D. CRABTREE (PhD, University of Minnesota) is Chair of Communication at Fairfield University, where she teaches courses in media studies, communication and social change, and globalization. Her research has focused on the role of media in social movements and revolution, media effects across cultures, and international service-learning.

ETSUKO FUJIMOTO (PhD, Arizona State University) is Assistant Professeor in the Department of Communication at Southern Oregon University. Her current research interests include negotiations, expressions, and representations of social and cultural identities, multiculturalism, and transnationalism.

KELLIE D. HAY (PhD, Ohio State University) is Assistant Professor in the Department of Rhetoric, Communication, and Journalism at Oakland University. She specializes in postcolonial theory, ethnography, and feminist cultural studies. She teaches communication theories and critical/cultural studies. Her current research grapples with theories of diaspora and how they are negotiated in Arab-American communities in the United States.

RADHA S. HEGDE (PhD, Ohio State University) teaches in the Department of Culture and Communication at New York University. Her research and teaching center on questions of postcoloniality, race, gender, and identity, with a focus on Third World women. Her work has appeared in journals such as *Communication Theory, Communication Studies, Women's Studies in Communication,* and *Violence Against Women.*

SUSAN L. KLINE (PhD, University of Illinois) is Associate Professor in the School of Journalism and Communication at Ohio State University. She has published on the social construction of identity, the development of communication capabilities, argumentation practices, social cognition and message design strategies, and communication practices in new media technologies. Her work has appeared in journals such as *Communication Research, Communication Education, Argumentation,* and *Journal of Social and Personal Relationships.*

WENSHU LEE (PhD, University of Southern California) is affiliated with San Jose State University. "In 1983, I crossed the Pacific Ocean from Taipei to Los Angeles to study for my PhD in communication arts and sciences. My scholarly locations have changed from a social scientist, to a critical intercultural communication scholar, to a postcolonial feminist, to (now) a transnational womanist along with my academic itineraries from the University of Southern California, to San Jose State University, to Bowling Green State University. Currently, I am interested in incorporating the politics of location into the issues of women, sexuality, labor, and justice in three areas of my daily life—the United States, Taiwan, and Mexico—between the 1960s and 2001. I welcome inquiries and cyberdialogues through e-mail (wenshulee@aol.com)."

SHEENA MALHOTRA (PhD, University of New Mexico) is Assistant Professor in the Department of Women's Studies at California State University, Northridge. She is an Indian citizen with experience in the Indian film and television industries. She worked as an executive producer and commissioning editor of programs for BiTV (Business India Television) and in the Indian film industry as an assistant director to Shekhar Kapur (director of *Bandit Queen* and *Elizabeth*). Her academic work from 1992 through 1999 focused on the cultural implications of satellite television in India, with particular interest in gender issues.

SUJATA MOORTI (PhD, University of Maryland) is Assistant Professor at Old Dominion University. Her research interests include transnational communicative practices, global media cultures, feminist media studies, and postcolonial theories. Her book, *Color of Rape: Gender and Race in Television's Public Spheres,* is forthcoming. She has published in *Social Text, Genders,* and *Journal of Film and Popular Culture,* among others.

THOMAS K. NAKAYAMA (PhD, University of Iowa) is Professor in the Hugh Downs School of Human Communication and Director of the Asian Pacific American Studies Program at Arizona State University. His research interests focus on questions of identity, particularly racial, sexual, national, and sociocultural ones, as they are constructed in public discourses. He has been a visiting scholar at the University of Iowa and the University of Maine and has been a Fulbright scholar at the Université de Mons-Hainaut in Belgium. His work has appeared in *Communication Theory, Critical Studies in Media Communication, International Journal of Intercultural Relations, Journal of Communication, Quarterly Journal of Speech,* and *Text and Performance Quarterly* as well as in various other journals, books, and texts.

ABHIK ROY (PhD, University of Kansas) is Assistant Professor in the Department of Human Communication Studies at Howard University. His research interests include intercultural communication, communication theory, and cultural studies and media. He is the author of several articles on media representations of gender, race, and aging across cultures.

MARYANNE SCHIFFMAN received her BA in economic development studies from the University of California, Berkeley. She currently is pursuing her doctorate in political science at the University of California, Santa Cruz, where she specializes in citizenship and public sphere issues in the countries of Colombia and Brazil.

FEDERICO A. SUBERVI-VÉLEZ (PhD, University of Wisconsin–Madison) is Professor of Communication and Graduate Adviser in the Department of Radio-TV-Film at the University of Texas at Austin. His teaching, research, and publications focus on the mass media and ethnic groups, especially Latinos in the United States. He also conducts research about mass communication and diversity in Brazil and about the media in Puerto Rico, his home country. He serves on academic editorial boards and as an adviser to public and private corporations that deal with diversity and media.

KARUDAPURAM E. SUPRIYA (PhD, University of Illinois at Urbana-Champaign) teaches intercultural and international communication in the Department of Communication at the University of Wisconsin– Milwaukee. She has published in interdisciplinary journals such as *Women and Performance* and a special issue on women and violence in *Hypatia: A Journal of Feminist Philosophy*. She also has written book chapters on white social identity and postcolonial theory in communication studies. She currently is a Cultures and Community fellow at the University of Wisconsin and was a fellow at the Center for Twenty-first Century Studies. Her book, *Shame and Recovery: Mapping Identity in an Asian Women's Shelter*, will be published by Peter Lang, New York.

GUST A. YEP (PhD, University of Southern California) is Professor of Speech and Communication Studies and Human Sexuality Studies at San Francisco State University. He is co-author of the forthcoming *Privacy and Disclosure of HIV/AIDS in Interpersonal Relationships* and editor of the forthcoming *Queering Communication.* His work has been published as chapters in numerous scholarly books and texts as well as in journals such as *Communication Quarterly; Hispanic Journal of Behavioral Sciences; International Quarterly of Community Health Education; Journal of Gay, Lesbian, and Bisexual Identity; Journal of Homosexuality;* and *Journal of Social Behavior and Personality.* He is the recipient of more than a dozen research grants and several teaching and community service awards.